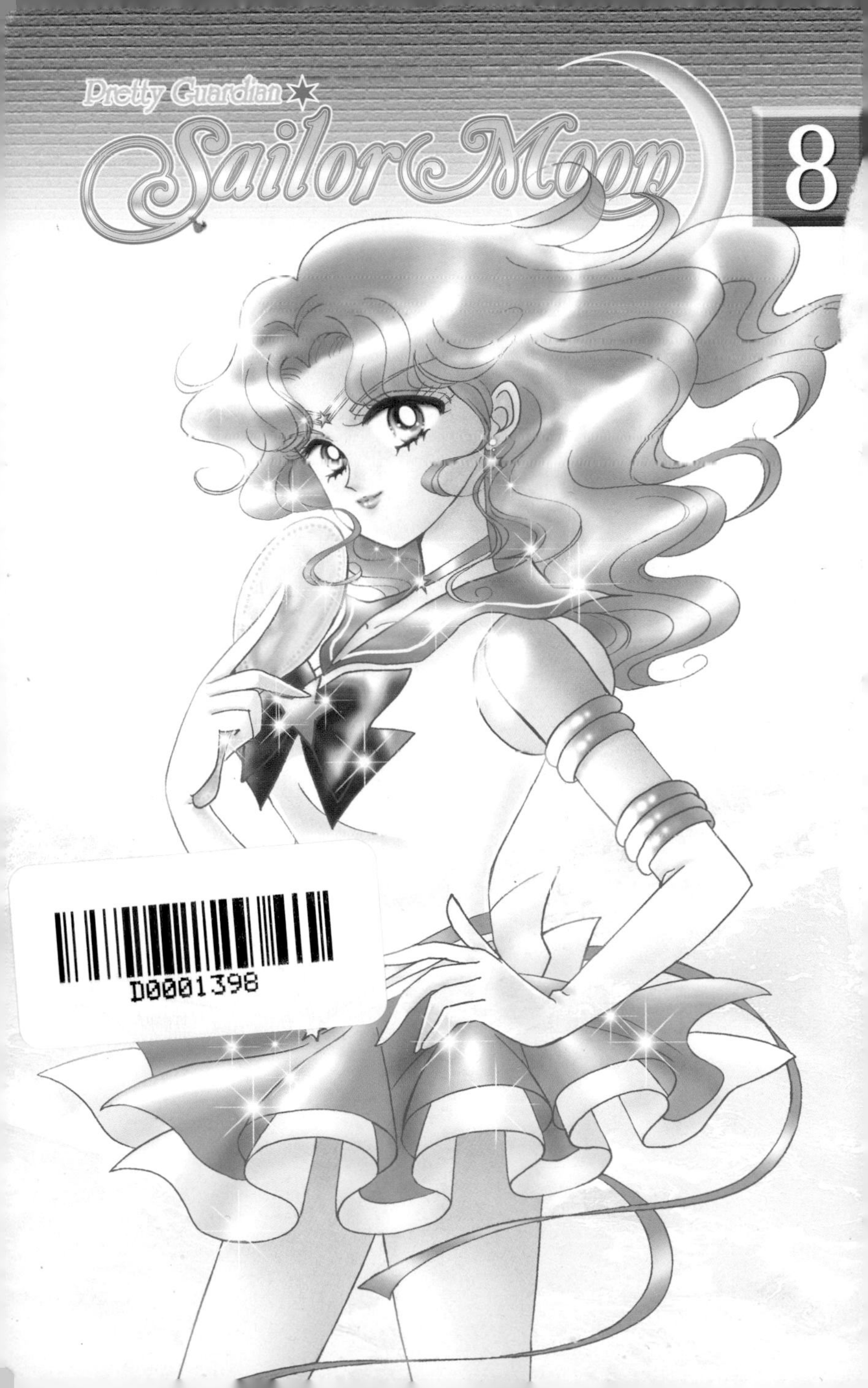
Pretty Guardian
Sailor Moon
8

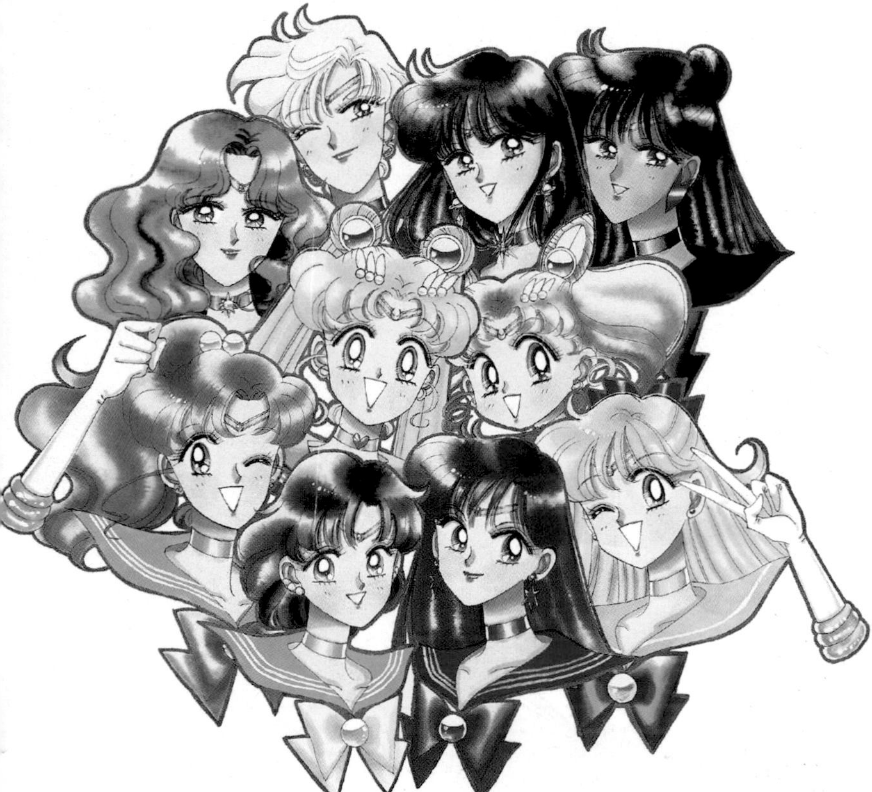

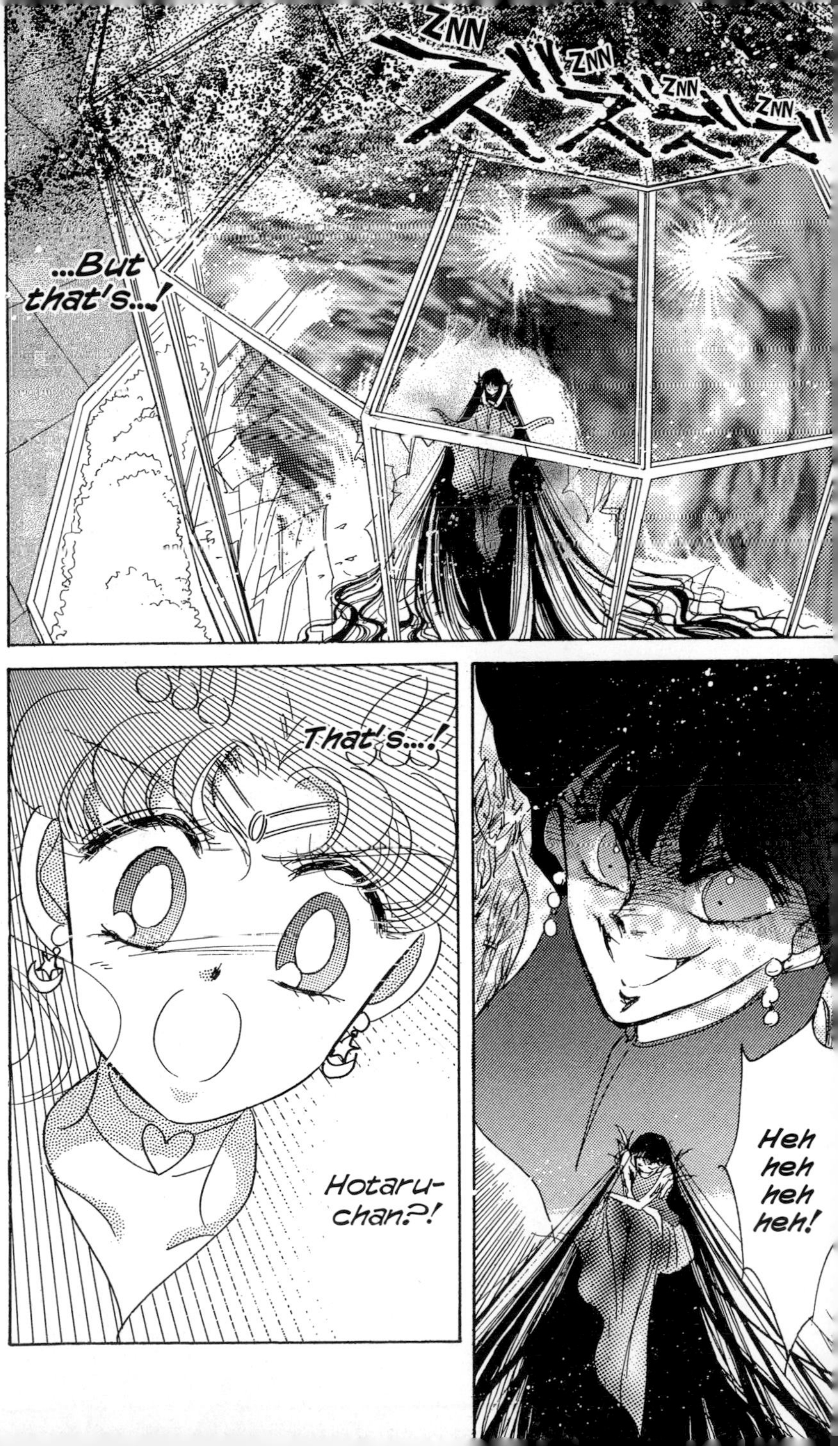
ZNN
ZNN
ZNN
ZNN
...But that's...!
Heh heh heh heh!
That's...!
Hotaru-chan?!

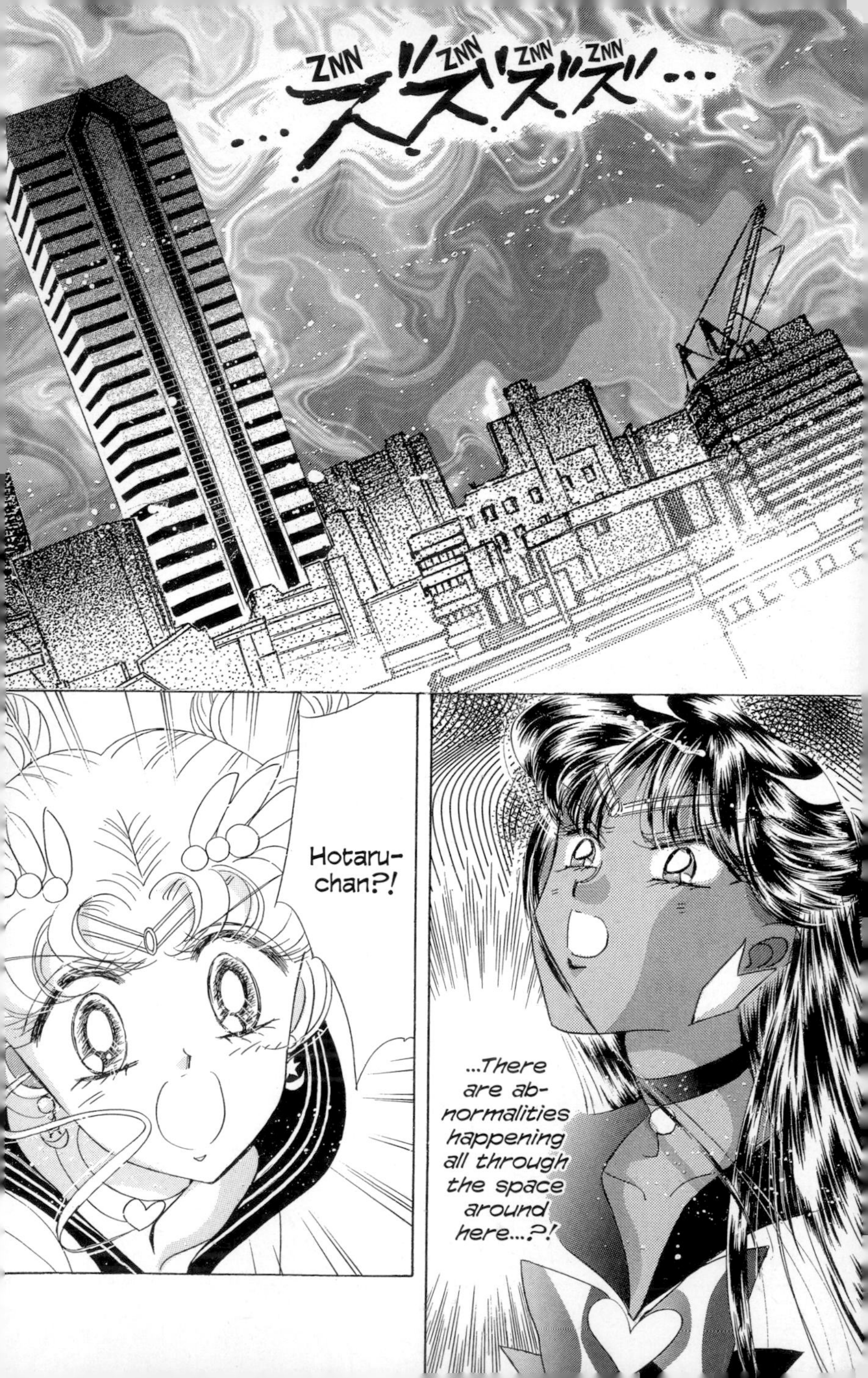
ZNN ZNN ZNN ZNN
…ズズズズ…
...There are ab-normalities happening all through the space around here...?!
Hotaru-chan?!

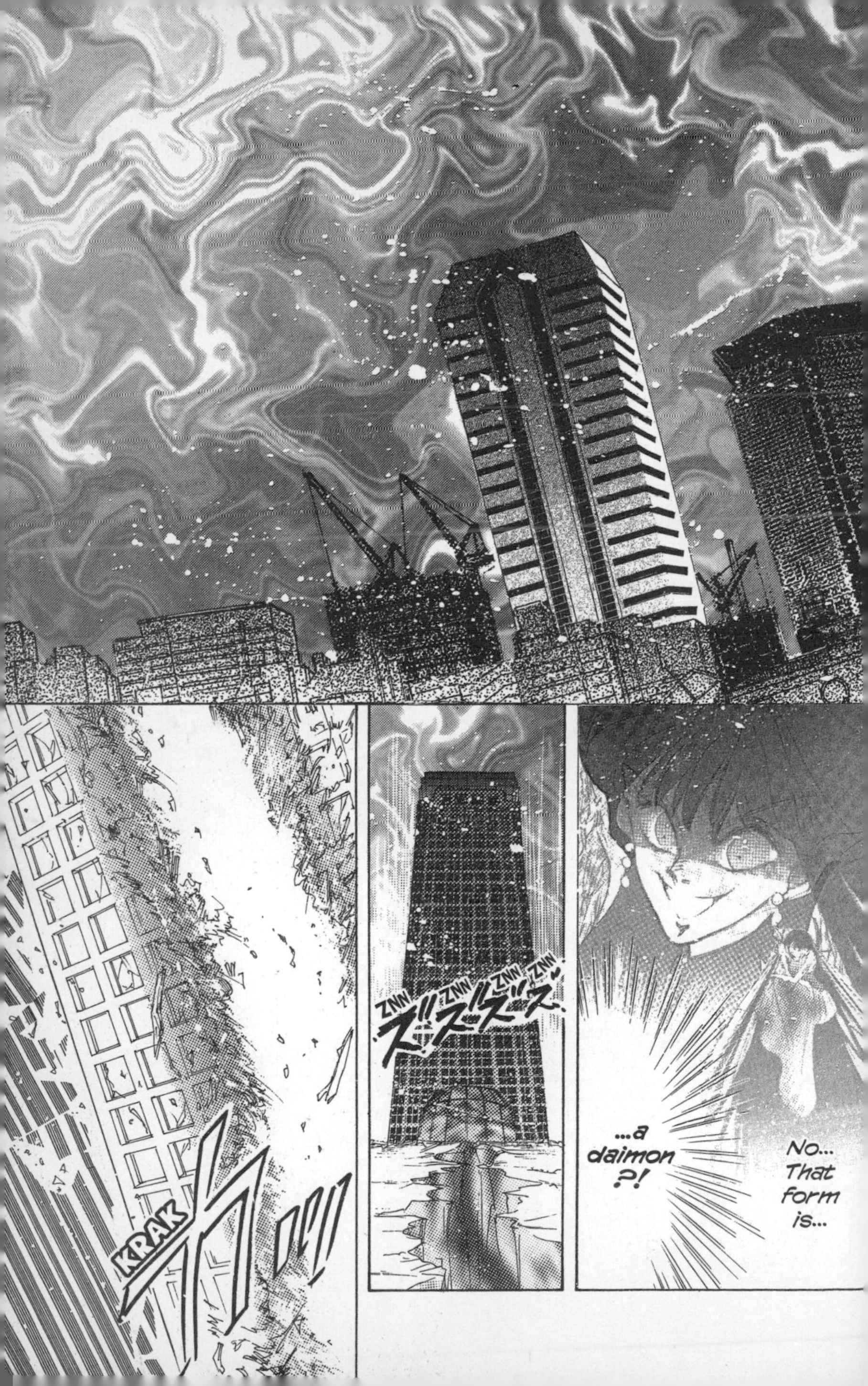
No... That form is...
...a daimon?!
ZNN
ZNN
ZNN
ZNN
KRAK

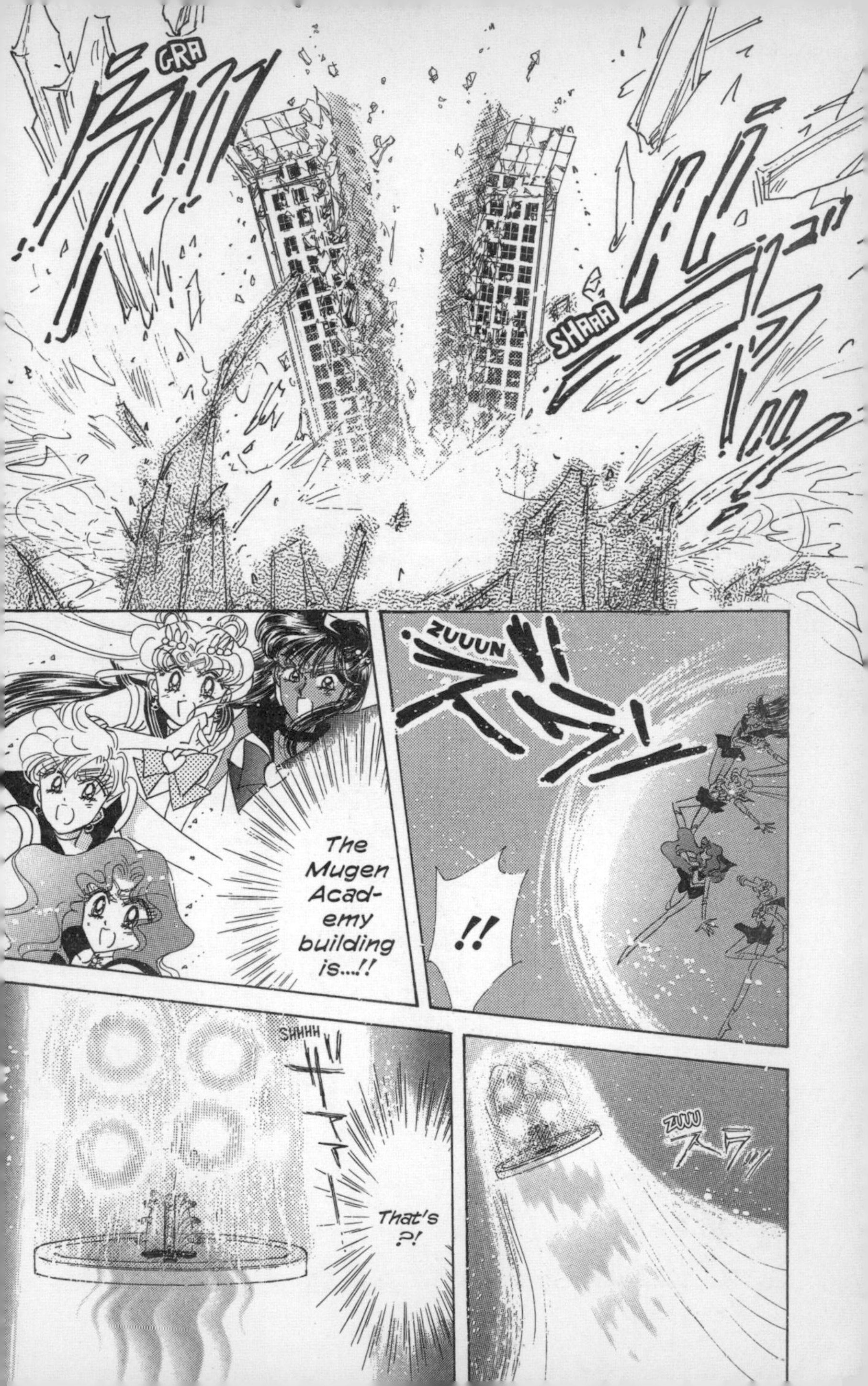
SHAAA
GRA
ZUUUN
!!
The Mugen Acad-emy building is...!!
ZUUU
SHHHH
That's ?!

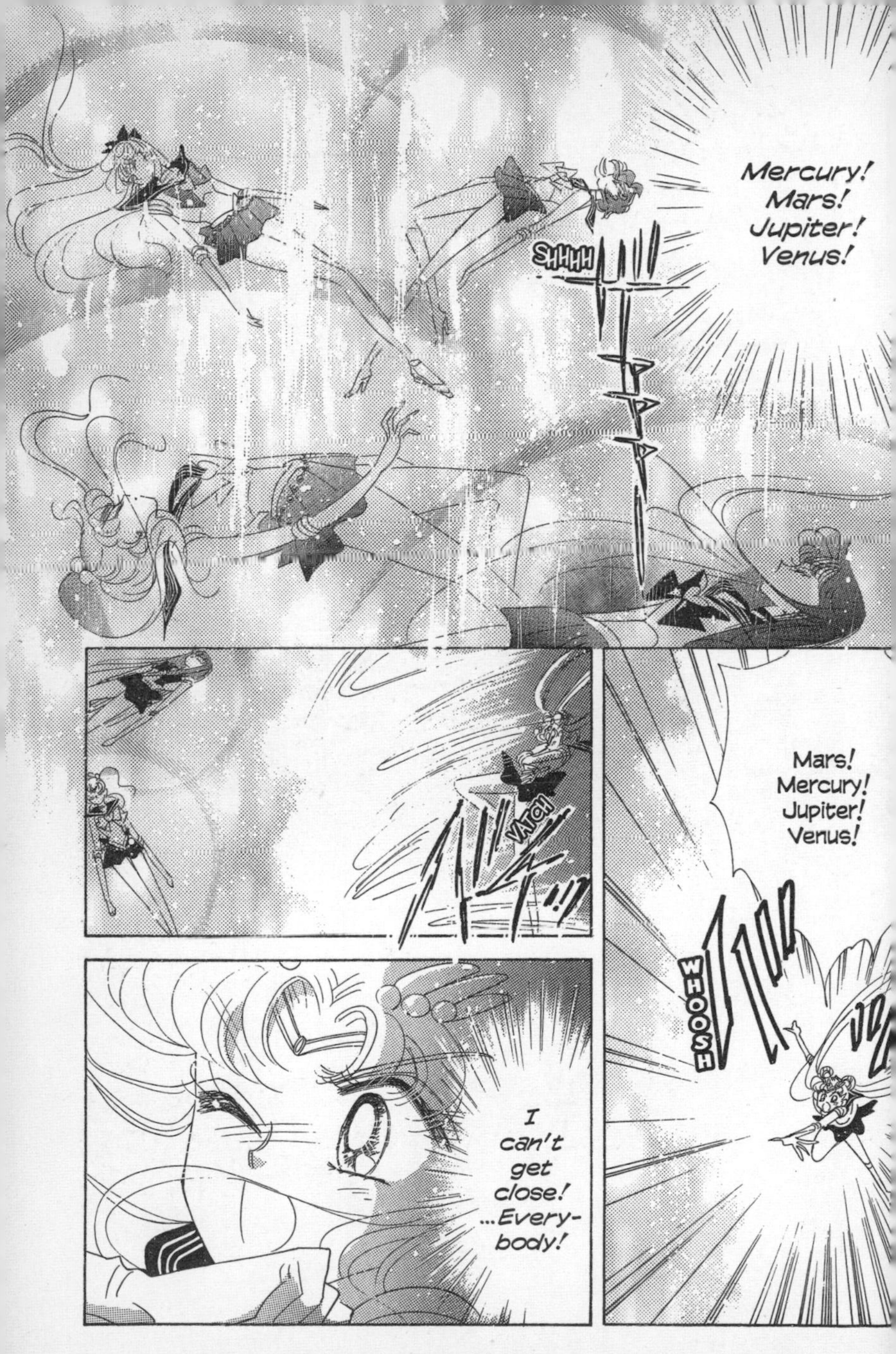
Mercury! Mars! Jupiter! Venus!
SHHHH
Mars! Mercury! Jupiter! Venus!
WHOOSH
VATCH
I can't get close! ...Every-body!

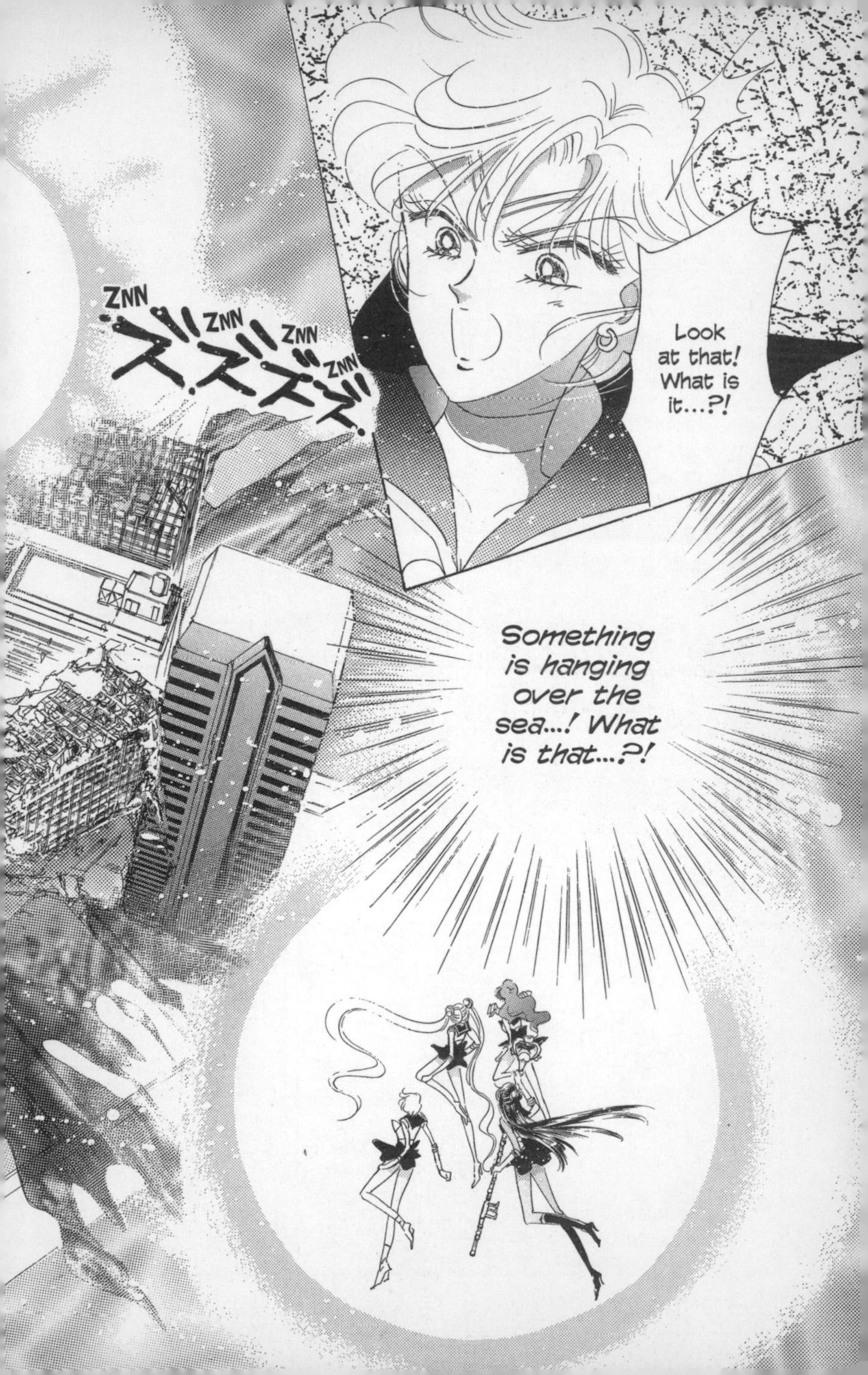
Look at that! What is it...?!
ZNN ZNN ZNN ZNN
ズズズズ
Something is hanging over the sea...! What is that...?!

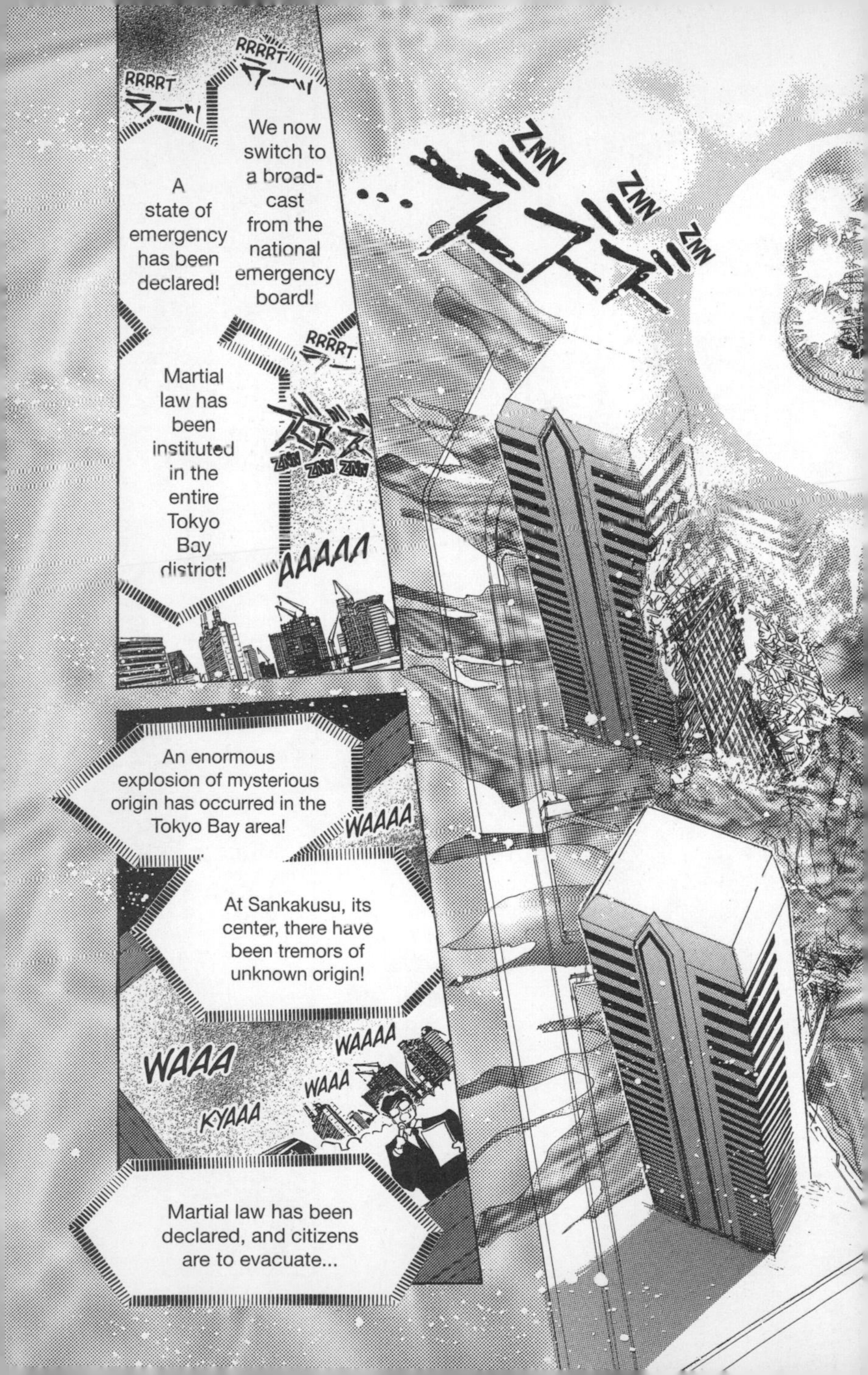
ZNN
ZNN
ZNN
RRRRT
We now switch to a broad-cast from the national emergency board!
RRRRT
A state of emergency has been declared!
RRRRT
ZNN ZNN ZNN
Martial law has been instituted in the entire Tokyo Bay district!
AAAAA
An enormous explosion of mysterious origin has occurred in the Tokyo Bay area!
WAAAA
At Sankakusu, its center, there have been tremors of unknown origin!
WAAAA
WAAA
WAAA
KYAAA
Martial law has been declared, and citizens are to evacuate...

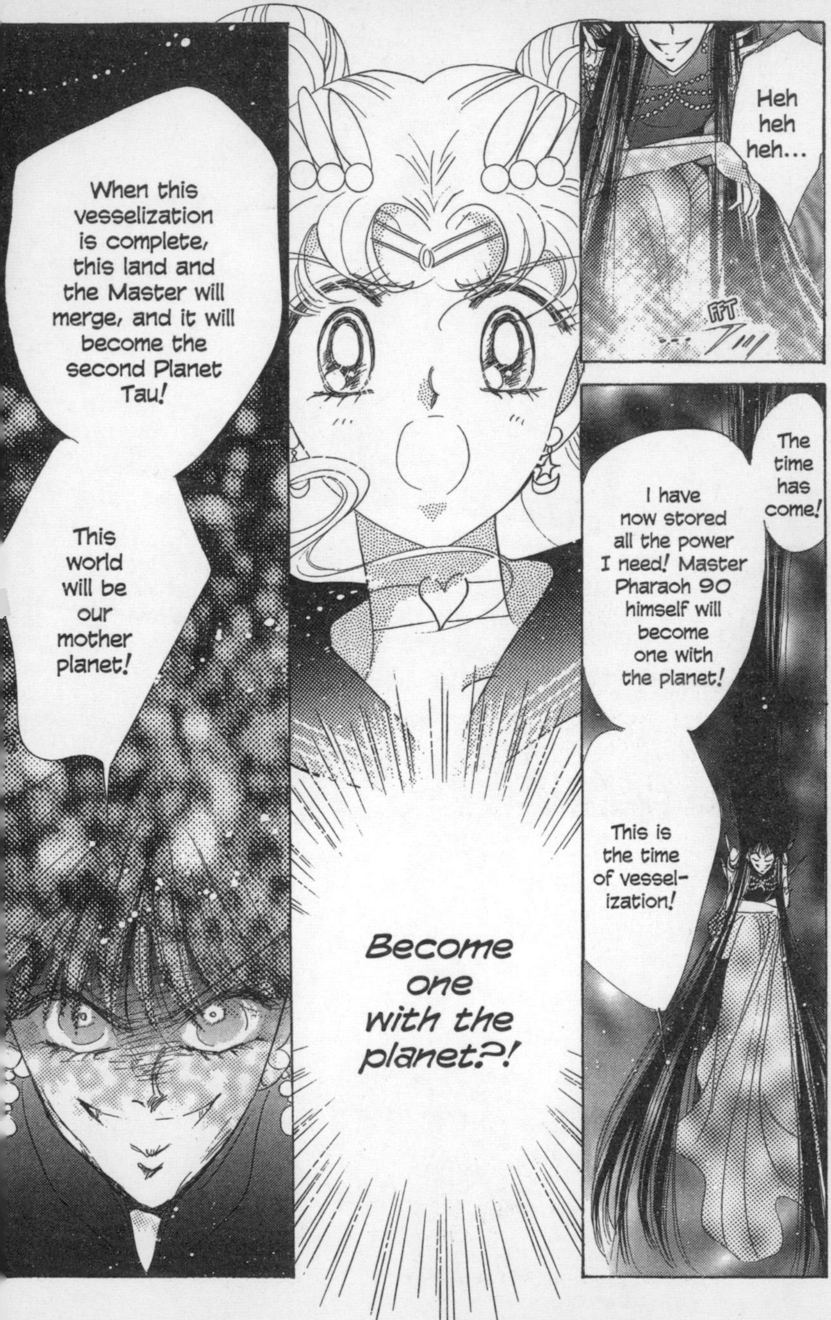
Heh heh heh...
FFT
The time has come!
I have now stored all the power I need! Master Pharaoh 90 himself will become one with the planet!
This is the time of vessel-ization!
Become one with the planet?!
When this vesselization is complete, this land and the Master will merge, and it will become the second Planet Tau!
This world will be our mother planet!

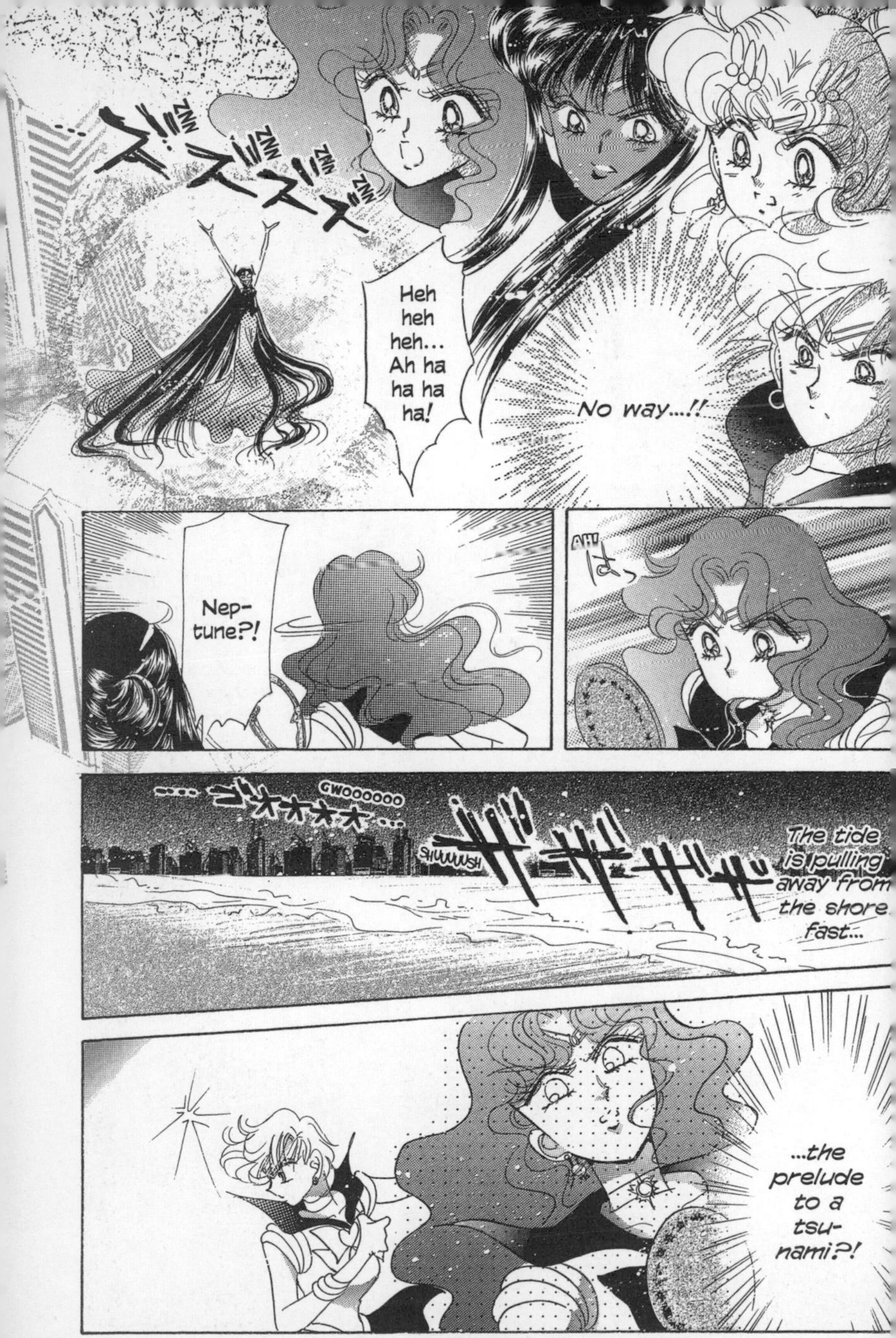
Heh heh heh... Ah ha ha ha ha!
No way...!!
ZNN
ZNN
ZNN
ZNN
AH!
Nep-tune?!
The tide is pulling away from the shore fast...
SHUUUUSH
GWOOOOOO
...the prelude to a tsu-nami?!

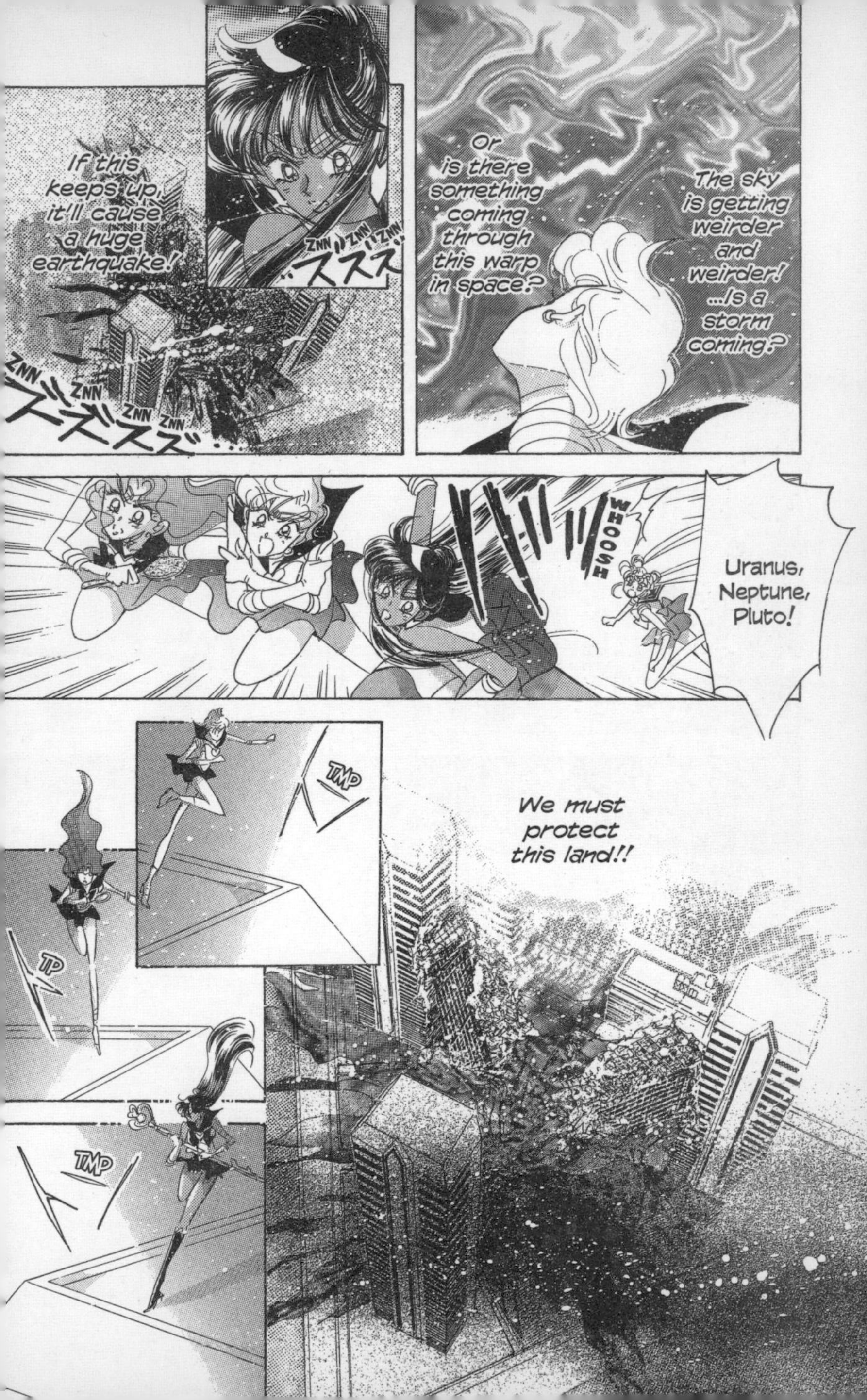
The sky is getting weirder and weirder! ...Is a storm coming?
Or is there something coming through this warp in space?
ZNN ZNN ZNN
If this keeps up, it'll cause a huge earthquake!
ZNN ZNN ZNN ZNN
Uranus, Neptune, Pluto!
WHOOSH
We must protect this land!!
TMP
TP
TMP

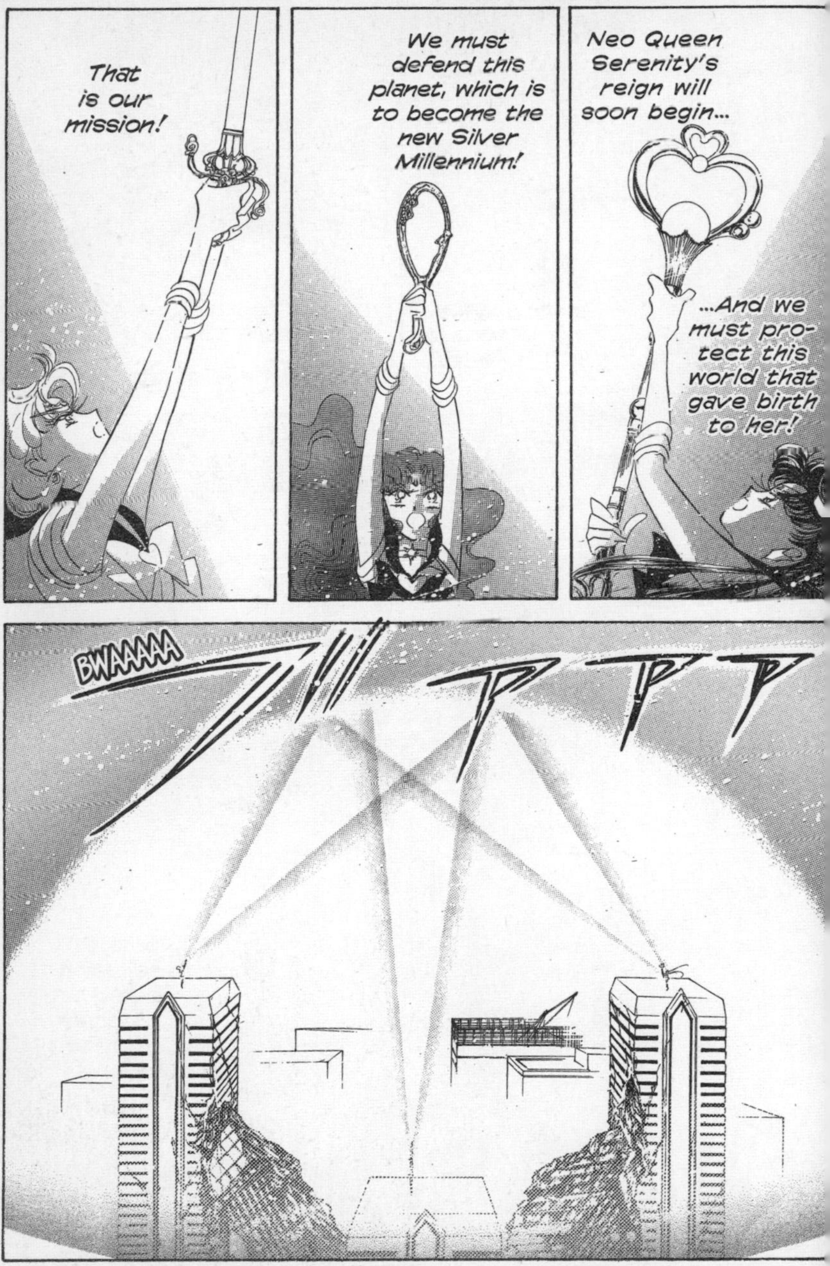
Neo Queen Serenity's reign will soon begin...
...And we must protect this world that gave birth to her!
We must defend this planet, which is to become the new Silver Millennium!
That is our mission!
BWAAAAA

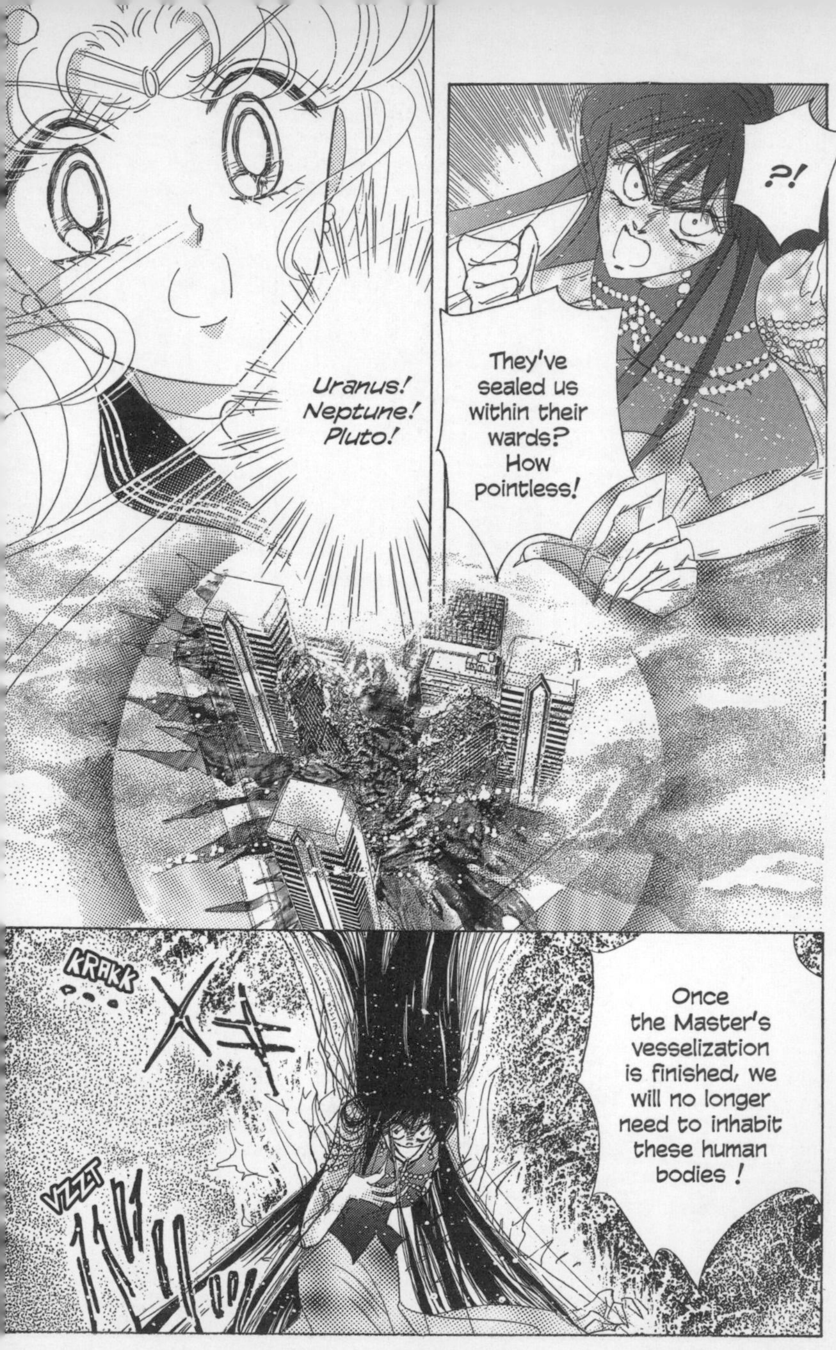
?!
They've sealed us within their wards? How pointless!
Uranus! Neptune! Pluto!
Once the Master's vesselization is finished, we will no longer need to inhabit these human bodies !
KRAKK
VZZZT

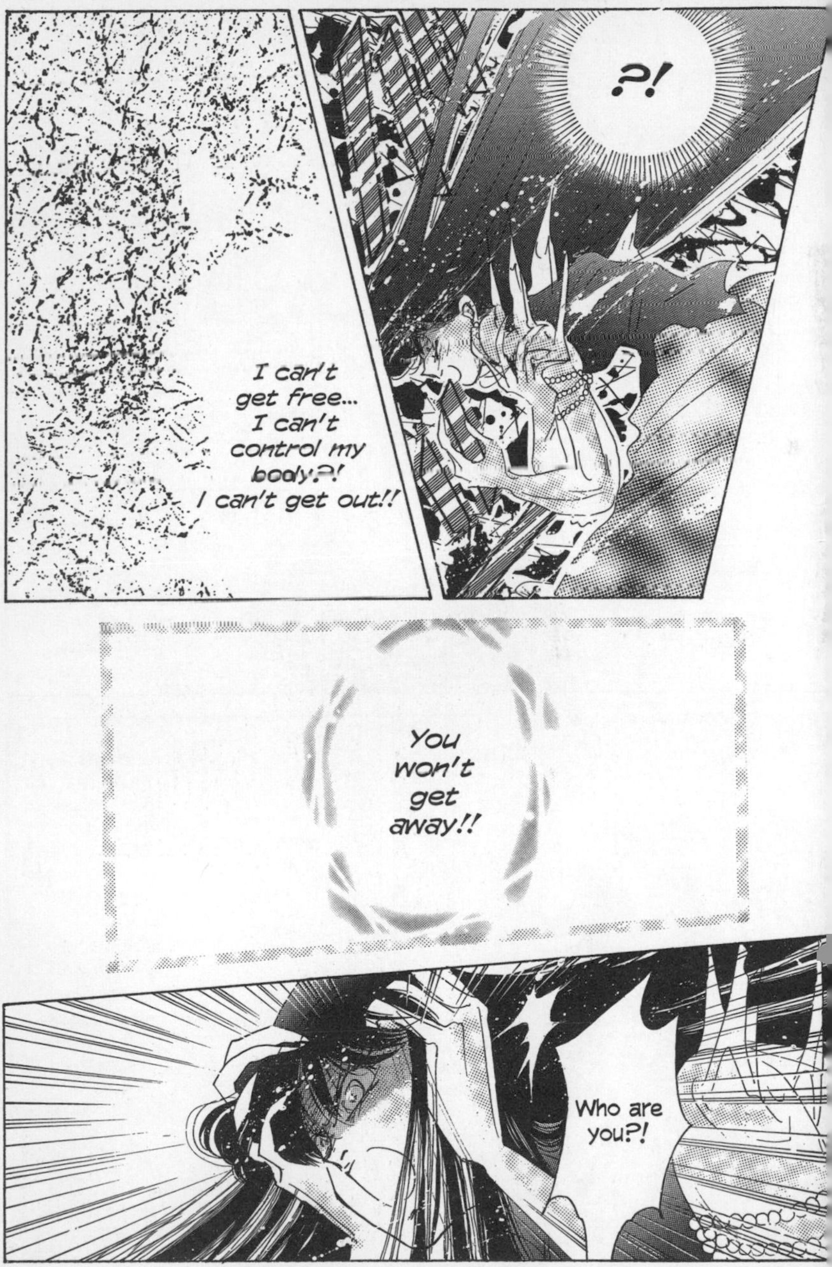
?!
I can't get free... I can't control my body?! I can't get out!!
You won't get away!!
Who are you?!

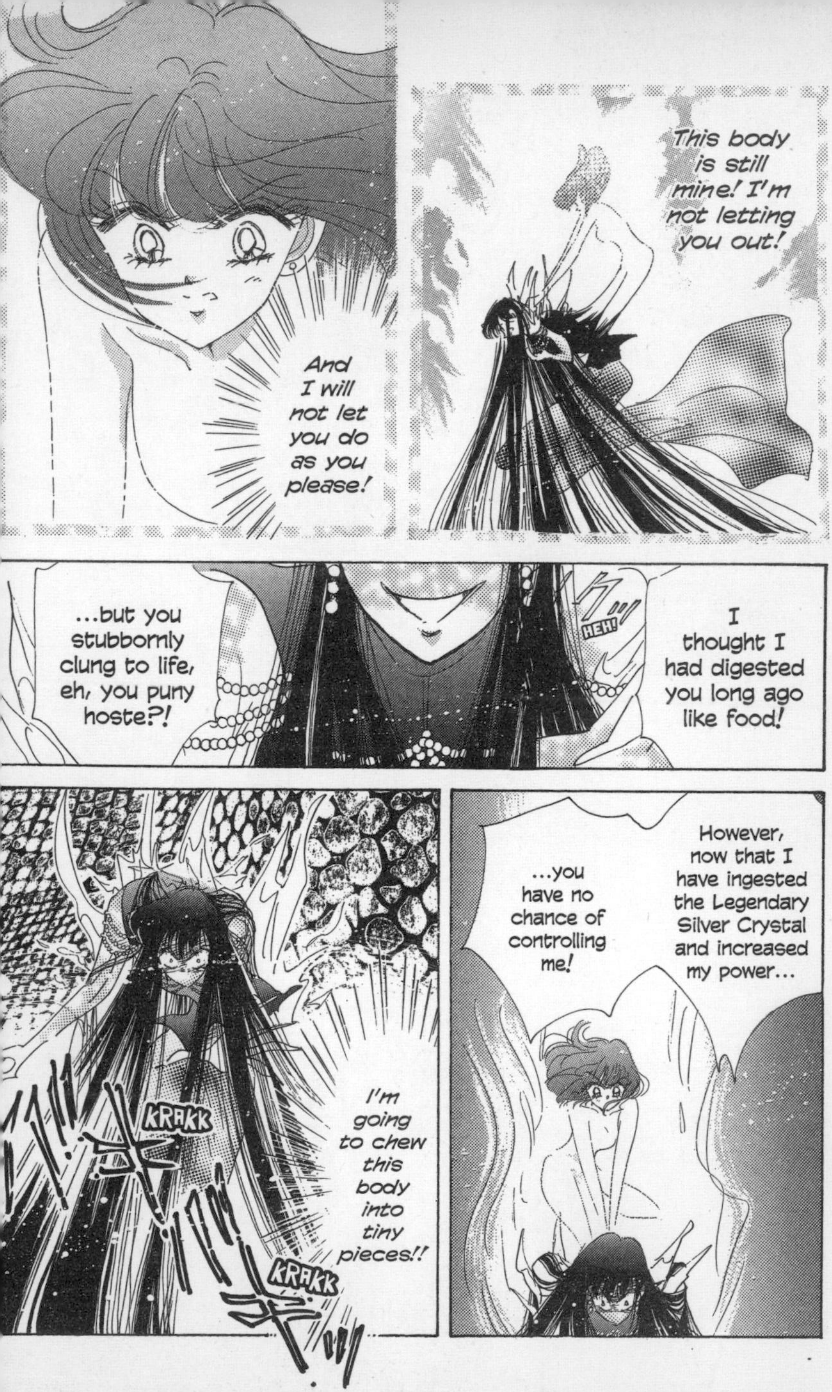
This body is still mine! I'm not letting you out!
And I will not let you do as you please!
I thought I had digested you long ago like food!
HEH!
...but you stubbornly clung to life, eh, you puny hoste?!
However, now that I have ingested the Legendary Silver Crystal and increased my power...
...you have no chance of controlling me!
I'm going to chew this body into tiny pieces!!
KRAKK
KRAKK

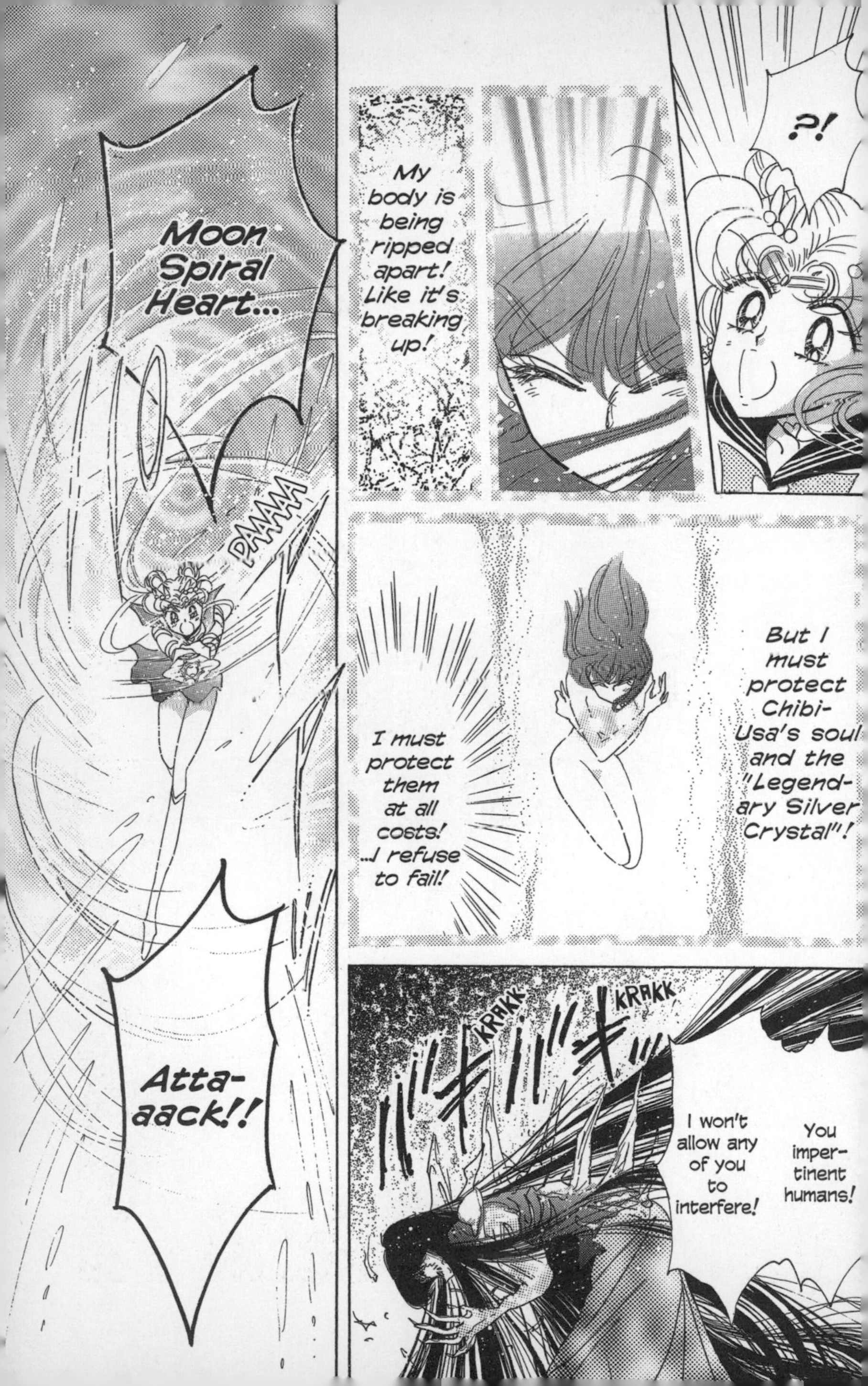
?!
My body is being ripped apart! Like it's breaking up!
But I must protect Chibi-Usa's soul and the "Legendary Silver Crystal"!
I must protect them at all costs! ...I refuse to fail!
KRAKK
KRAKK
バキバキッ
You imper-tinent humans!
I won't allow any of you to interfere!
Moon Spiral Heart...
PAAAAA
Atta-aack!!

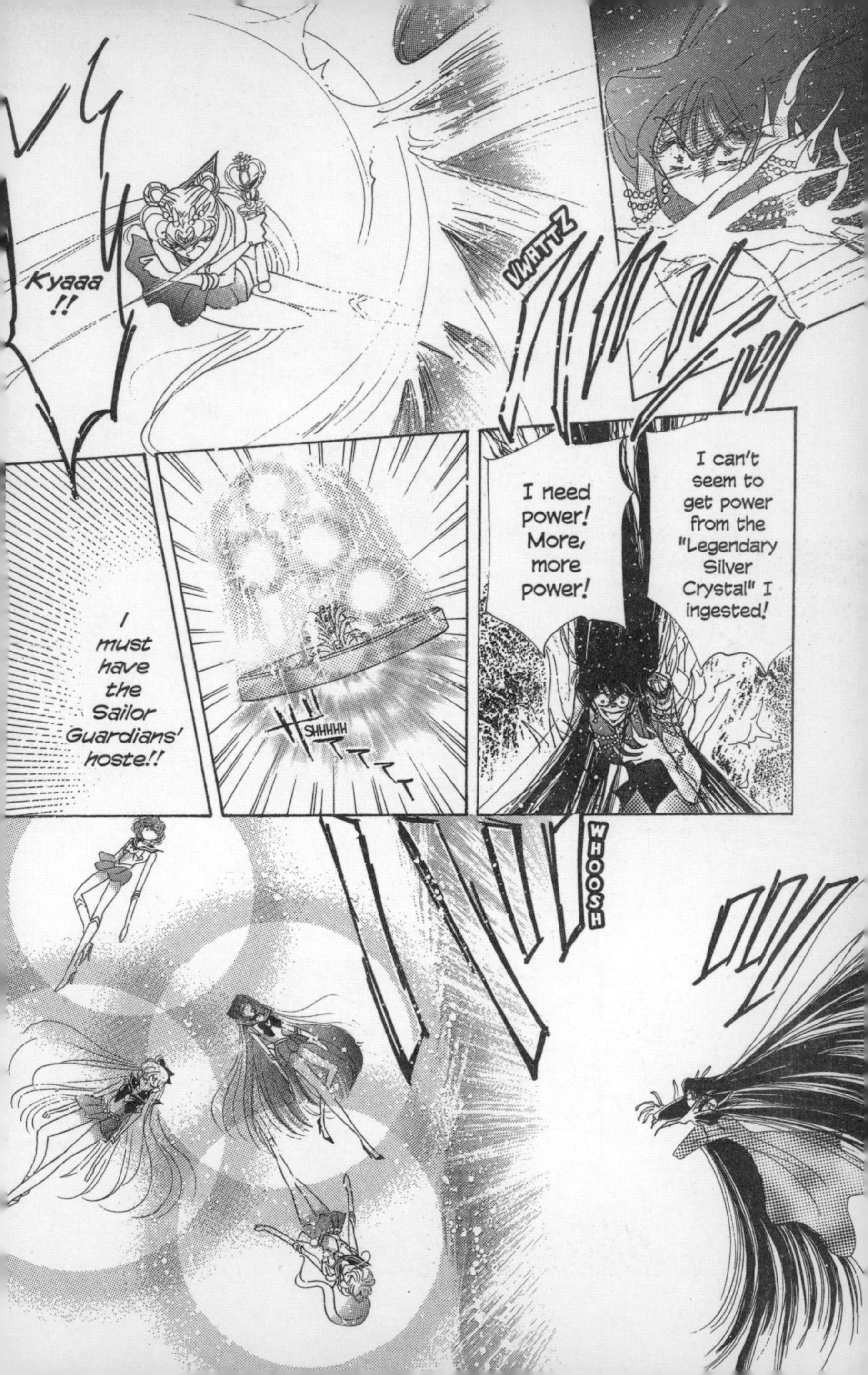
VWATTZ
Kyaaa!!
I can't seem to get power from the "Legendary Silver Crystal" I ingested!
I need power! More, more power!
SHHHHH
I must have the Sailor Guardians' hoste!!
WHOOSH

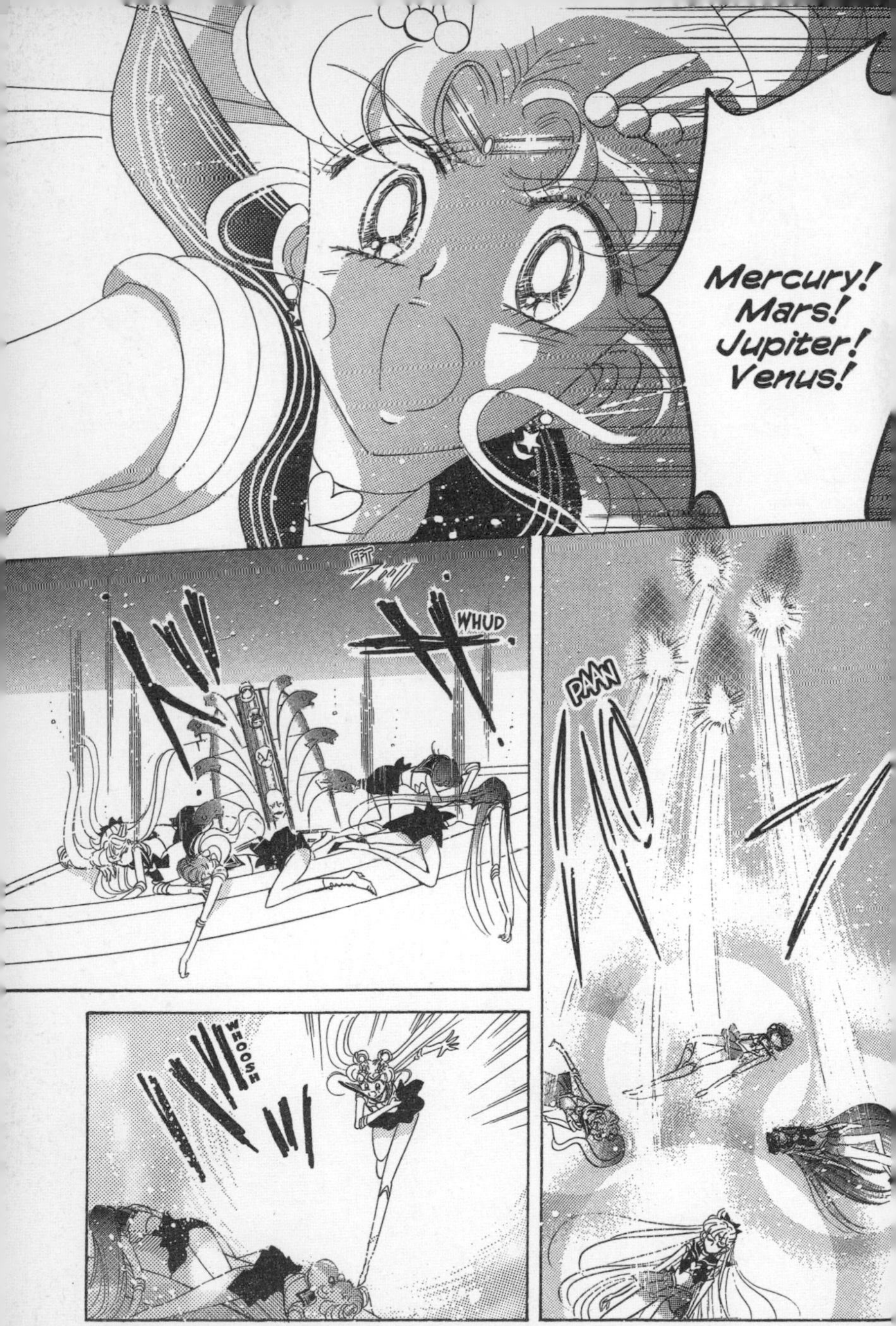
Mercury!
Mars!
Jupiter!
Venus!
PAAN
FFT
WHUD
WHOOSH

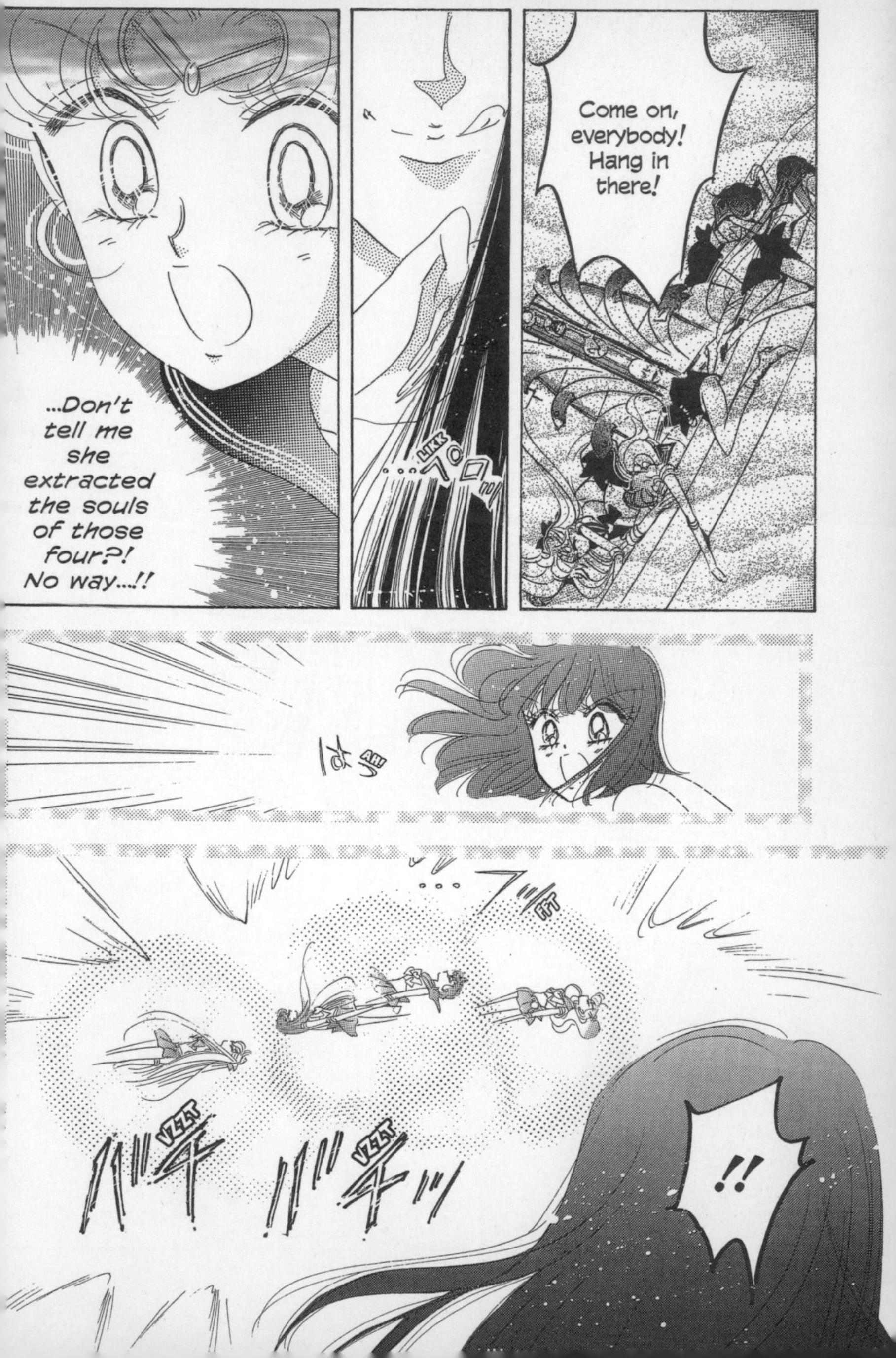
Come on, everybody! Hang in there!
LIKK
...Don't tell me she extracted the souls of those four?! No way...!!
AH!
FFT
VZZZT
VZZZT
!!

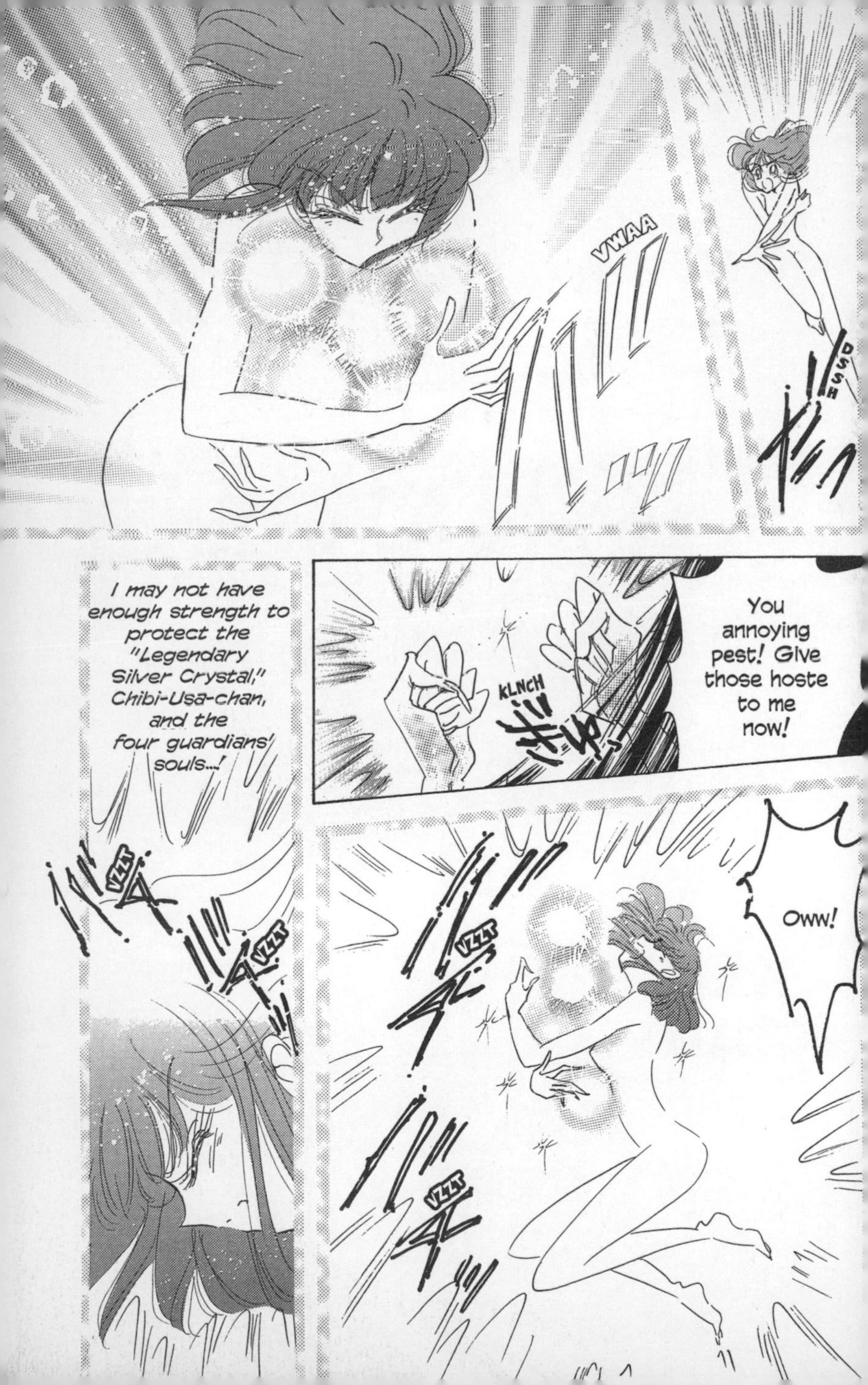
DSSH
VWAA
You annoying pest! Give those hoste to me now!
KLNCH
I may not have enough strength to protect the "Legendary Silver Crystal," Chibi-Usa-chan, and the four guardians' souls...!
Oww!
VZZT
VZZT
VZZT
VZZT

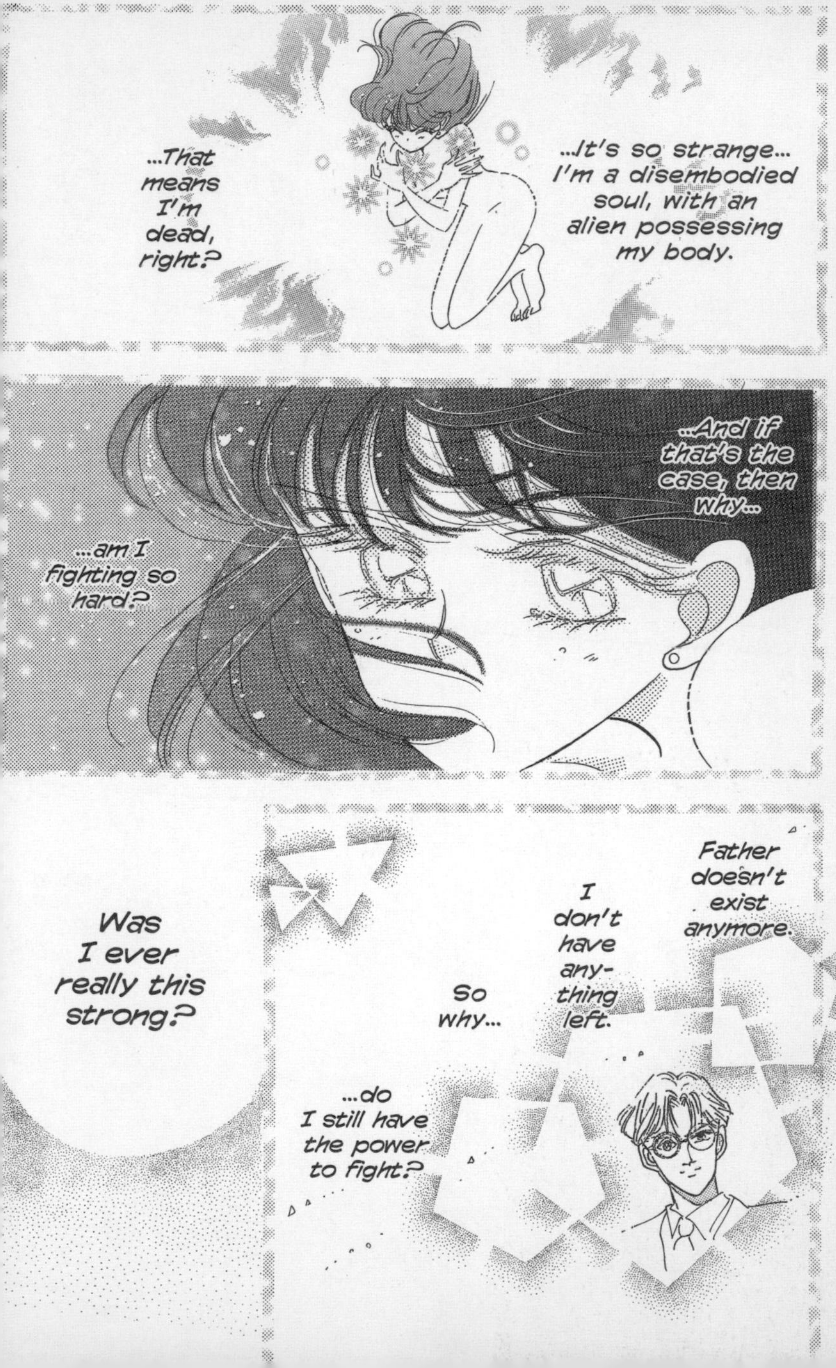
...It's so strange... I'm a disembodied soul, with an alien possessing my body.
...That means I'm dead, right?
...And if that's the case, then why...
...am I fighting so hard?
Father doesn't exist anymore.
I don't have any-thing left.
So why...
...do I still have the power to fight?
Was I ever really this strong?

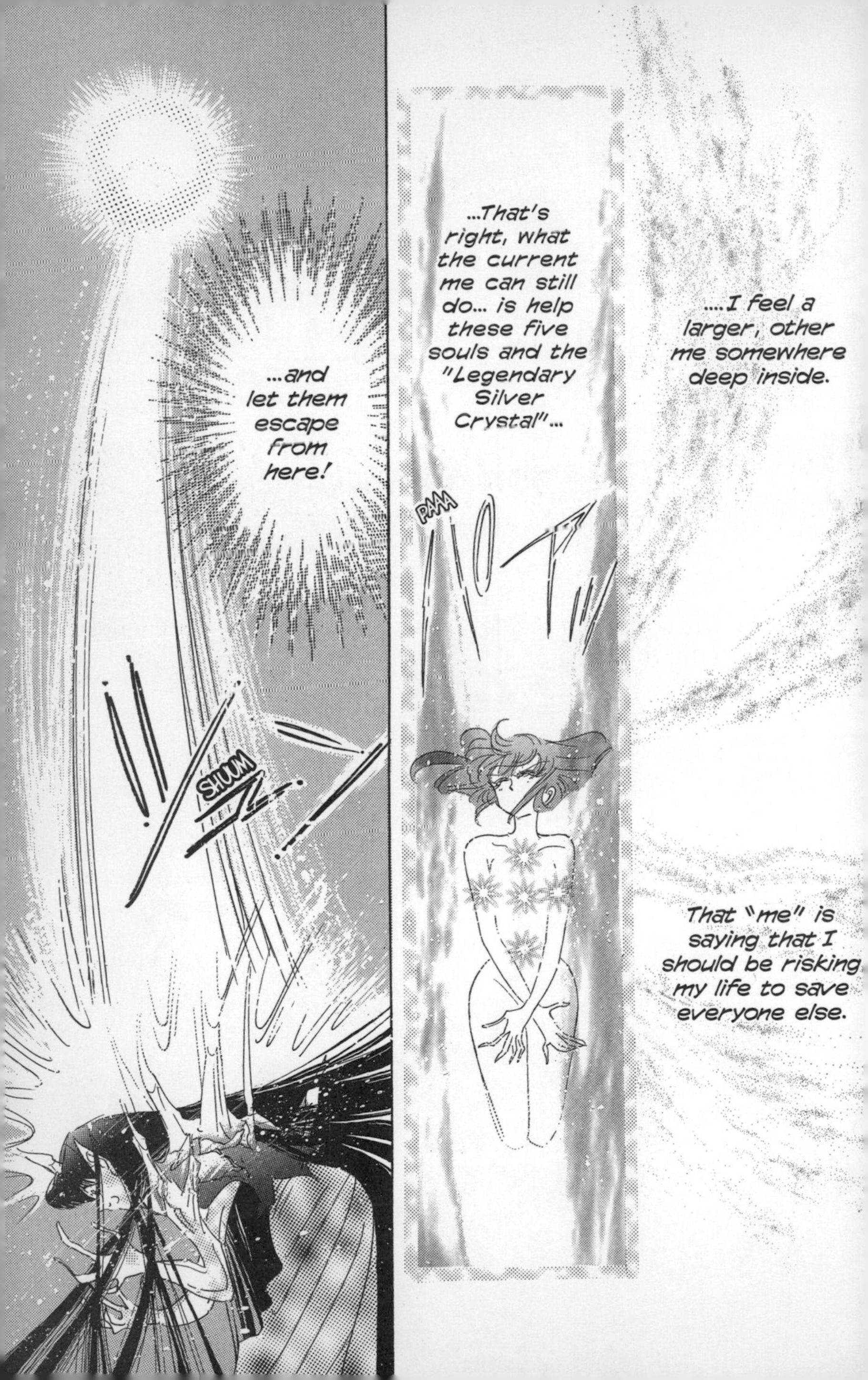
....I feel a larger, other me somewhere deep inside.
That "me" is saying that I should be risking my life to save everyone else.
...That's right, what the current me can still do... is help these five souls and the "Legendary Silver Crystal"...
PAAA
...and let them escape from here!
SHUUM

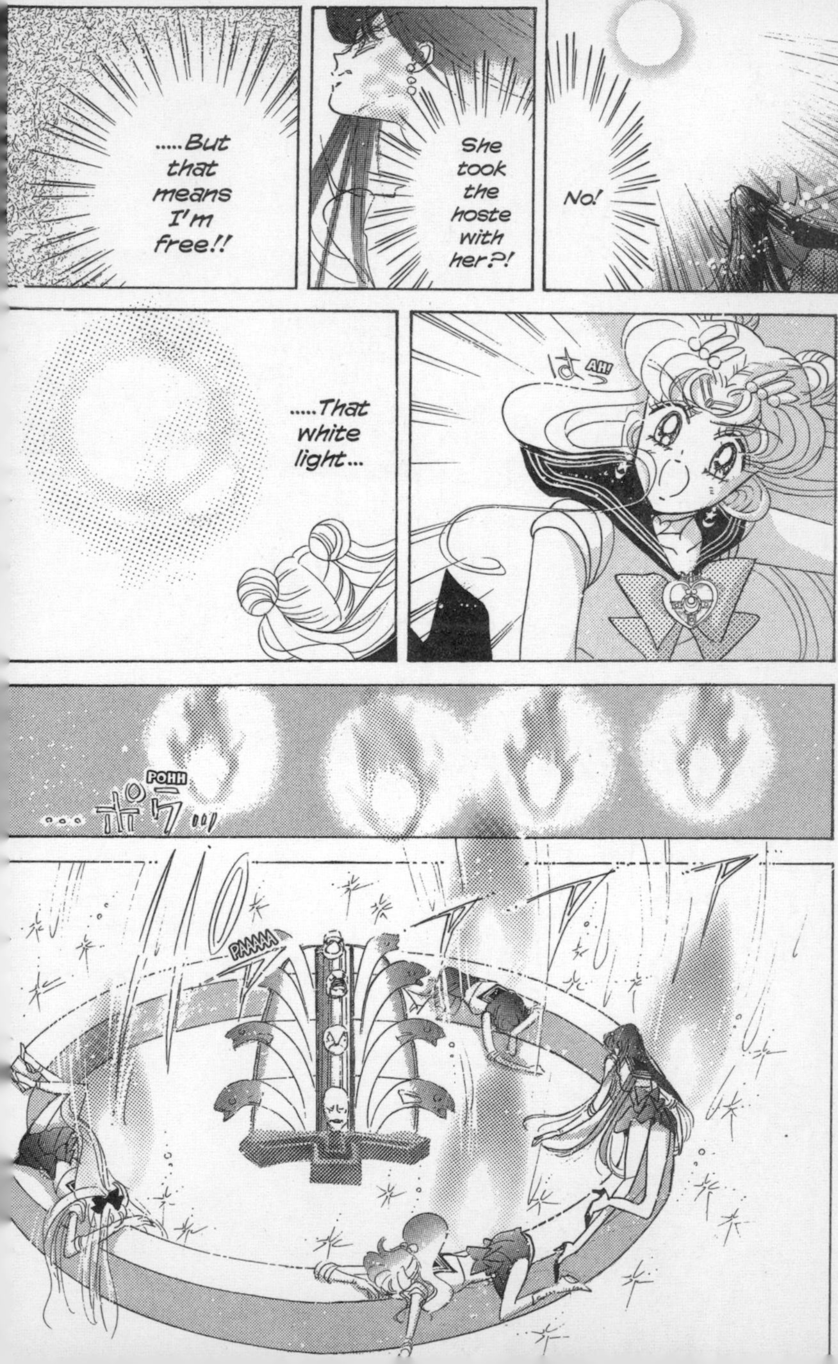
No!
She took the hoste with her?!
.....But that means I'm free!!
AH!
.....That white light...
POHH
PAAAAA

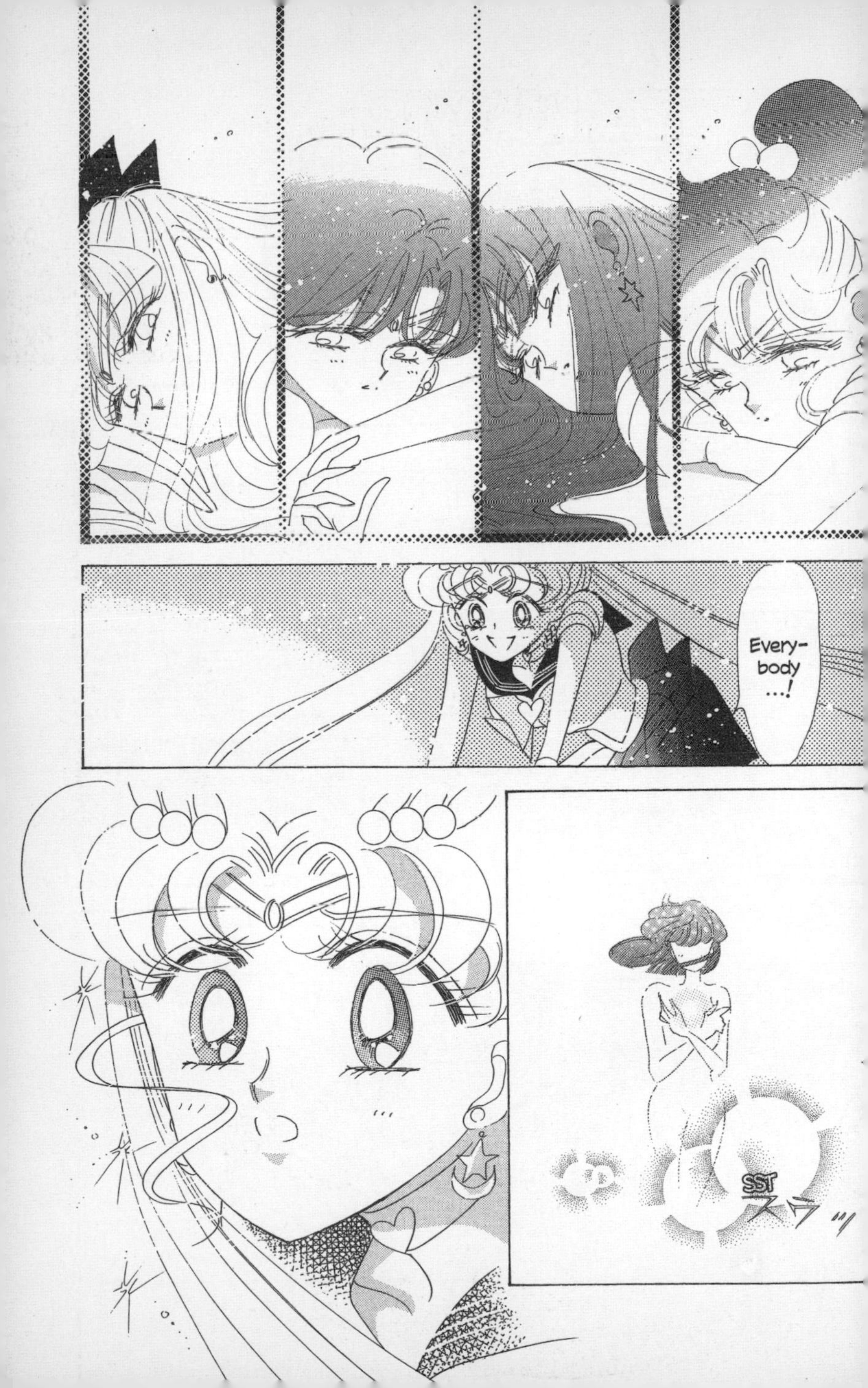
Every-
body
...!
SST

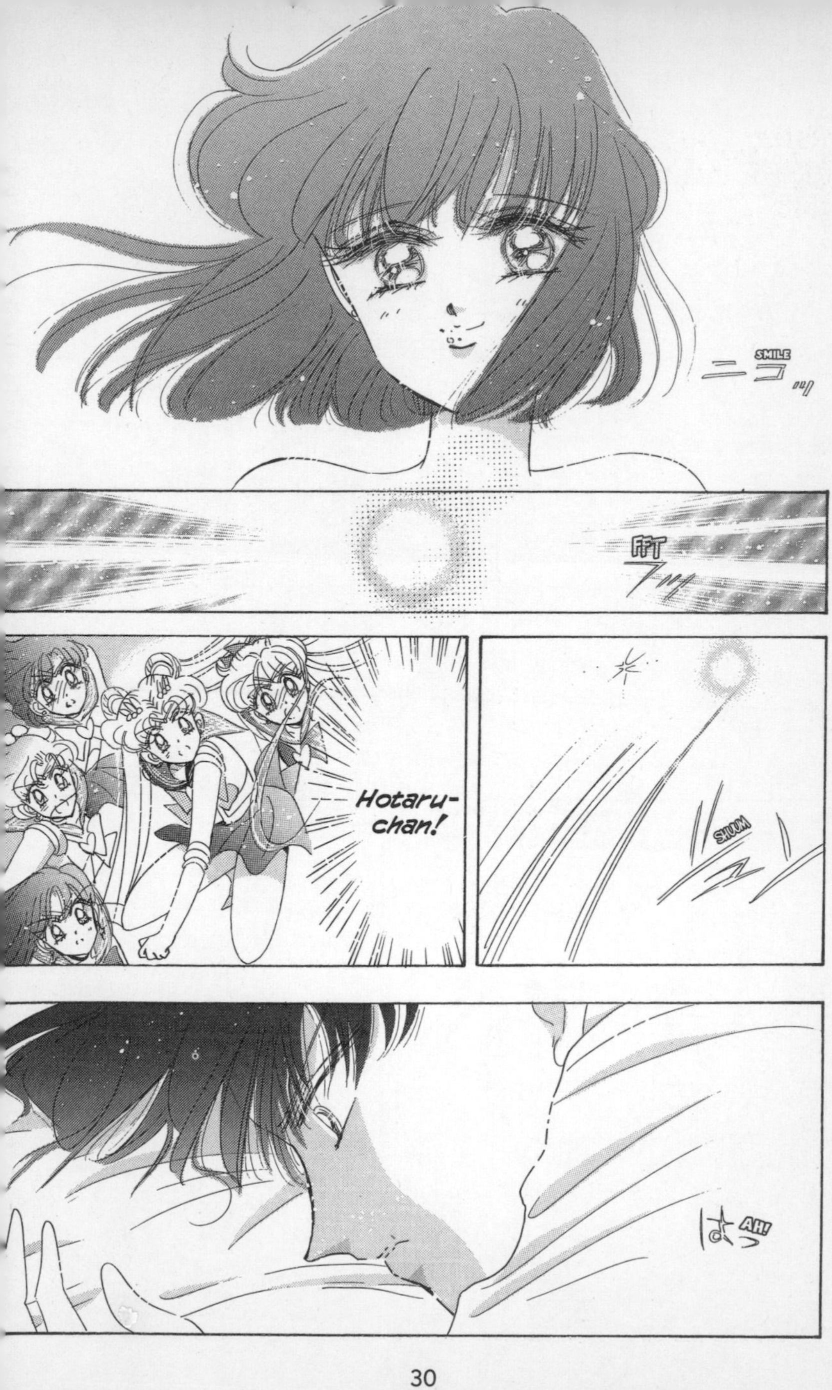
SMILE
ニコッ
FFT
フッ
SHUUM
Hotaru-chan!
はっ
AH!

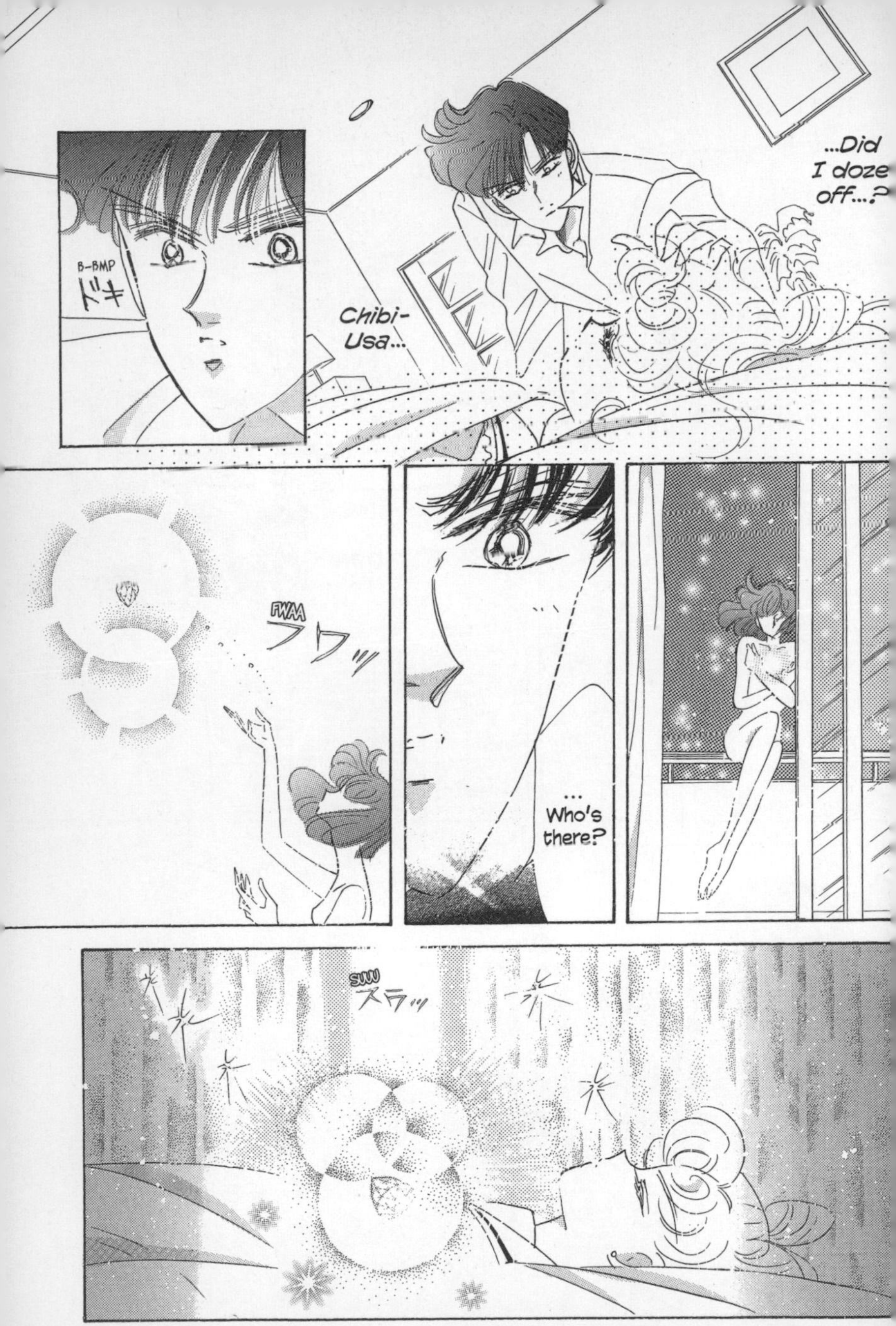
...Did I doze off...?
Chibi-Usa...
B-BMP
ドキ
... Who's there?
FWAA
フワッ
SUUU
スラッ

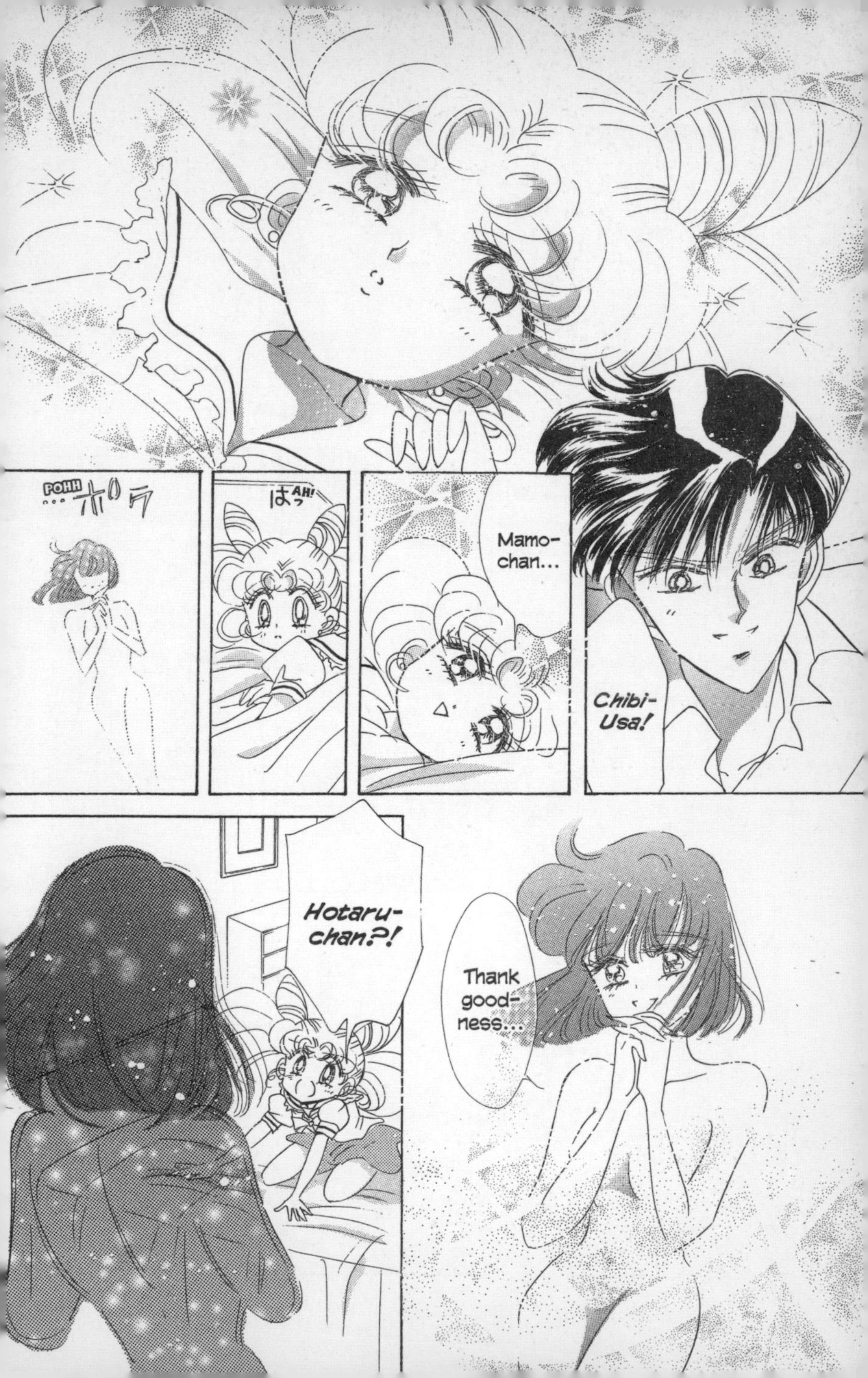
Chibi-Usa!
Mamo-chan...
AH!
POHH
Thank goodness...
Hotaru-chan?!

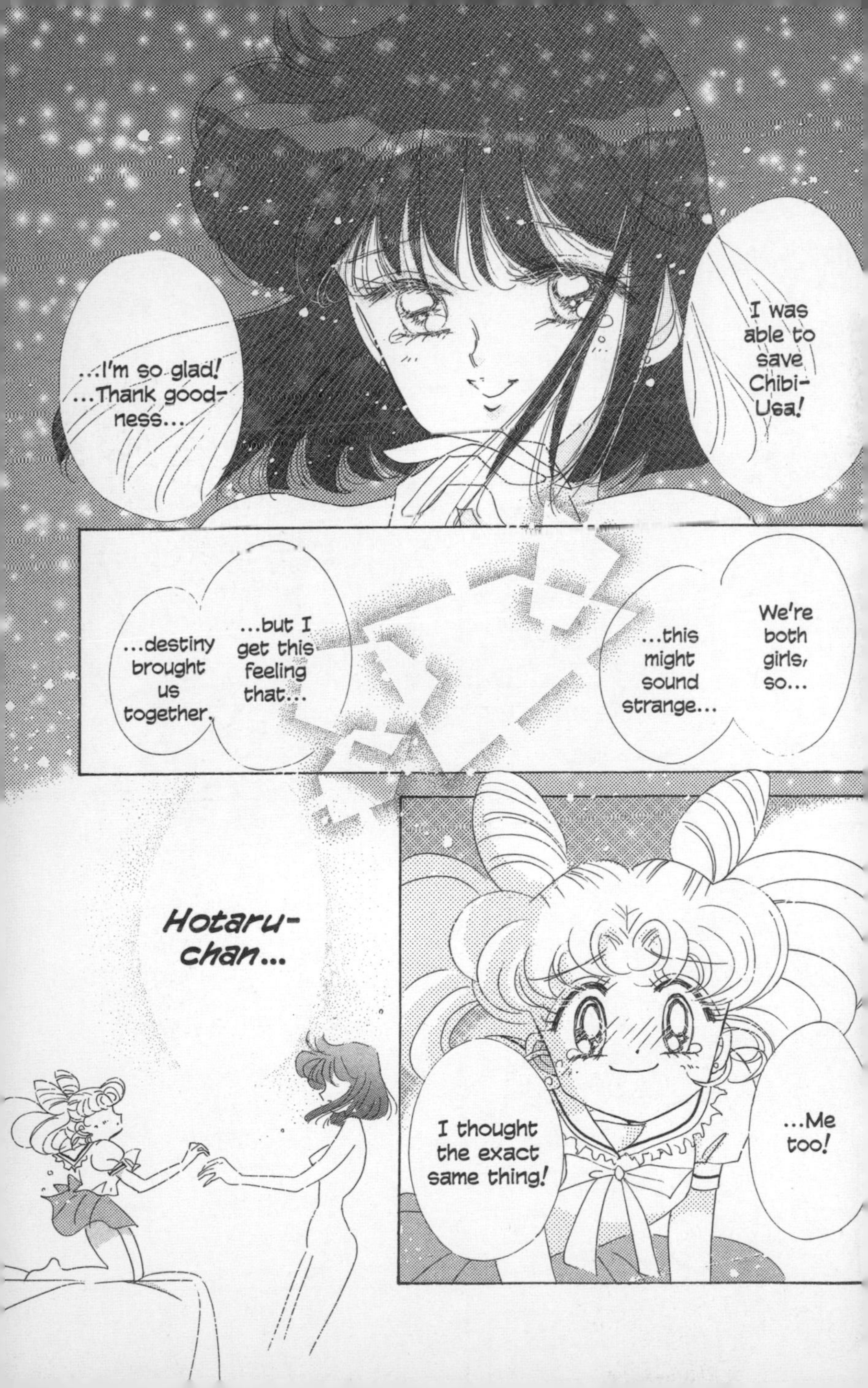
I was able to save Chibi-Usa!
...I'm so glad! ...Thank goodness...
We're both girls, so...
...this might sound strange...
...but I get this feeling that...
...destiny brought us together.
...Me too!
I thought the exact same thing!
Hotaru-chan...

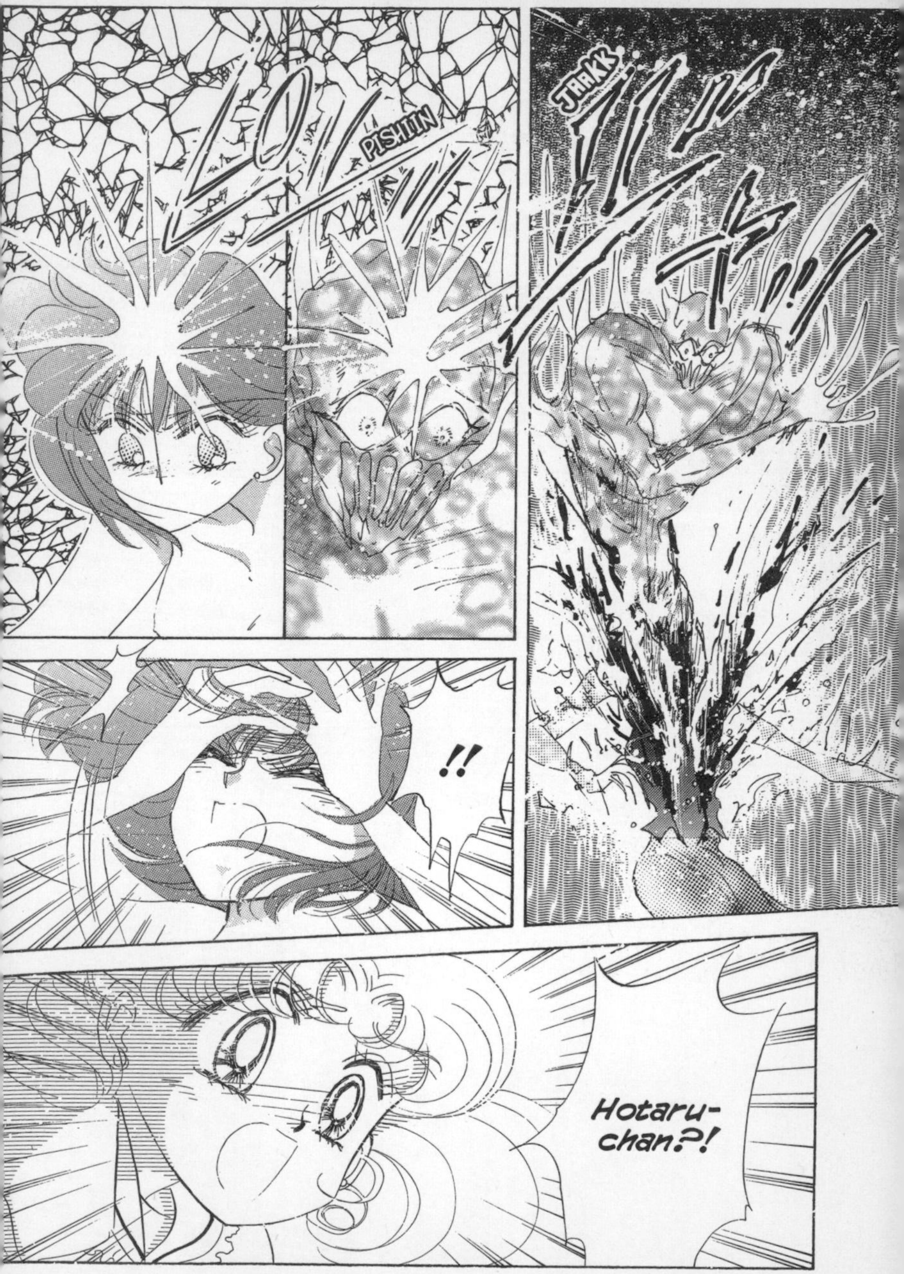
JAAKK
PISHIIN
!!
Hotaru-
chan?!

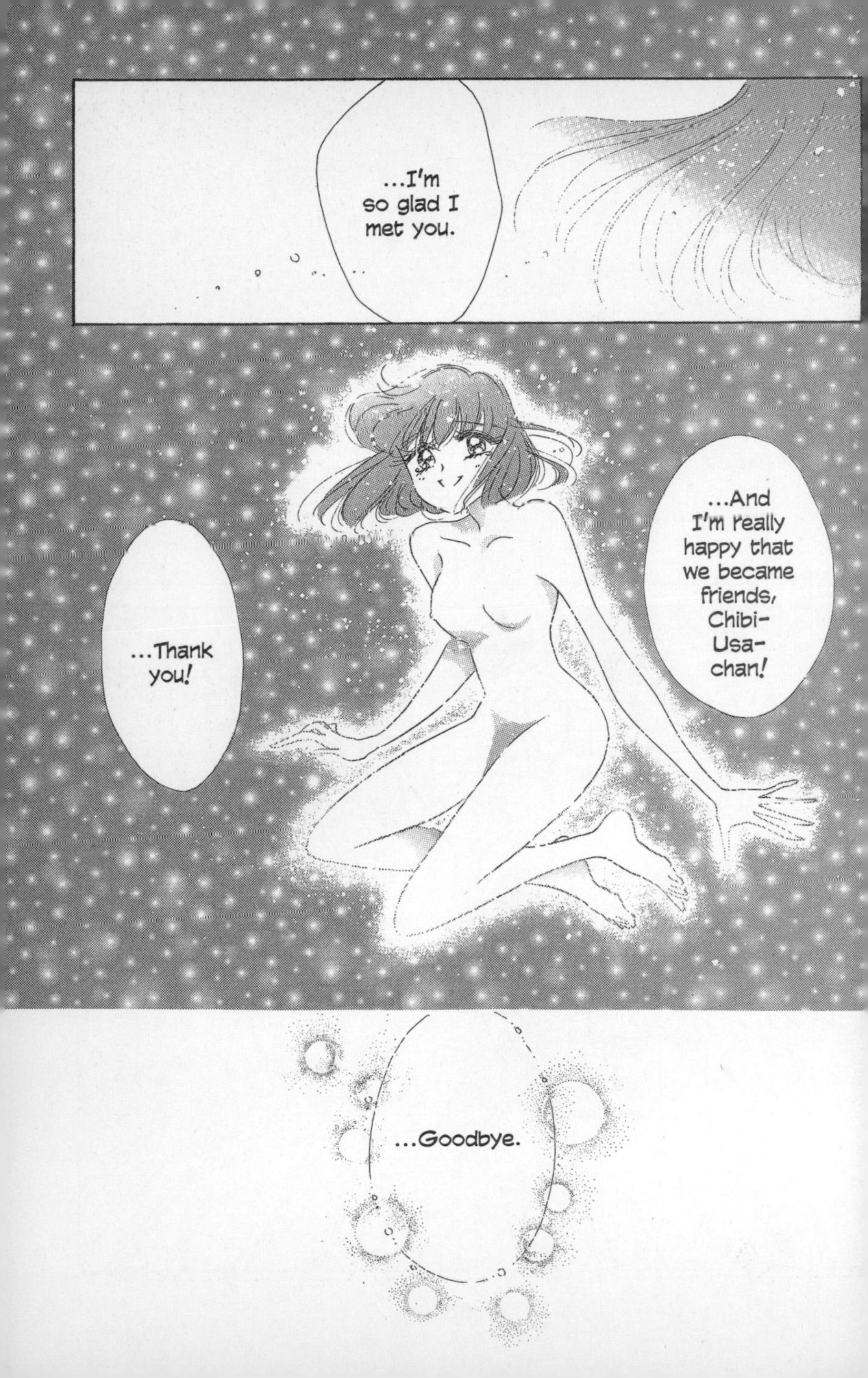
...I'm so glad I met you.
...And I'm really happy that we became friends, Chibi-Usa-chan!
...Thank you!
...Goodbye.

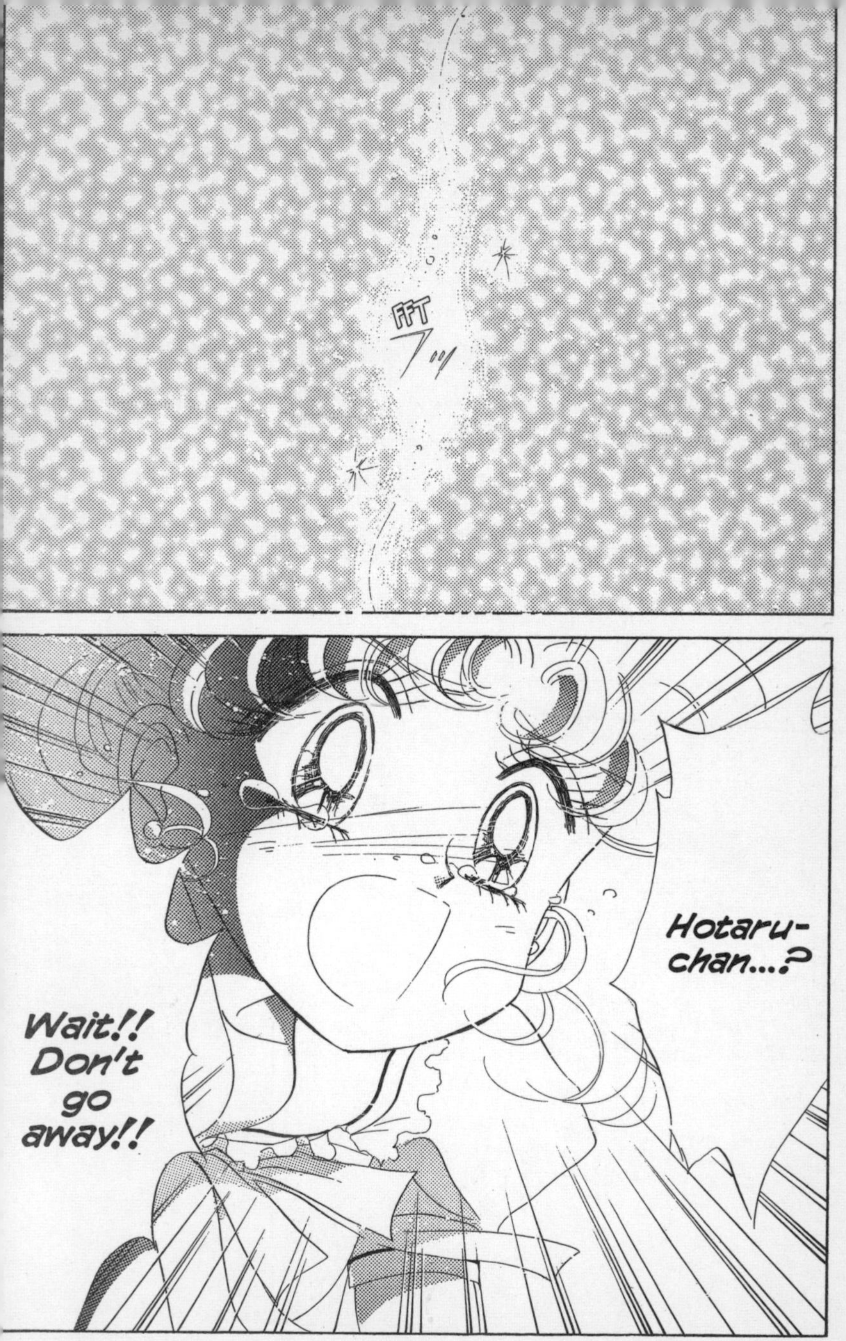
FFT
フッ
Hotaru-chan...?
Wait!! Don't go away!!

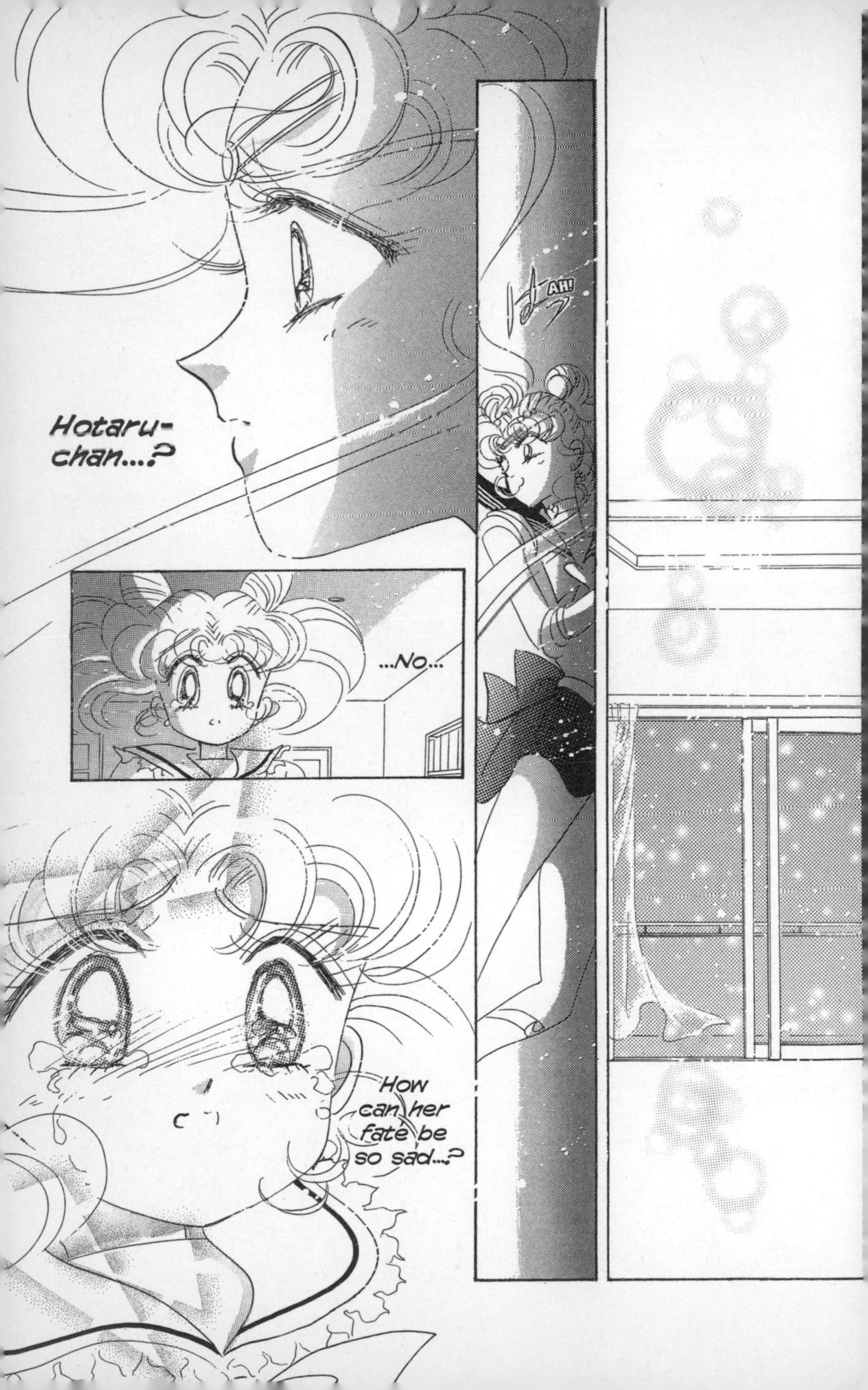
はっ
AH!
Hotaru-chan...?
...No...
How can her fate be so sad...?

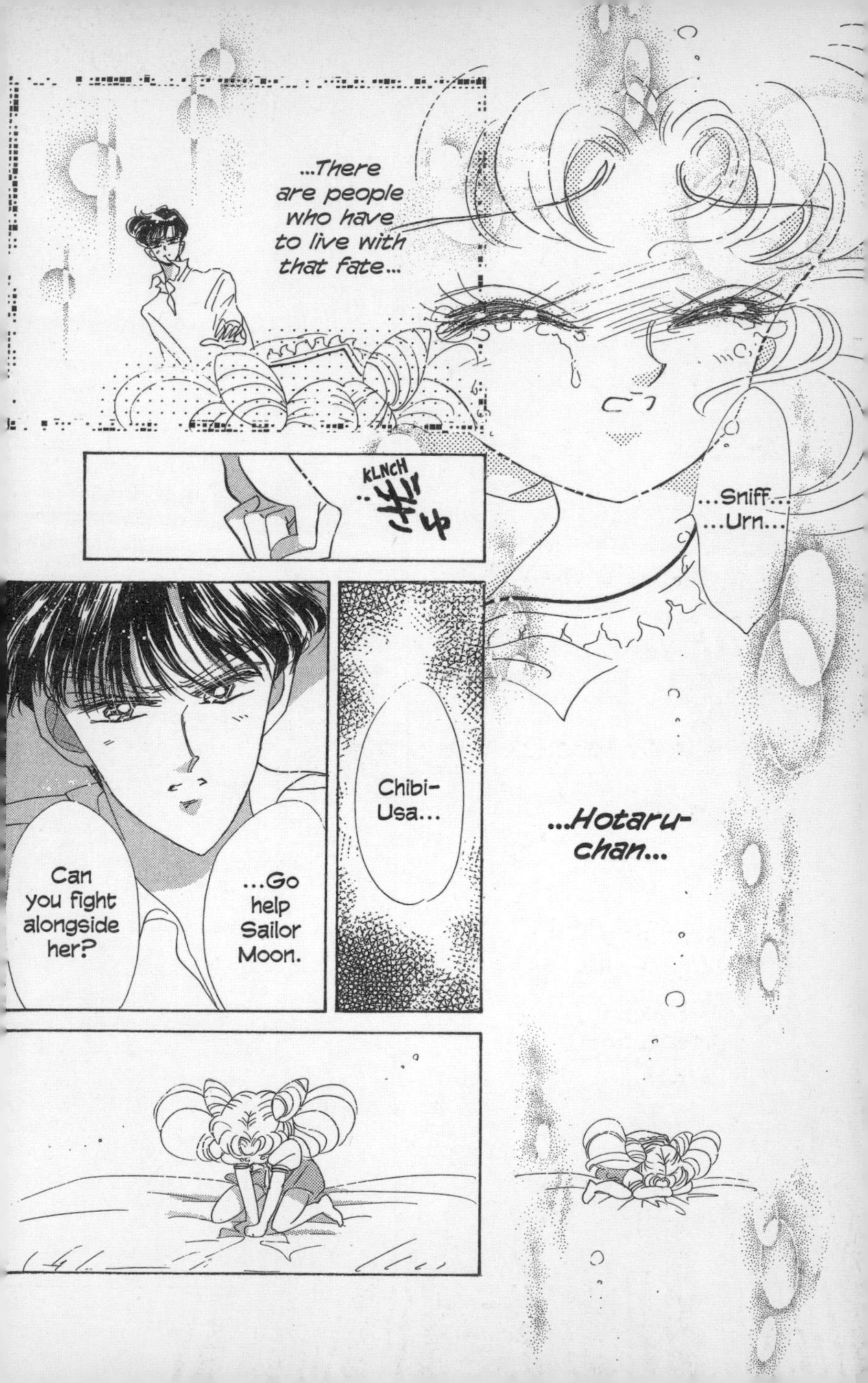
...There are people who have to live with that fate...
...Sniff... ...Urn...
...Hotaru-chan...
KLNCH
ぎゅ
Chibi-Usa...
...Go help Sailor Moon.
Can you fight alongside her?

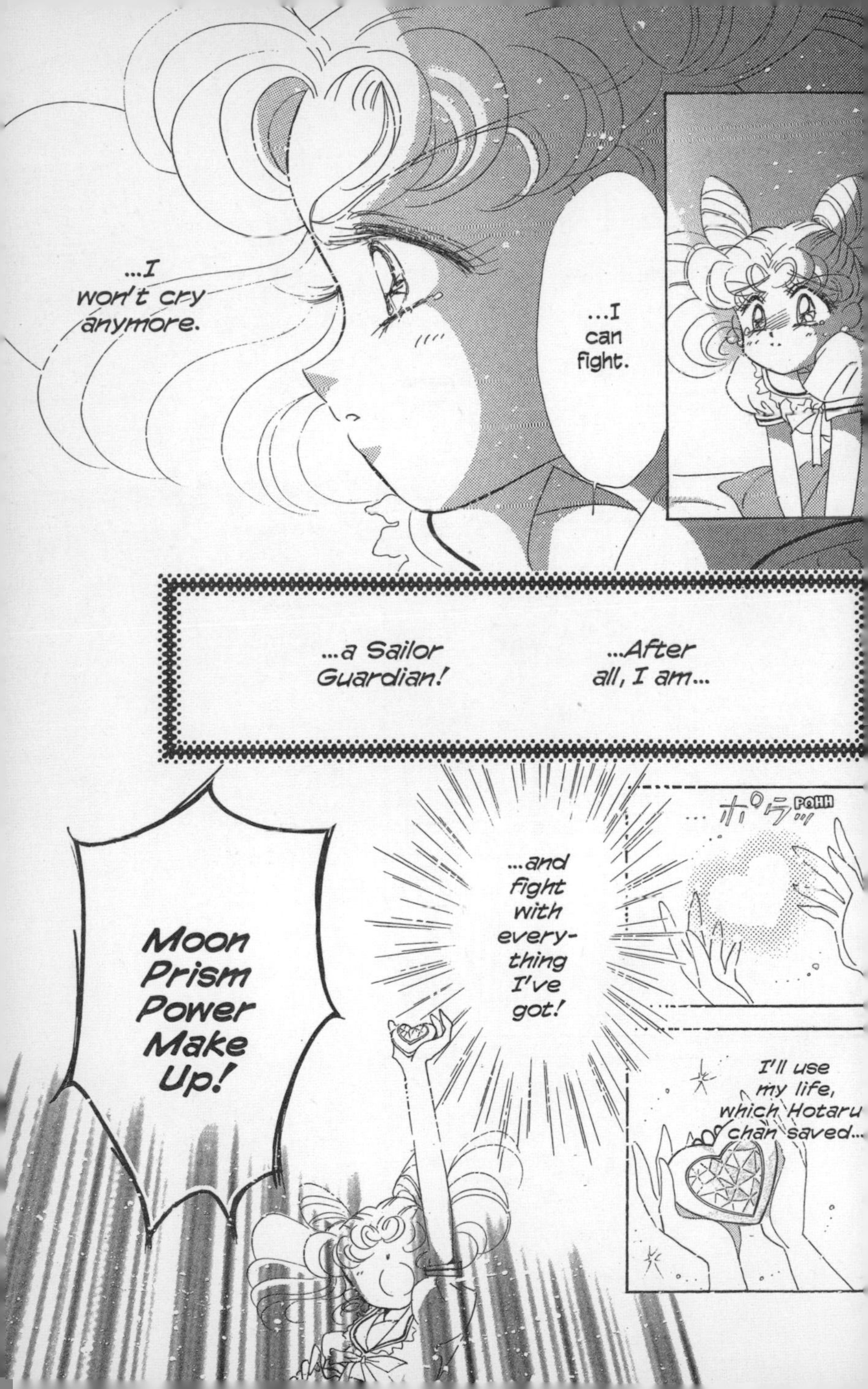
...I can fight.
...I won't cry anymore.
...After all, I am...
...a Sailor Guardian!
POHH
I'll use my life, which Hotaru chan saved...
...and fight with everything I've got!
Moon Prism Power Make Up!

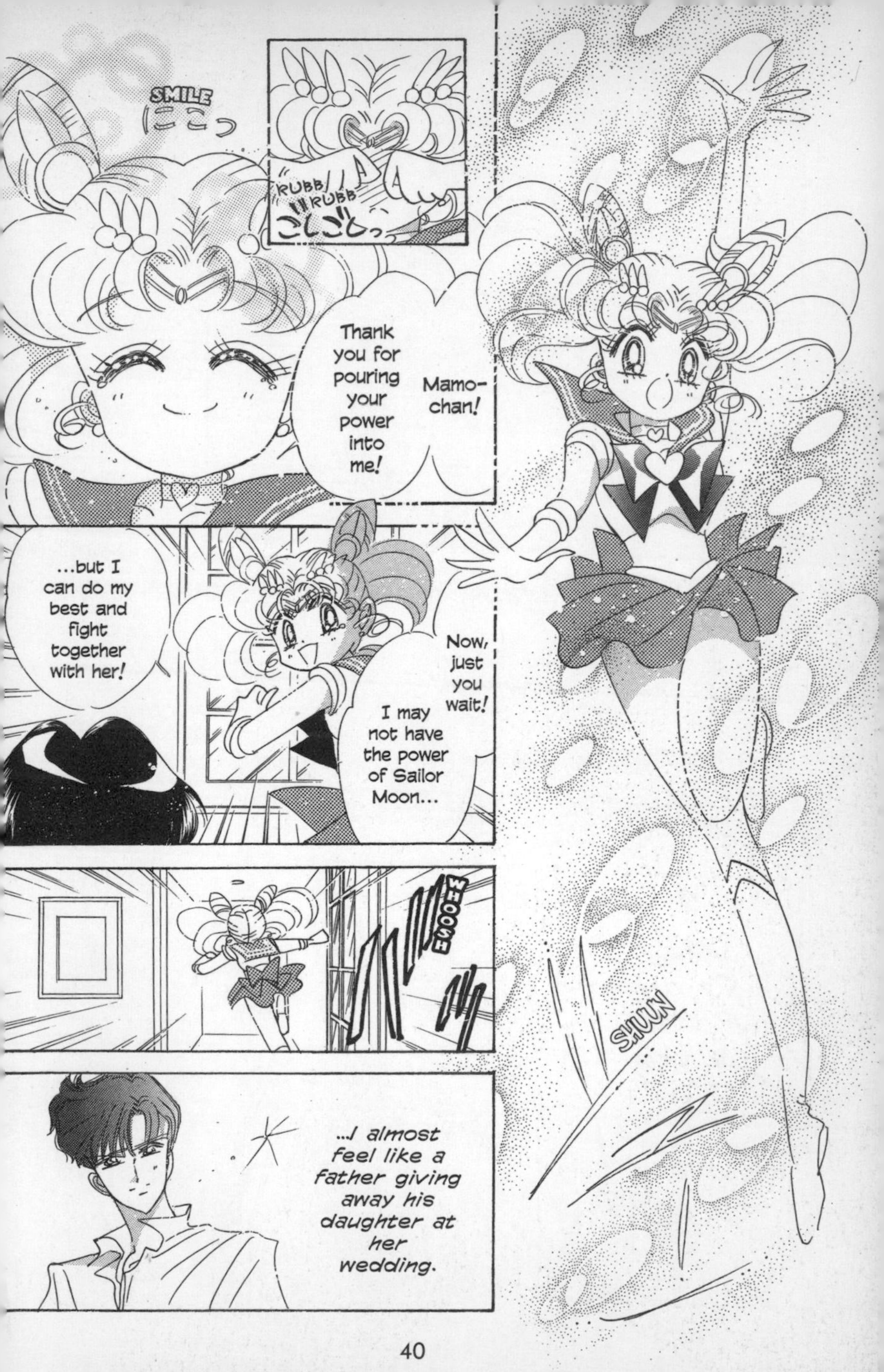
SHUUN
RUBB RUBB
ごしごしっ
SMILE
にこっ
Mamo-chan!
Thank you for pouring your power into me!
Now, just you wait!
I may not have the power of Sailor Moon...
...but I can do my best and fight together with her!
WHOOSH
...I almost feel like a father giving away his daughter at her wedding.

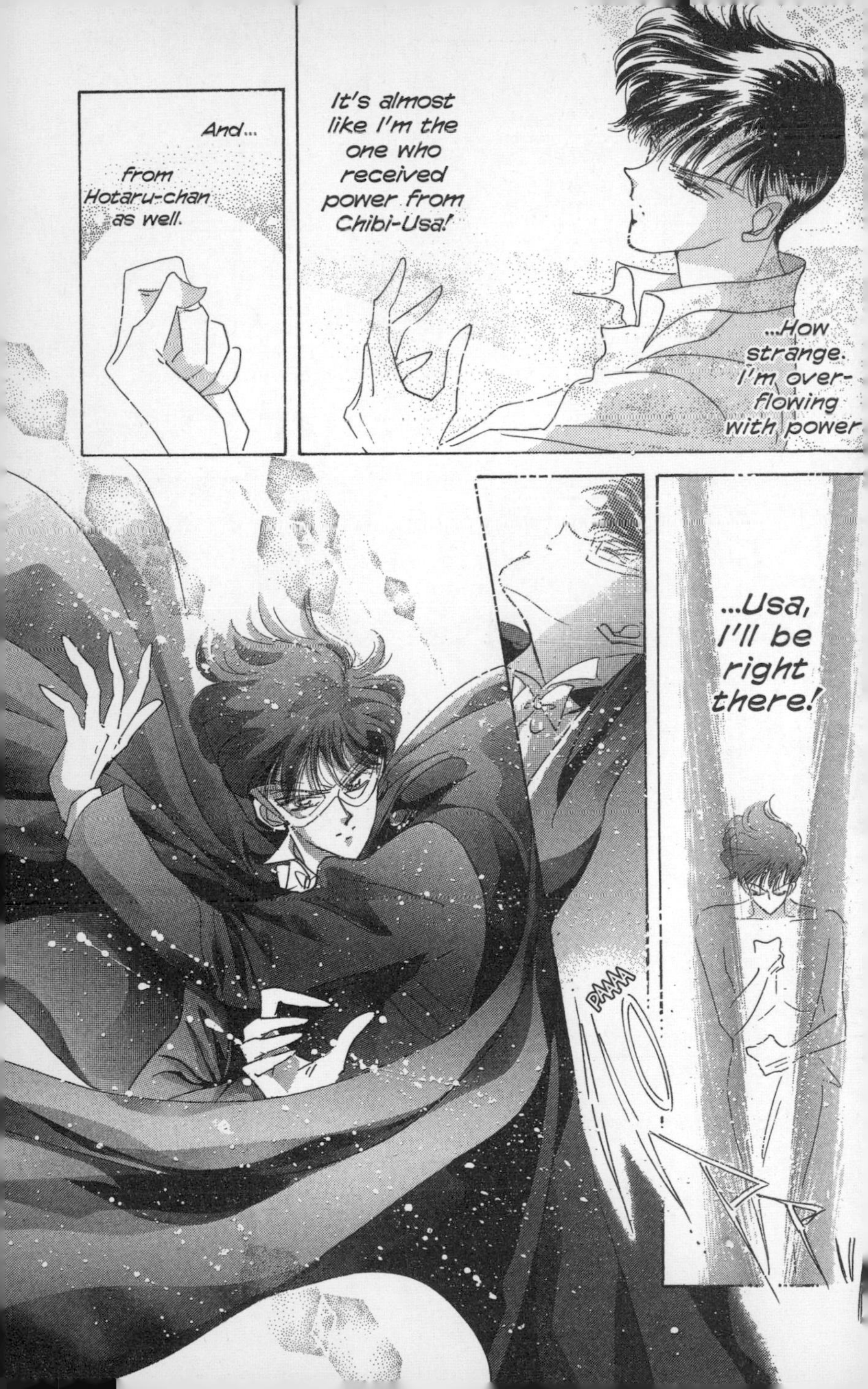
...How strange. I'm over-flowing with power
It's almost like I'm the one who received power from Chibi-Usa!
And...
from Hotaru-chan as well.
...Usa, I'll be right there!
PAAAA

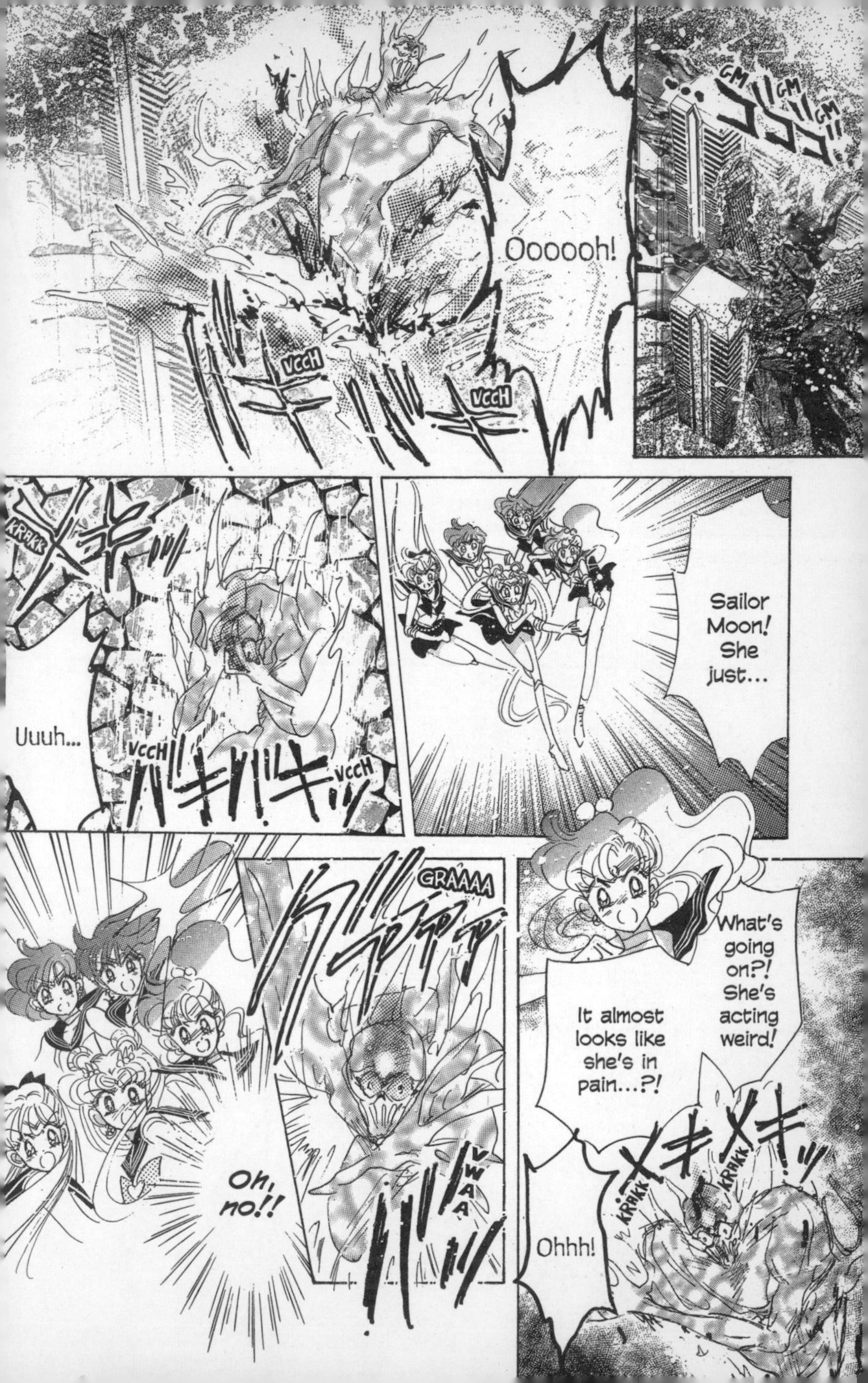
GM GM GM
Oooooh!
VCCH
VCCH
Sailor Moon! She just...
KRAKK
Uuuh...
VCCH
VCCH
What's going on?! She's acting weird!
It almost looks like she's in pain...?!
KRAKK
KRAKK
Ohhh!
GRAAAA
VWAA
Oh, no!!

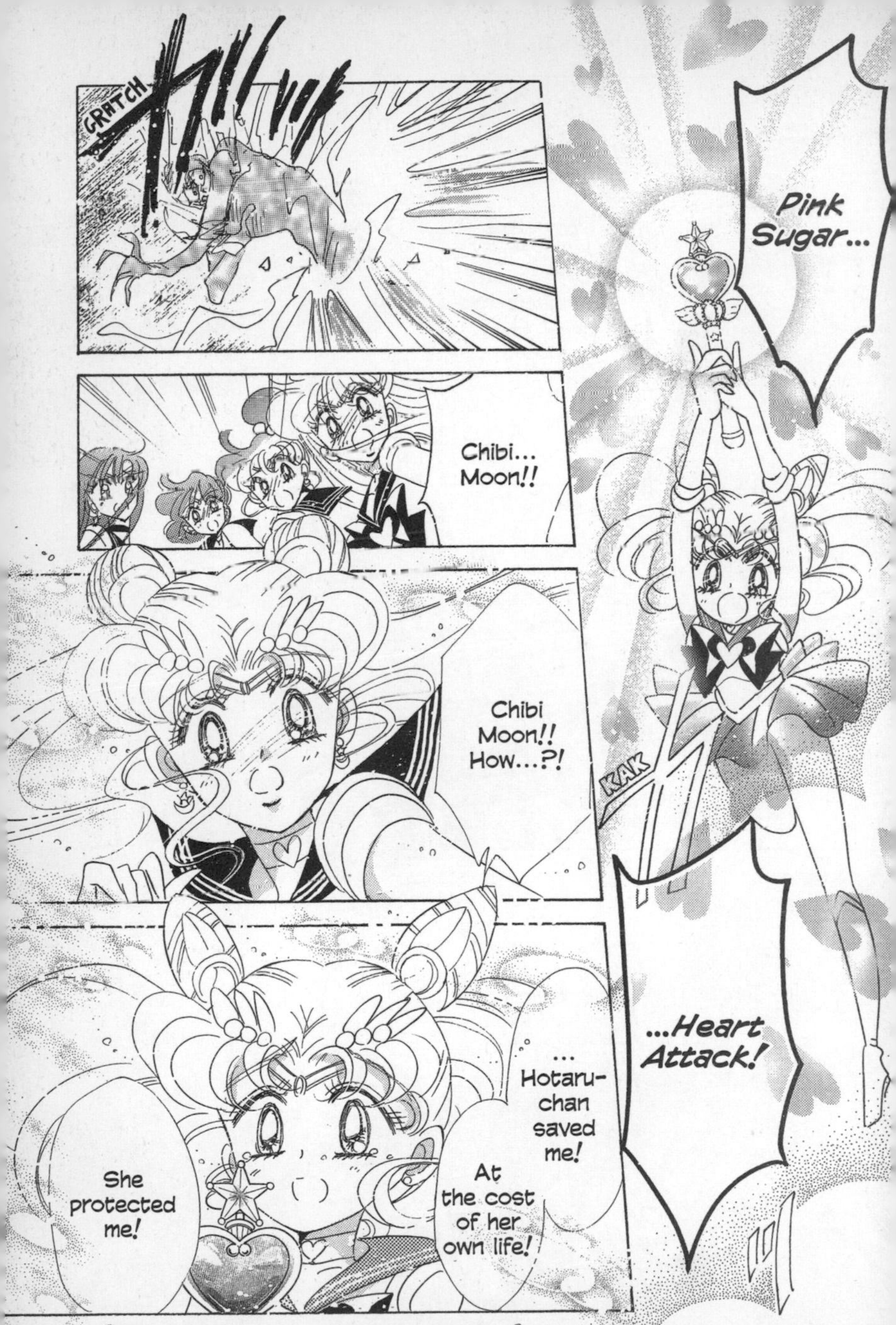
Pink Sugar...
KAK
...Heart Attack!
GRATCH
Chibi... Moon!!
Chibi Moon!! How...?!
...Hotaru-chan saved me!
At the cost of her own life!
She protected me!

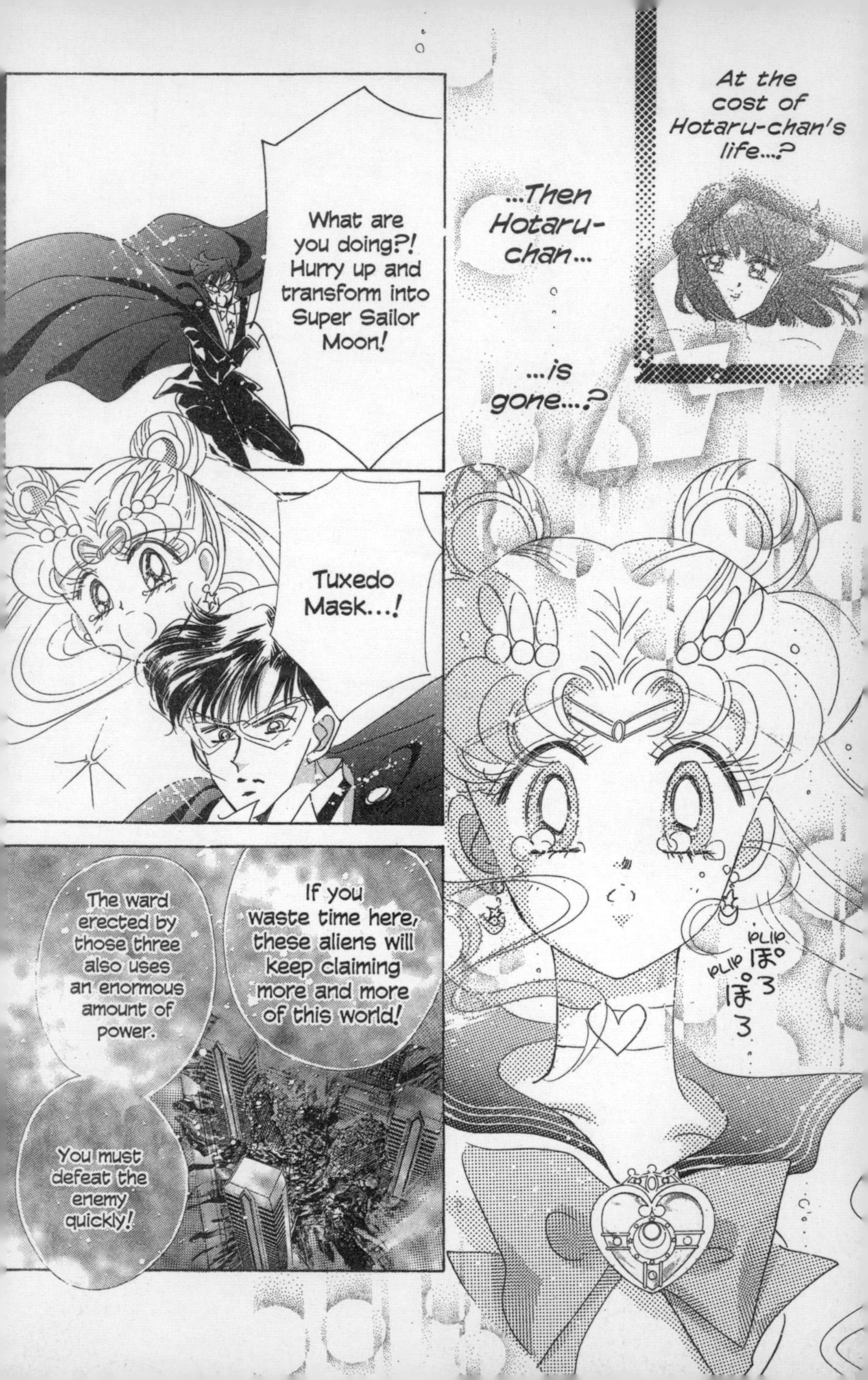
At the cost of Hotaru-chan's life...?
...Then Hotaru-chan...
...is gone...?
ぽろ plip
ぽろ plip
What are you doing?! Hurry up and transform into Super Sailor Moon!
Tuxedo Mask...!
If you waste time here, these aliens will keep claiming more and more of this world!
The ward erected by those three also uses an enormous amount of power.
You must defeat the enemy quickly!

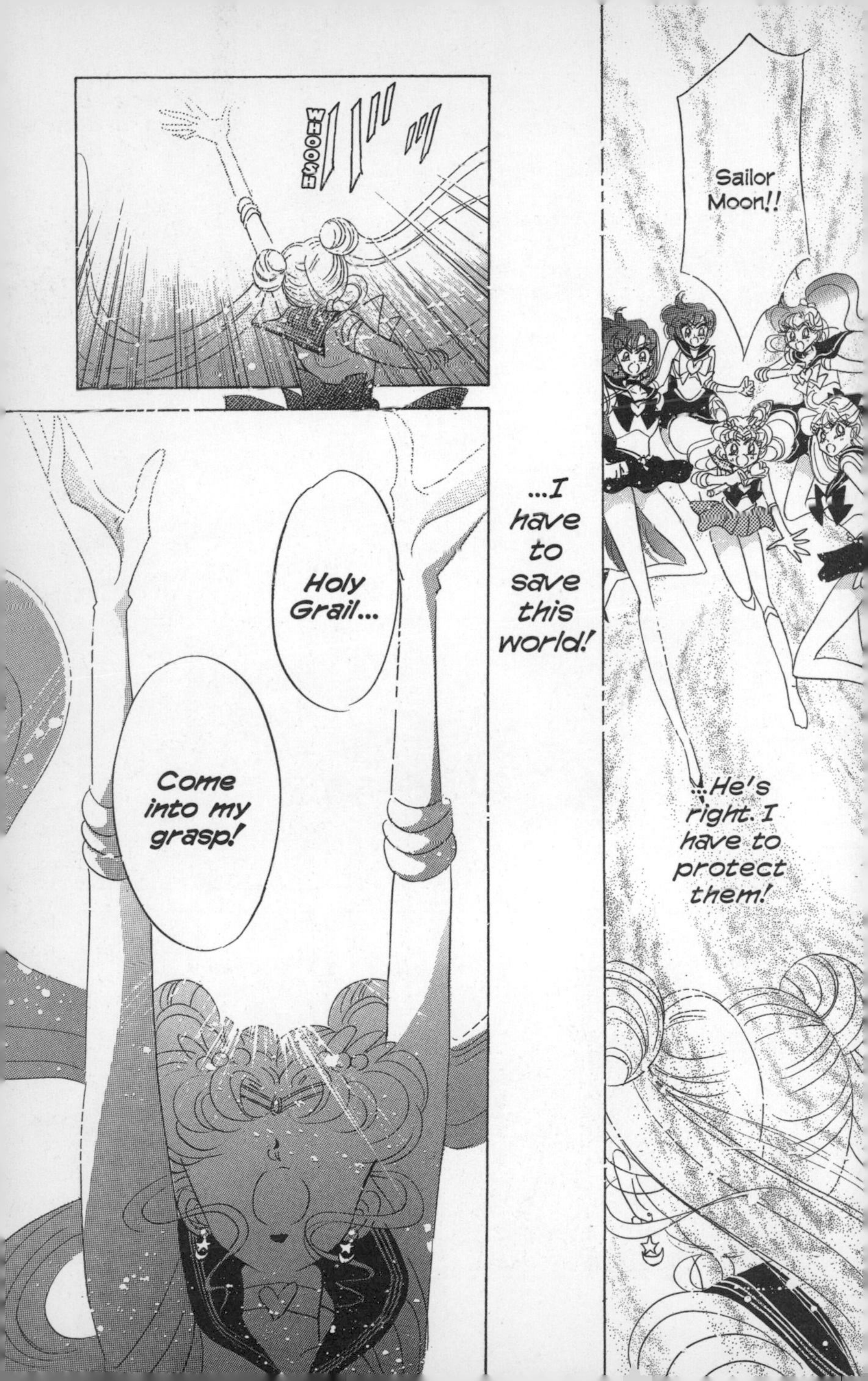
Sailor Moon!!
...He's right. I have to protect them!
...I have to save this world!
WHOOSH
Holy Grail...
Come into my grasp!

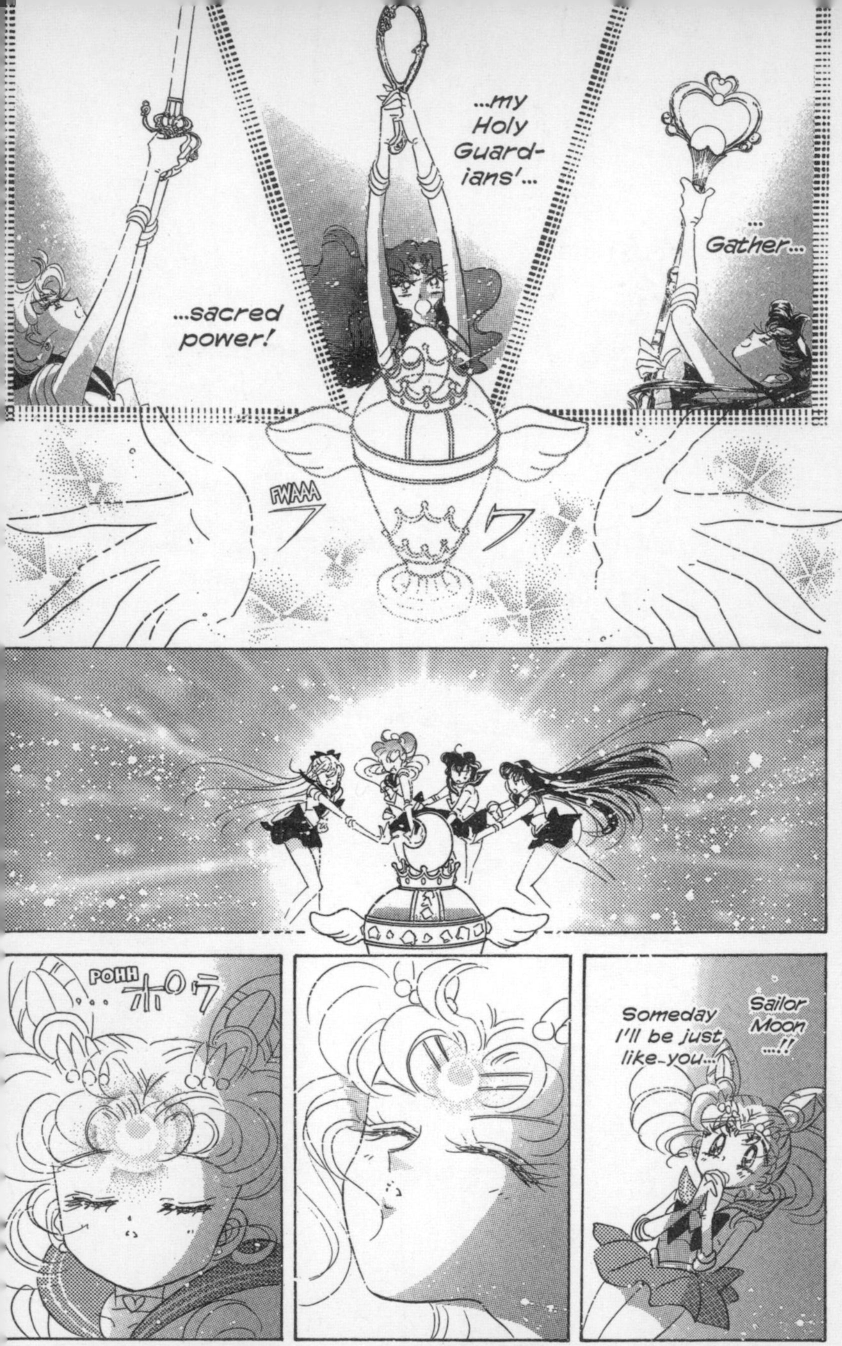

... Gather...
...my Holy Guard-ians'...
...sacred power!
FWAAA
Sailor Moon ...!!
Someday I'll be just like-you...
POHH
...

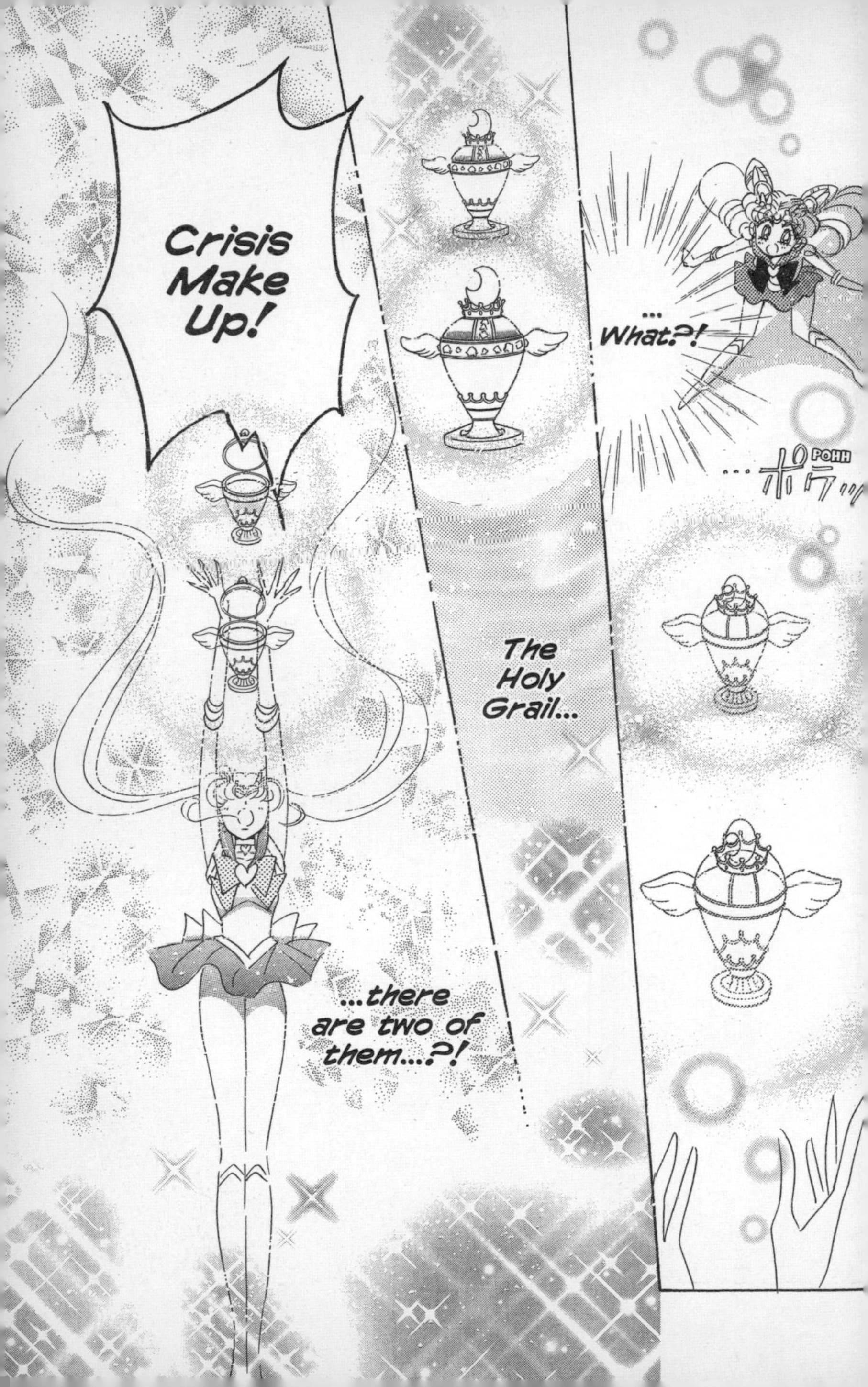
...What?!
...ポワッ
POHH
The Holy Grail...
Crisis Make Up!
...there are two of them...?!

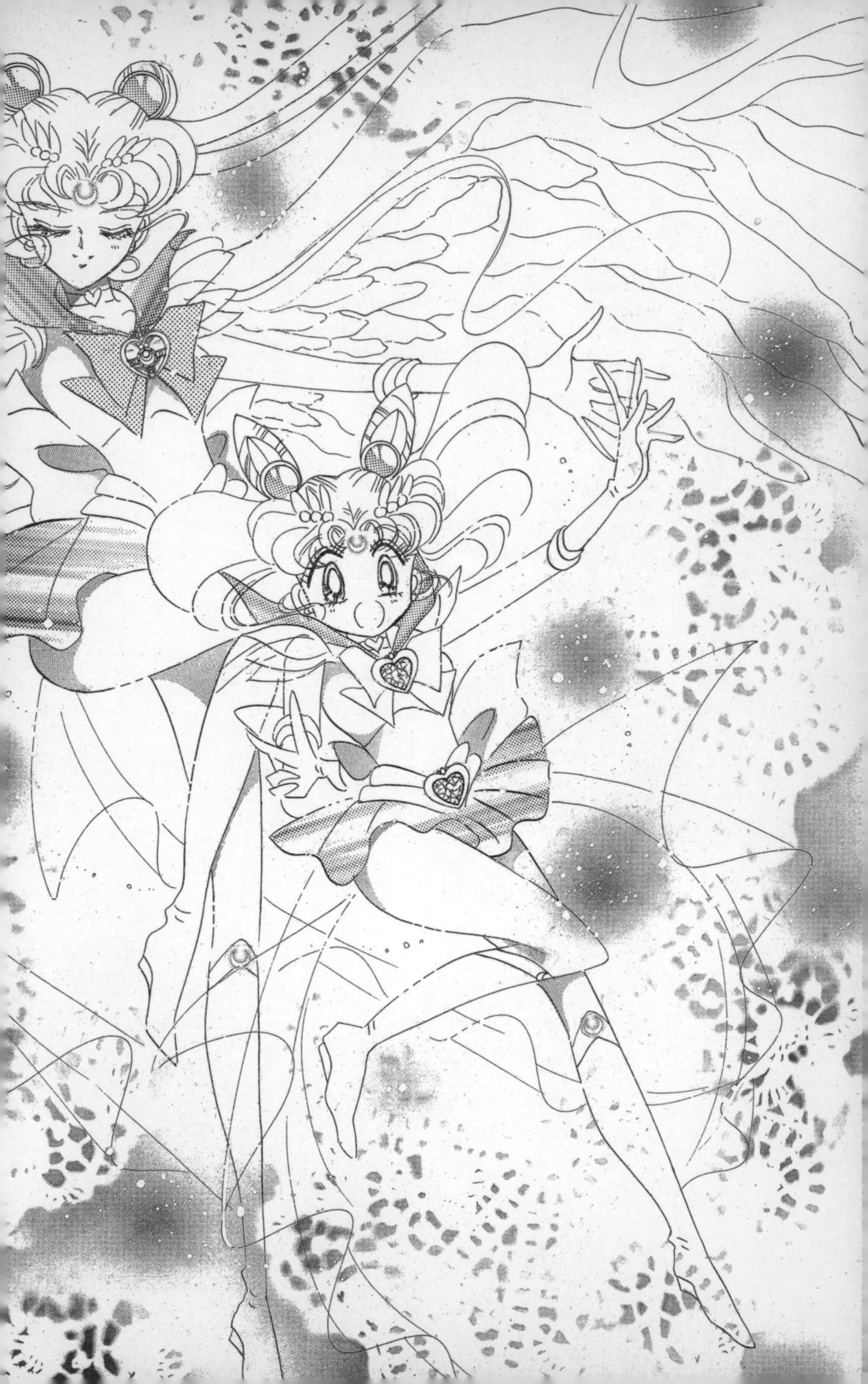

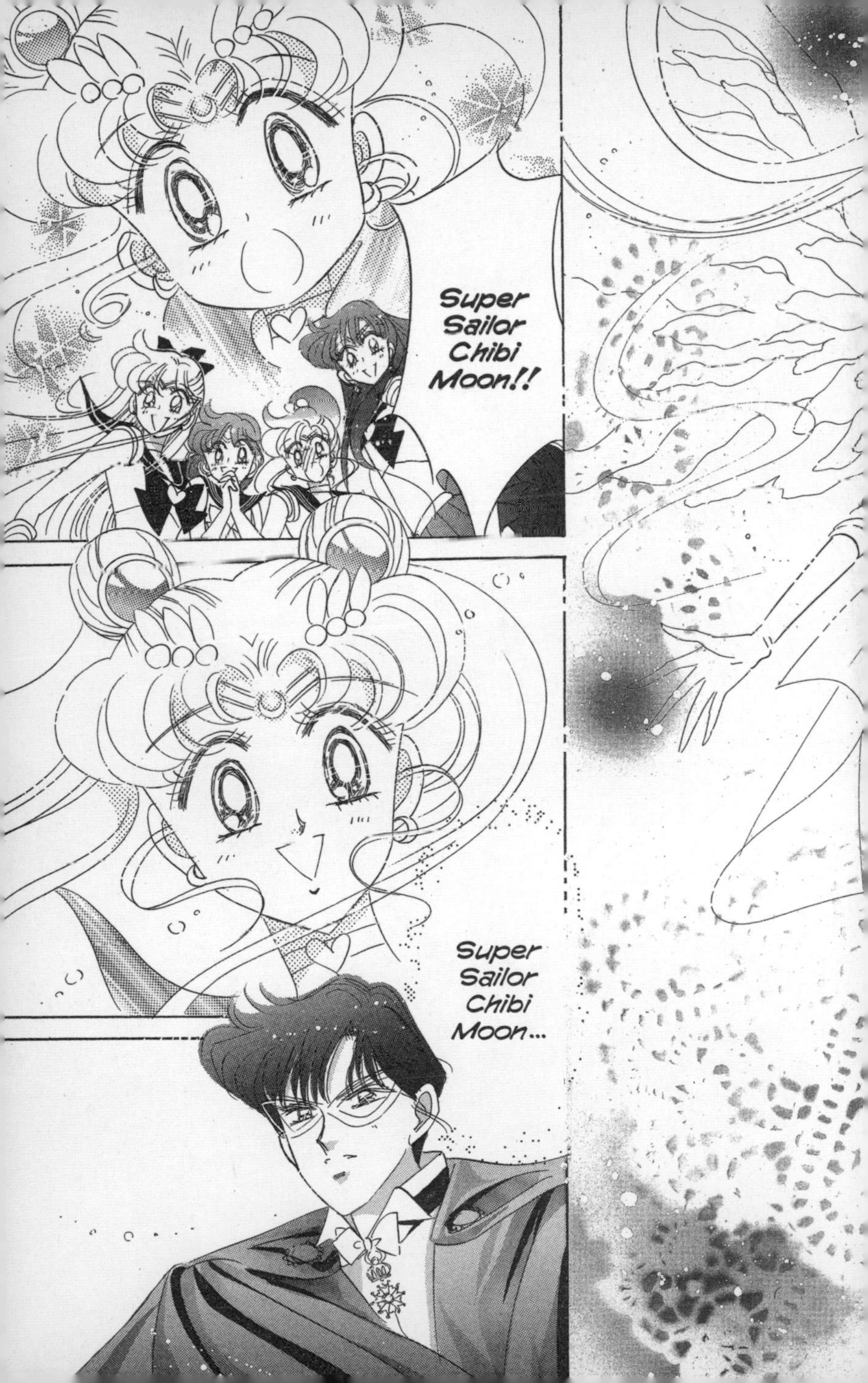
Super Sailor Chibi Moon!!
Super Sailor Chibi Moon...

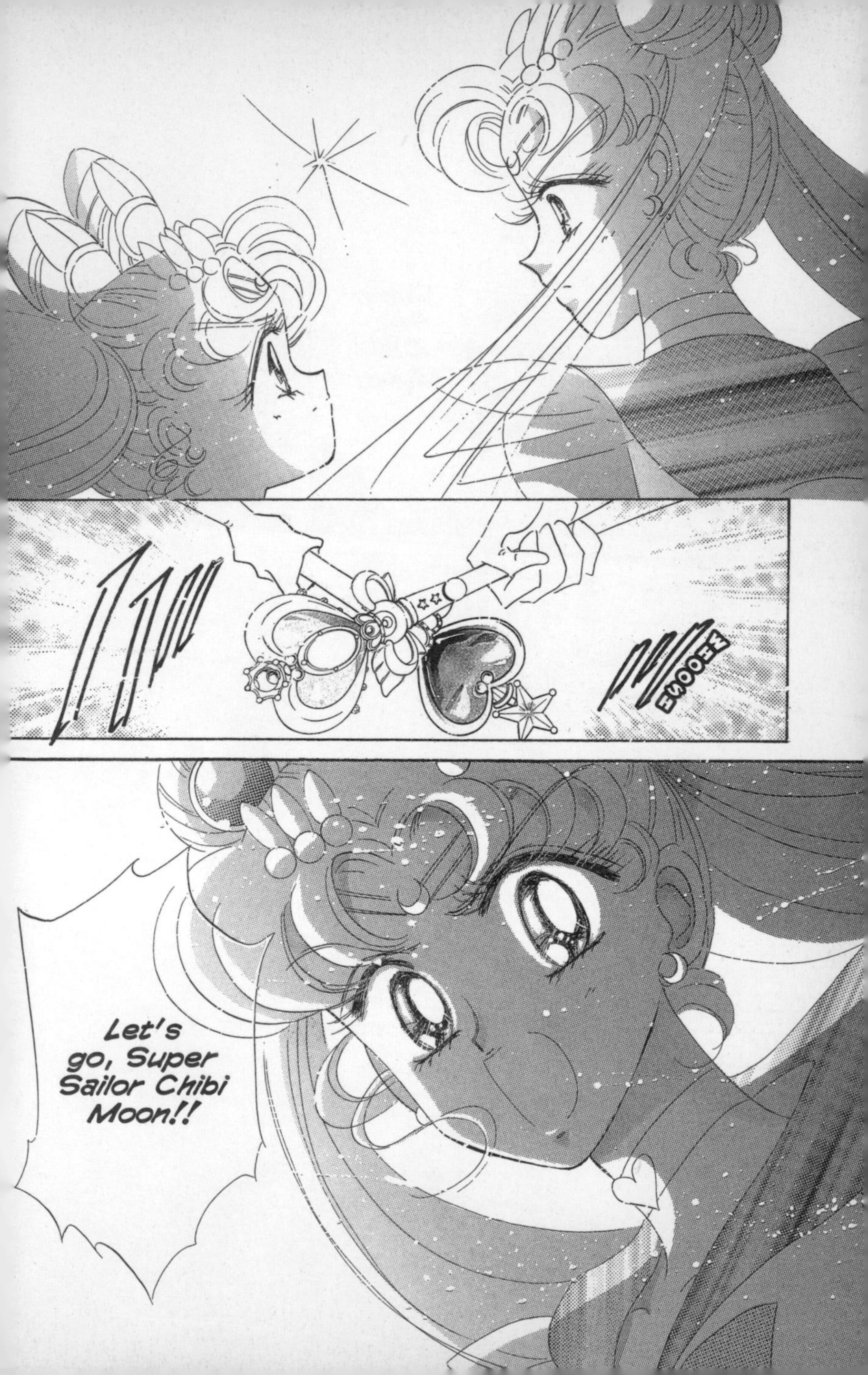
WHOOSH
Let's go, Super Sailor Chibi Moon!!

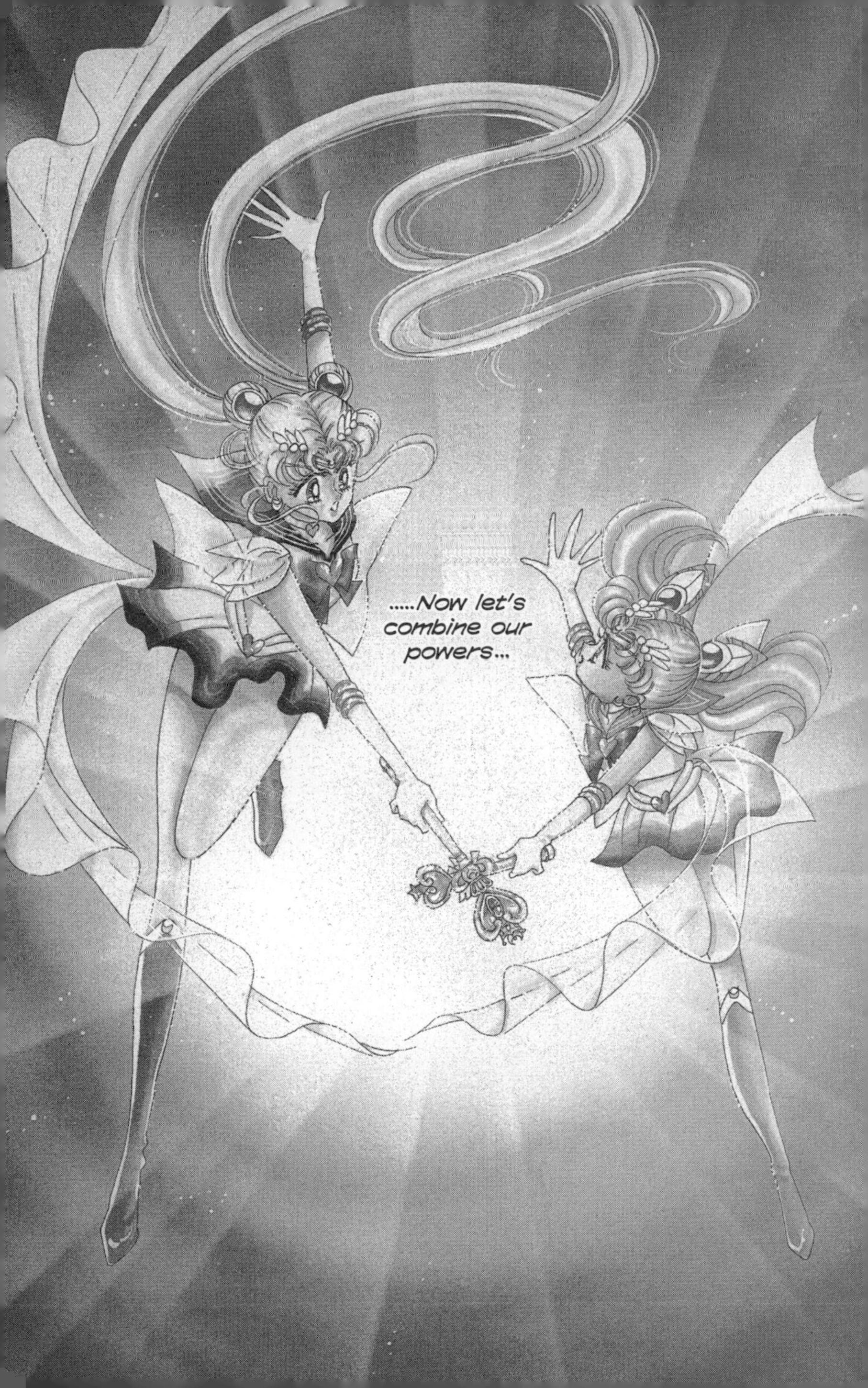
.....Now let's combine our powers...

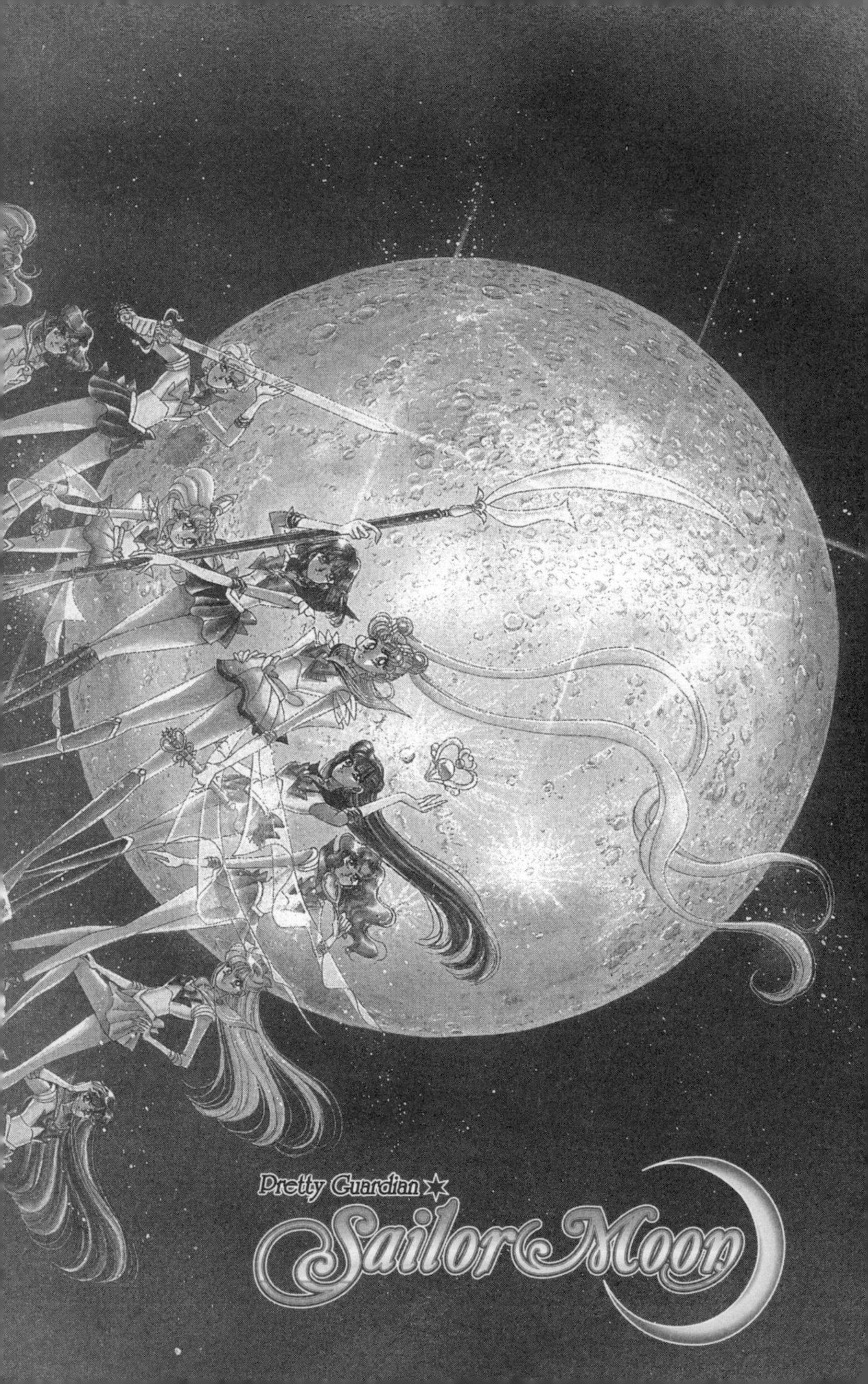
Pretty Guardian
Sailor Moon

Act 37 Infinity 11, Infinite -- Judge

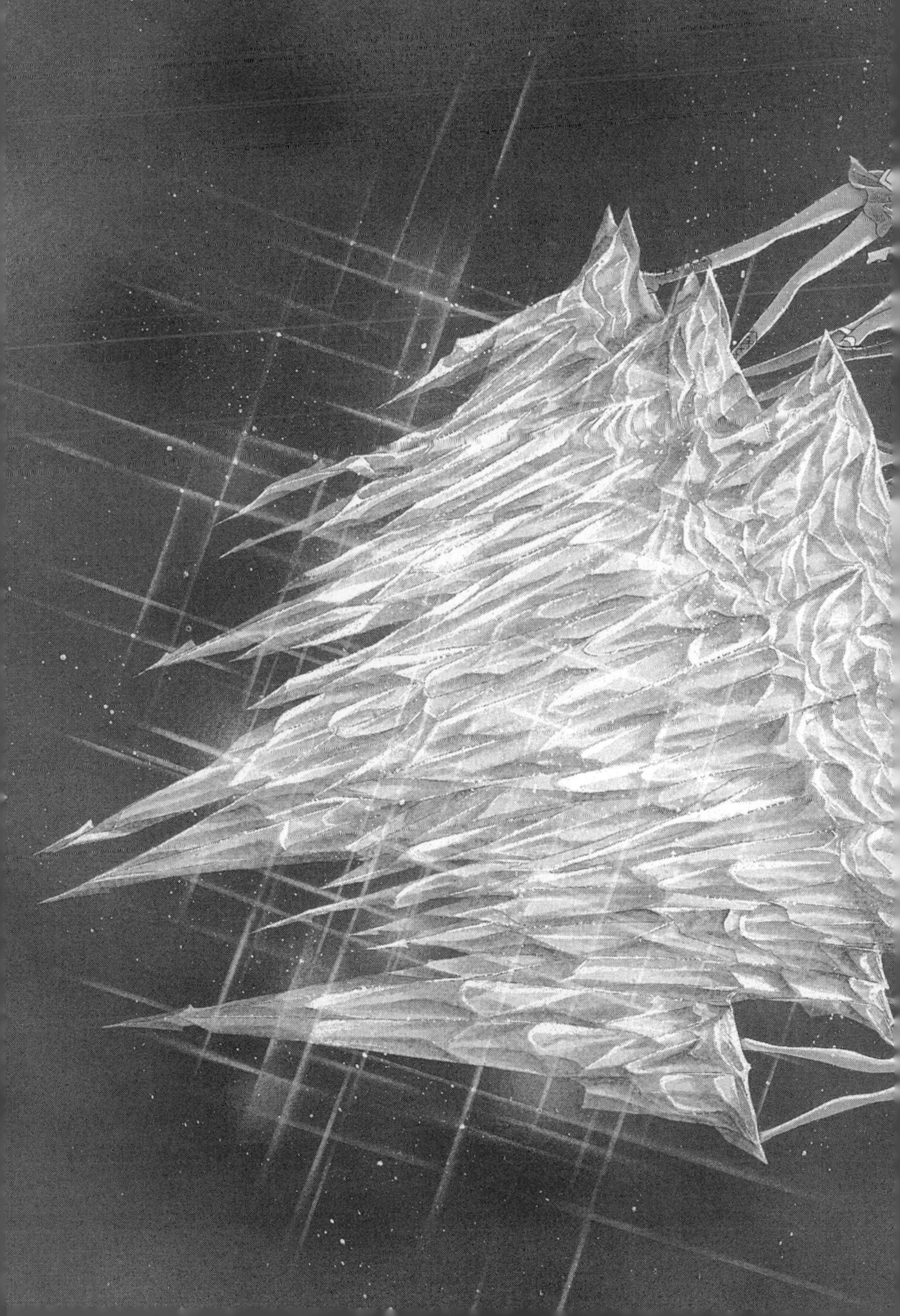

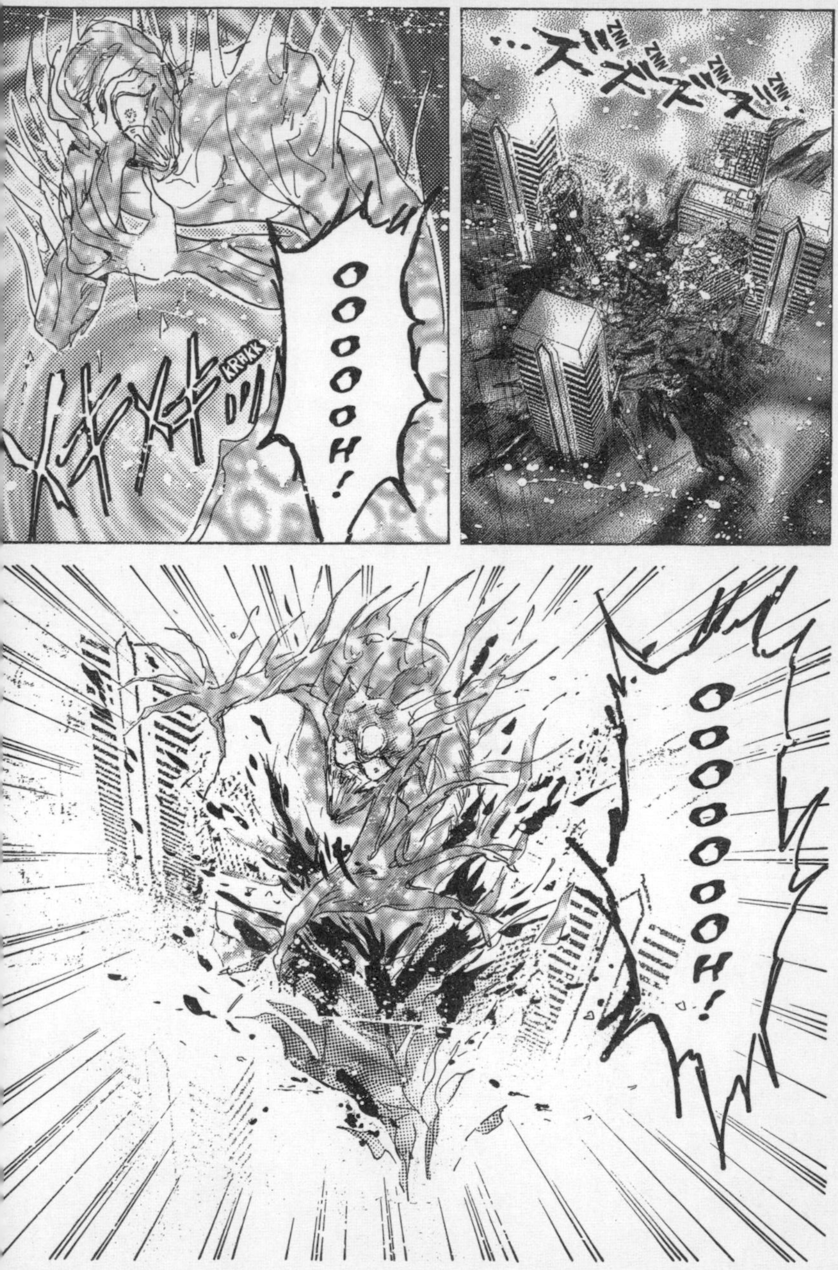
...
ZNN ZNN ZNN ZNN
OOOOOH!
KRAKK
OOOOOOOH!

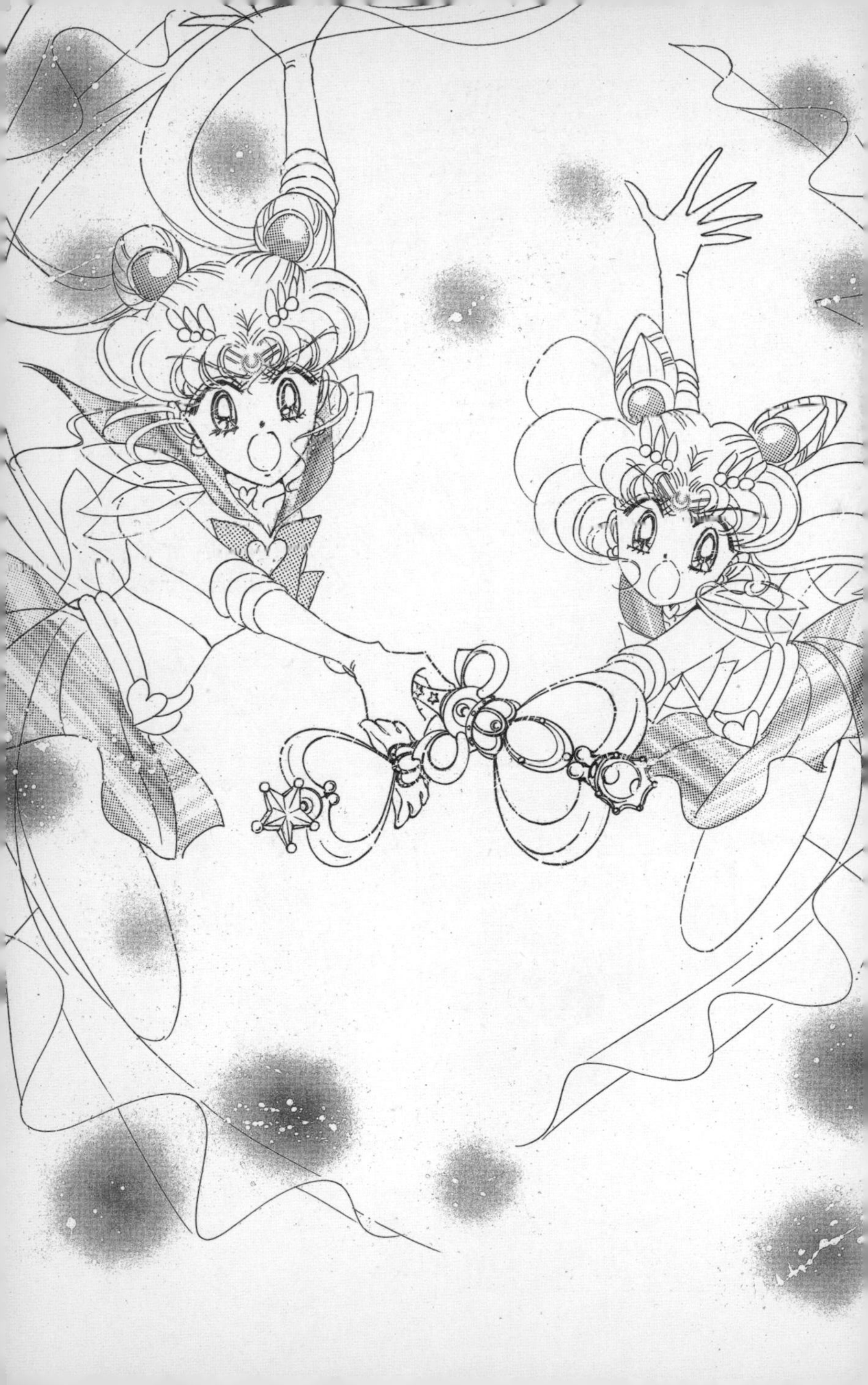

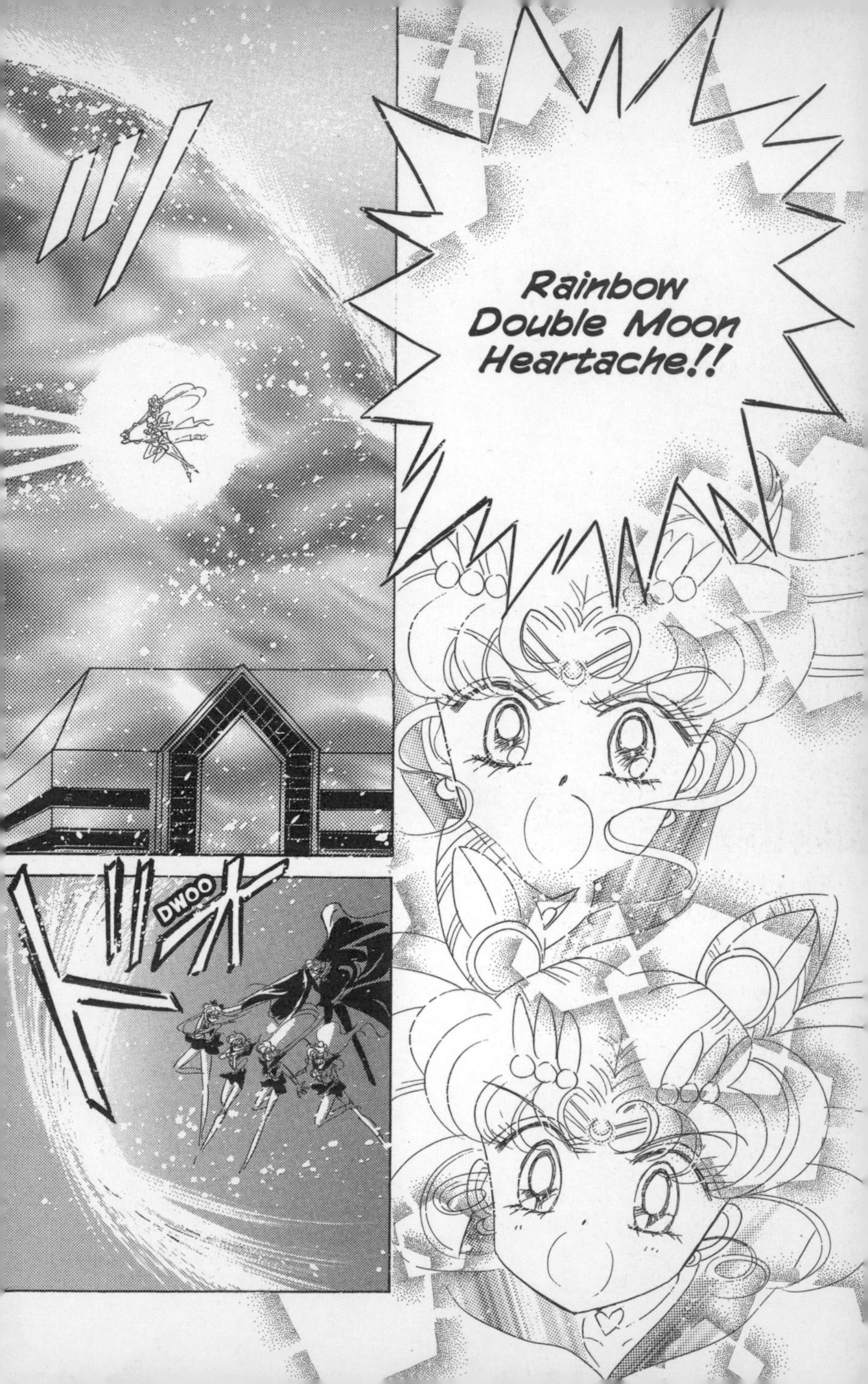
Rainbow Double Moon Heartache!!
DWOO

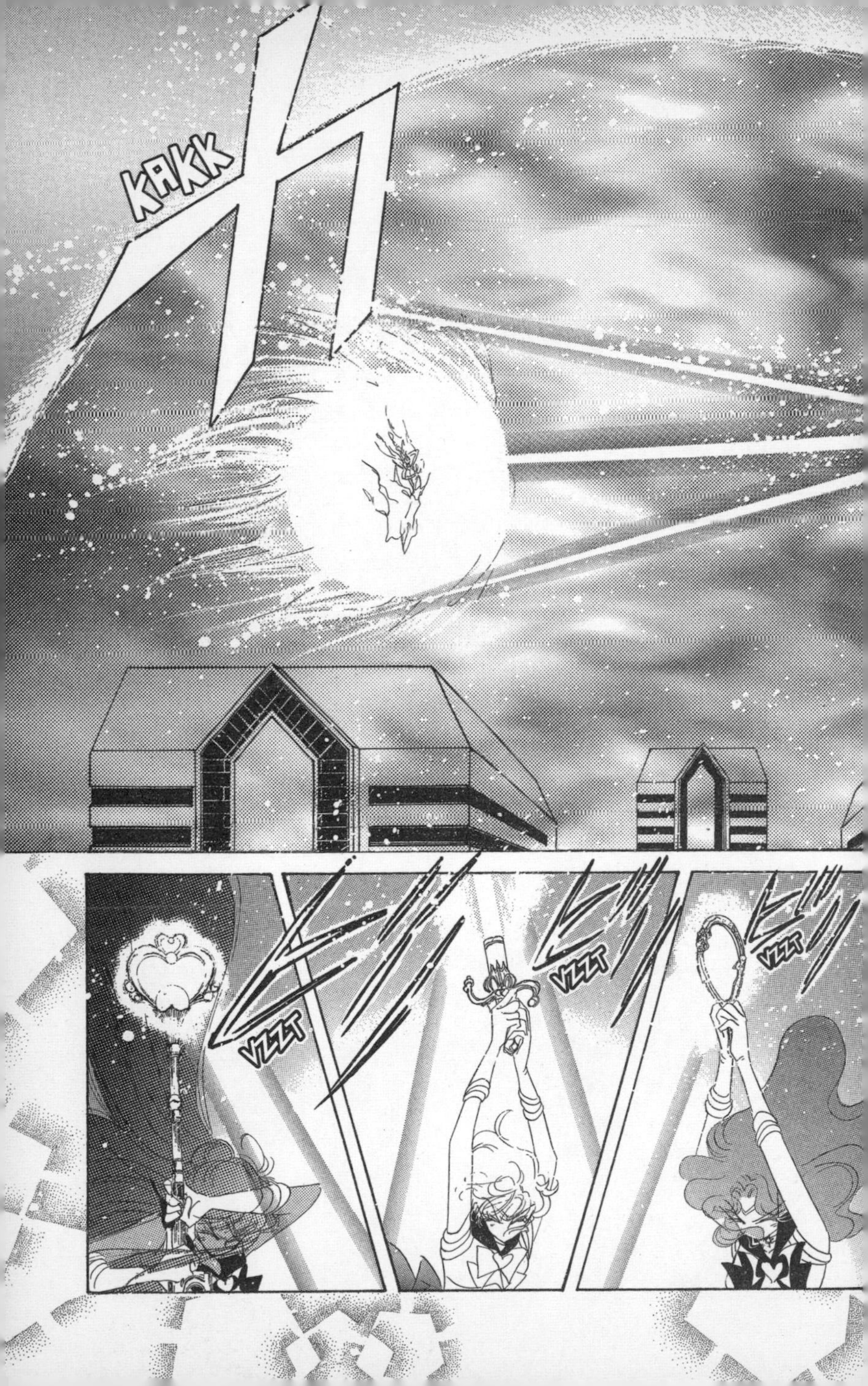
KAKK
VZZT
VZZT
VZZZT

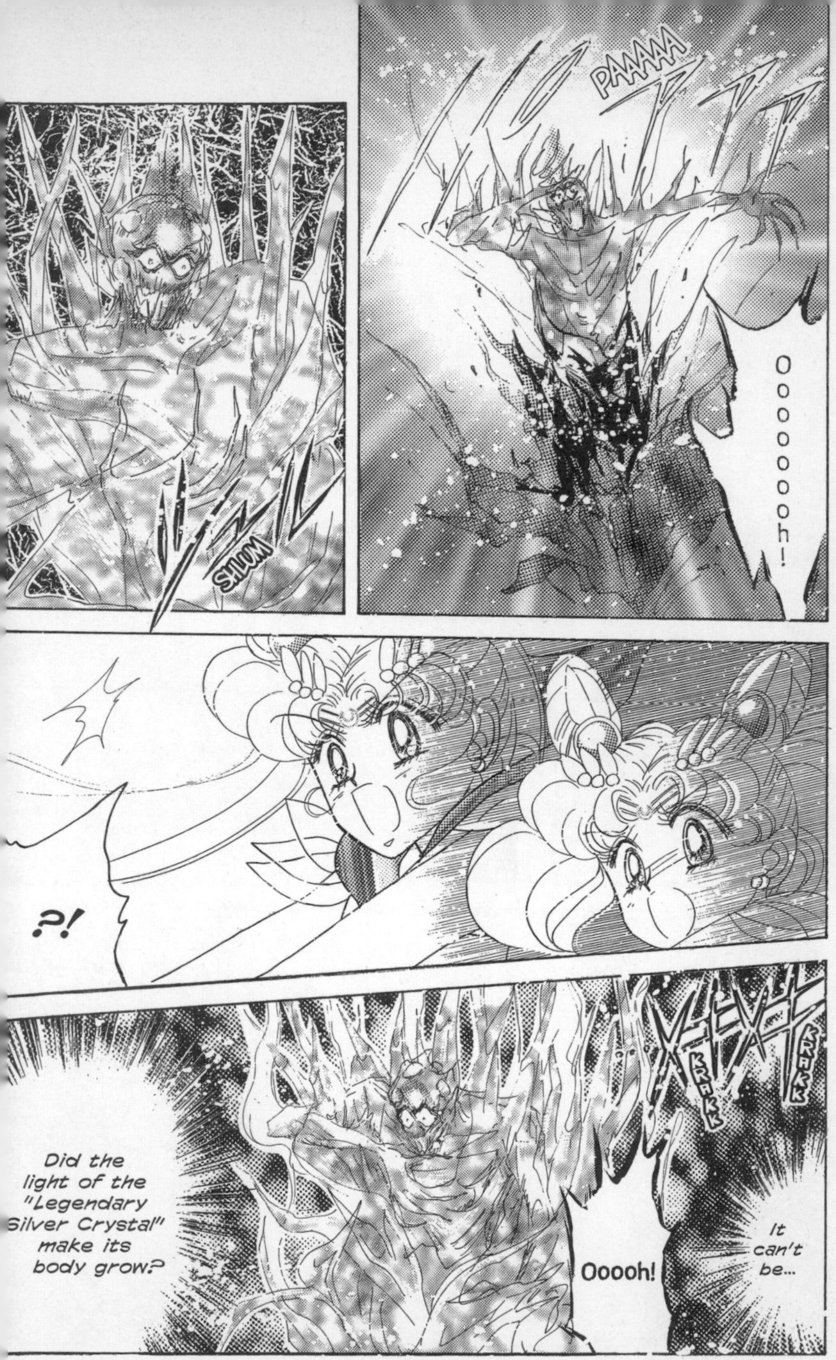
PAAAAA
Oooooooh!
SHLUM
?!
KRAKK
KRAKK
It can't be...
Ooooh!
Did the light of the "Legendary Silver Crystal" make its body grow?

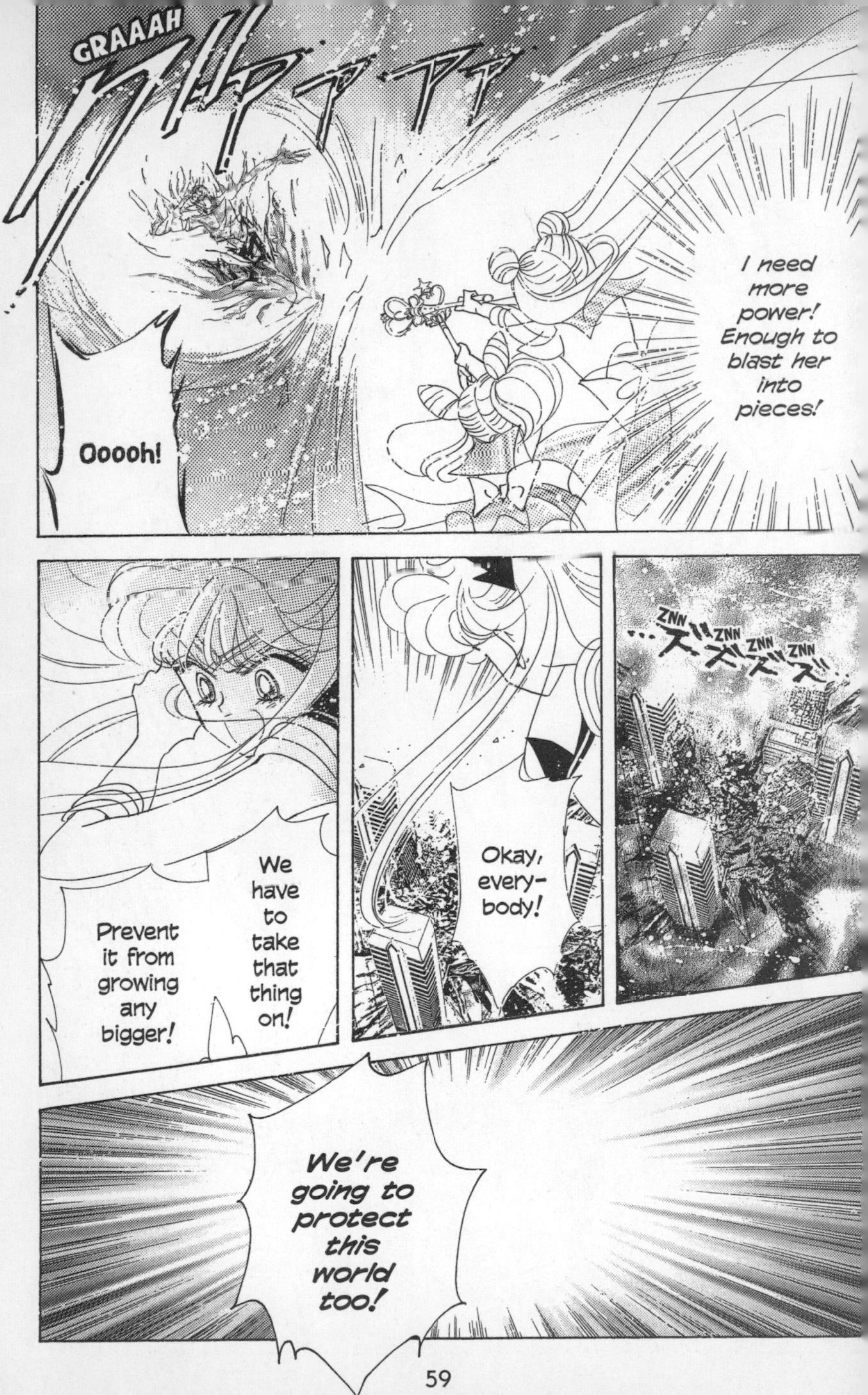
GRAAAH
I need more power! Enough to blast her into pieces!
Ooooh!
...ZNN ZNN ZNN ZNN...
Okay, every-body!
We have to take that thing on!
Prevent it from growing any bigger!
We're going to protect this world too!

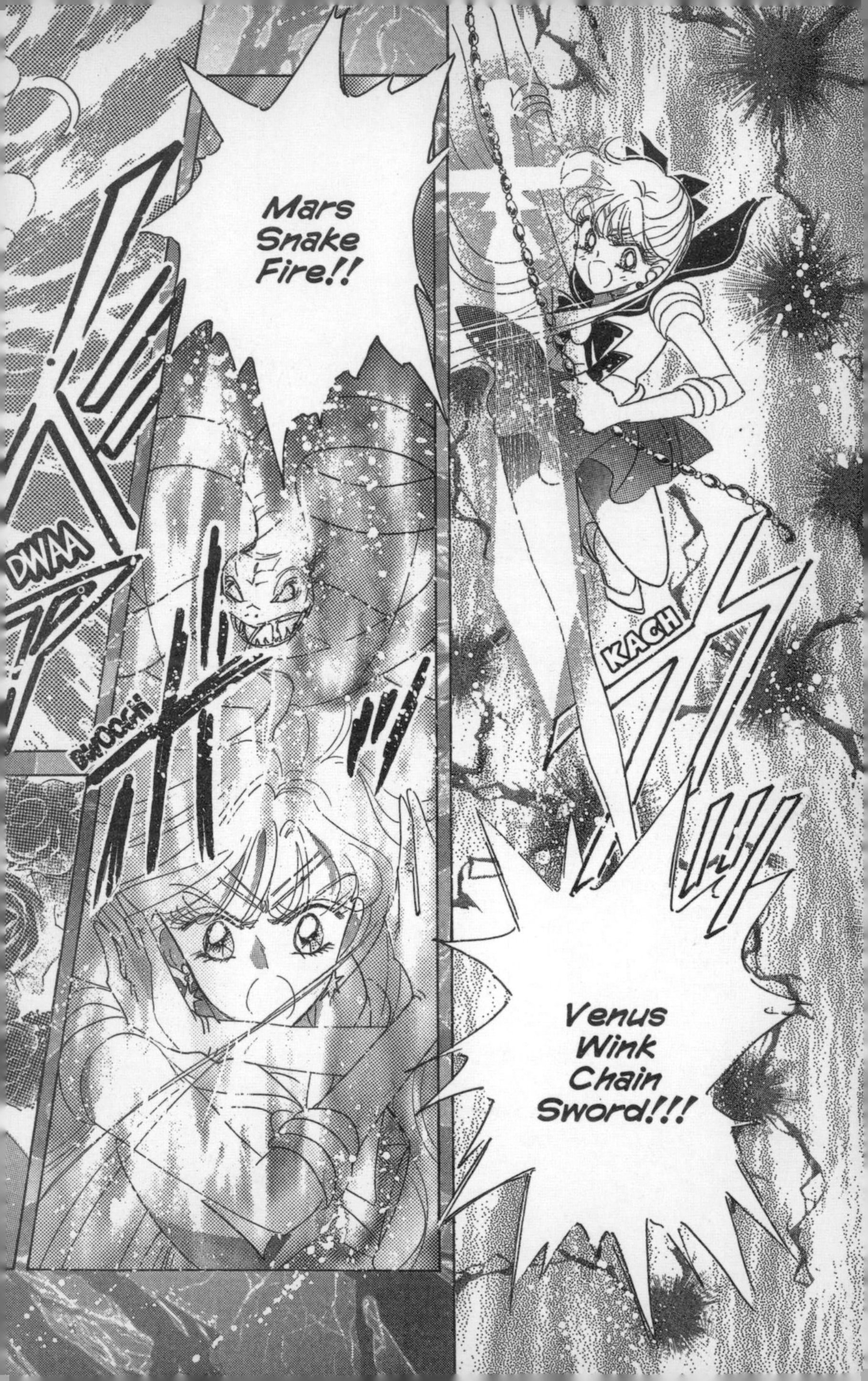
KACH
Venus Wink Chain Sword!!!
Mars Snake Fire!!
DWAA
BWOOSH

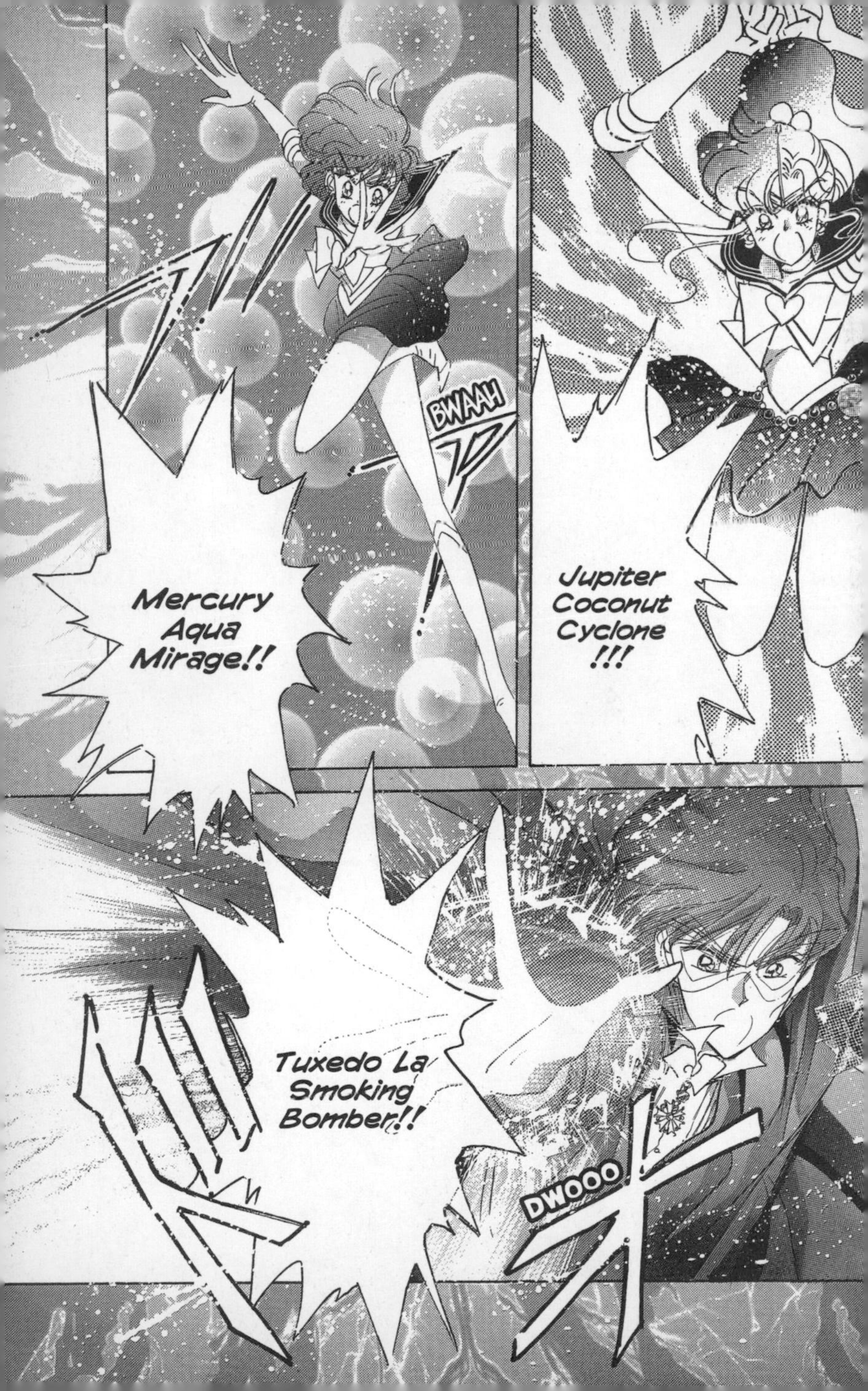
Jupiter Coconut Cyclone !!!
BWAAH
Mercury Aqua Mirage!!
Tuxedo La Smoking Bomber!!
DWOOO

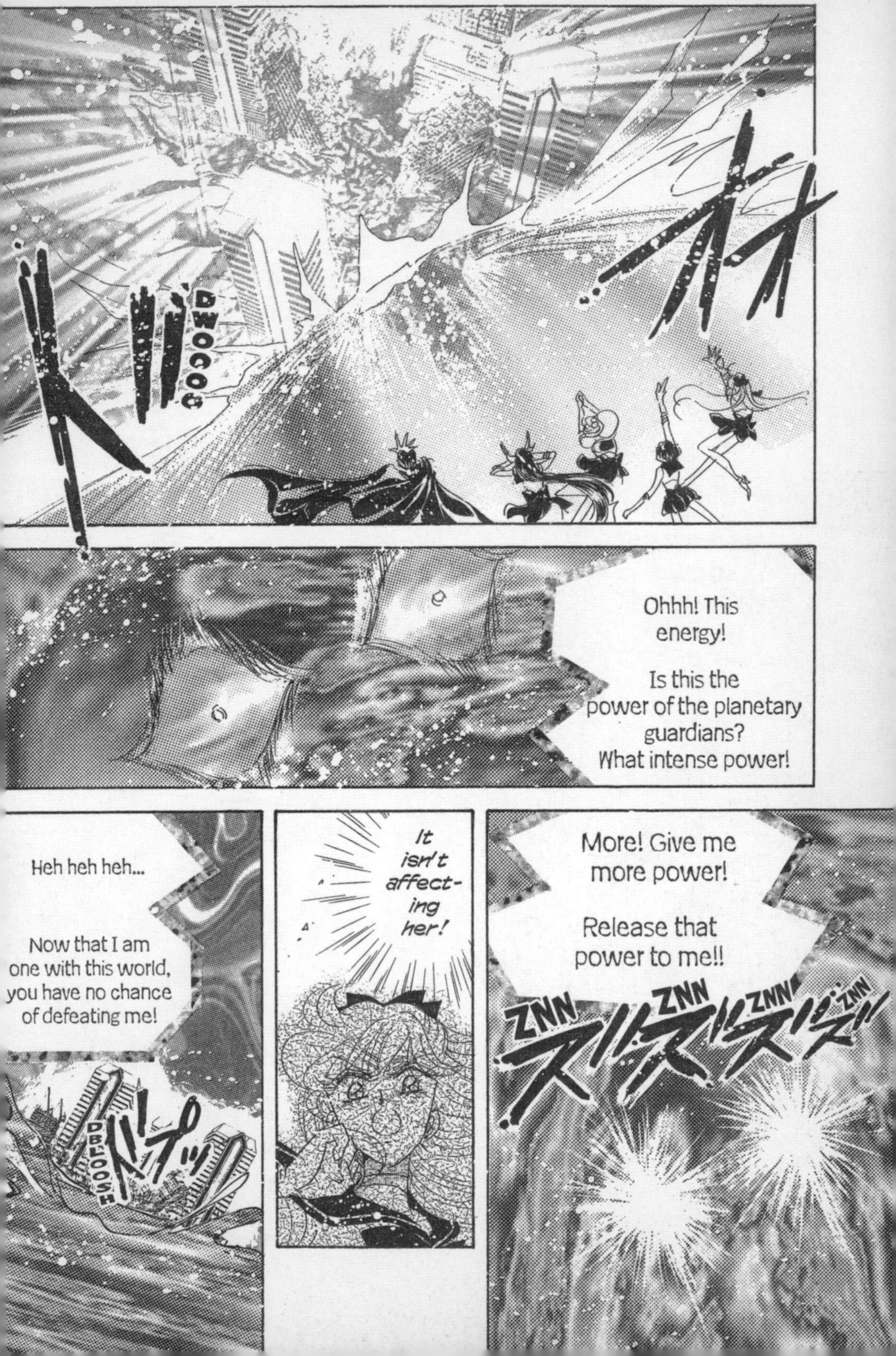
DWOOOO
Ohhh! This energy!
Is this the power of the planetary guardians? What intense power!
More! Give me more power!
Release that power to me!!
ZNN ZNN ZNN ZNN
It isn't affect-ing her!
Heh heh heh...
Now that I am one with this world, you have no chance of defeating me!
DBLOOSH

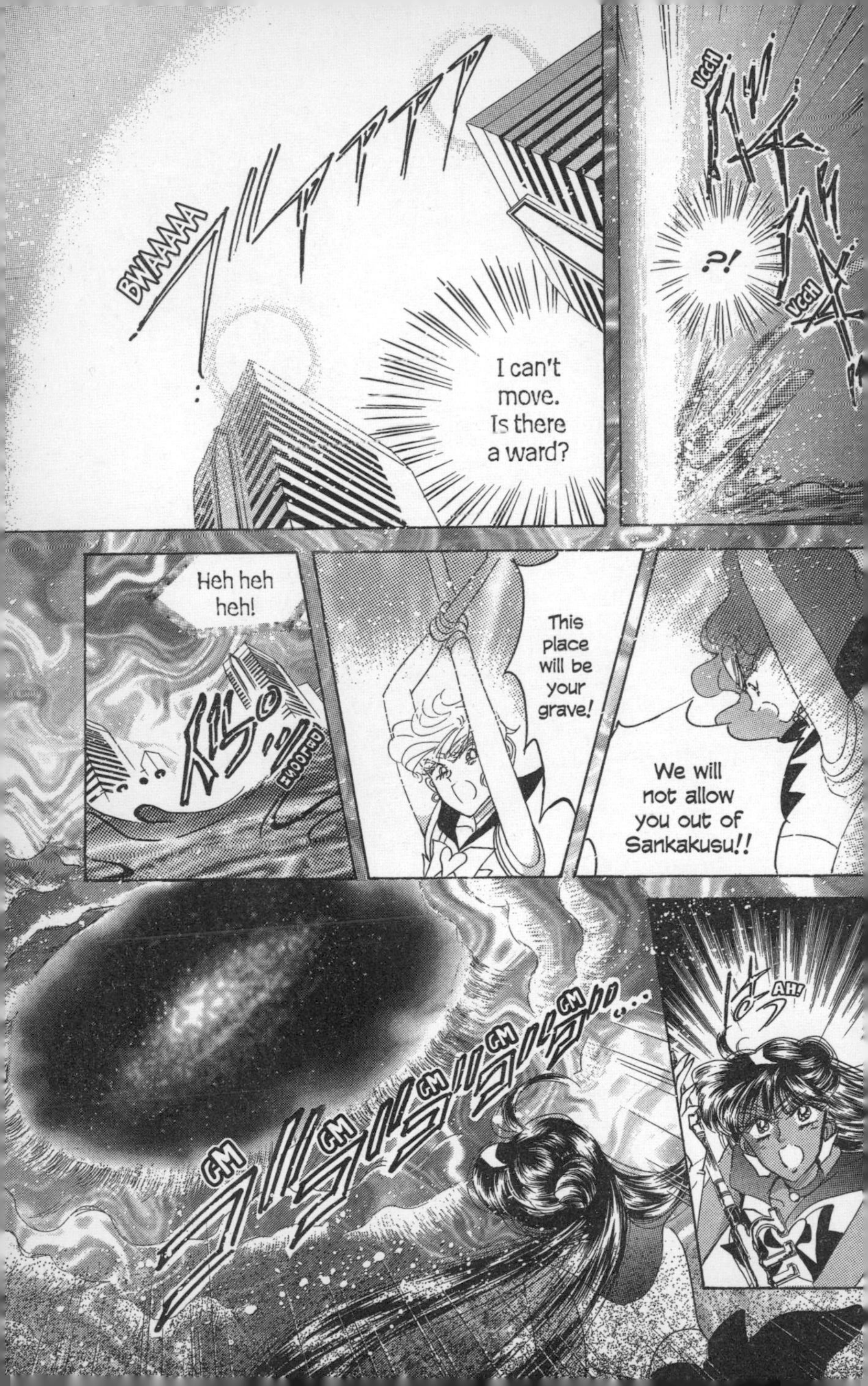
VCCH
?!
VCCH
BWAAAAA
I can't move. Is there a ward?
We will not allow you out of Sankakusu!!
This place will be your grave!
Heh heh heh!
FWOOSH
AH!
GM
GM
GM
GM
GM

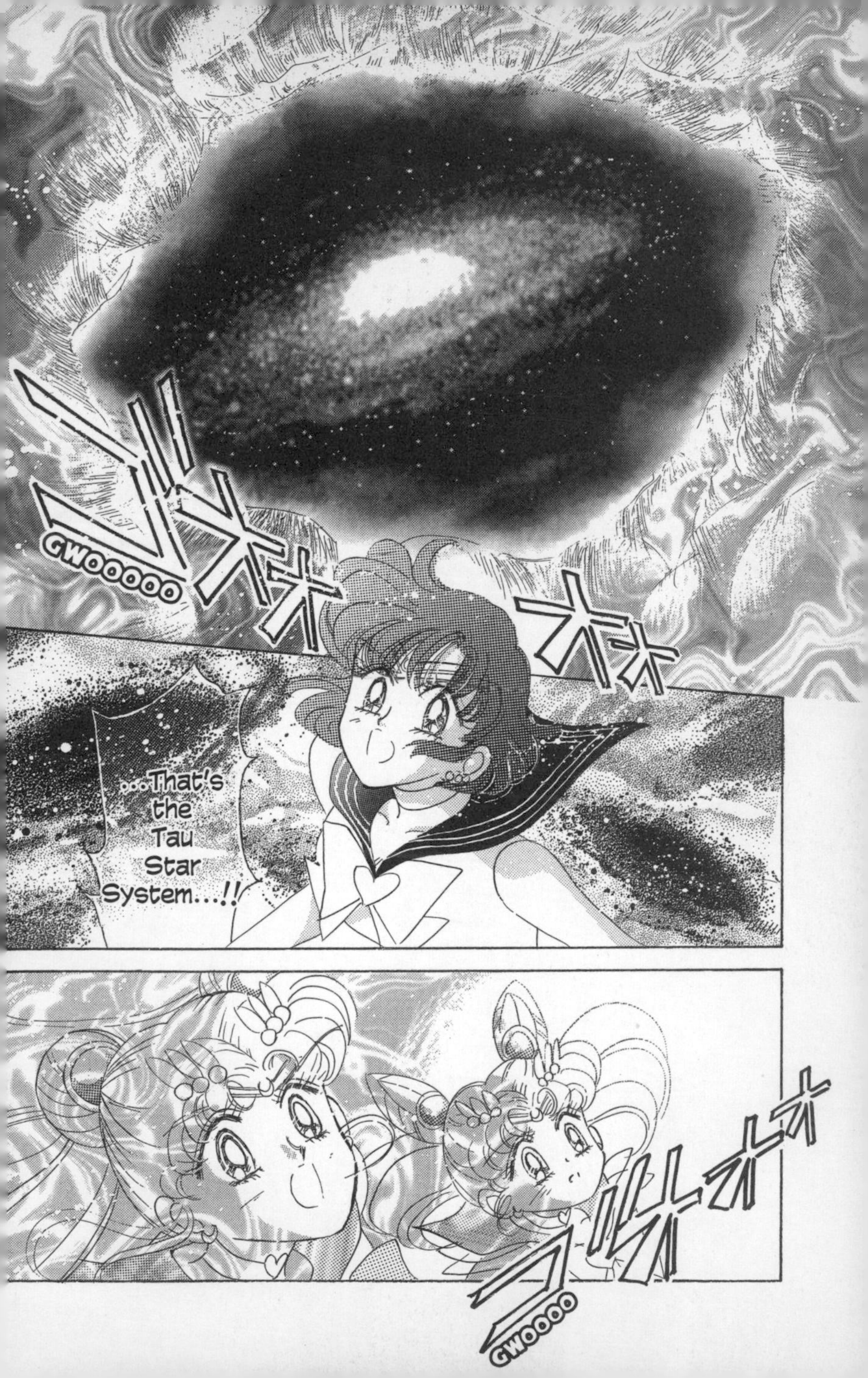
GWOOOOOO
...That's the Tau Star System...!!
GWOOOO

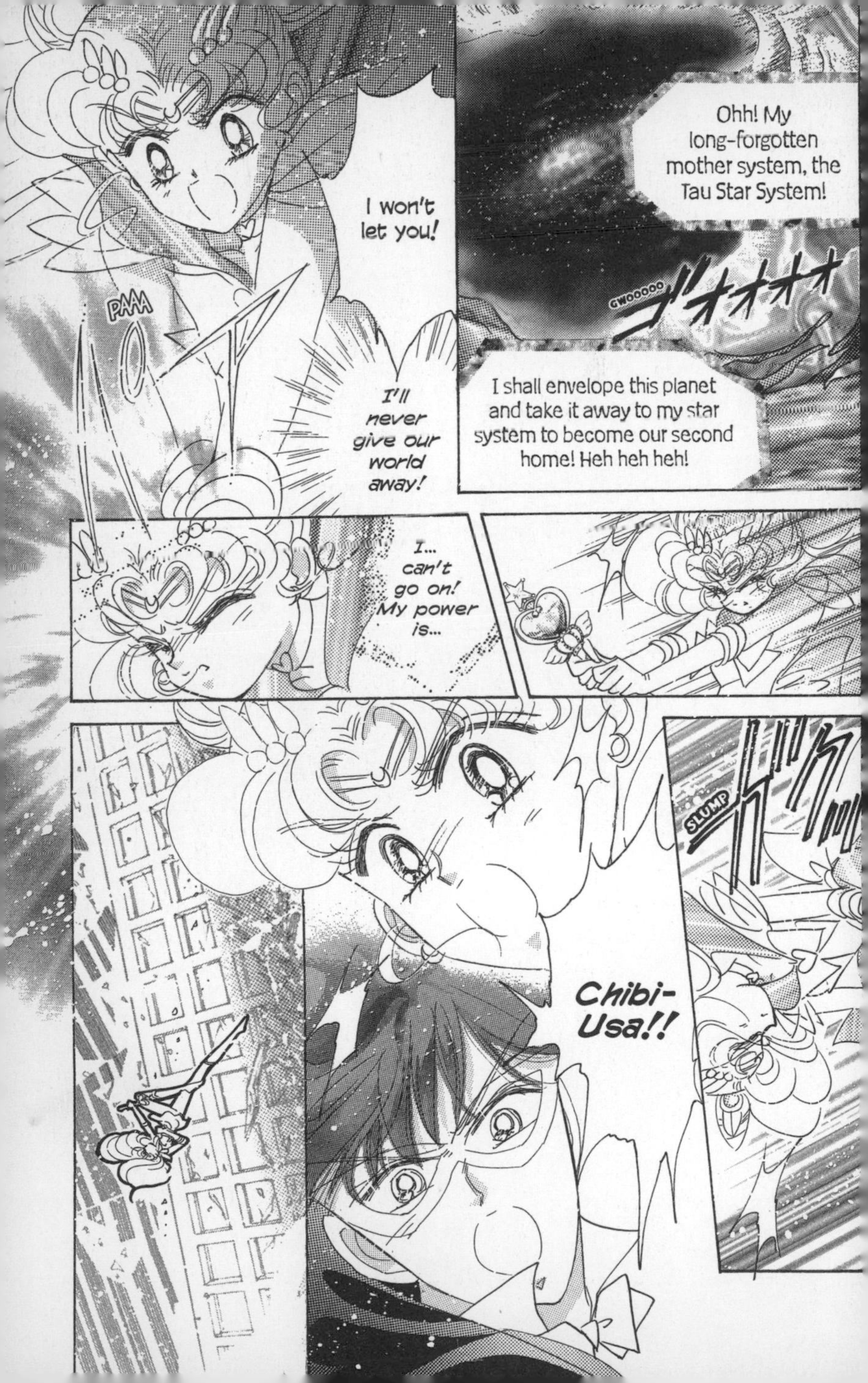
Ohh! My long-forgotten mother system, the Tau Star System!
GWOOOOO
ゴオオオオ
I shall envelope this planet and take it away to my star system to become our second home! Heh heh heh!
I won't let you!
PAAA
I'll never give our world away!
I... can't go on! My power is...
SLUMP
Chibi-Usa!!

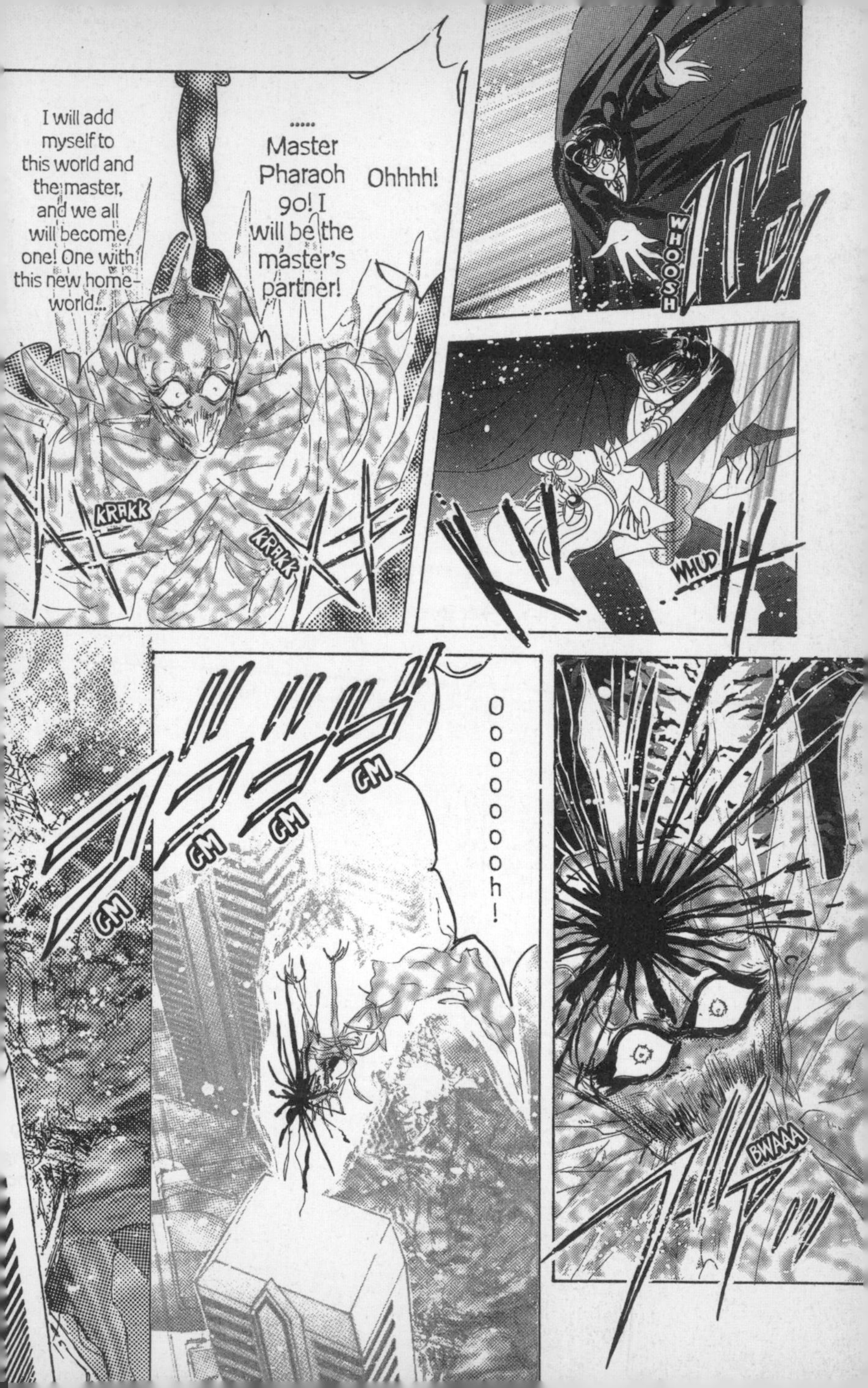
WHOOSH
WHUD
Ohhhh!
...... Master Pharaoh 90! I will be the master's partner!
I will add myself to this world and the master, and we all will become one! One with this new home-world...
KRAKK
KRAKK
BWAAA
Oooooooooh!
GM
GM
GM
GM
GM

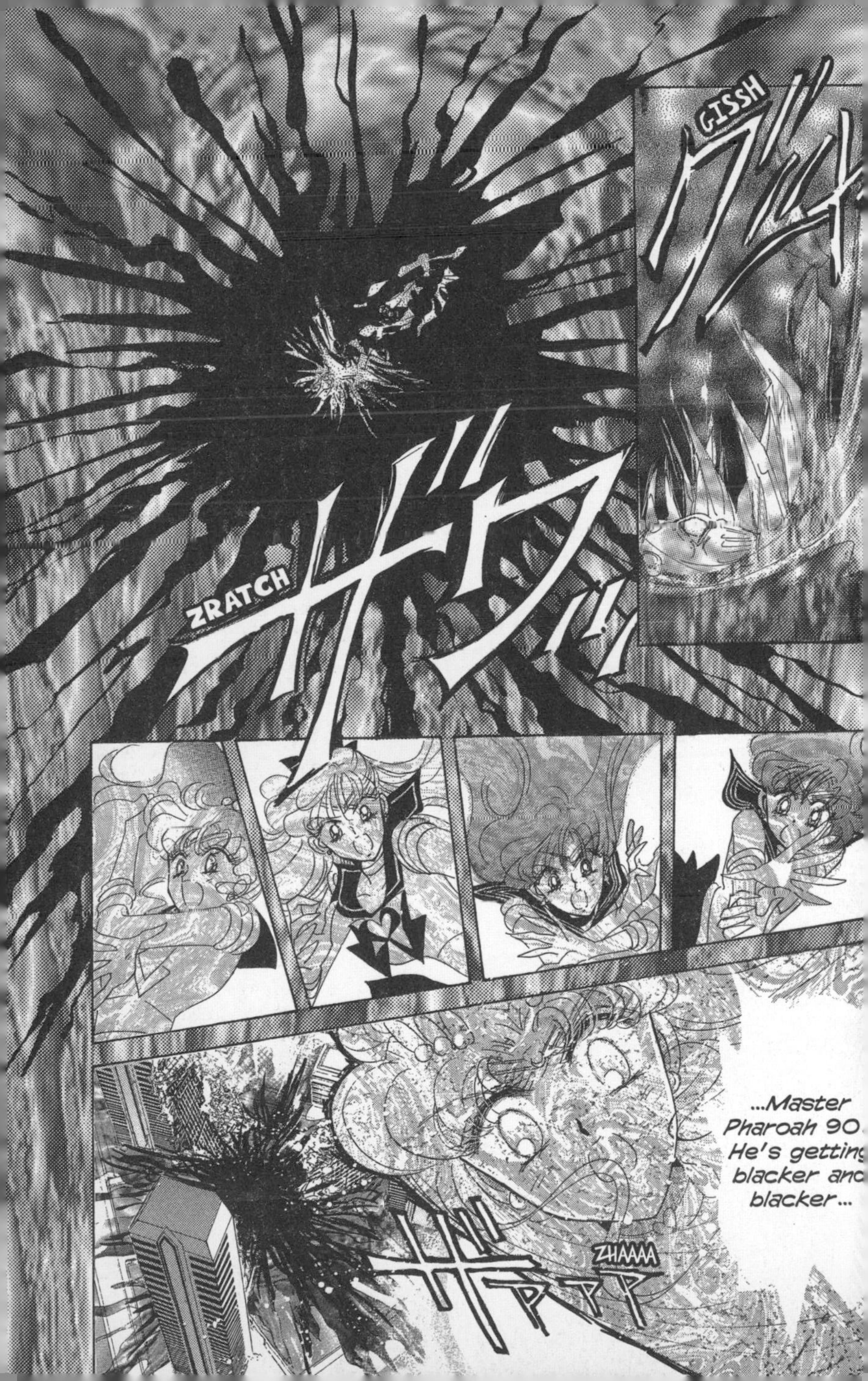
GISSH
ZRATCH
...Master Pharoah 90... He's getting blacker and blacker...
ZHAAAA

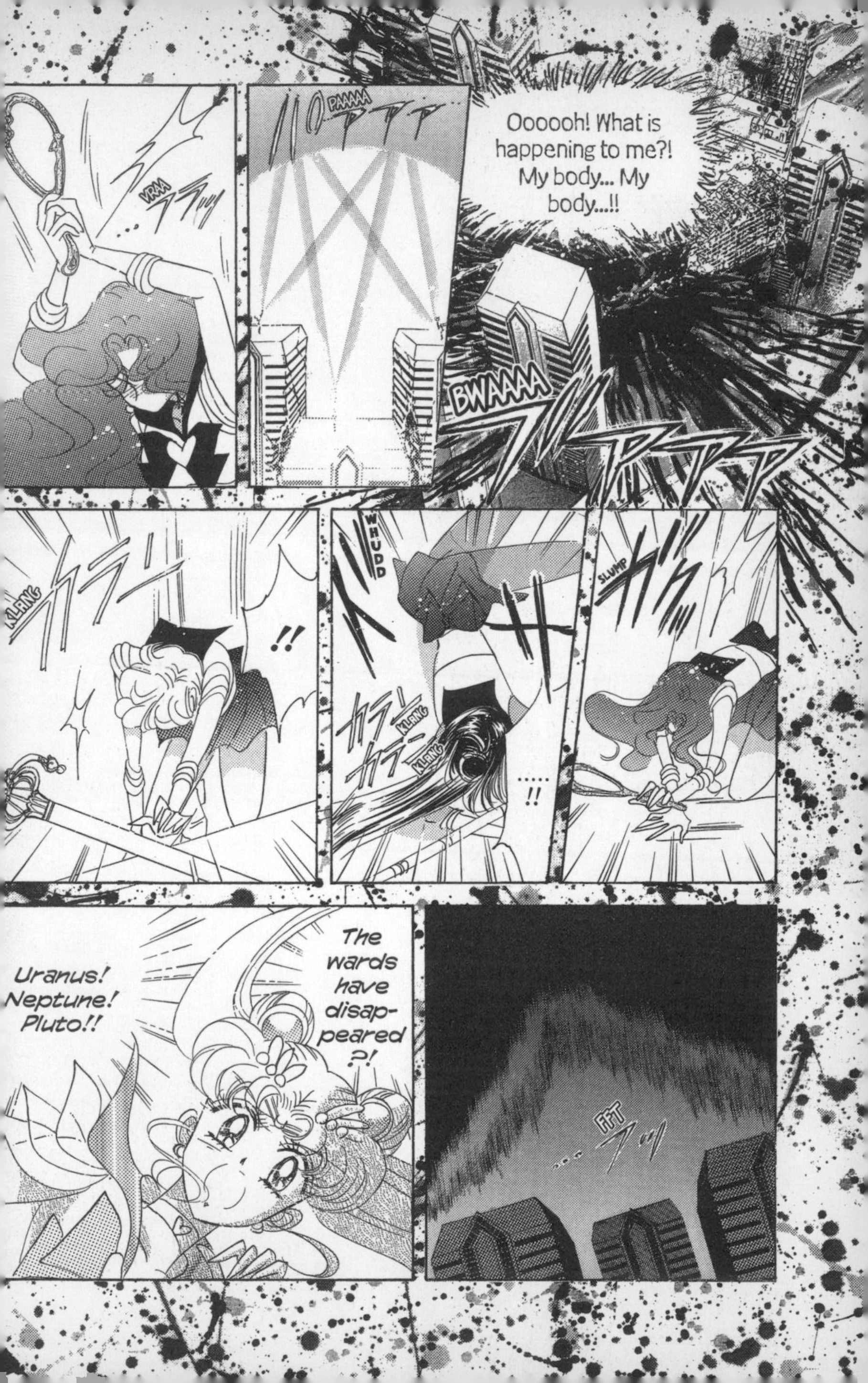
Oooooh! What is happening to me?! My body... My body...!!
BWAAAA
PAAAAA
VRAA
...
SLUMP
WHUDD
KLANG
KLANG
.....
!!
KLANG
!!
FFT
...
The wards have disap-peared?!
Uranus! Neptune! Pluto!!

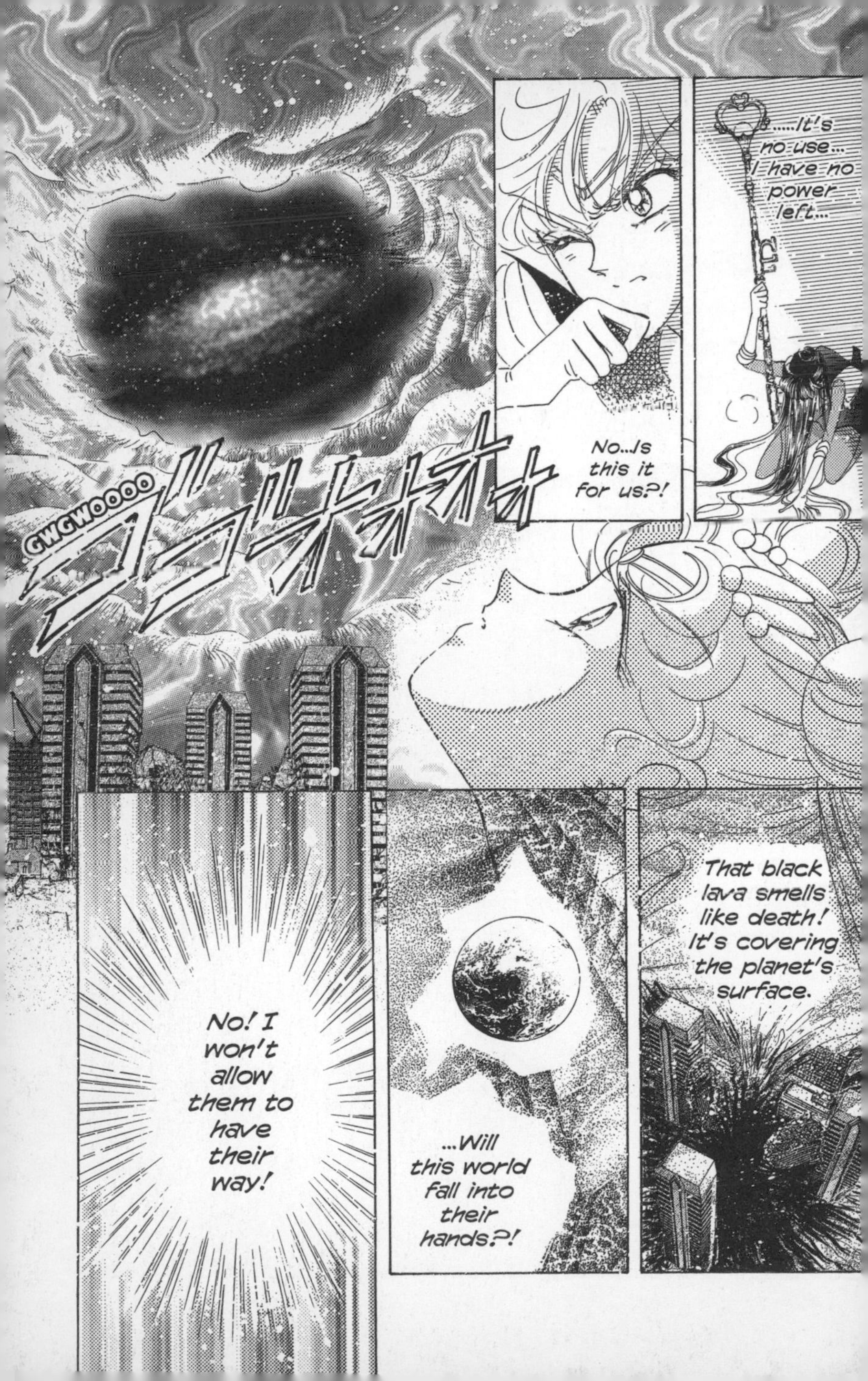

.....It's no use... I have no power left...
No...Is this it for us?!
GWGWOOOO
That black lava smells like death! It's covering the planet's surface.
...Will this world fall into their hands?!
No! I won't allow them to have their way!

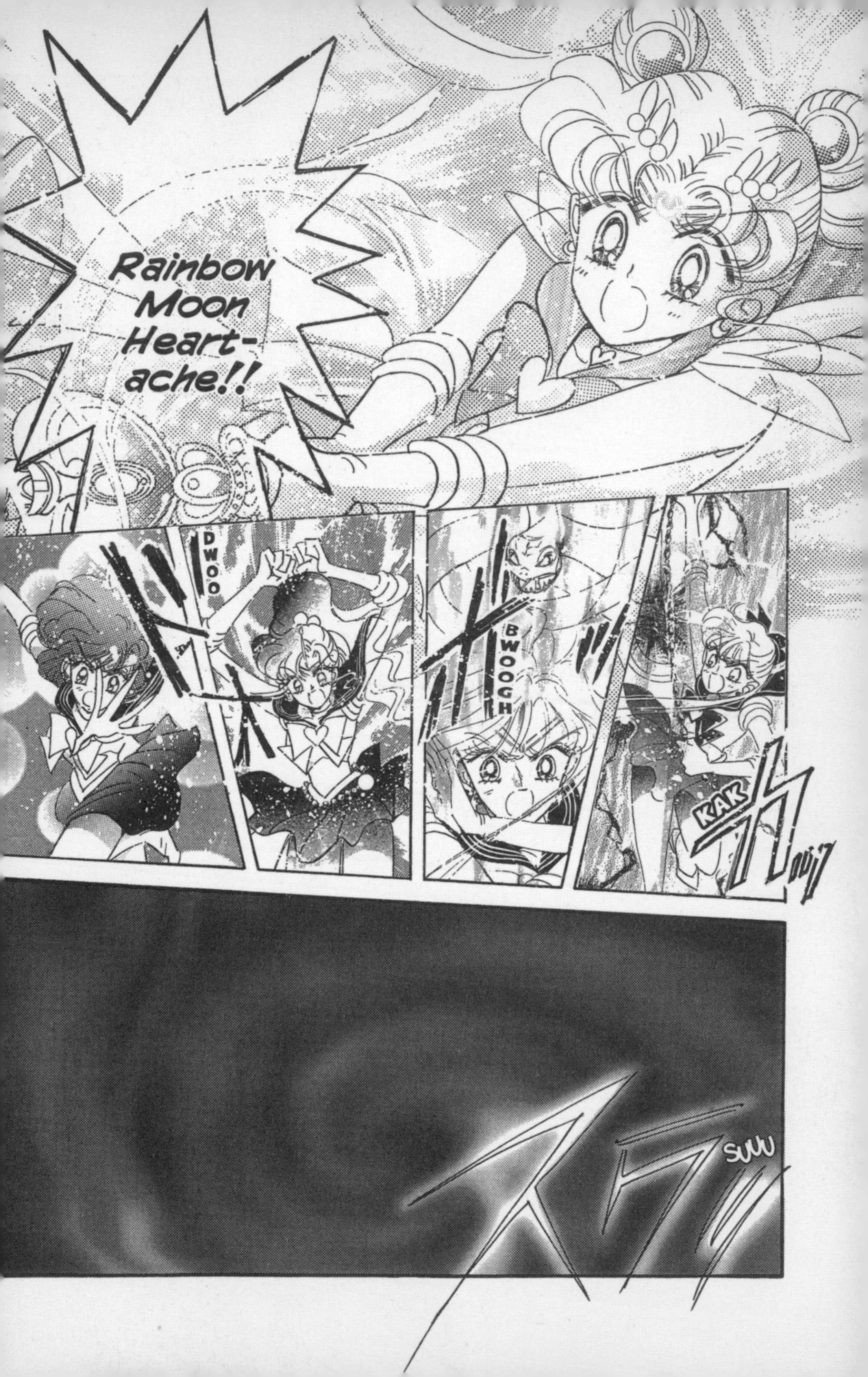
Rainbow Moon Heart-ache!!
KAK
BWOOGH
DWOO
SUUU

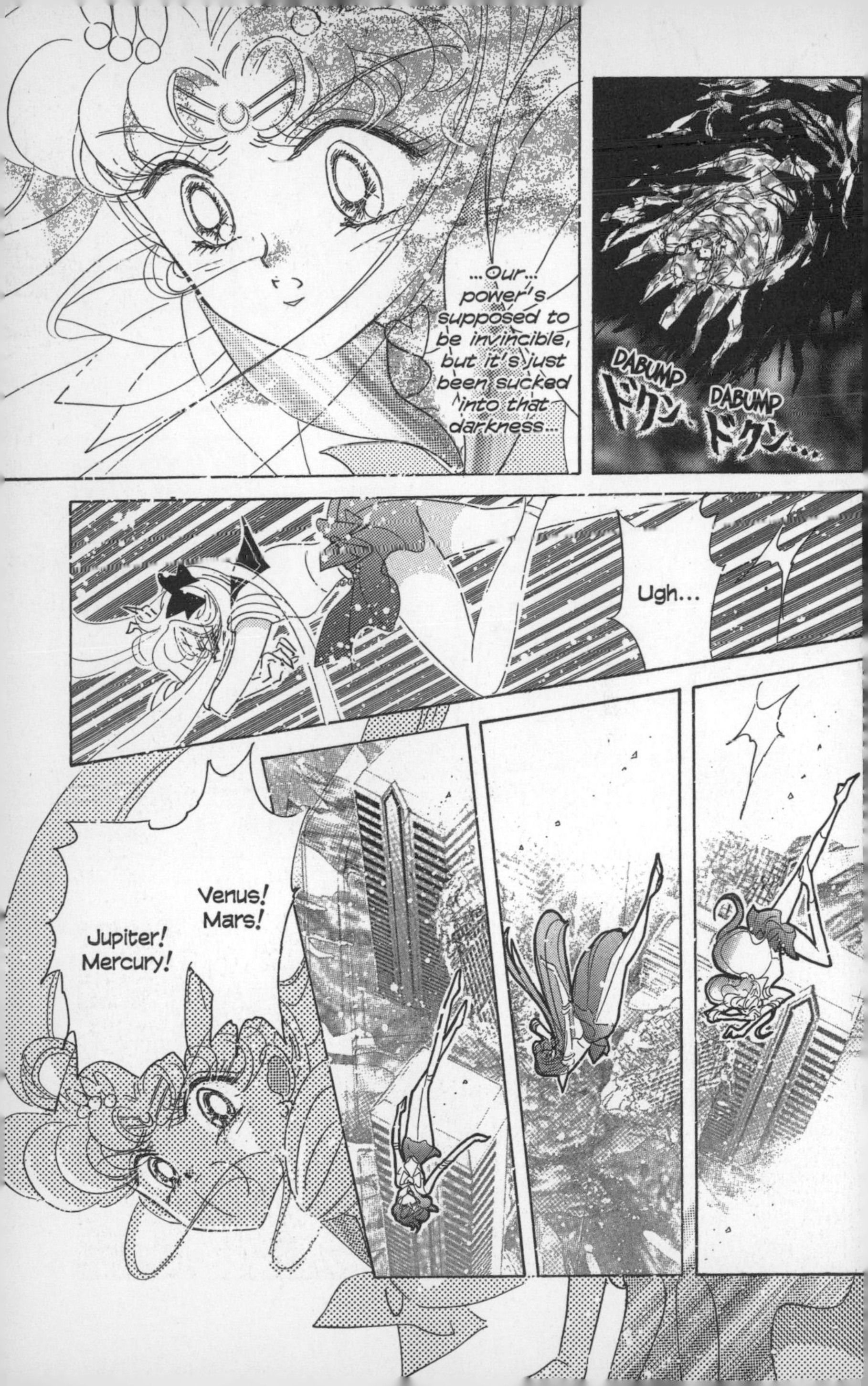
DABUMP ドクン
DABUMP ドクン...
...Our... power's supposed to be invincible, but it's just been sucked into that darkness...
Ugh...
Venus! Mars!
Jupiter! Mercury!

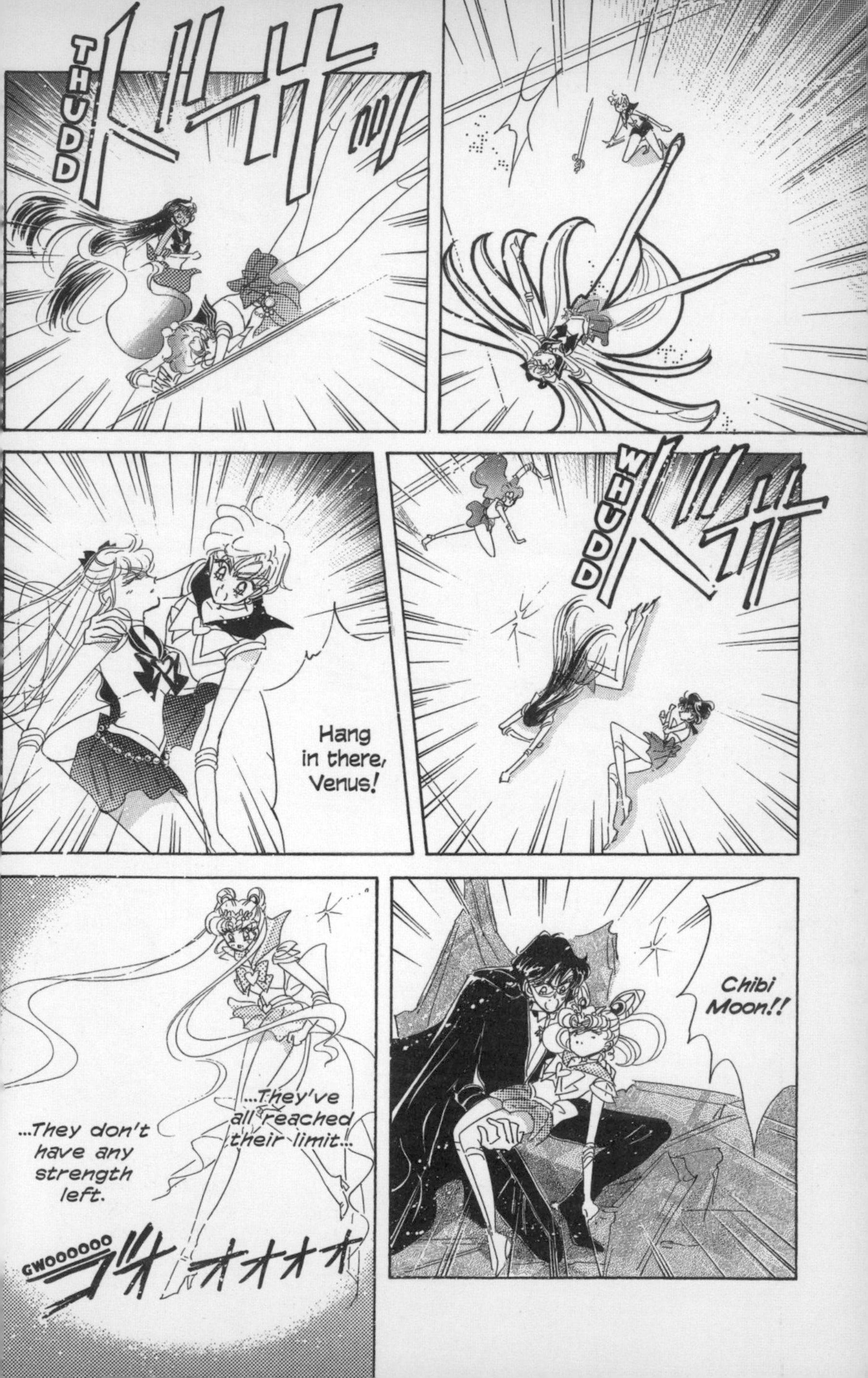
THUDD
WHUDD
Hang in there, Venus!
Chibi Moon!!
...They've all reached their limit...
...They don't have any strength left.
GWOOOOOO

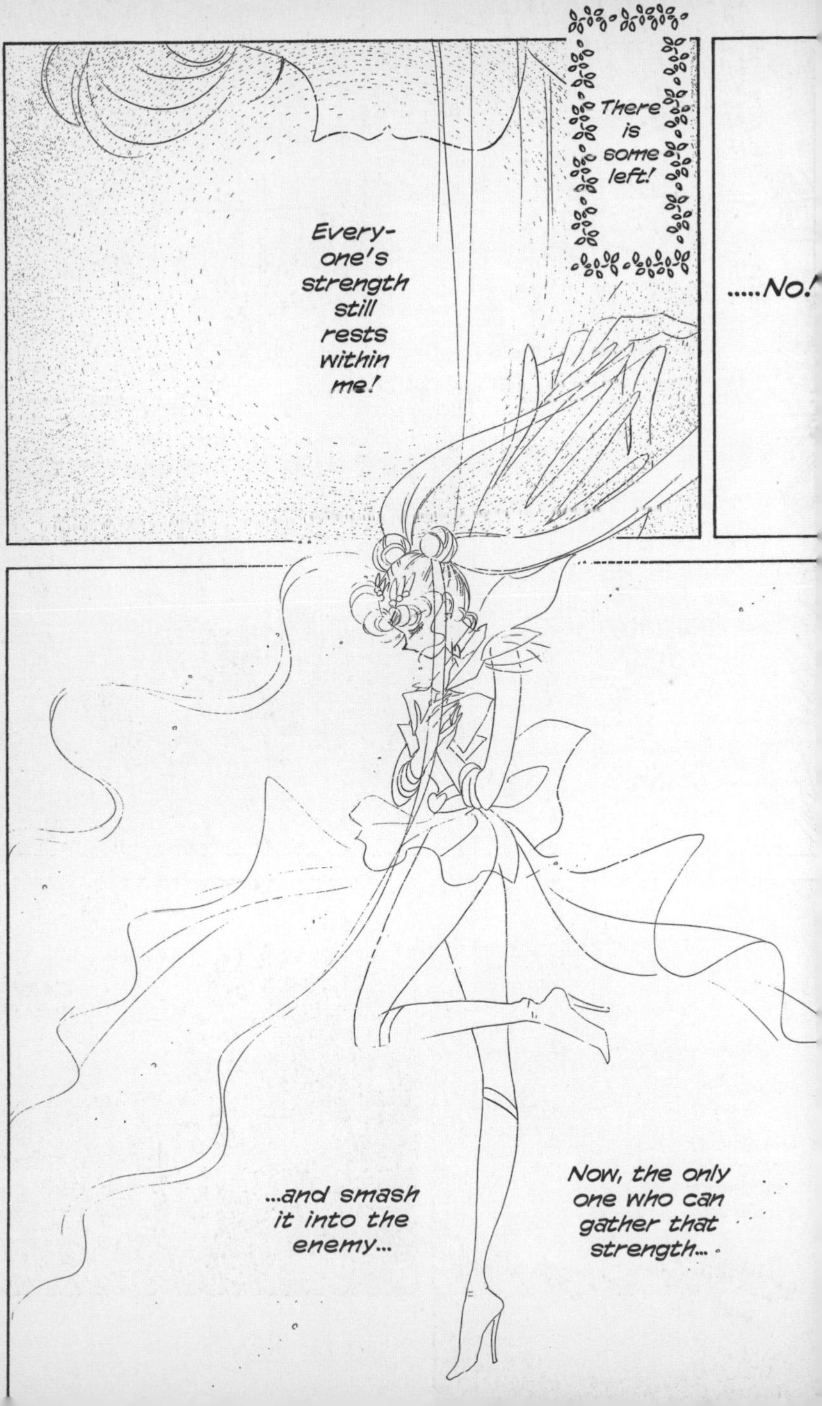
.....No!
There is some left!
Every-one's strength still rests within me!
Now, the only one who can gather that strength...
...and smash it into the enemy...

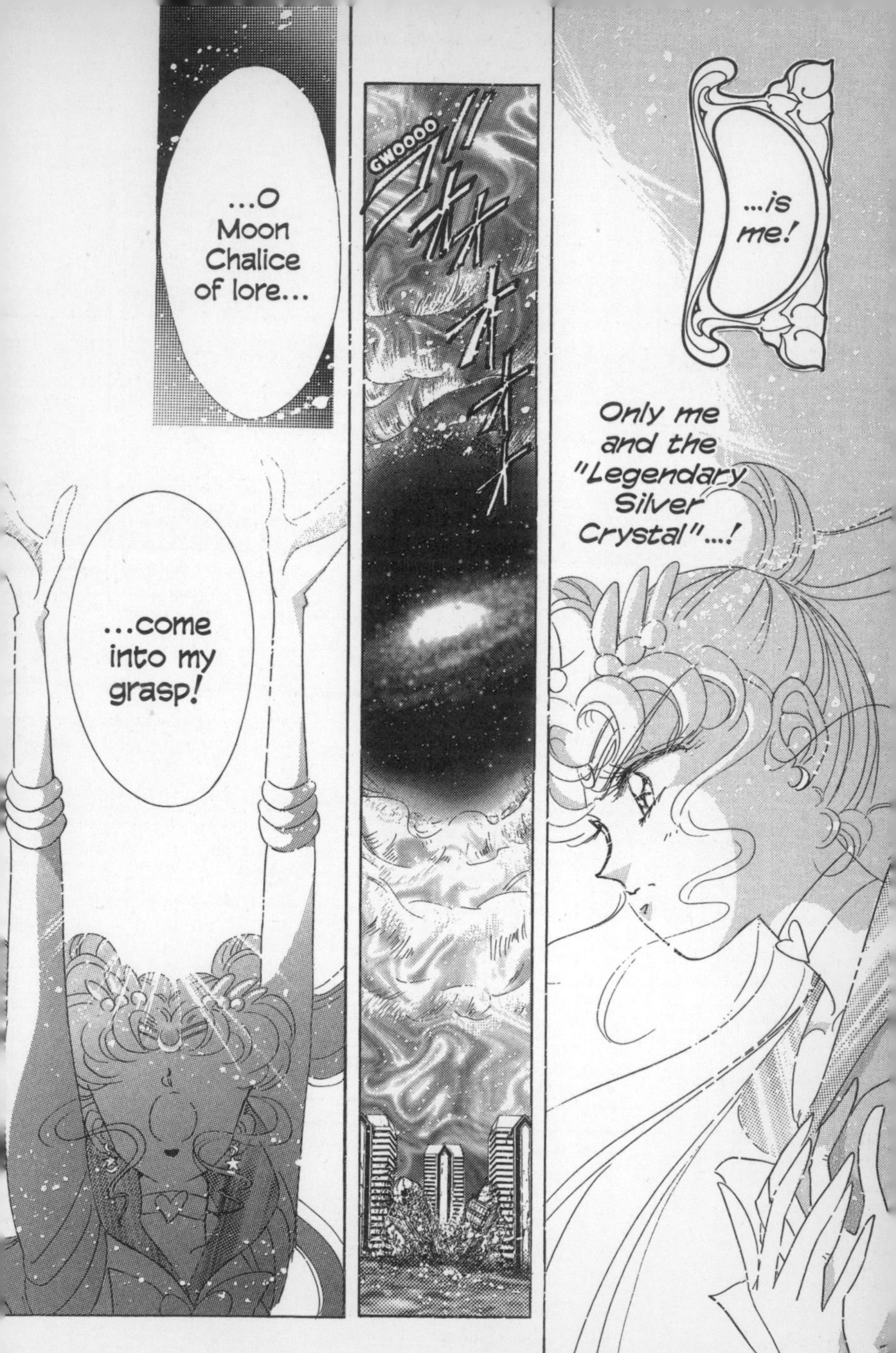

...is me!
Only me and the "Legendary Silver Crystal"...!
GWOOOO
...O Moon Chalice of lore...
...come into my grasp!

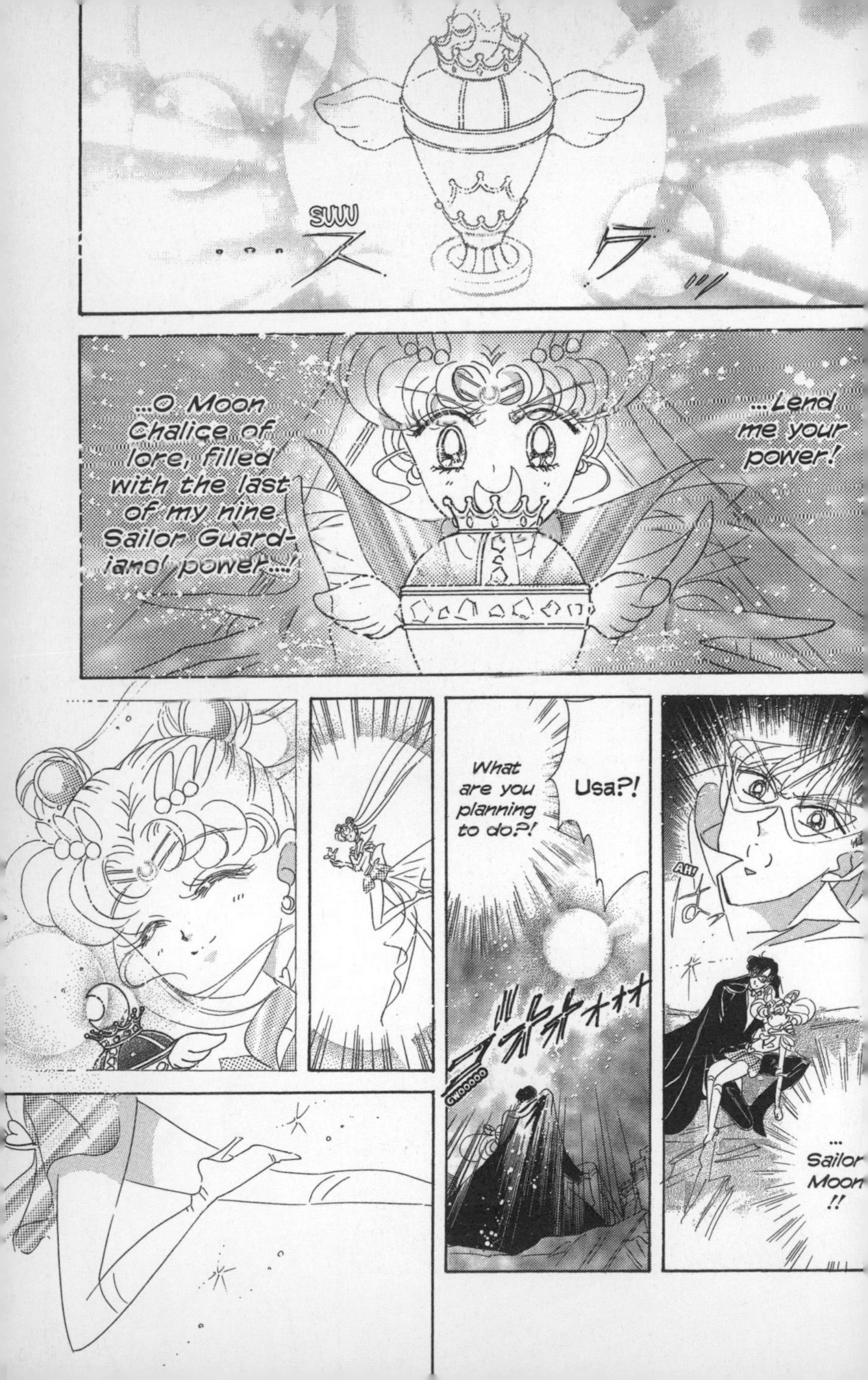
SUUU
...Lend me your power!
...O Moon Chalice of lore, filled with the last of my nine Sailor Guardians' power...!
AH!
...Sailor Moon!!
Usa?!
What are you planning to do?!
GWOOOOO

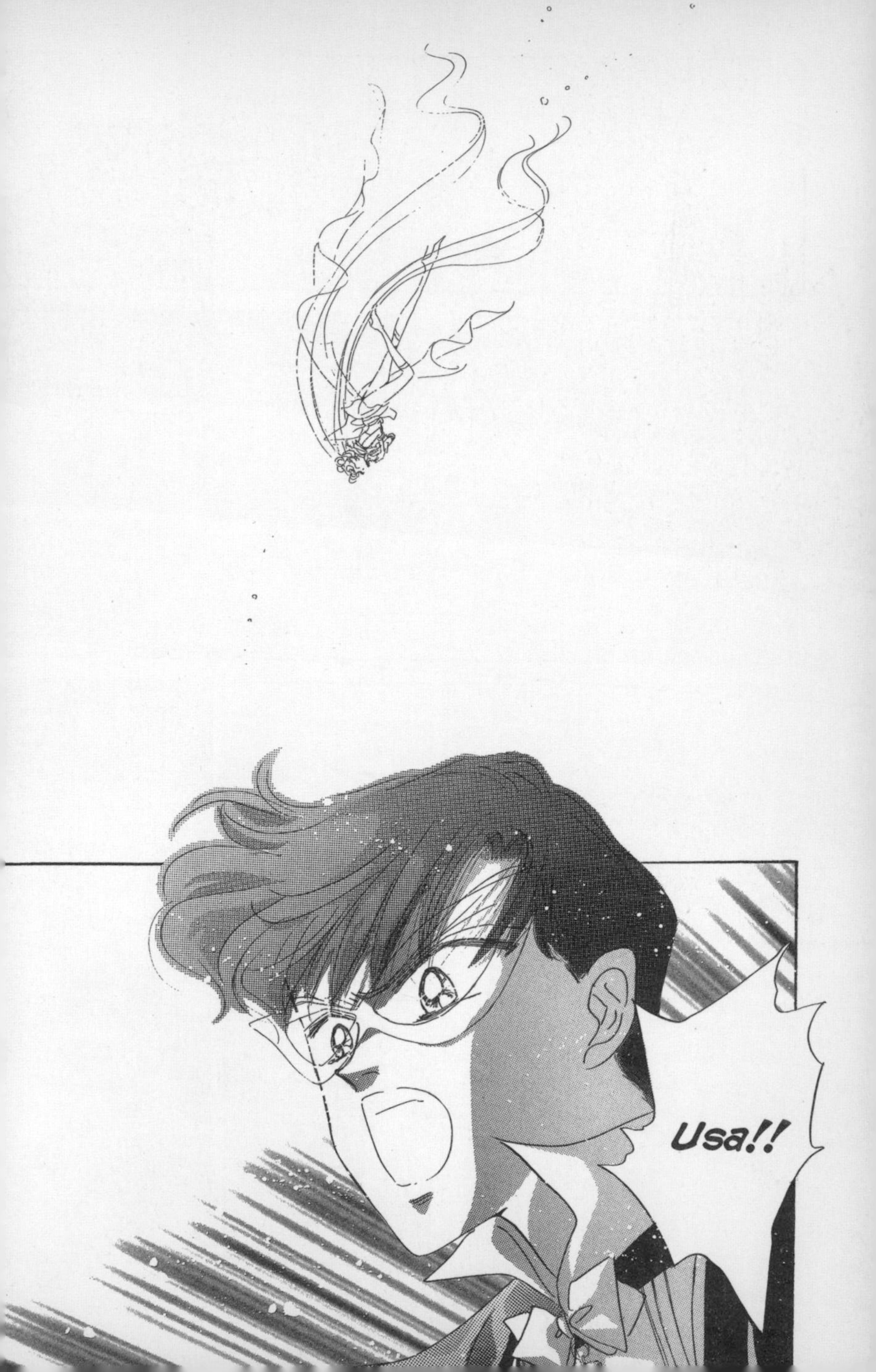
Usa!!

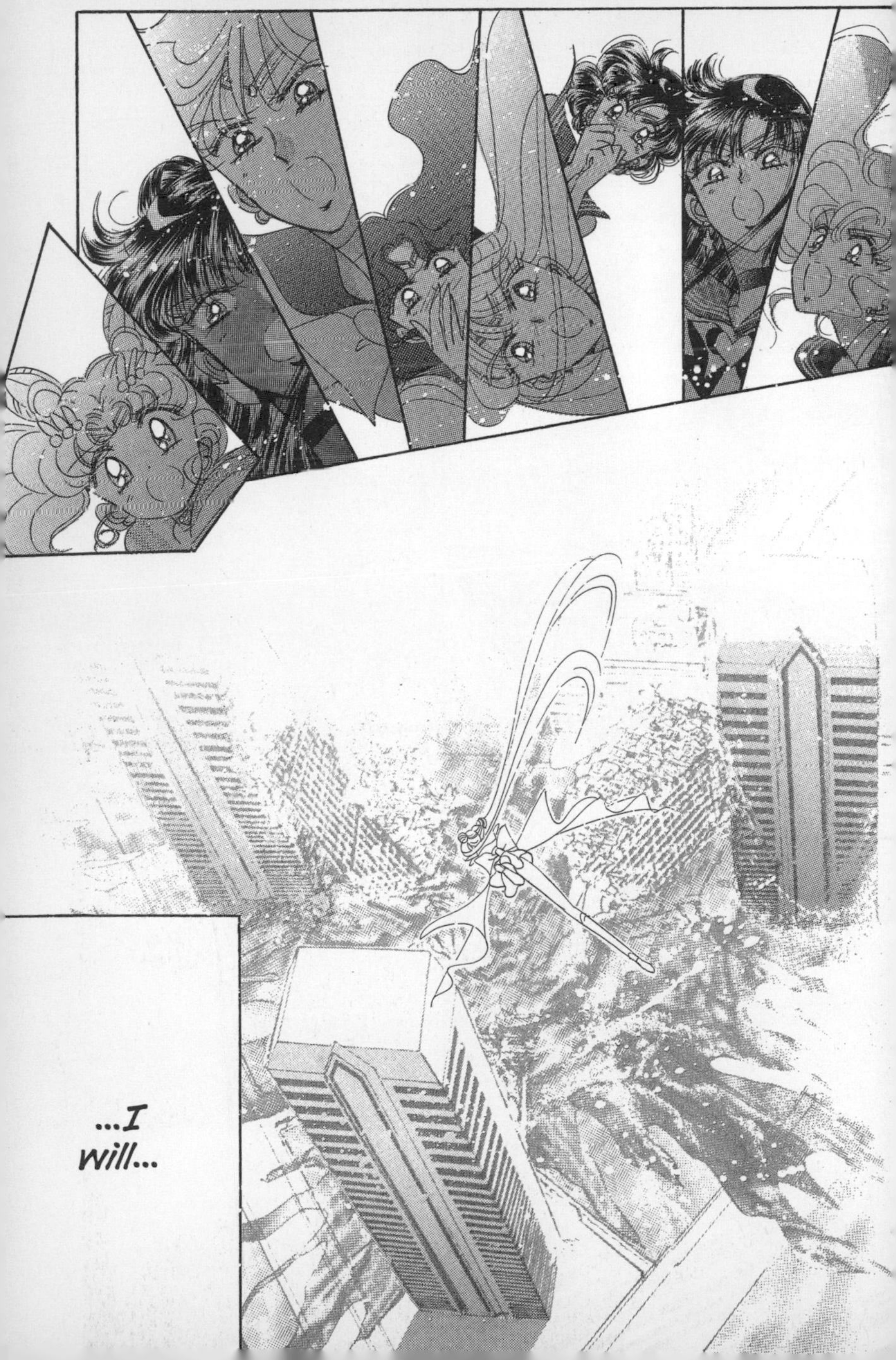
...I will...

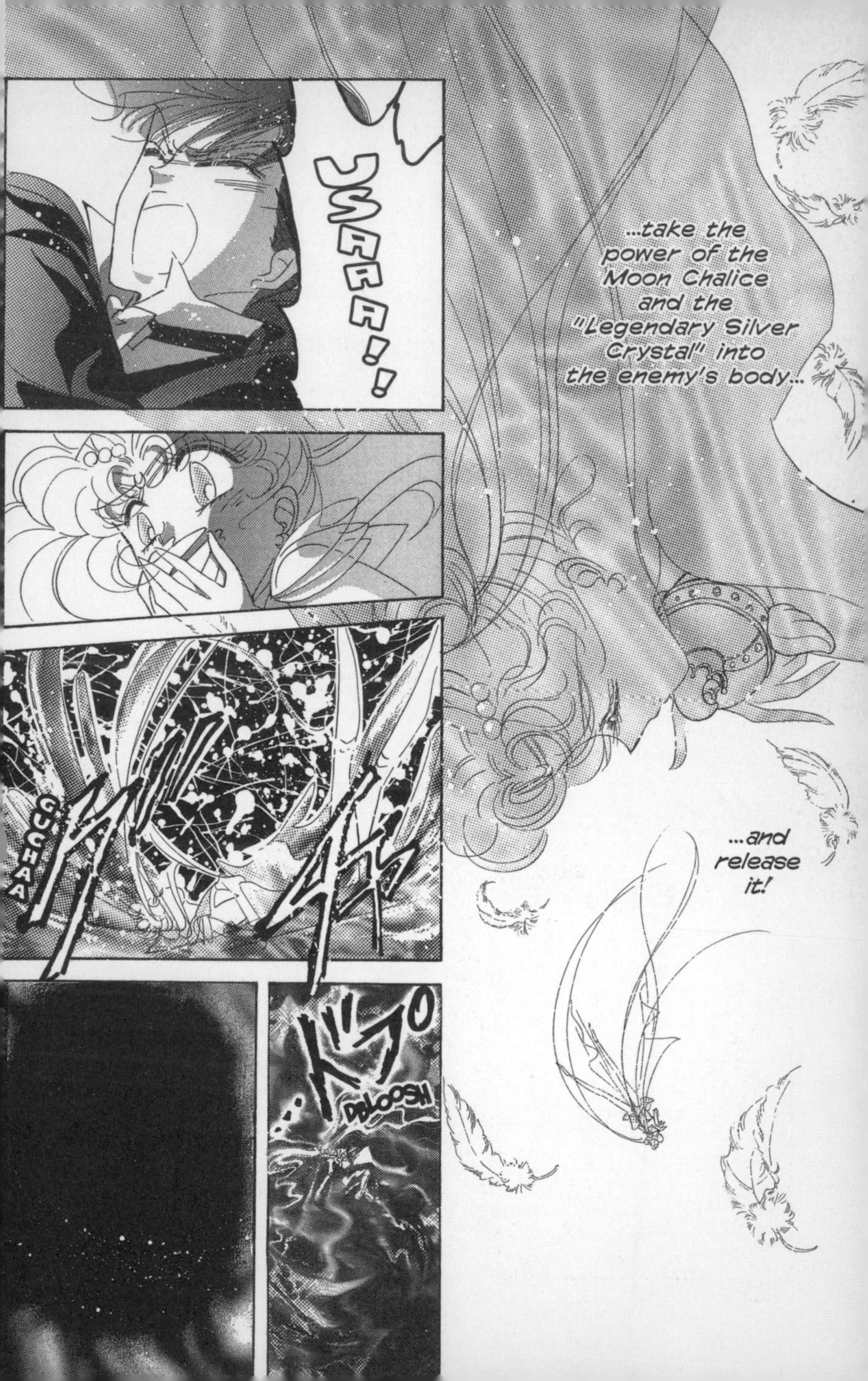
...take the power of the Moon Chalice and the "Legendary Silver Crystal" into the enemy's body...
...and release it!
USAAA!!
GUCHAA
...
DBLOOSH

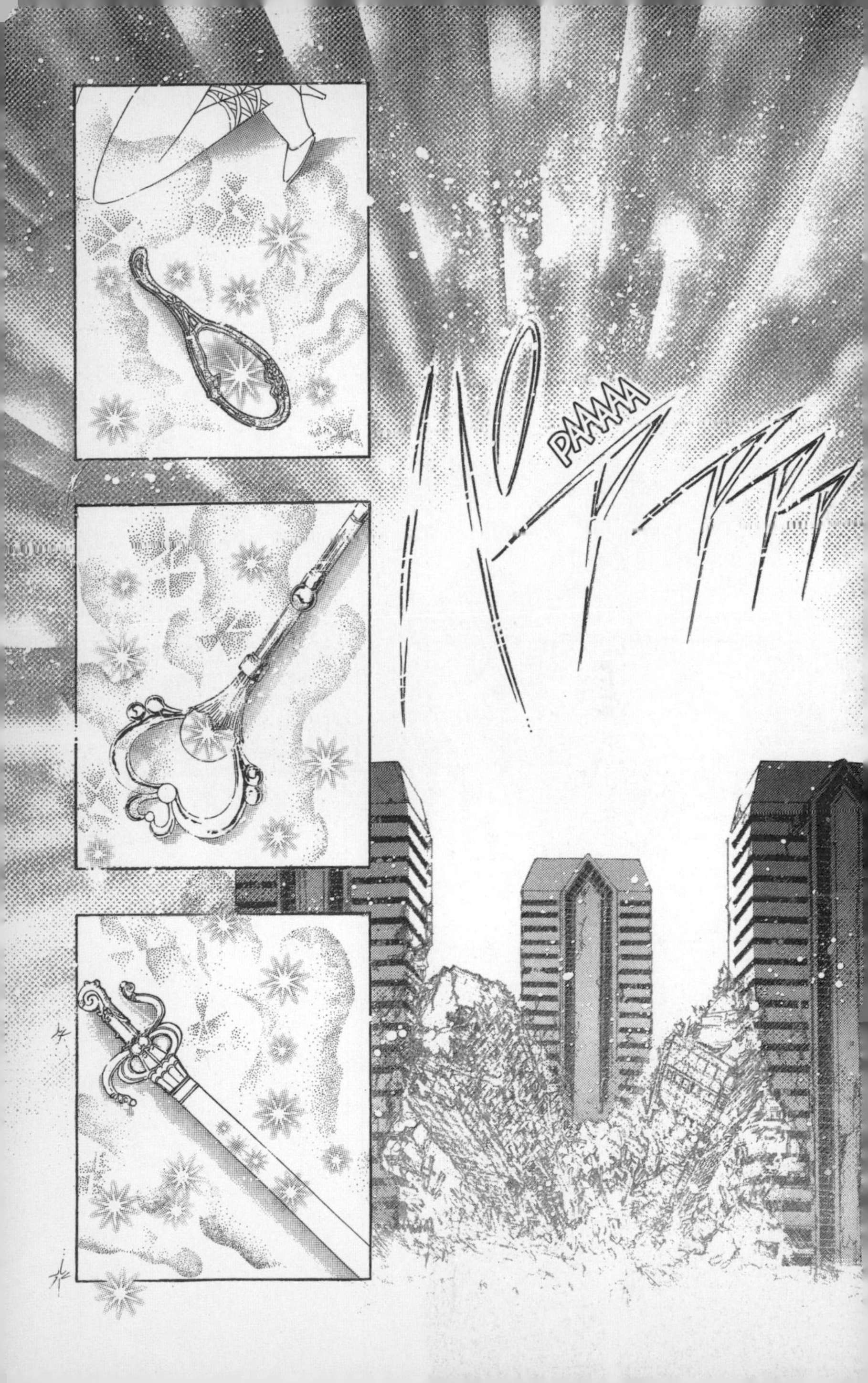
PAAAAA

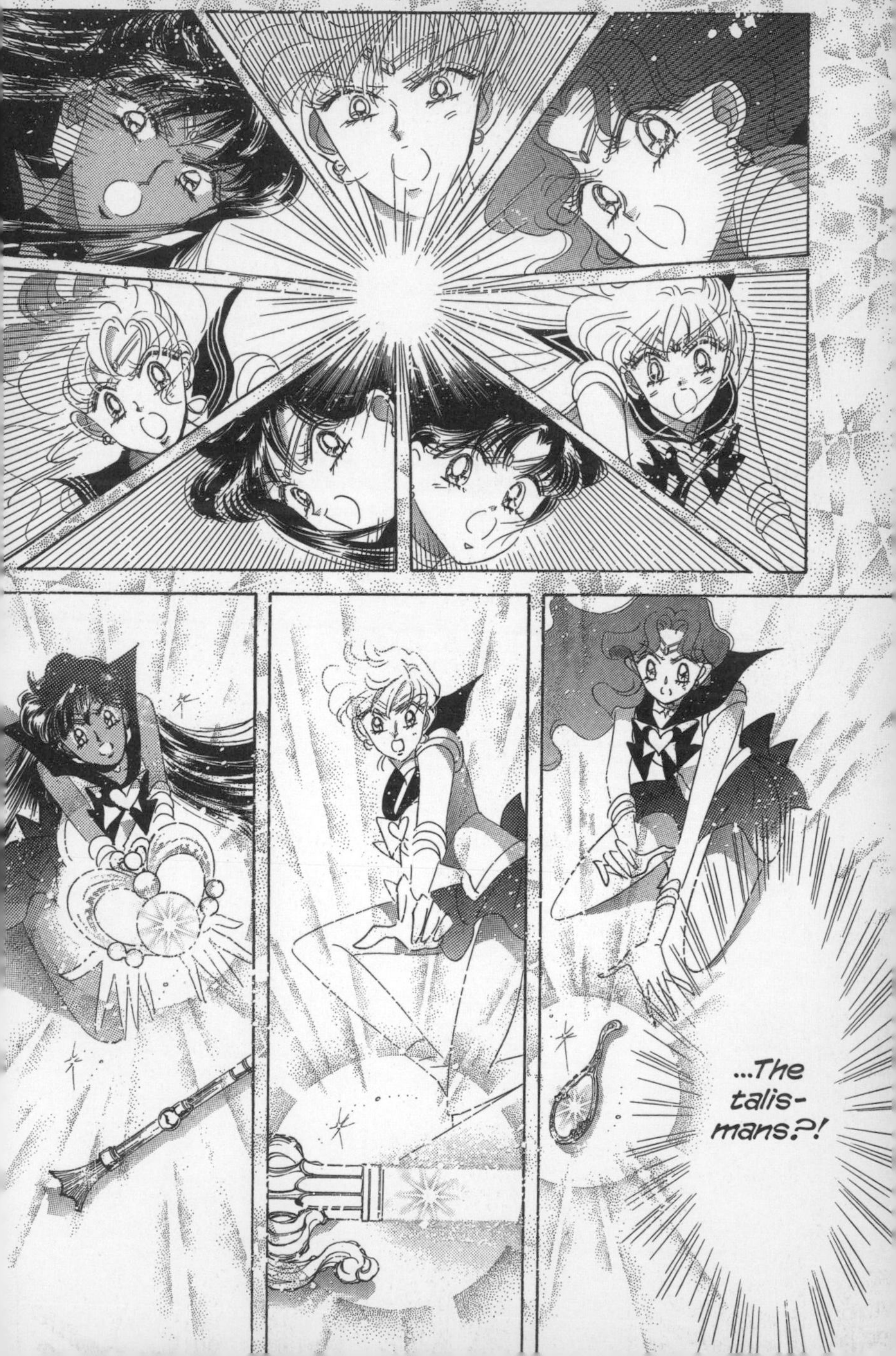
...The talis-mans?!

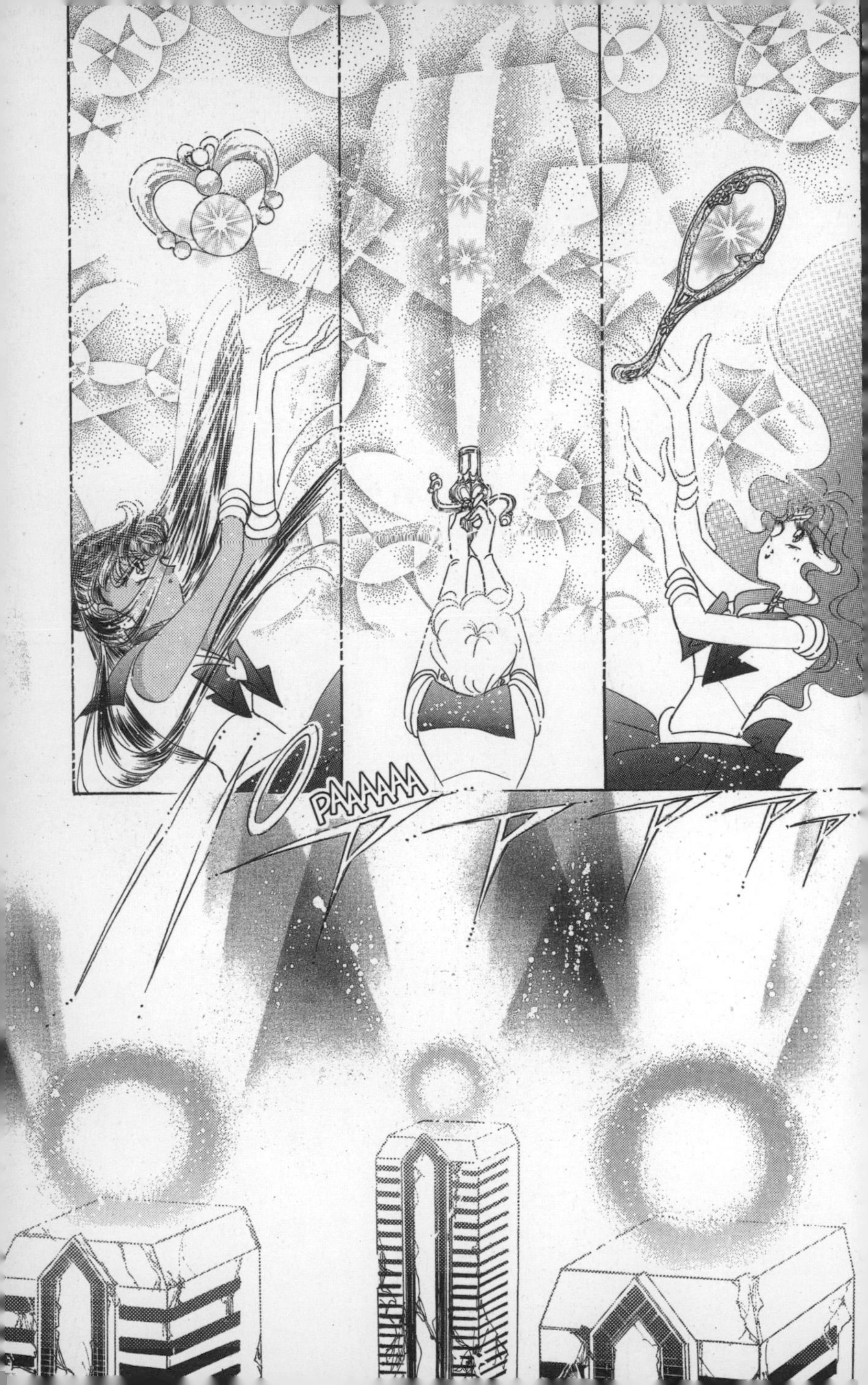
PAAAAAA

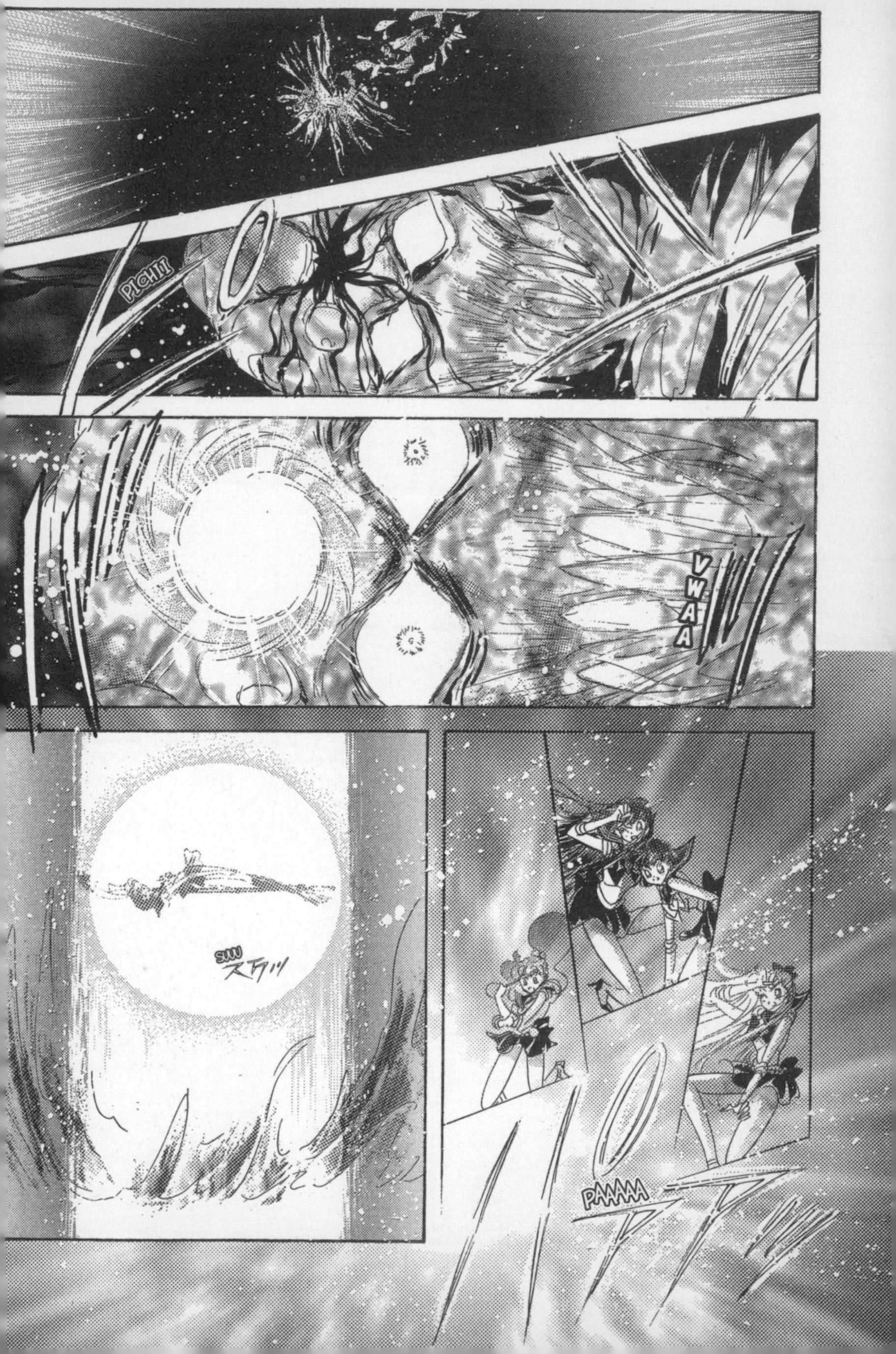
PICHII
VWAAA
PAAAAA
SUUU
スウッ

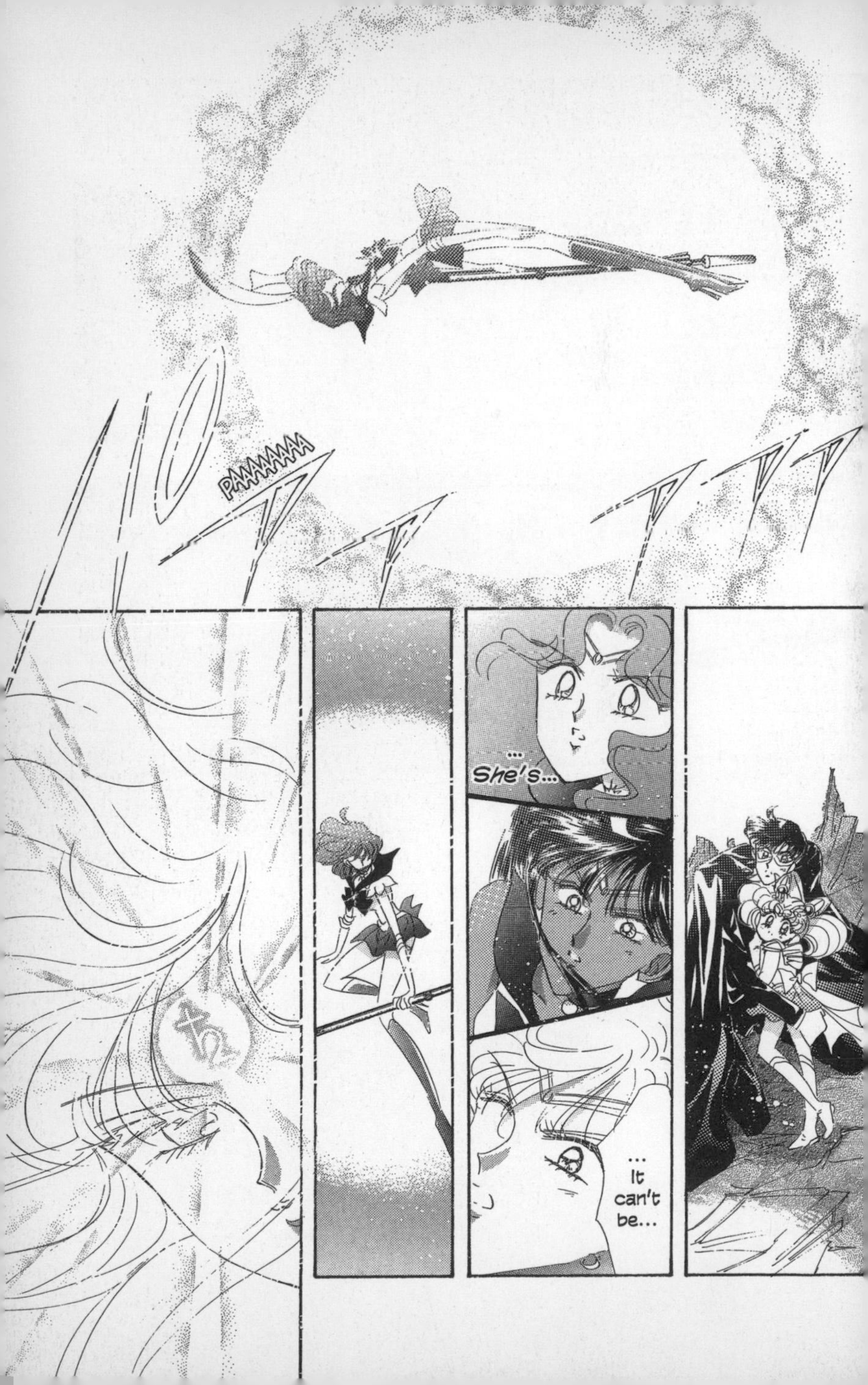
PAAAAAAA
... She's...
... It can't be...

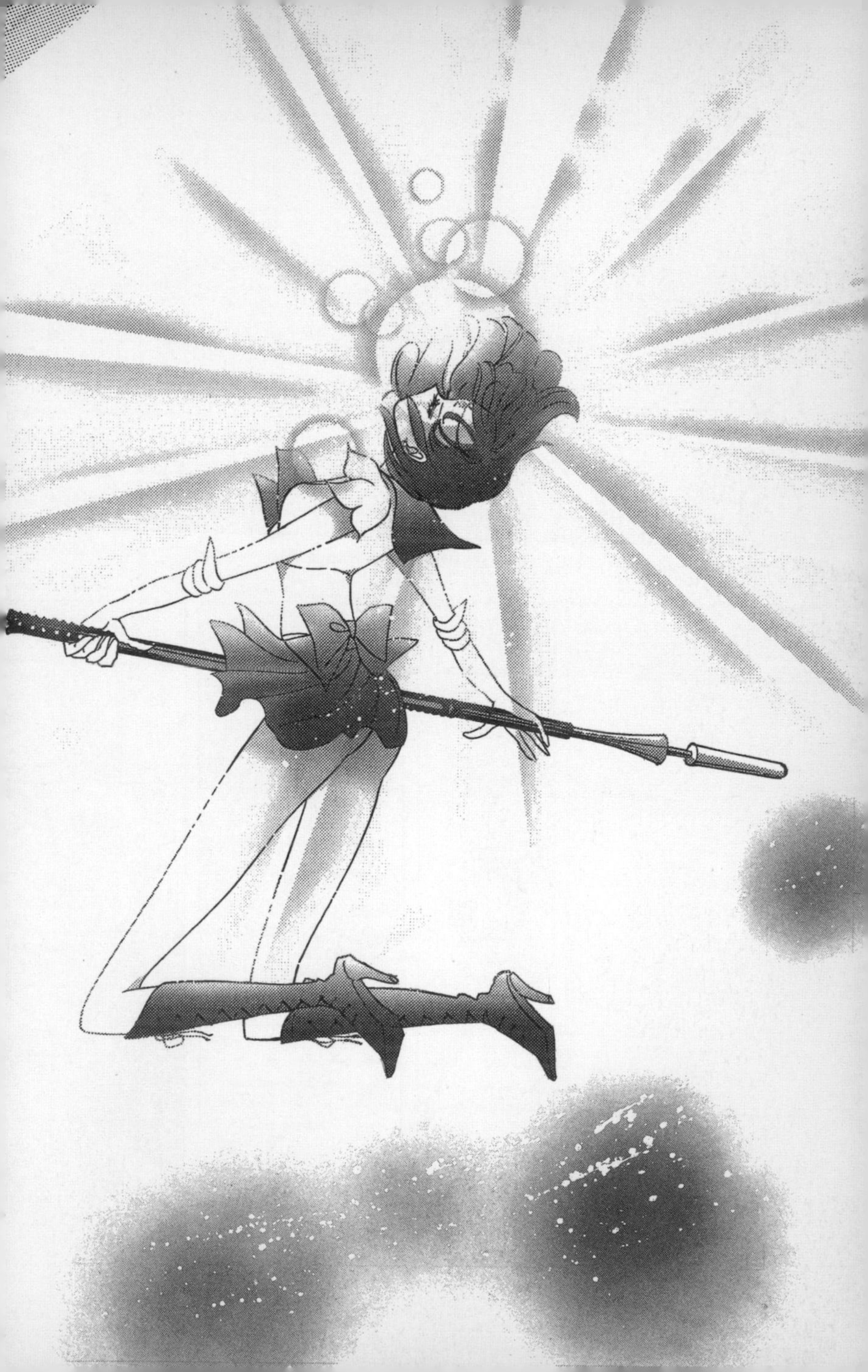

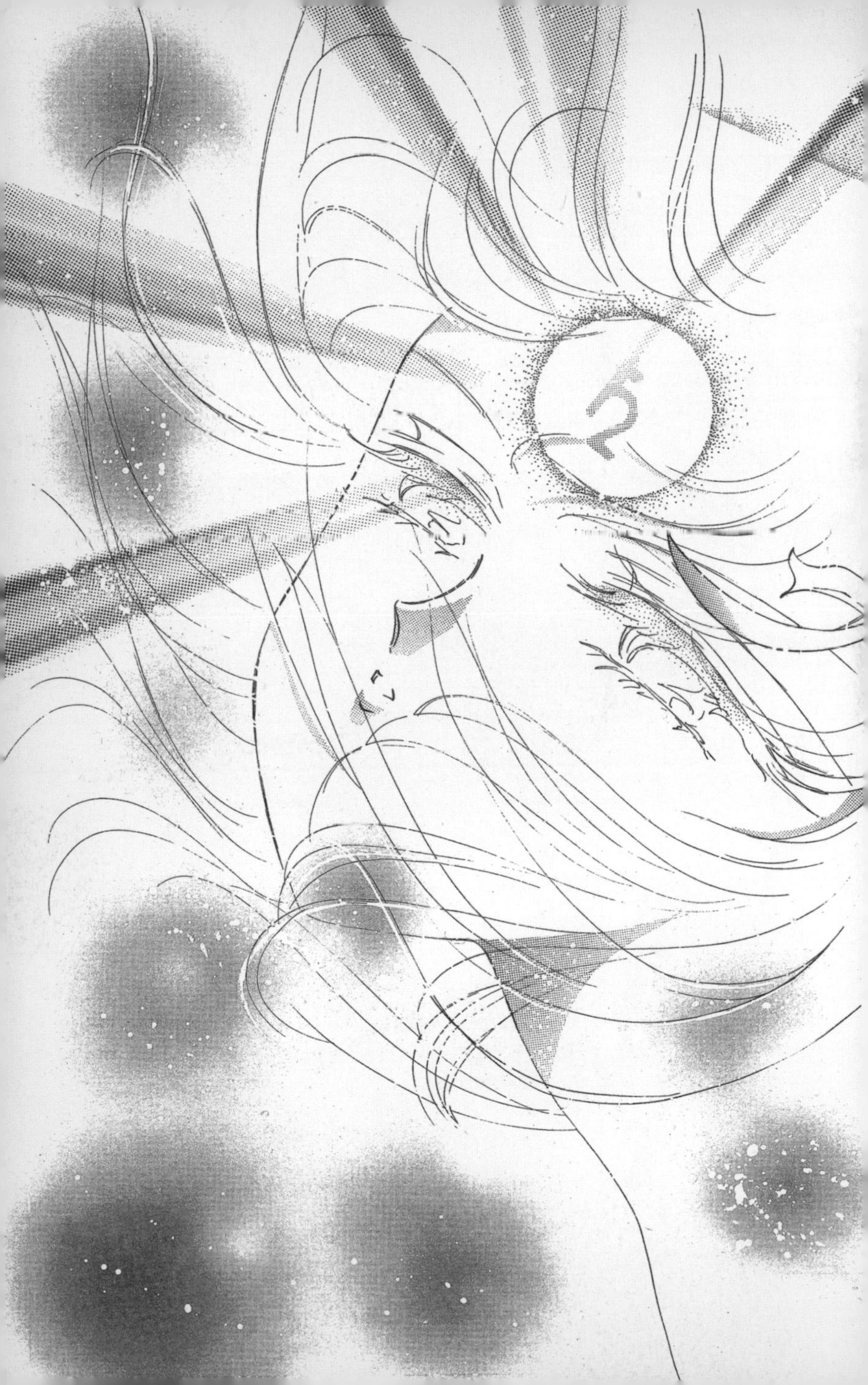

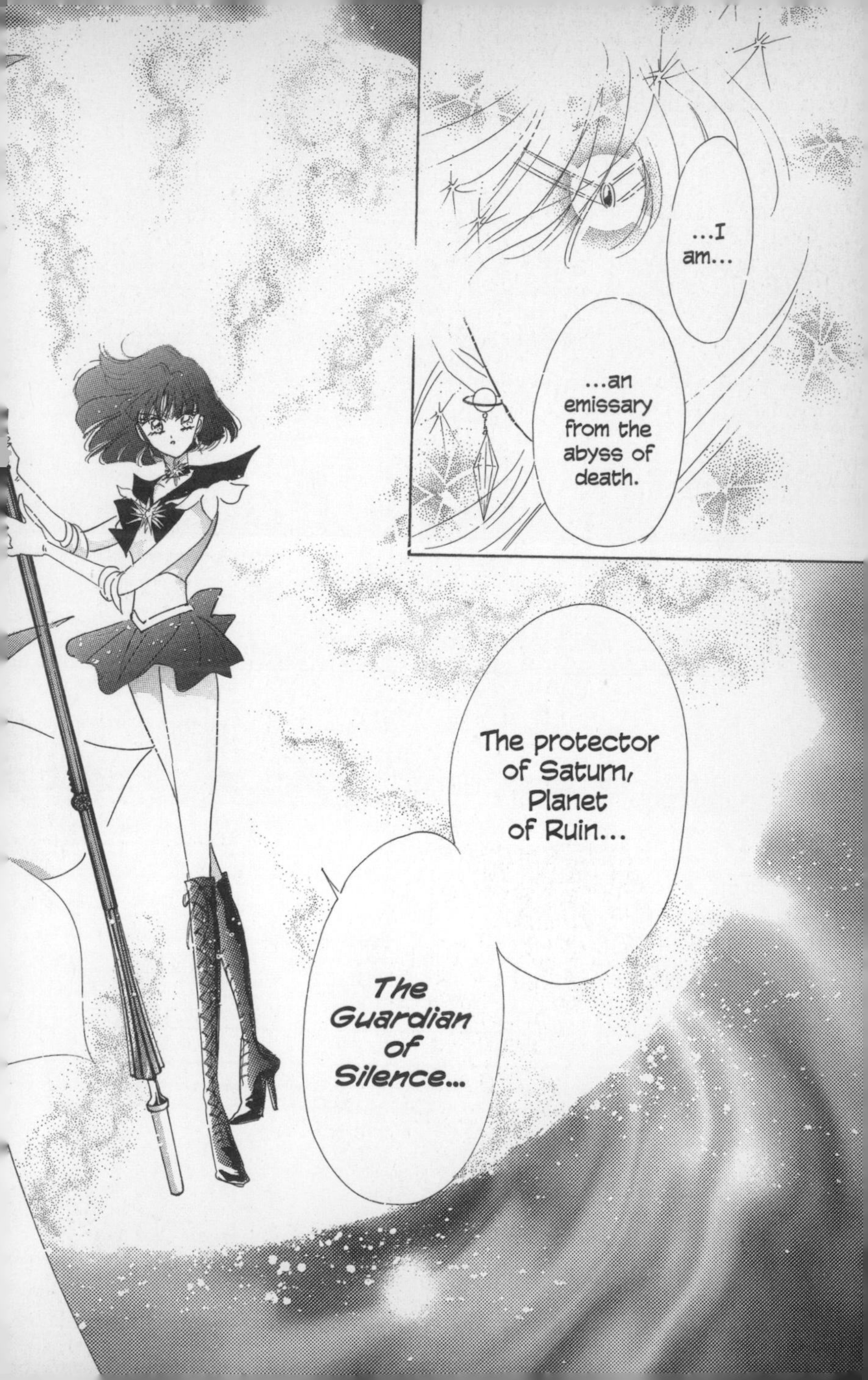
...I am...
...an emissary from the abyss of death.
The protector of Saturn, Planet of Ruin...
The Guardian of Silence...

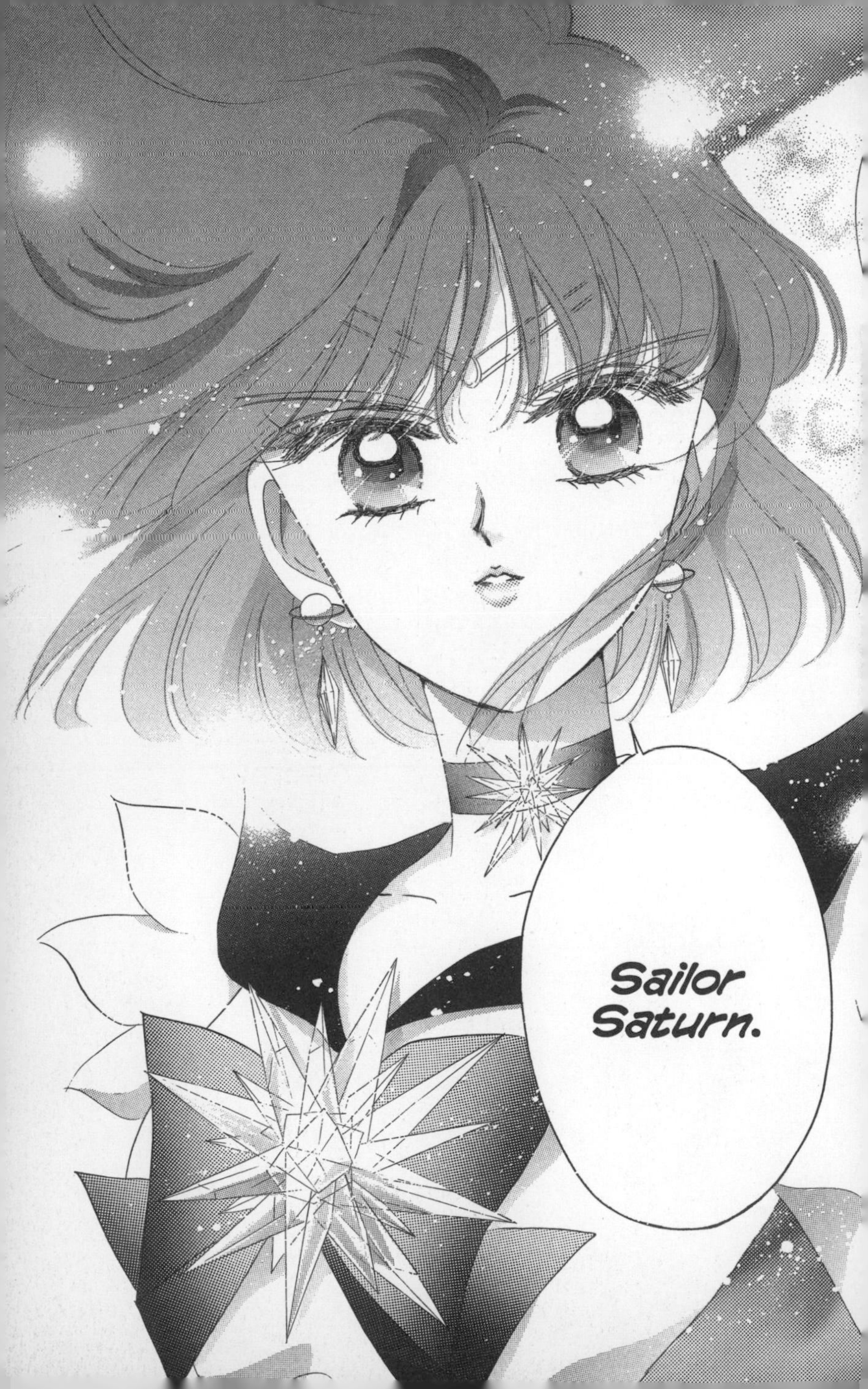
Sailor Saturn.

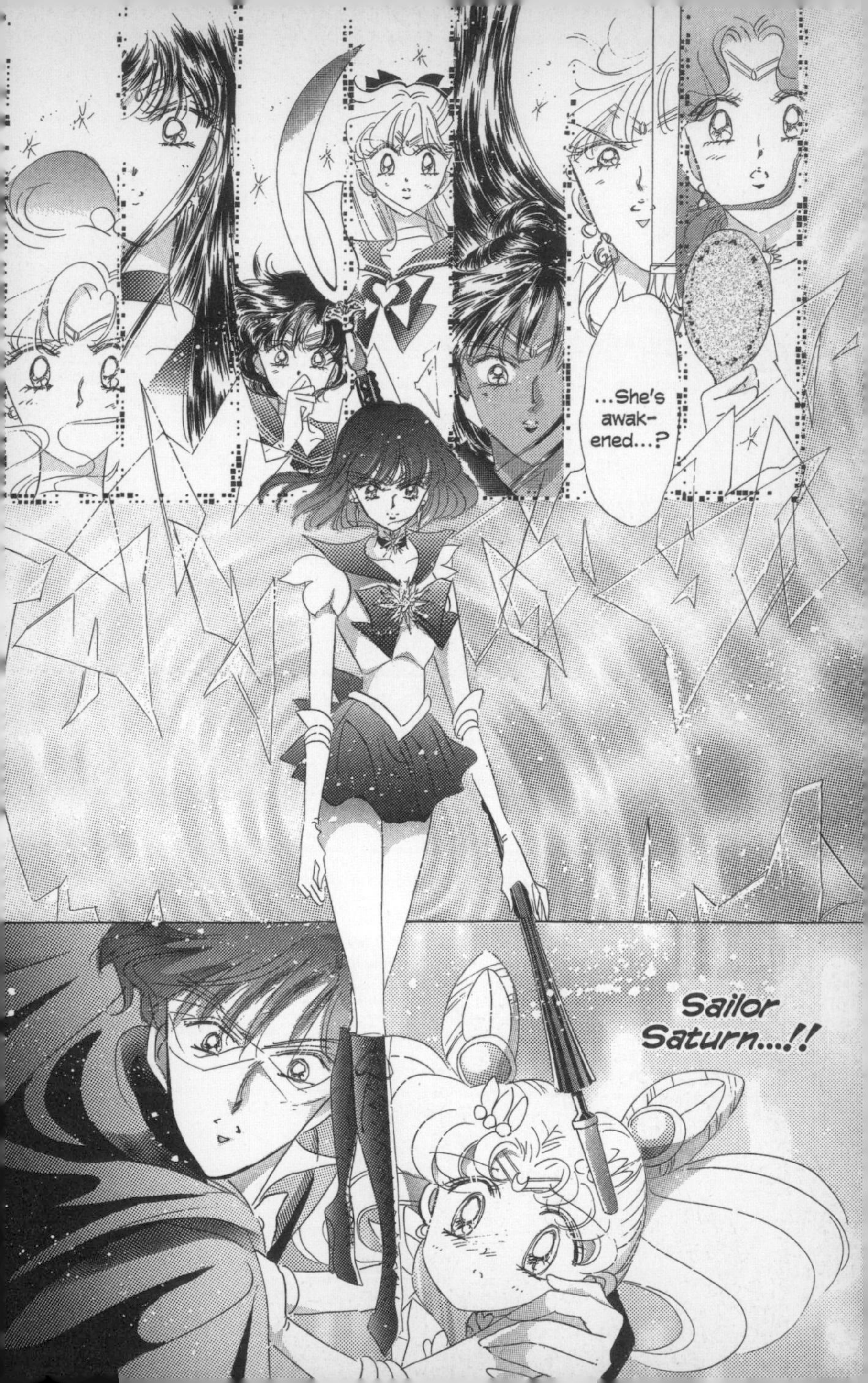
...She's awak-ened...?
Sailor Saturn...!!

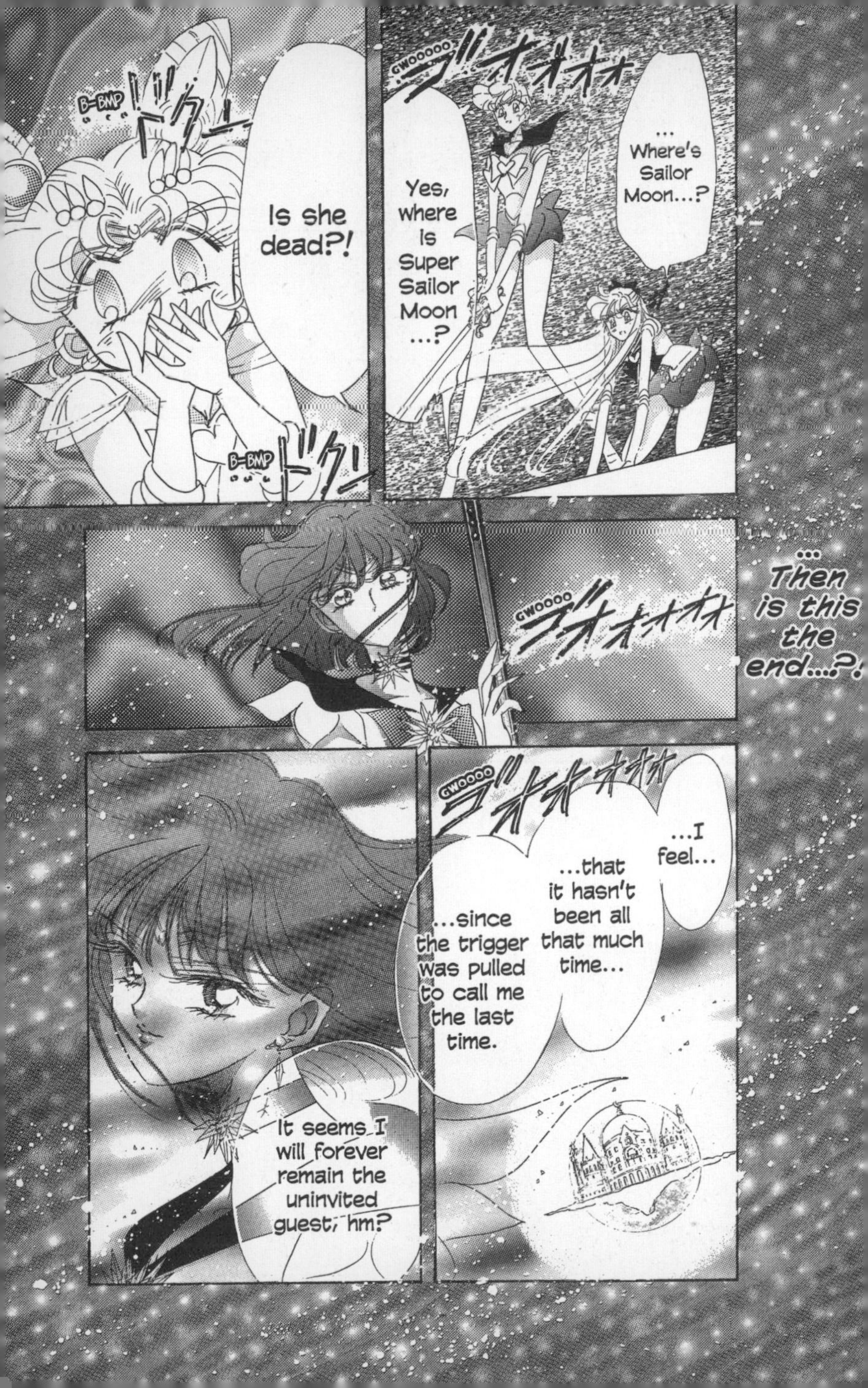
GWOOOOO
... Where's Sailor Moon...?
Yes, where is Super Sailor Moon ...?
B-BMP
Is she dead?!
B-BMP
GWOOOO
... Then is this the end...?!
GWOOOO
...I feel...
...that it hasn't been all that much time...
...since the trigger was pulled to call me the last time.
It seems I will forever remain the uninvited guest, hm?

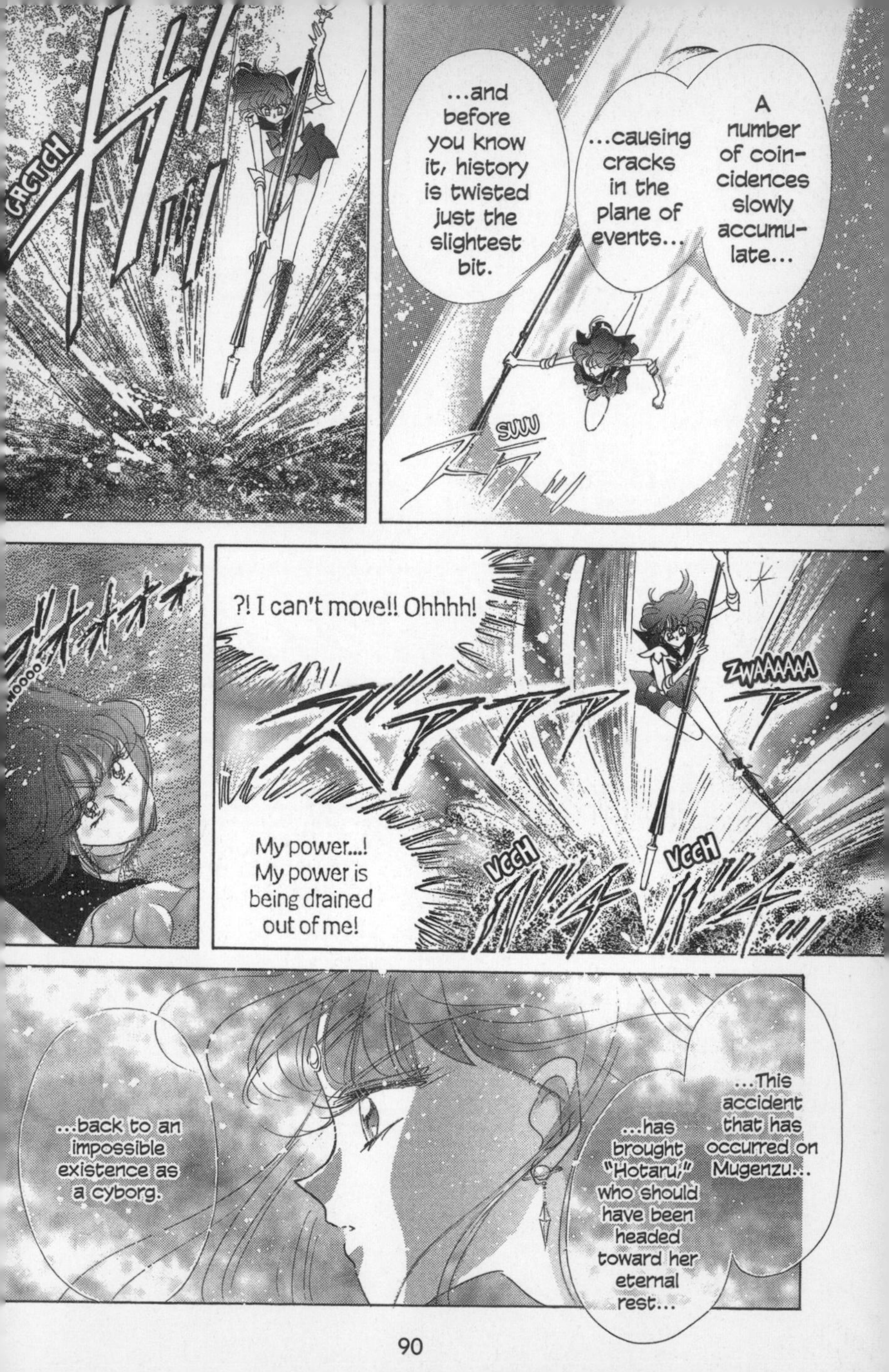
A number of coin-cidences slowly accumu-late...
...causing cracks in the plane of events...
...and before you know it, history is twisted just the slightest bit.
SWUU
CRTCH
?! I can't move!! Ohhhh!
ZWAAAAAA
My power...! My power is being drained out of me!
VCCH
VCCH
WOOOO
...This accident that has occurred on Mugenzu...
...has brought "Hotaru," who should have been headed toward her eternal rest...
...back to an impossible existence as a cyborg.

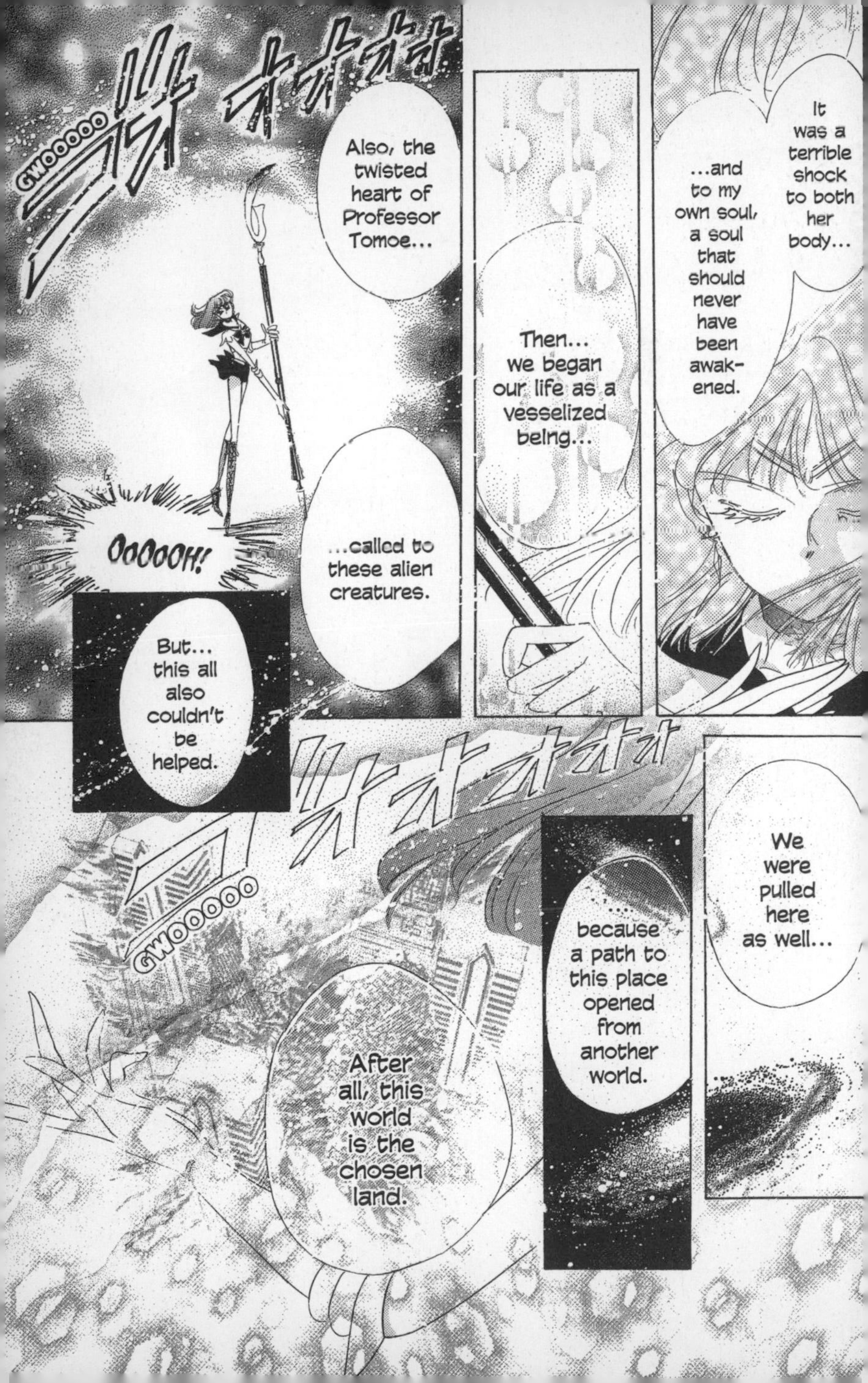
It was a terrible shock to both her body...
...and to my own soul, a soul that should never have been awakened.
Then... we began our life as a vesselized being...
GWOOOOO
Also, the twisted heart of Professor Tomoe...
...called to these alien creatures.
OOOOOH!
But... this all also couldn't be helped.
We were pulled here as well...
because a path to this place opened from another world.
GWOOOOOO
After all, this world is the chosen land.

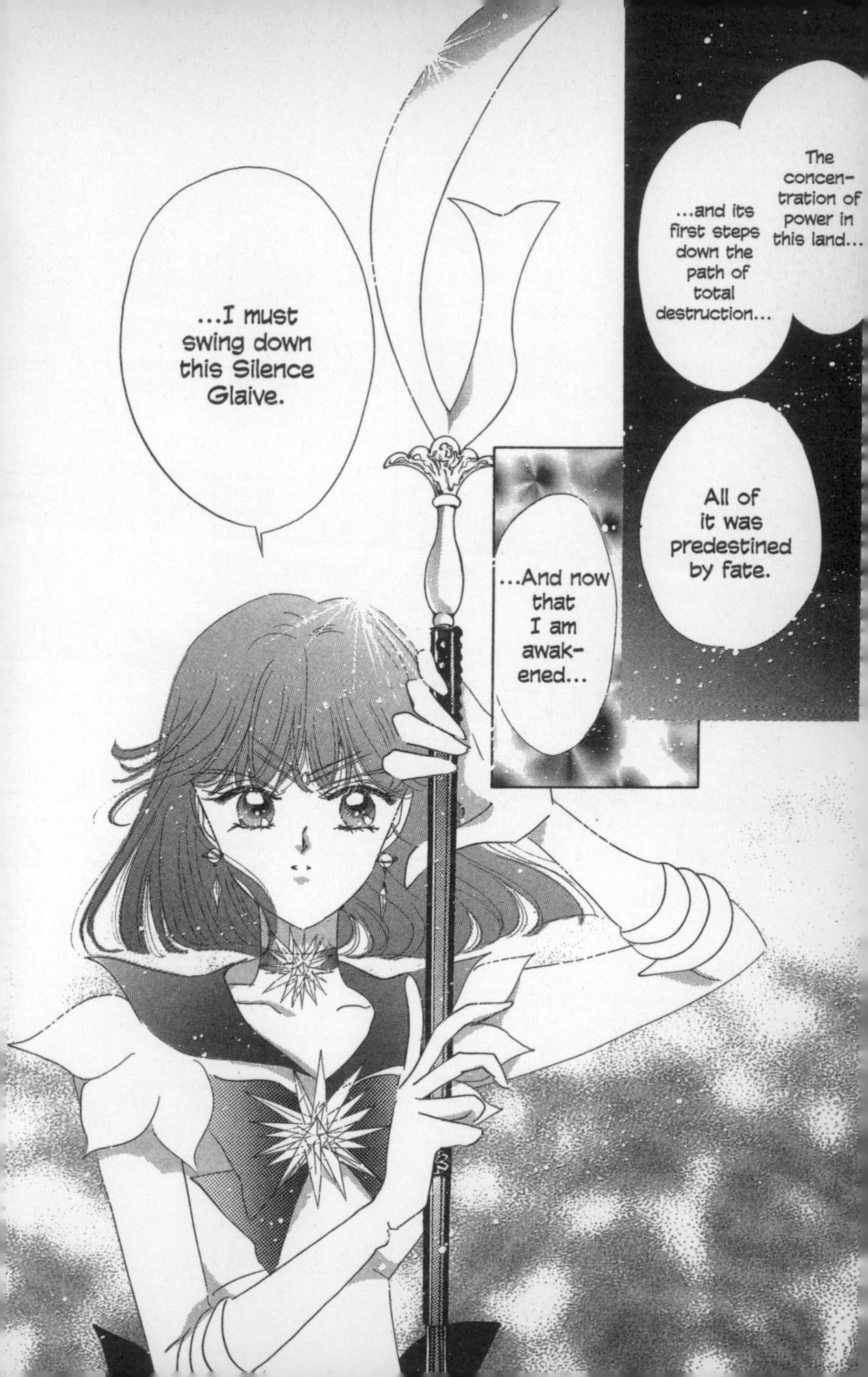
The concentration of power in this land...
...and its first steps down the path of total destruction...
All of it was predestined by fate.
...And now that I am awakened...
...I must swing down this Silence Glaive.

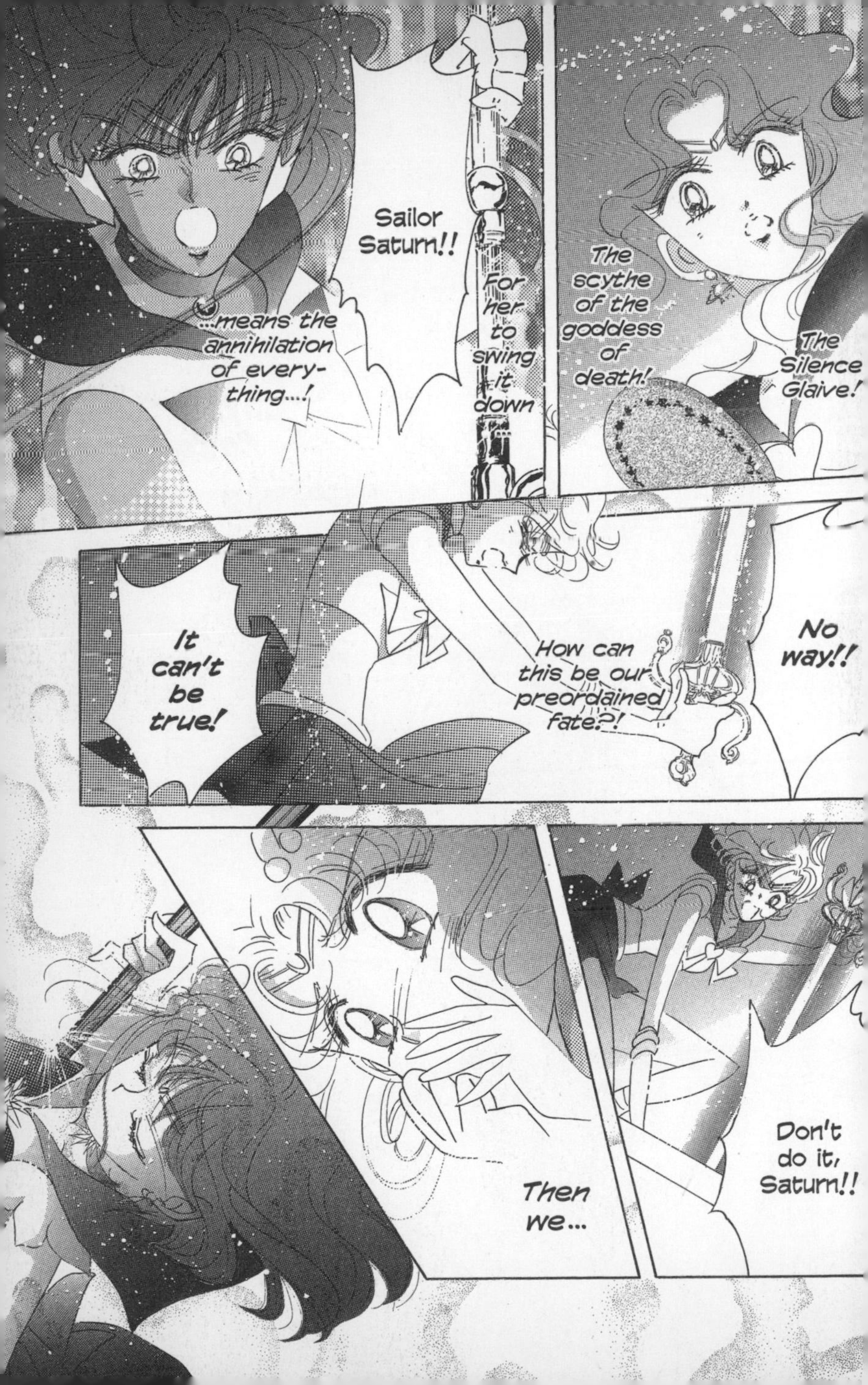

The Silence Glaive!
The scythe of the goddess of death!
Sailor Saturn!!
For her to swing it down...
...means the annihilation of every-thing...!
No way!!
How can this be our preordained fate?!
It can't be true!
Don't do it, Saturn!!
Then we...

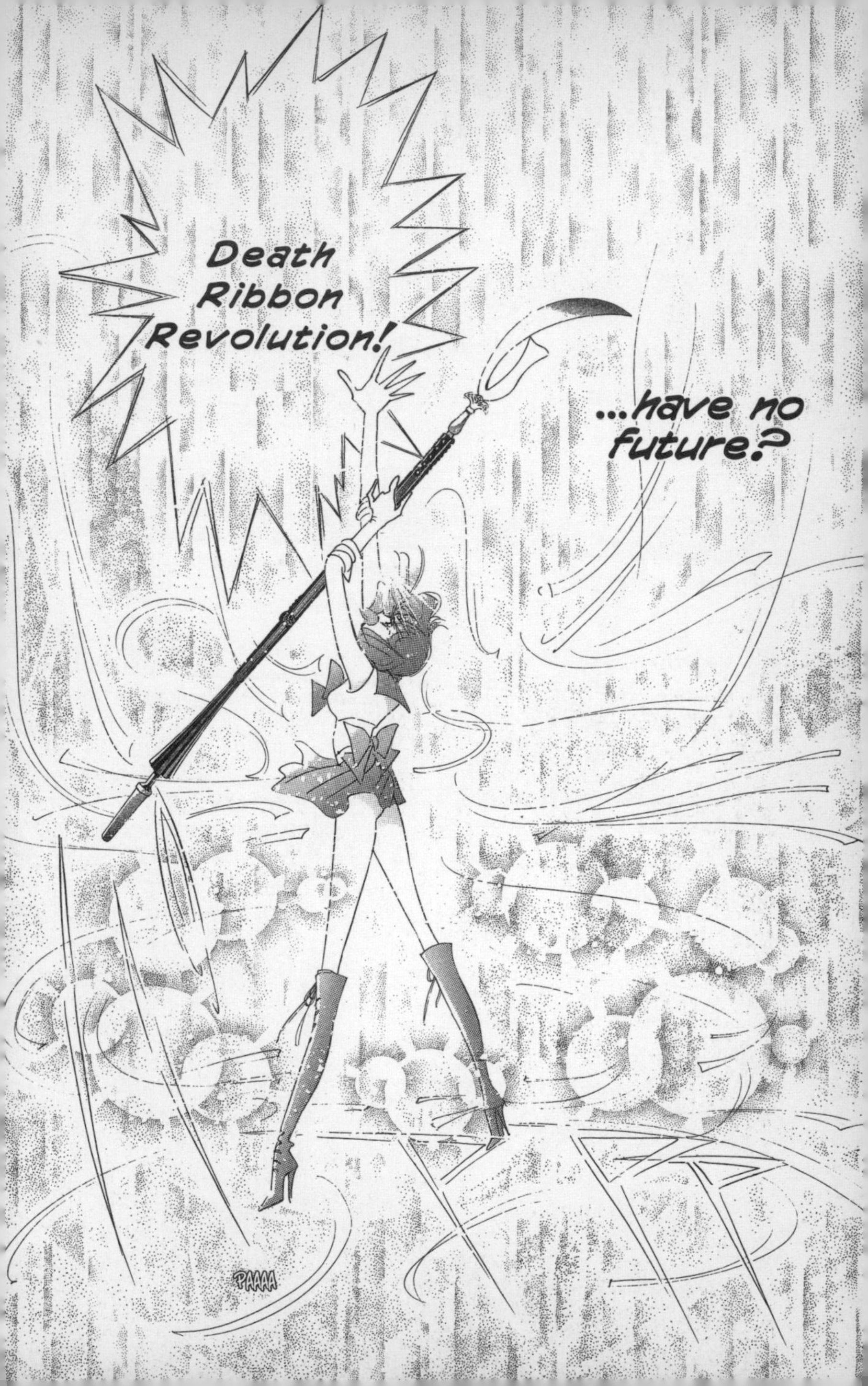
...have no future?
Death Ribbon Revolution!
PAAAA

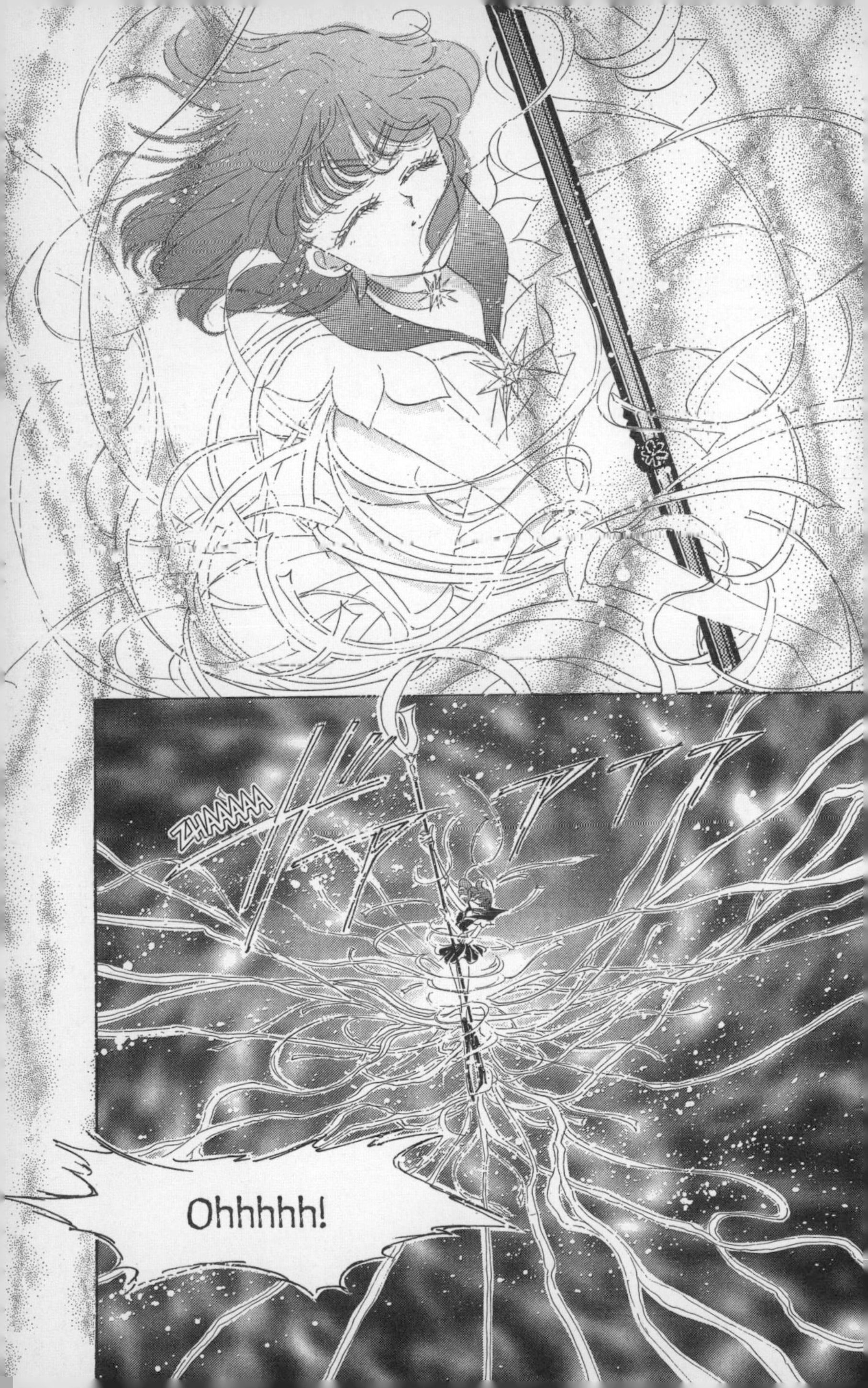
ZHAAAAA
Ohhhhh!

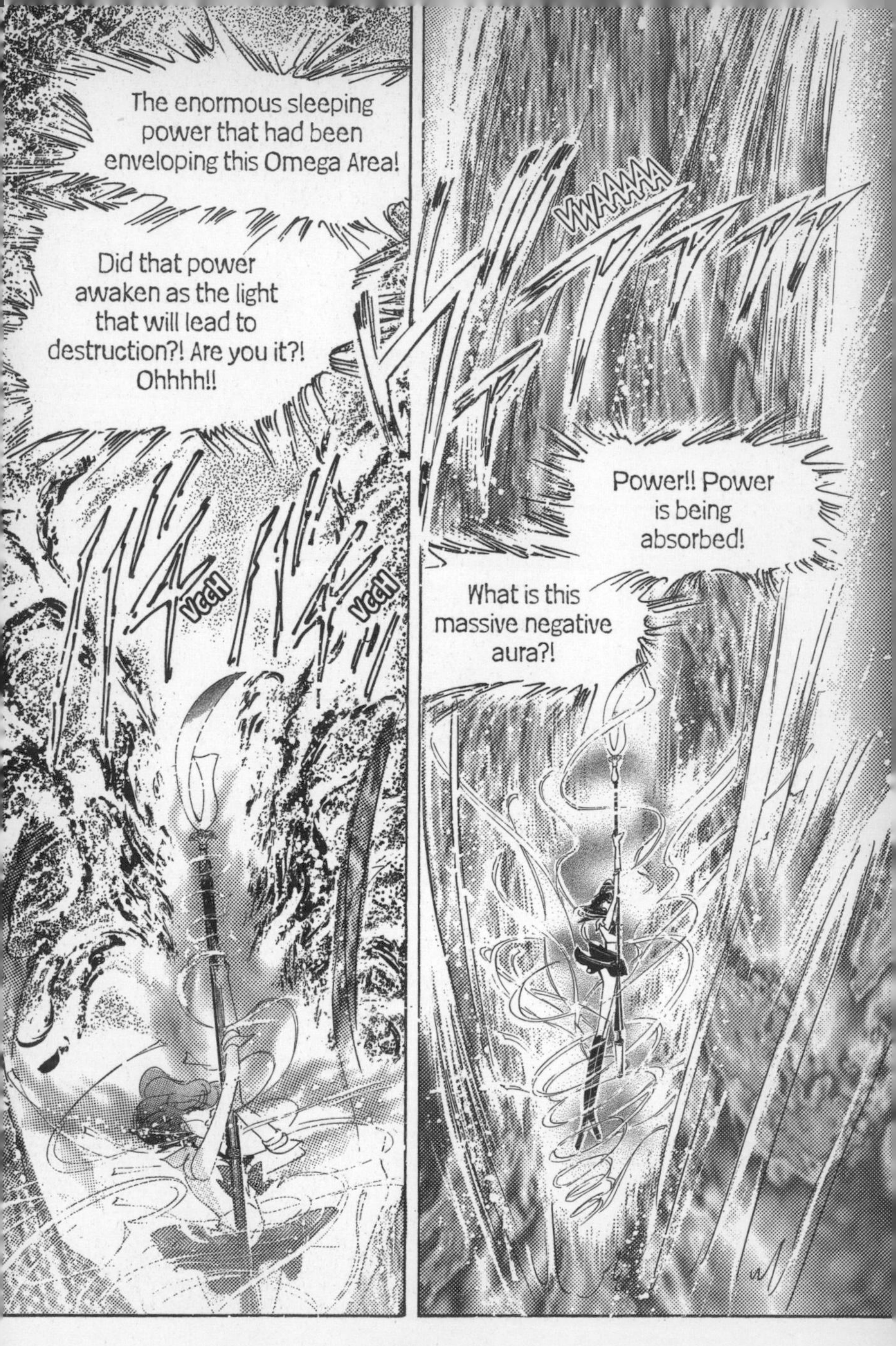
VWAAAAA
Power!! Power is being absorbed!
What is this massive negative aura?!
The enormous sleeping power that had been enveloping this Omega Area!
Did that power awaken as the light that will lead to destruction?! Are you it?! Ohhhh!!
VCCH
VCCH

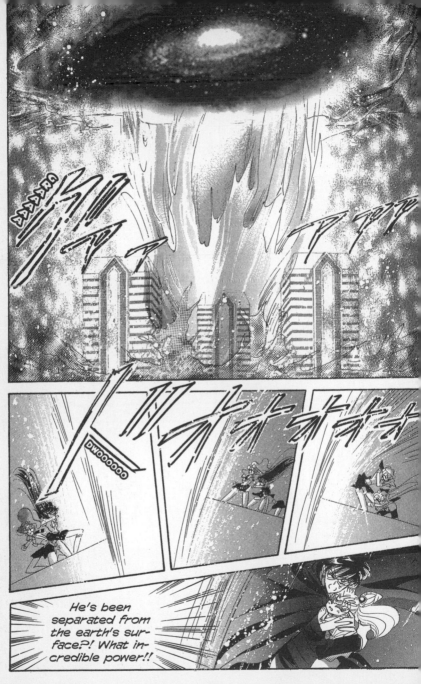

He's been separated from the earth's surface?! What incredible power!!

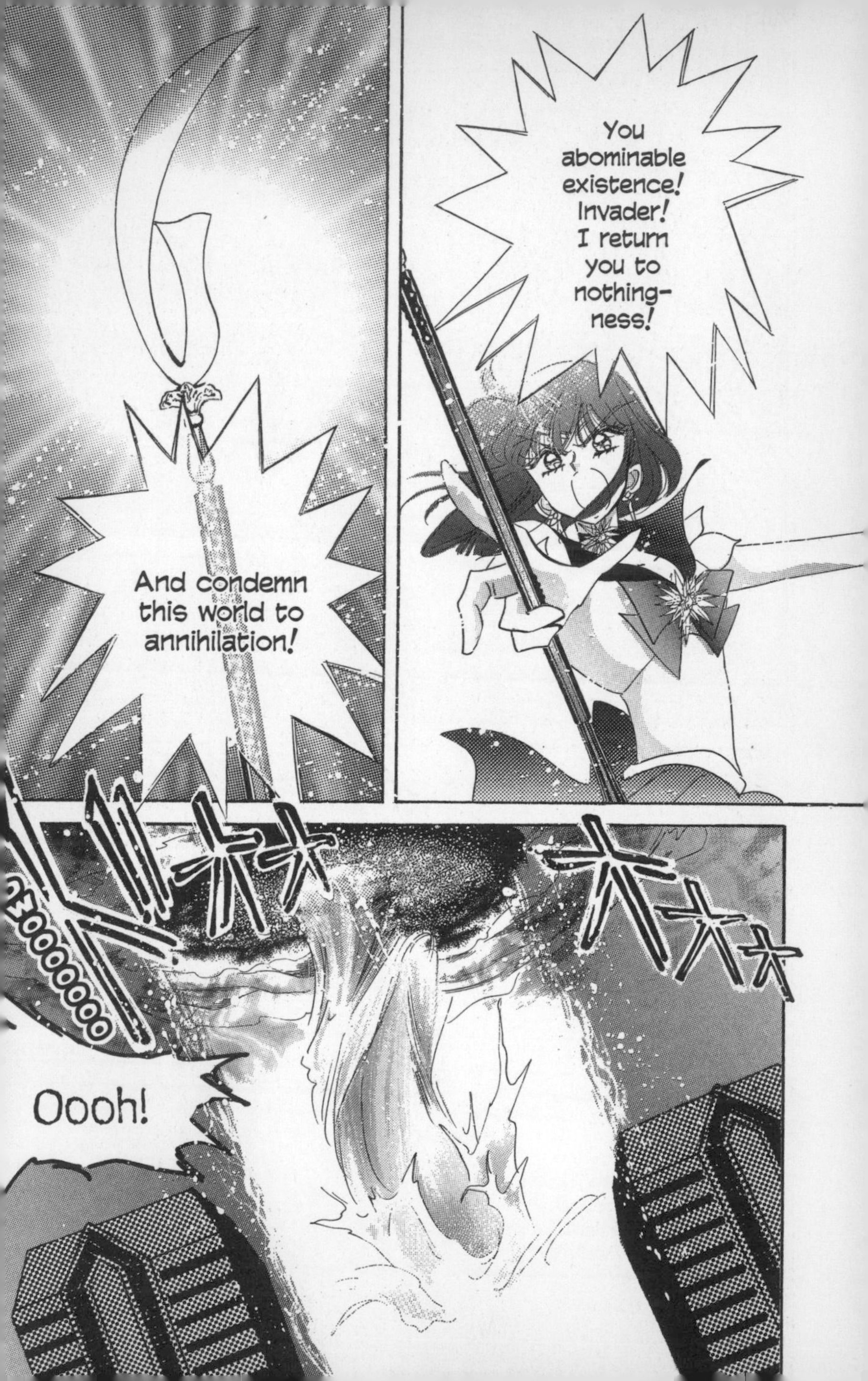
You abominable existence! Invader! I return you to nothing-ness!
And condemn this world to annihilation!
Oooh!

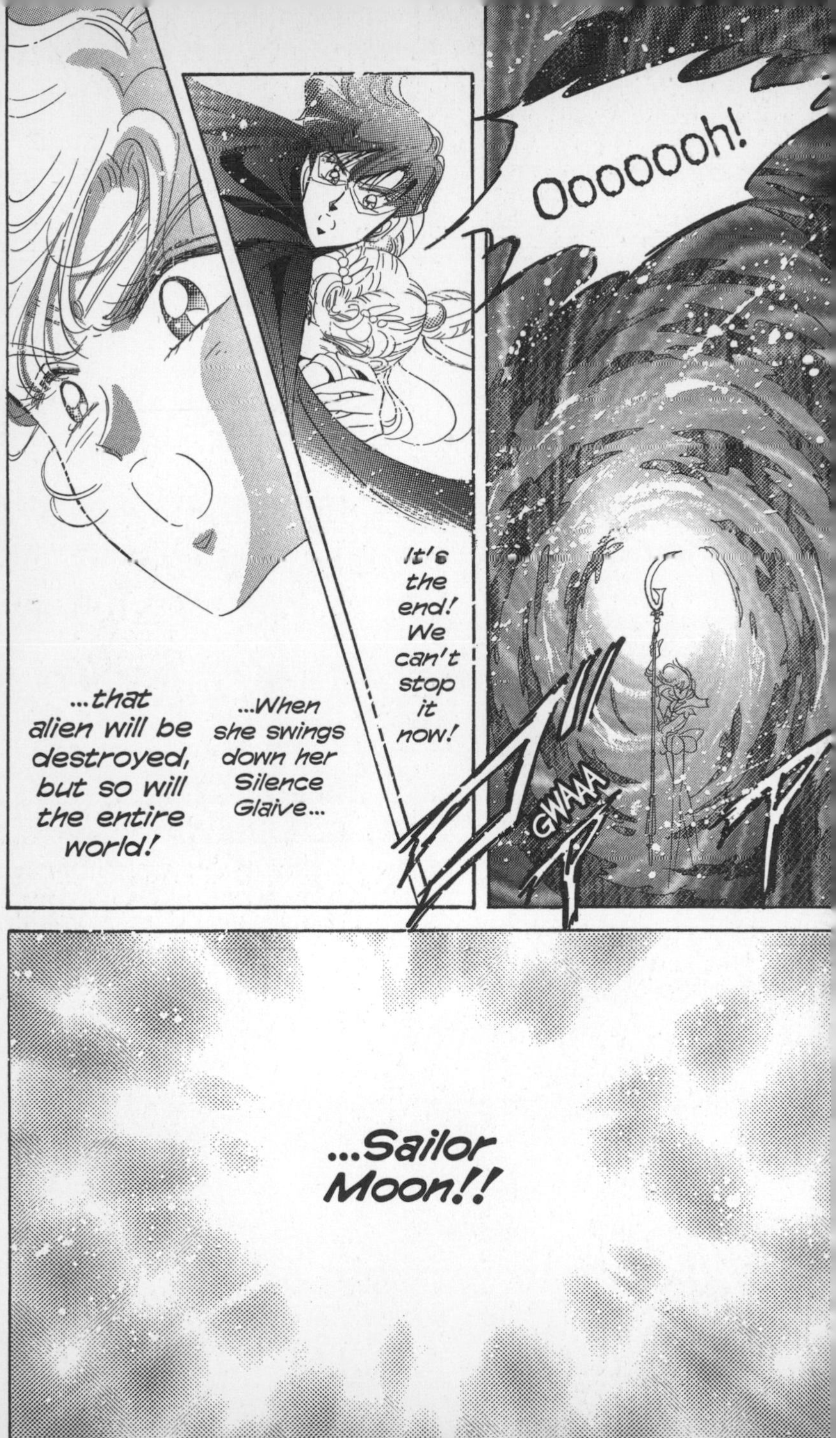
Ooooooh!
GWAAA
It's the end! We can't stop it now!
...When she swings down her Silence Glaive...
...that alien will be destroyed, but so will the entire world!
...Sailor Moon!!

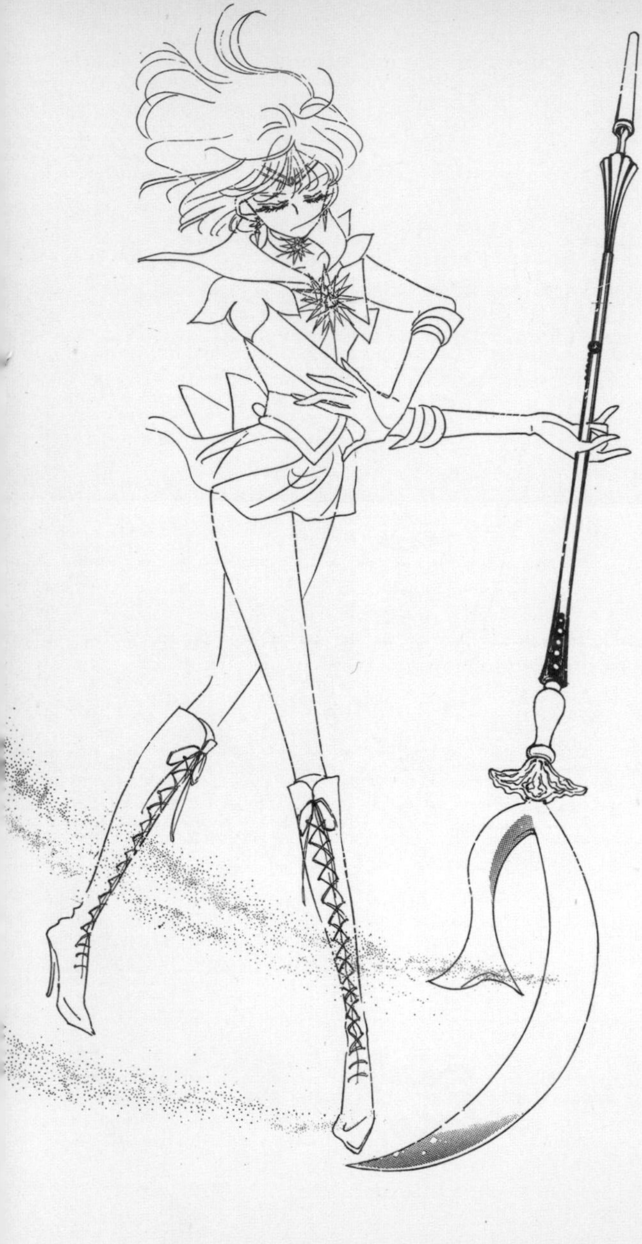

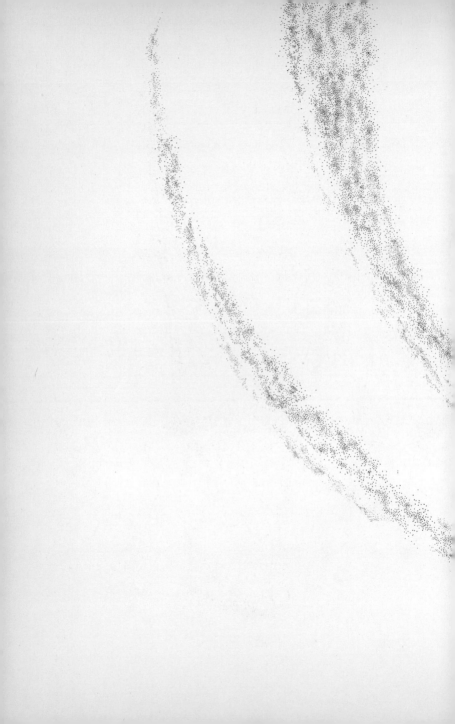

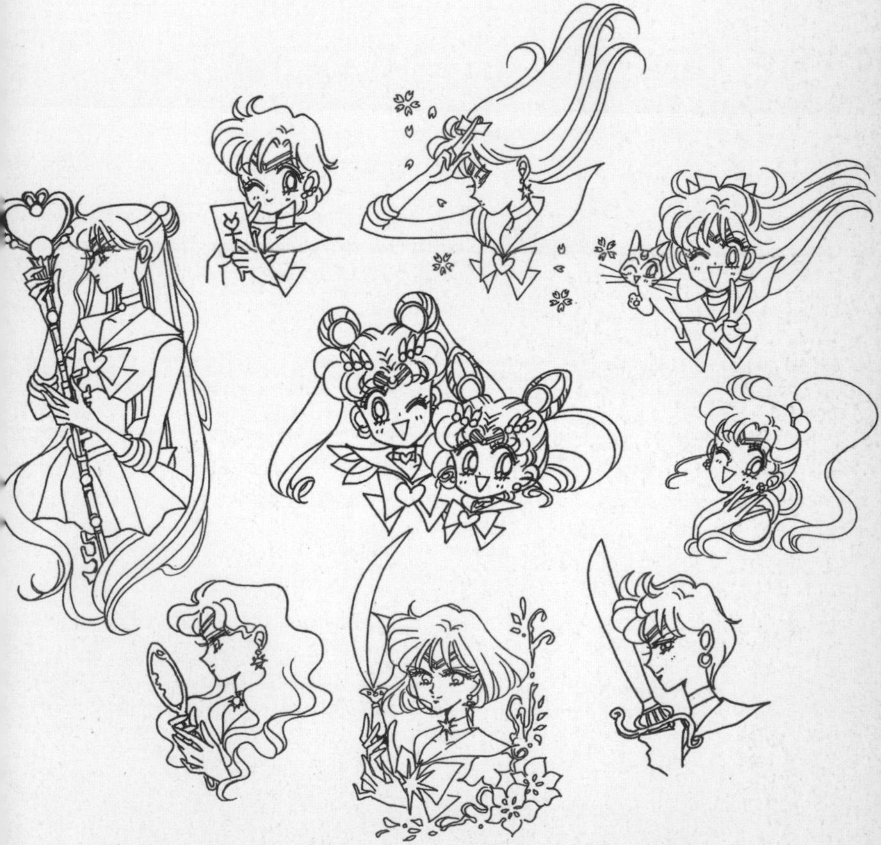

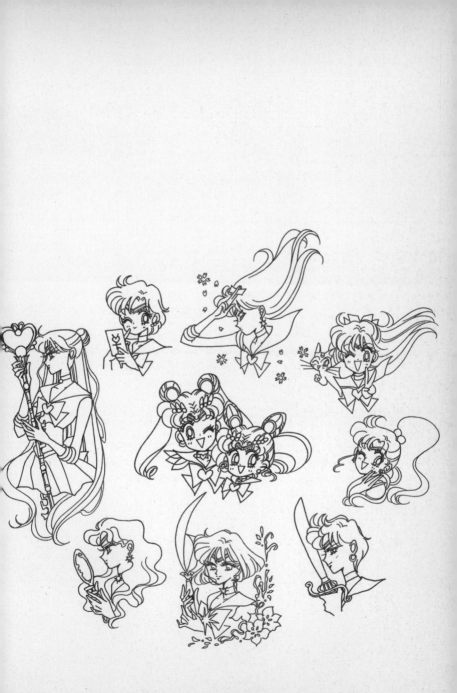

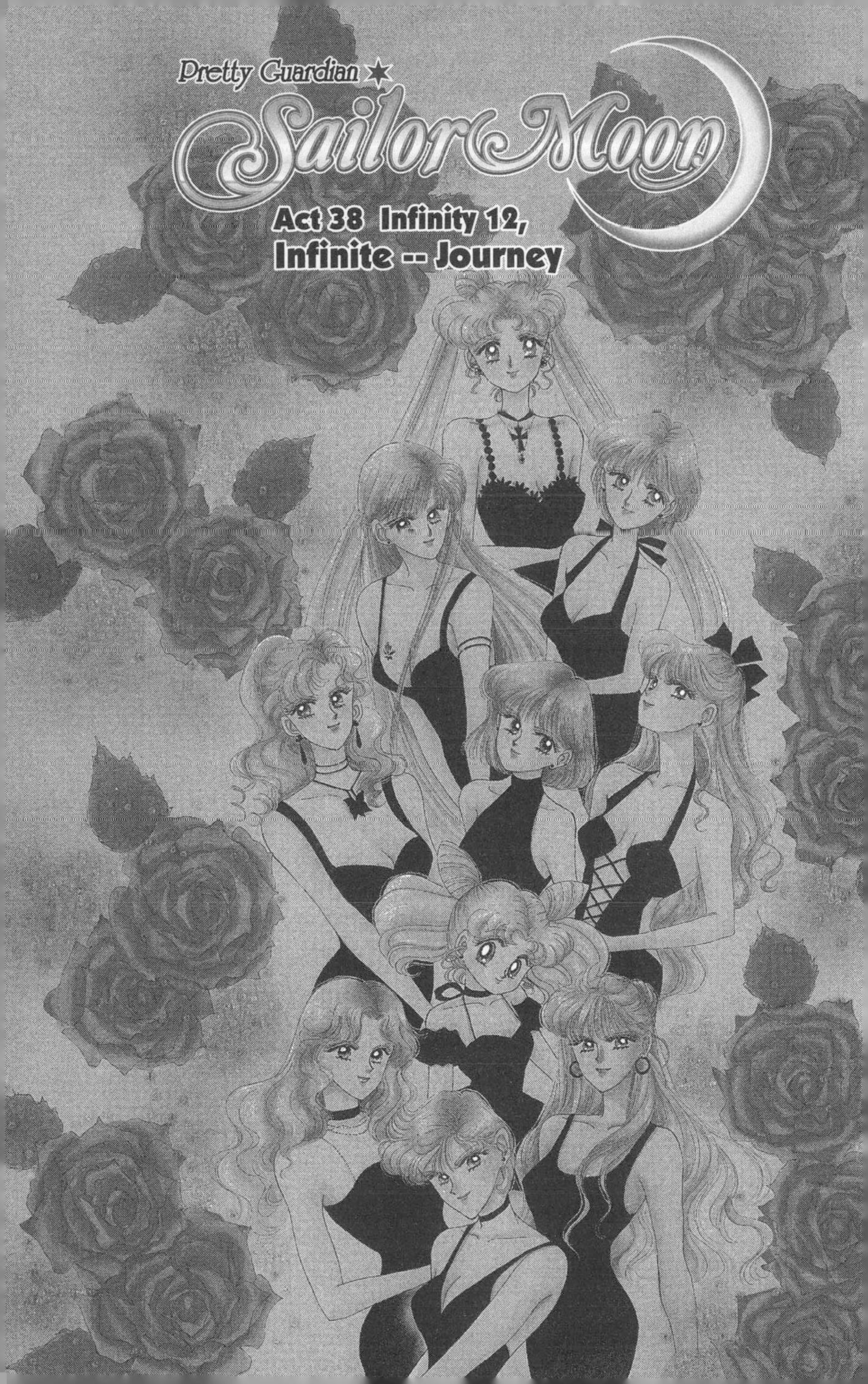
Pretty Guardian
Sailor Moon
Act 38 Infinity 12,
Infinite -- Journey

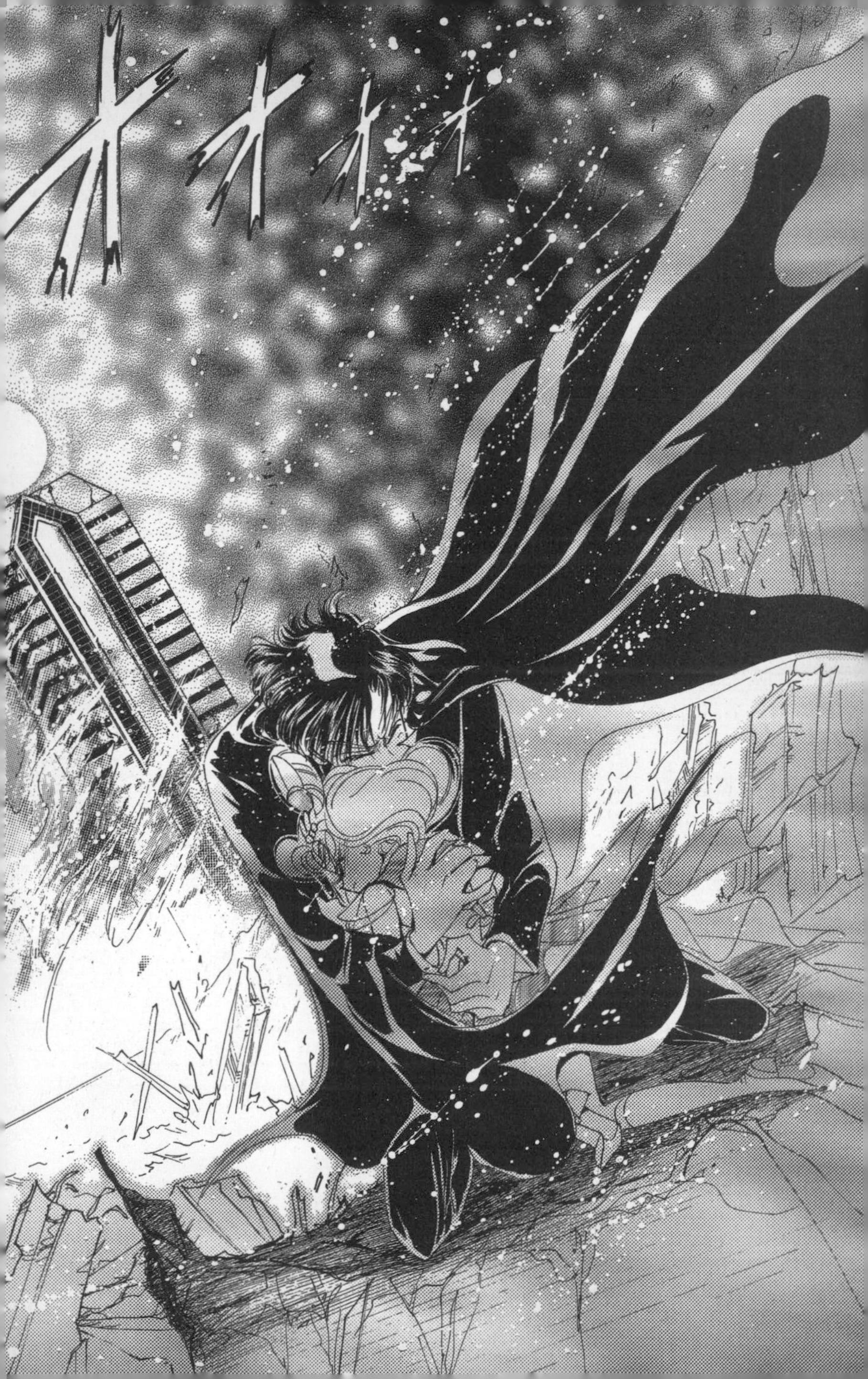
オオオオ

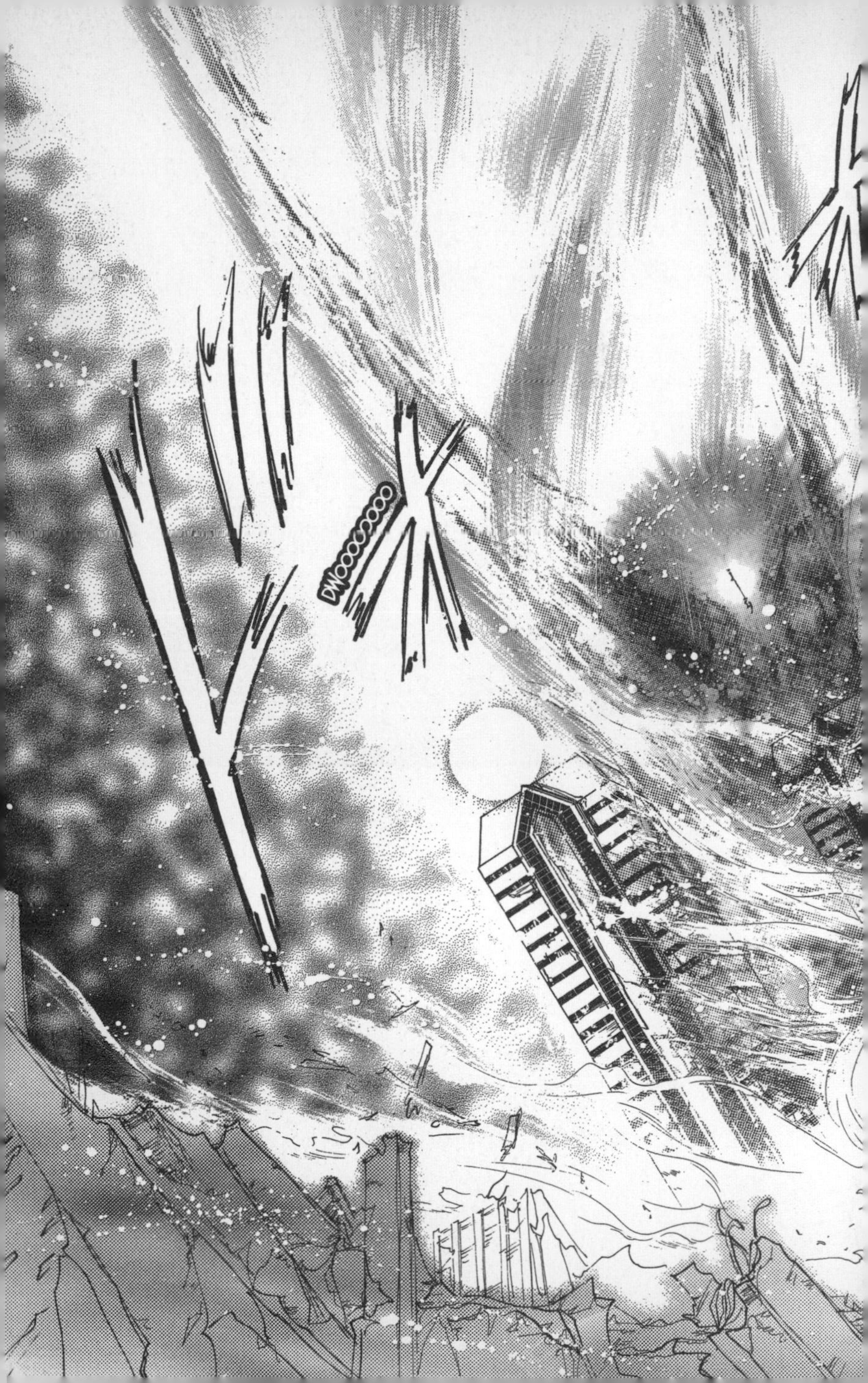
DWOOOOOOOO

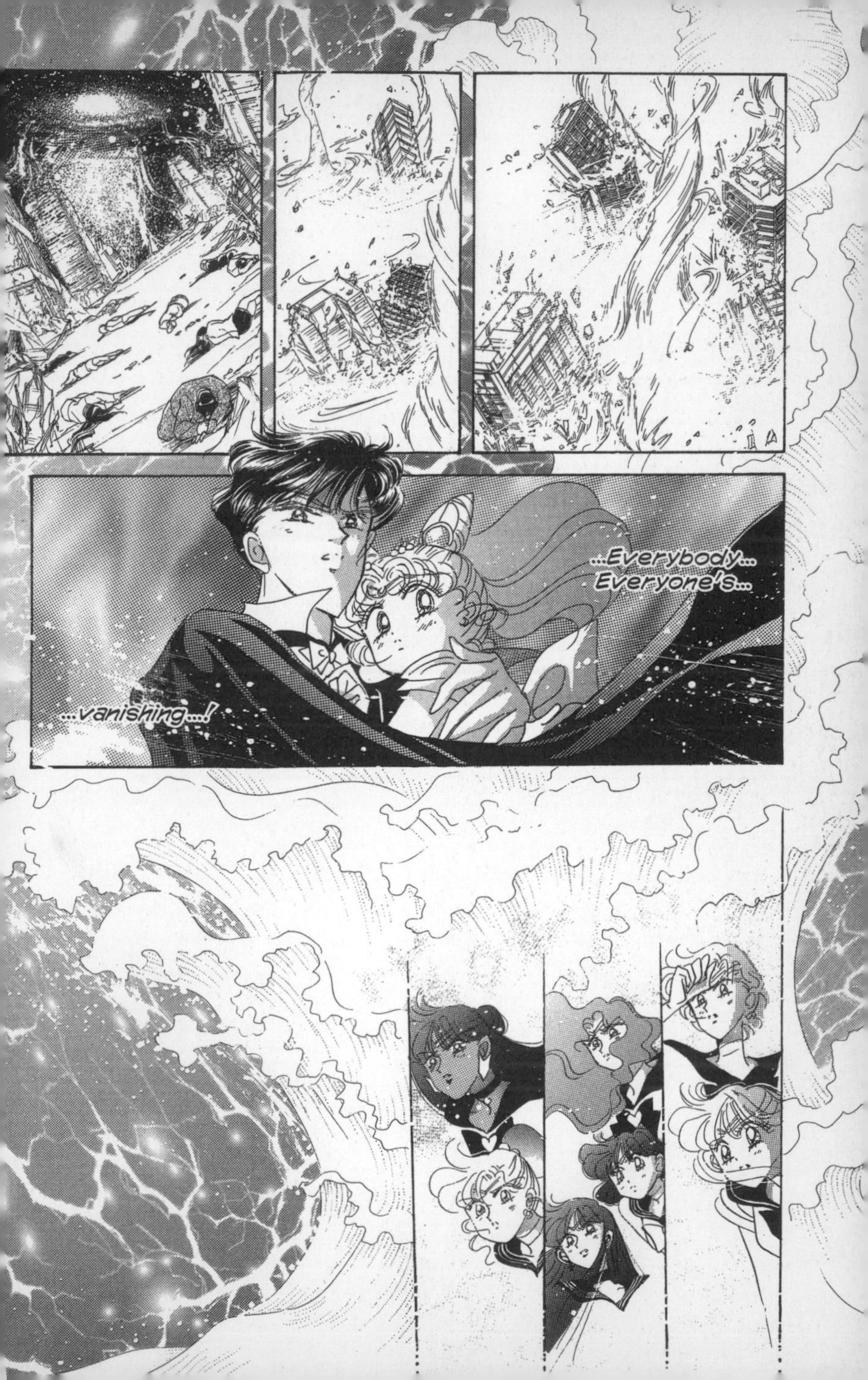
...Everybody...
Everyone's...
...vanishing...!

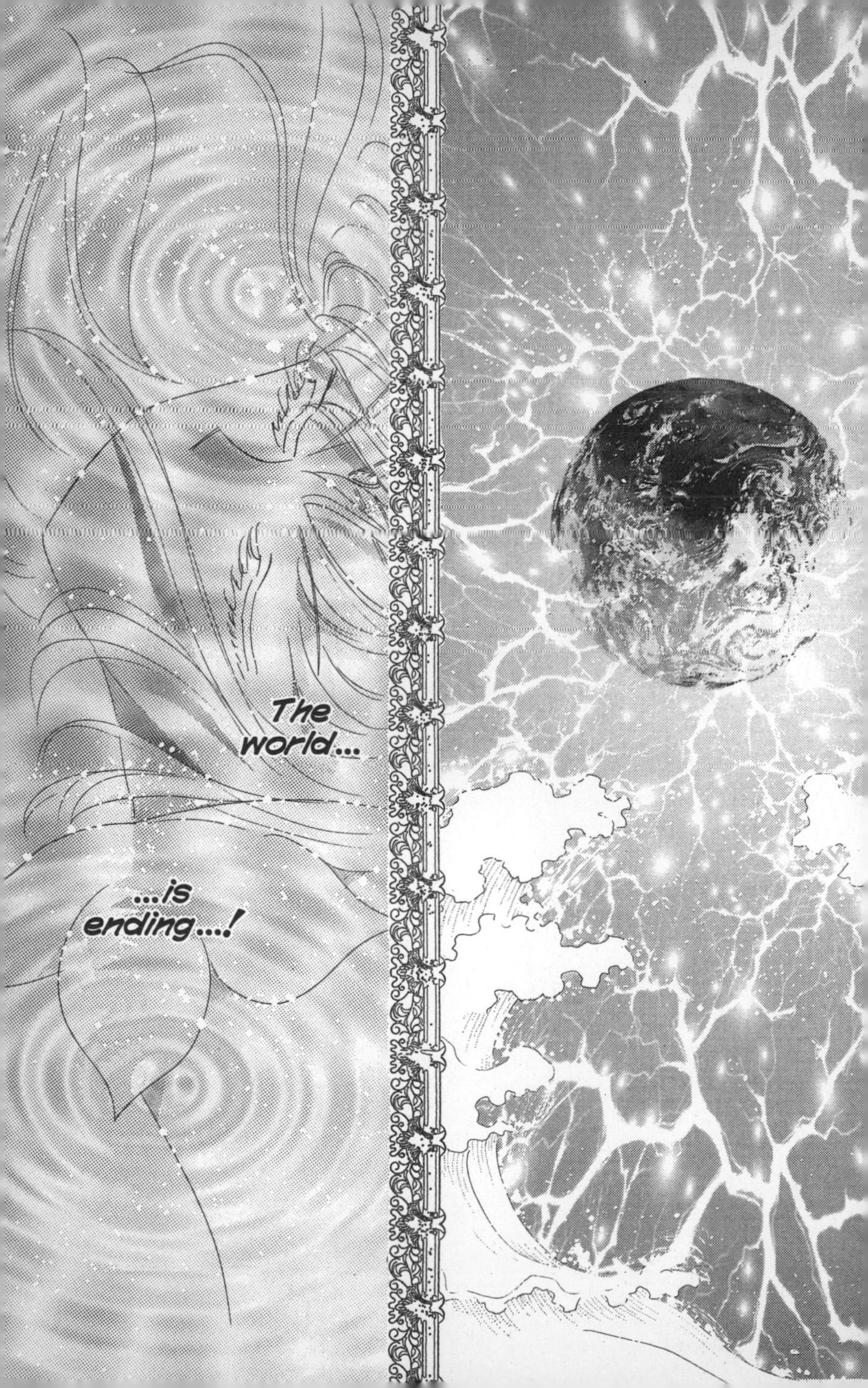
The world...
...is ending...!

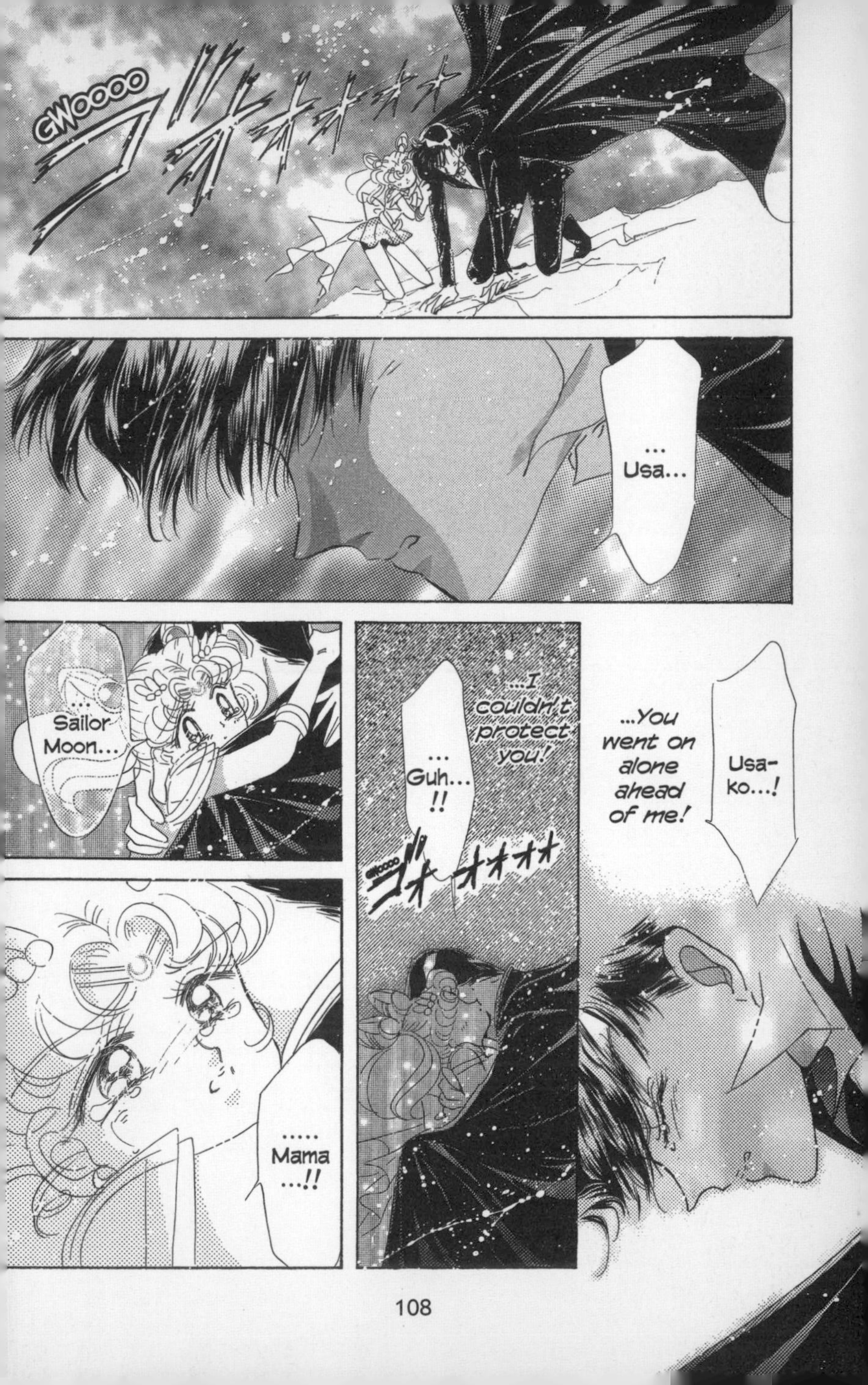
GWOOOO
... Usa...
Usa-ko...!
...You went on alone ahead of me!
...I couldn't protect you!
... Guh... !!
GWOOO
... Sailor Moon...
..... Mama ...!!

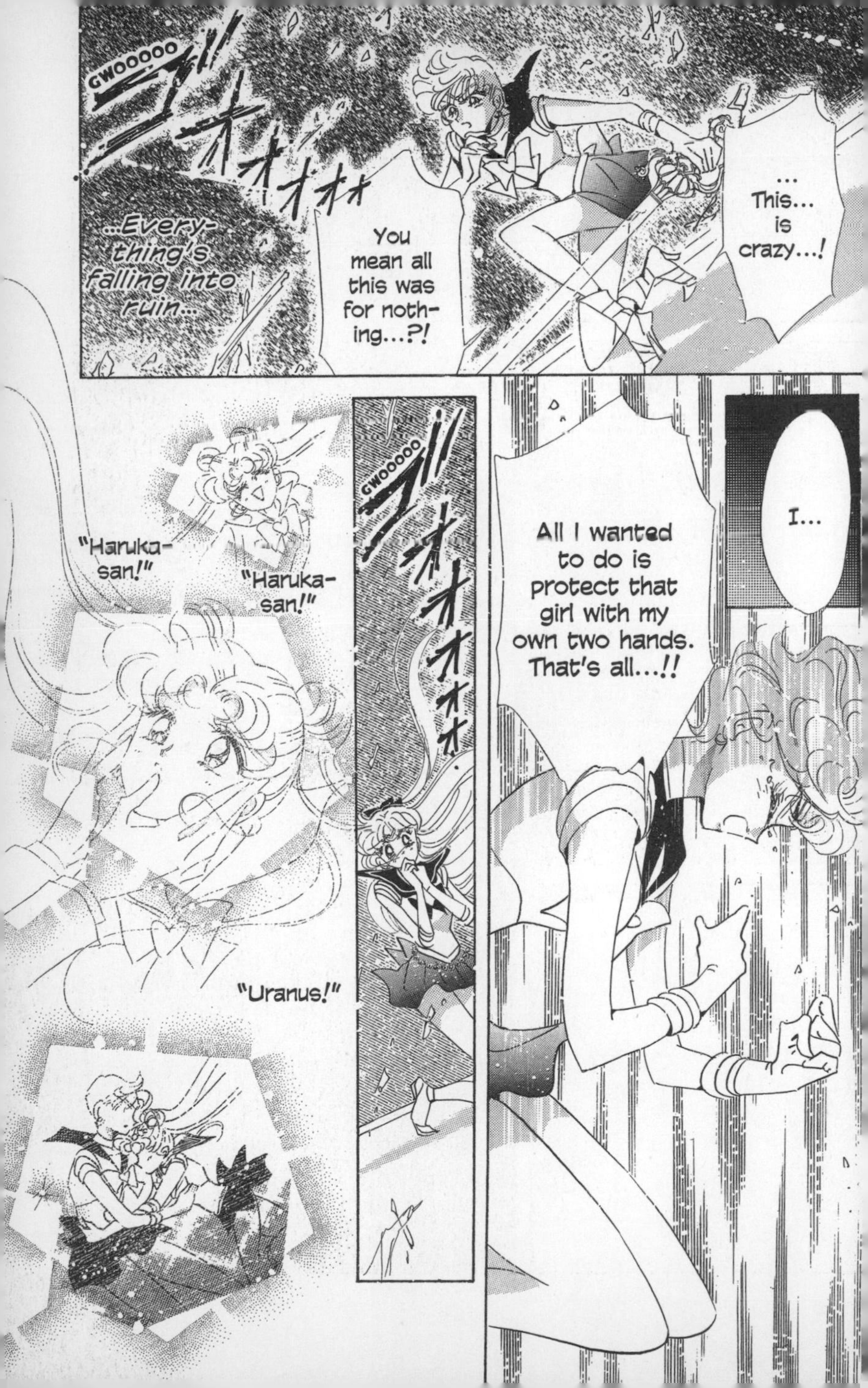
... This... is crazy...!
You mean all this was for nothing...?!
...Everything's falling into ruin...
GWOOOOO
I...
All I wanted to do is protect that girl with my own two hands. That's all...!!
GWOOOOO
"Haruka-san!"
"Haruka-san!"
"Uranus!"

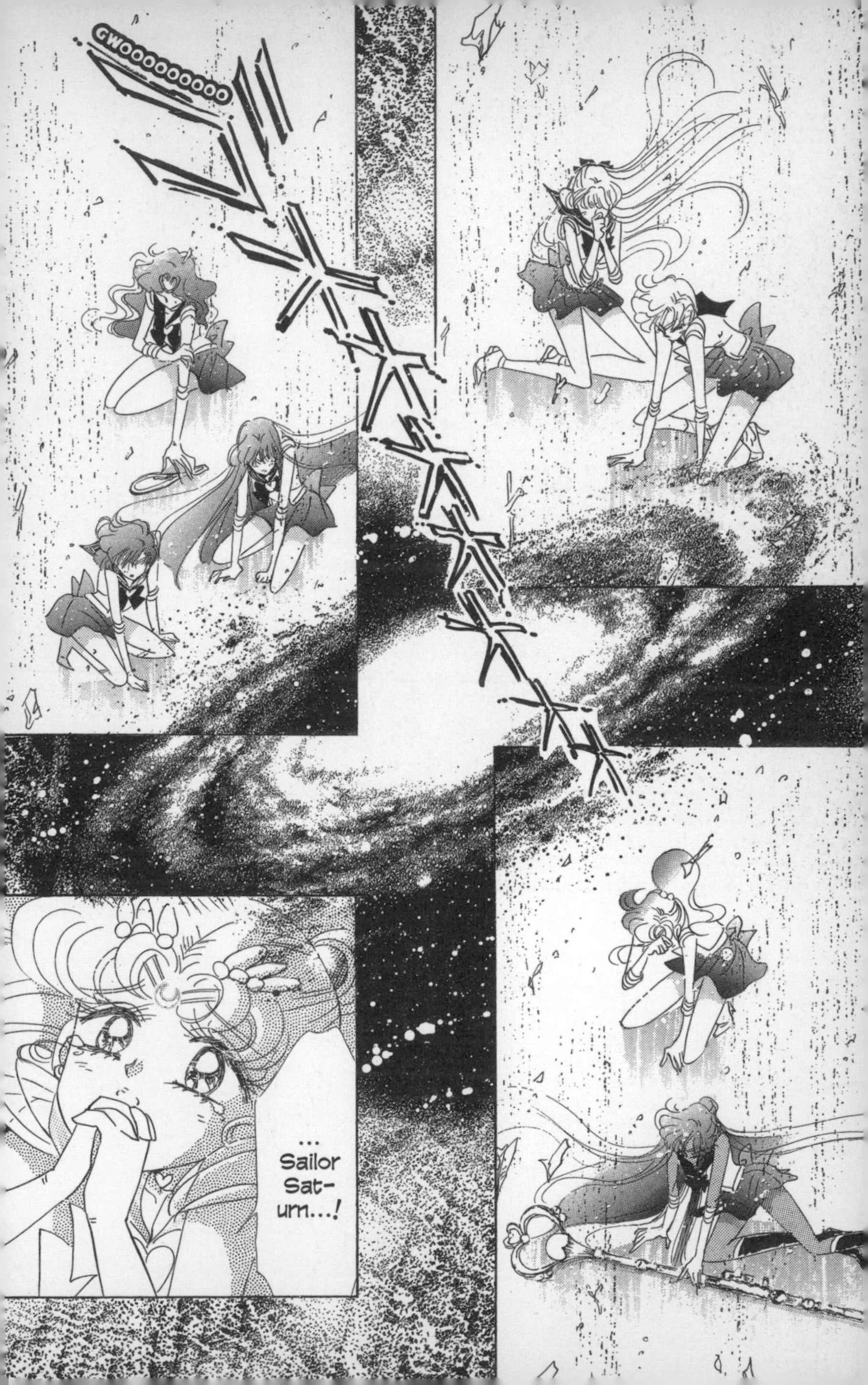
GWOOOOOOOOOO
... Sailor Sat-urn...!

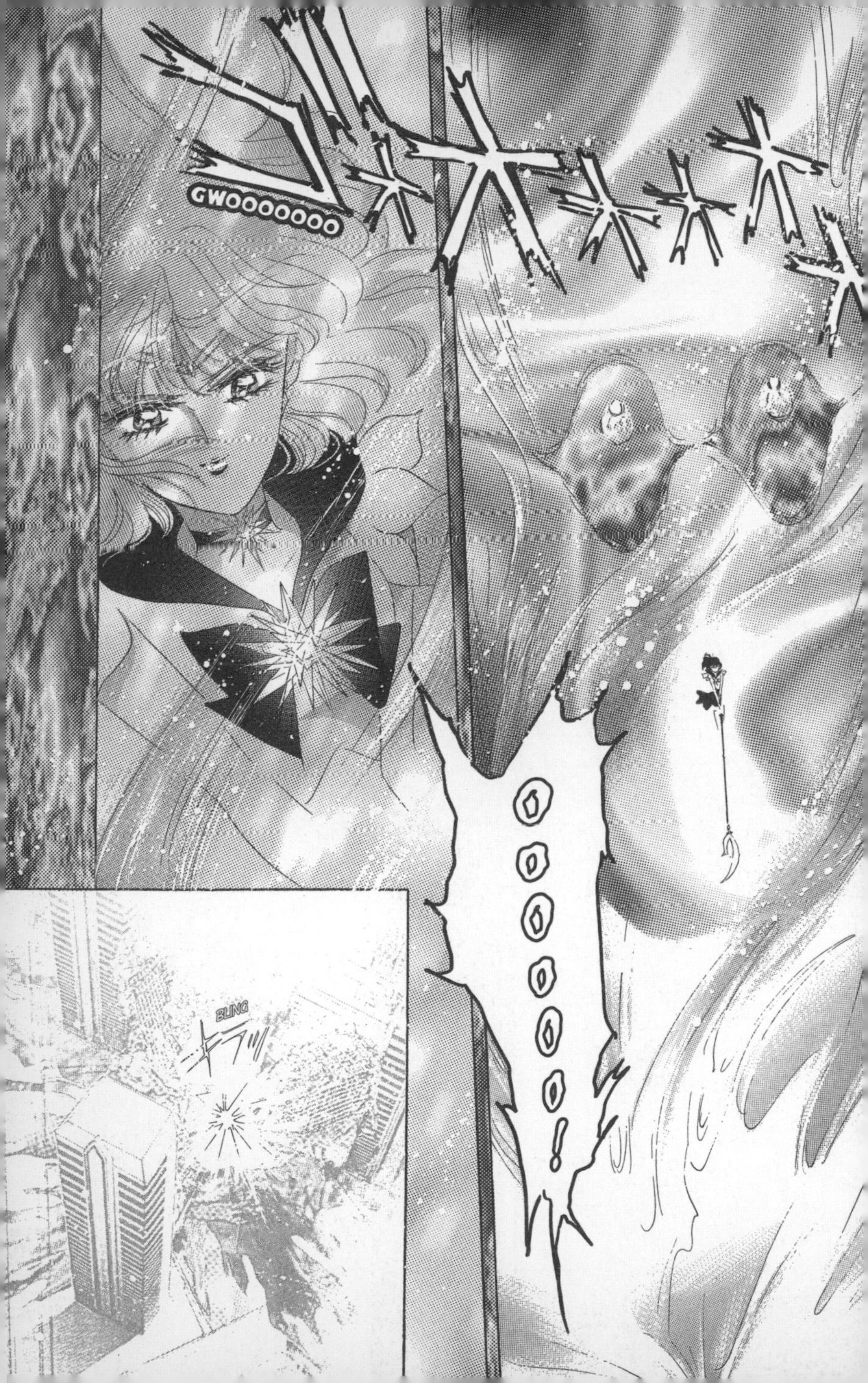
GWOOOOOOO
OOOOOOOO!
BLING

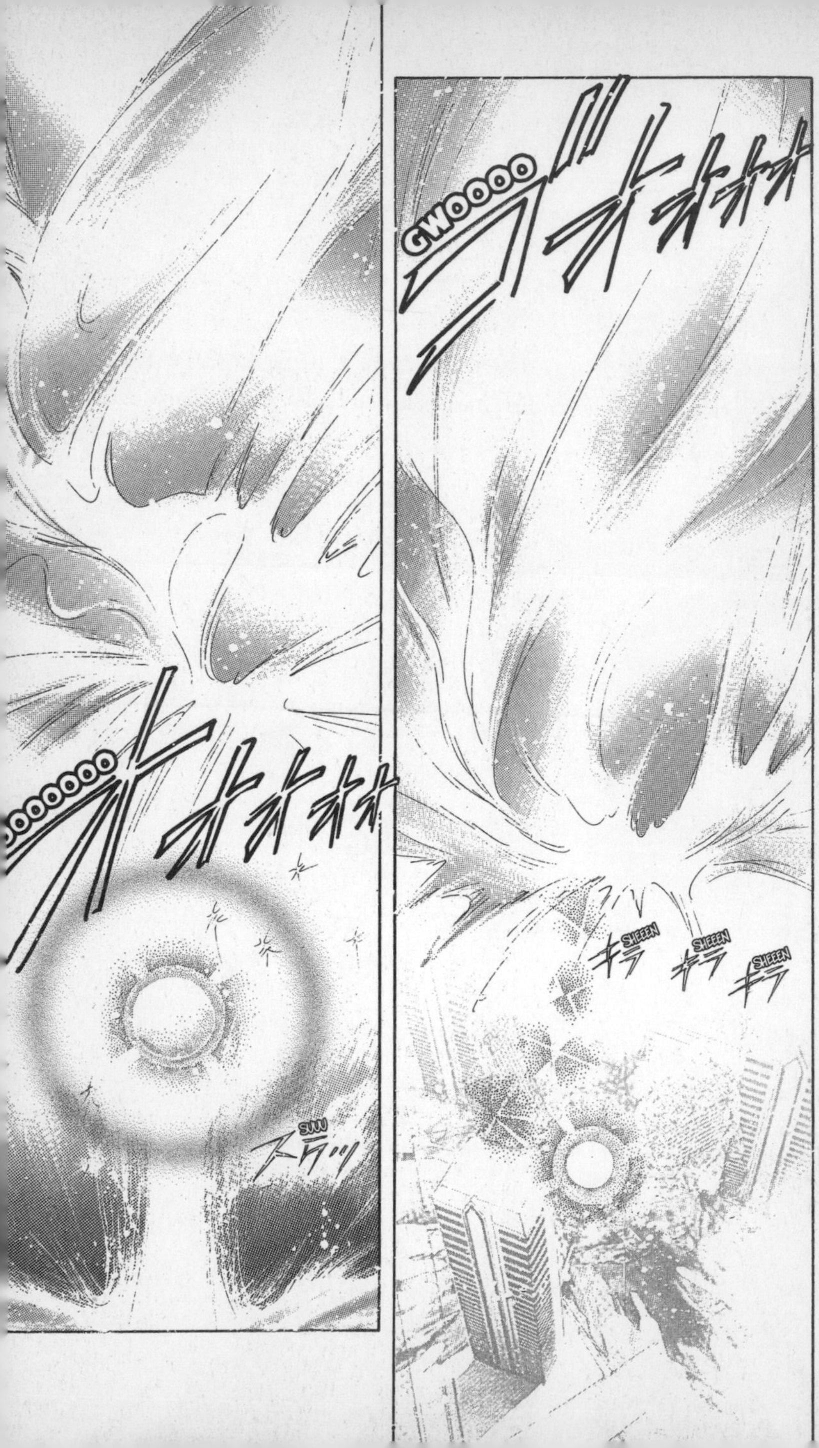
GWOOOO
SHEEEN
キラ
SHEEEN
キラ
SHEEEN
キラ
OOOOOOO
SUUU

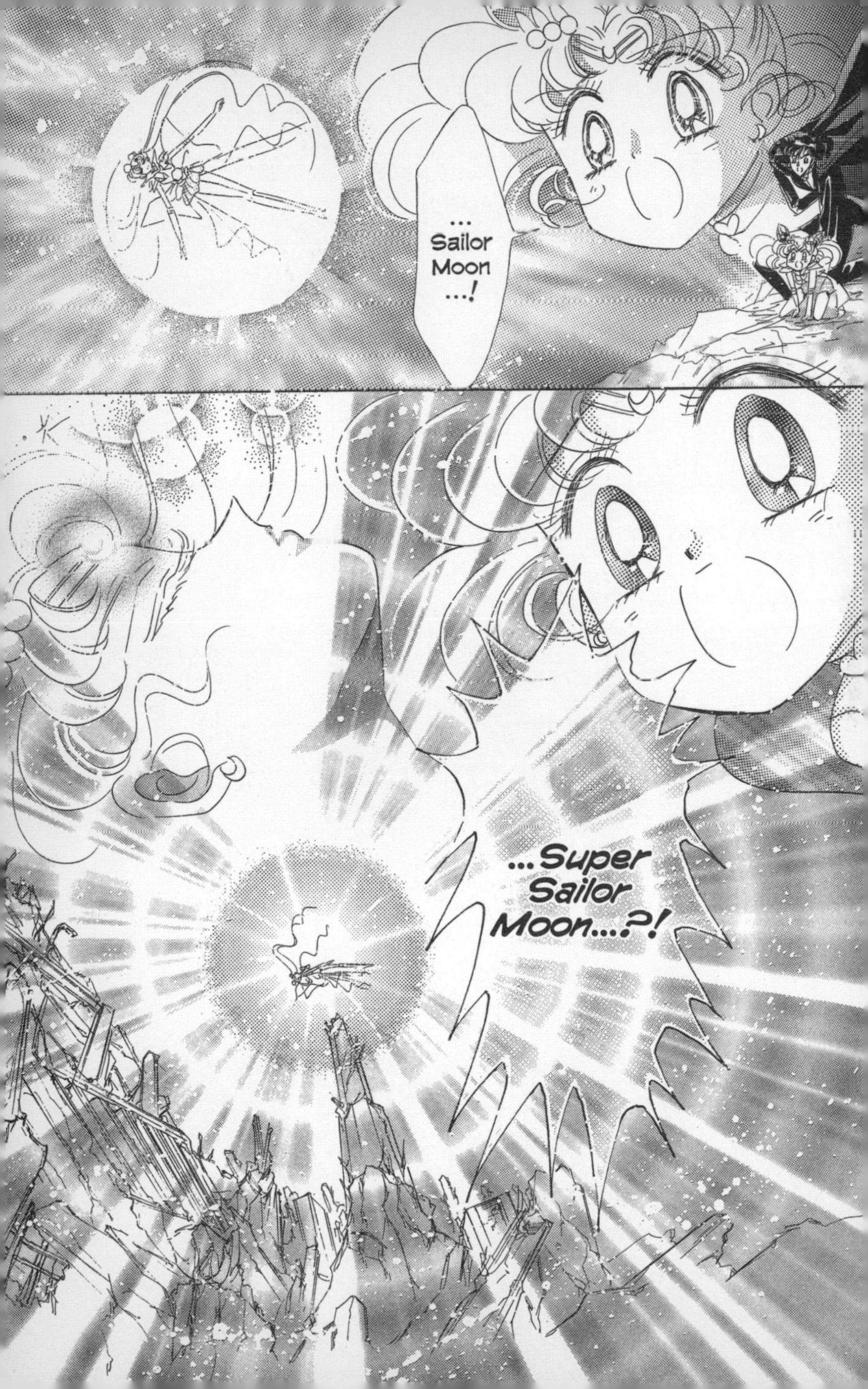
... Sailor Moon ...!
...Super Sailor Moon...?!

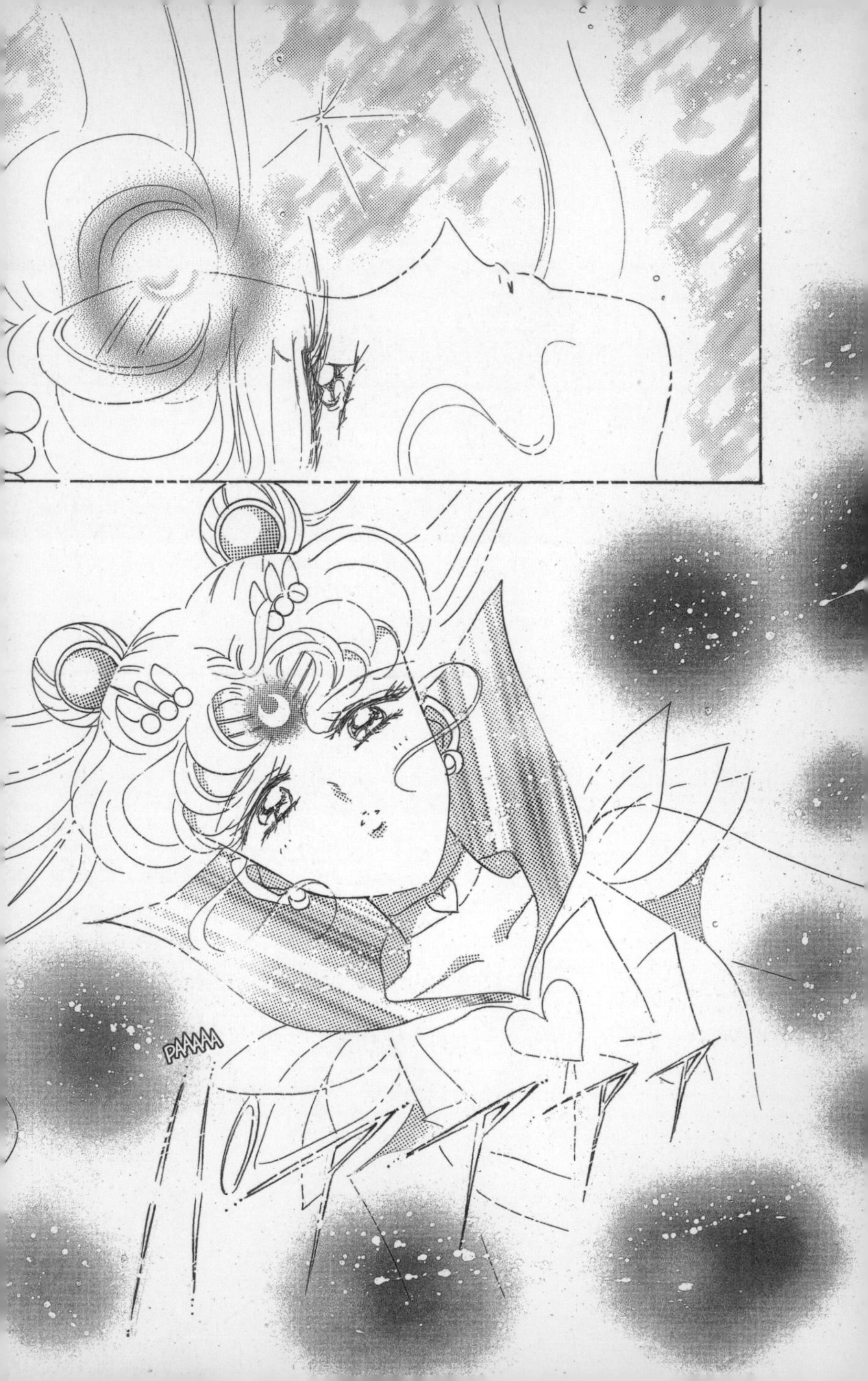
PAAAAA

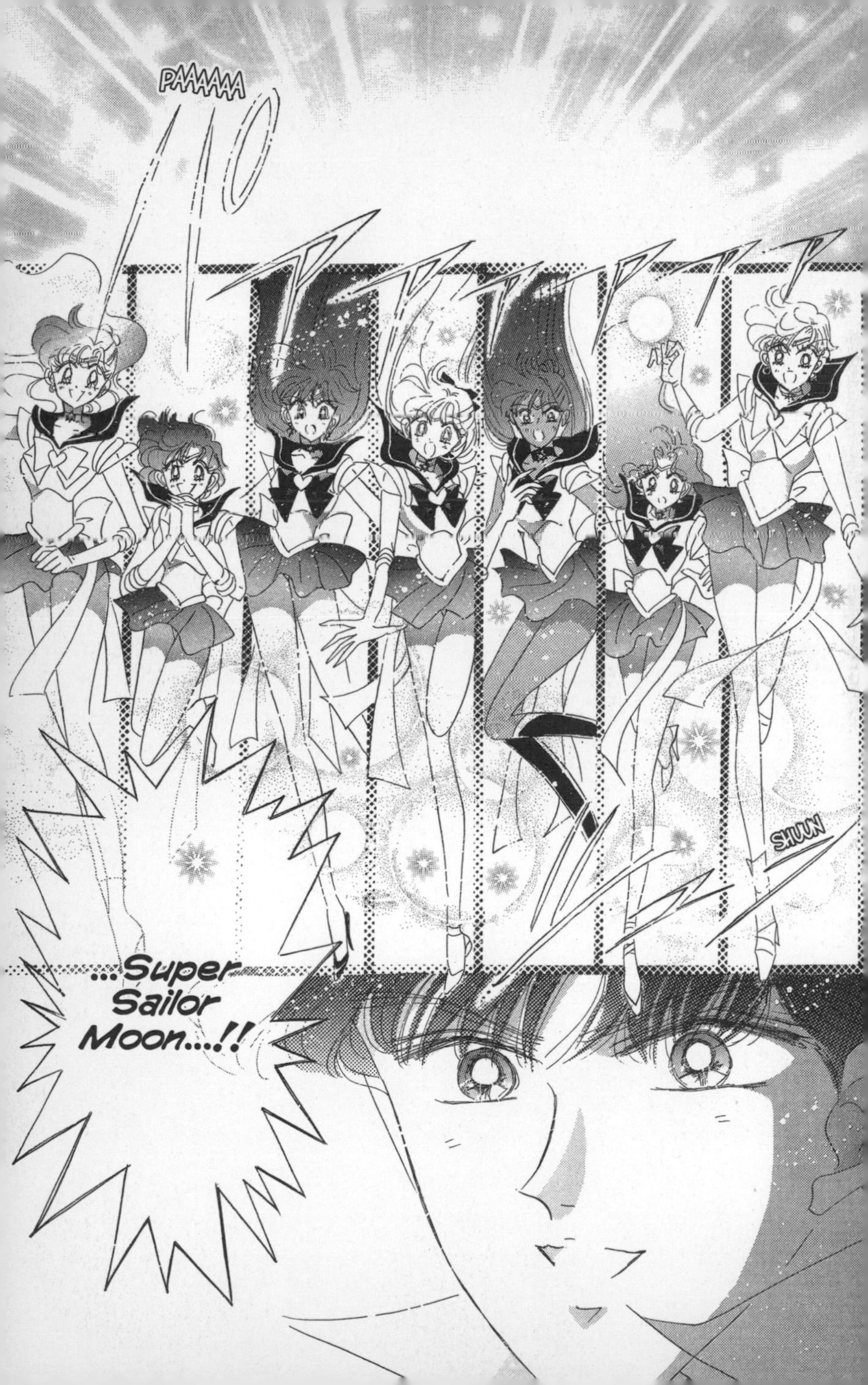
PAAAAAA
SHUUN
...Super Sailor Moon...!!

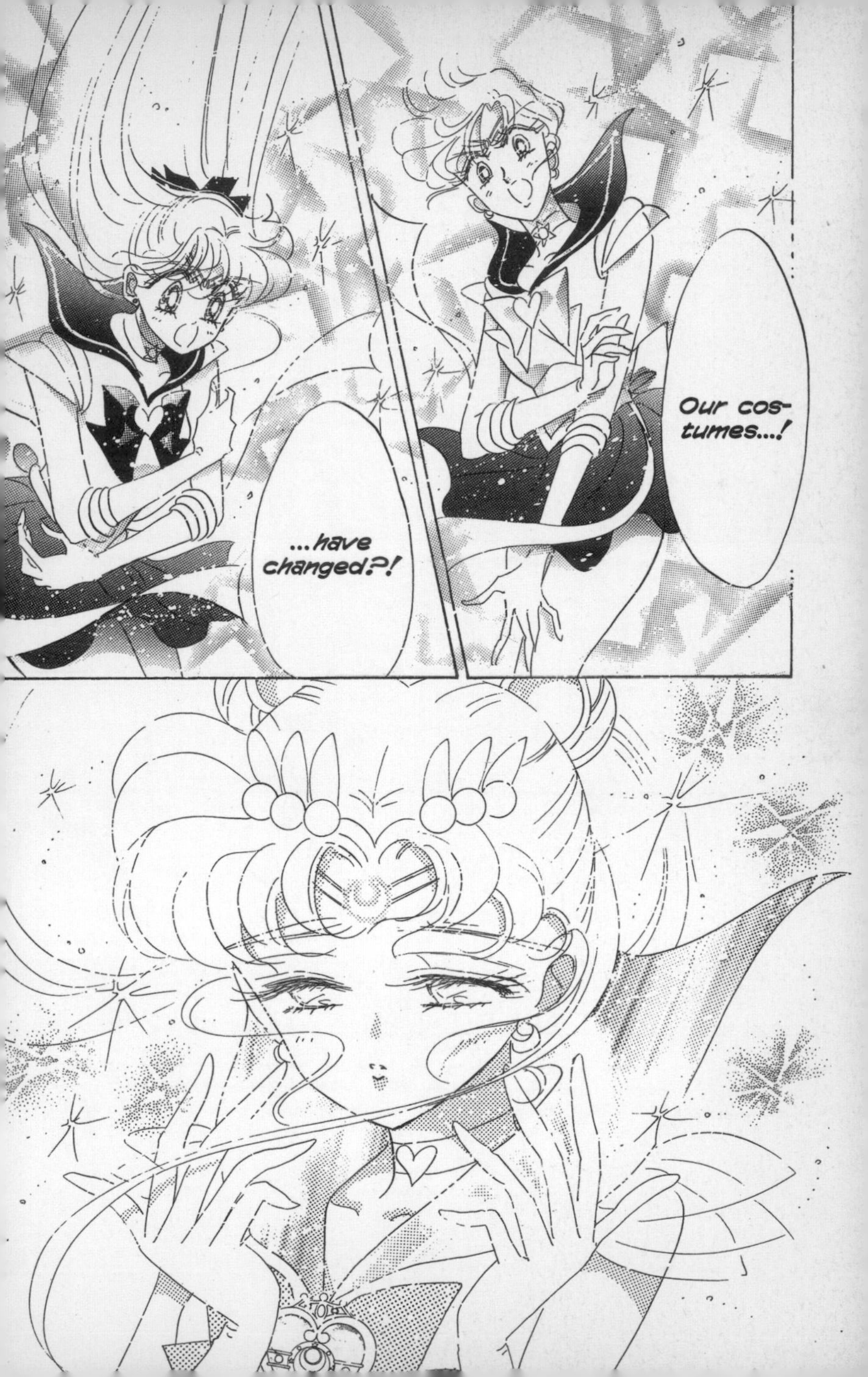
Our cos-
tumes...!
...have
changed?!

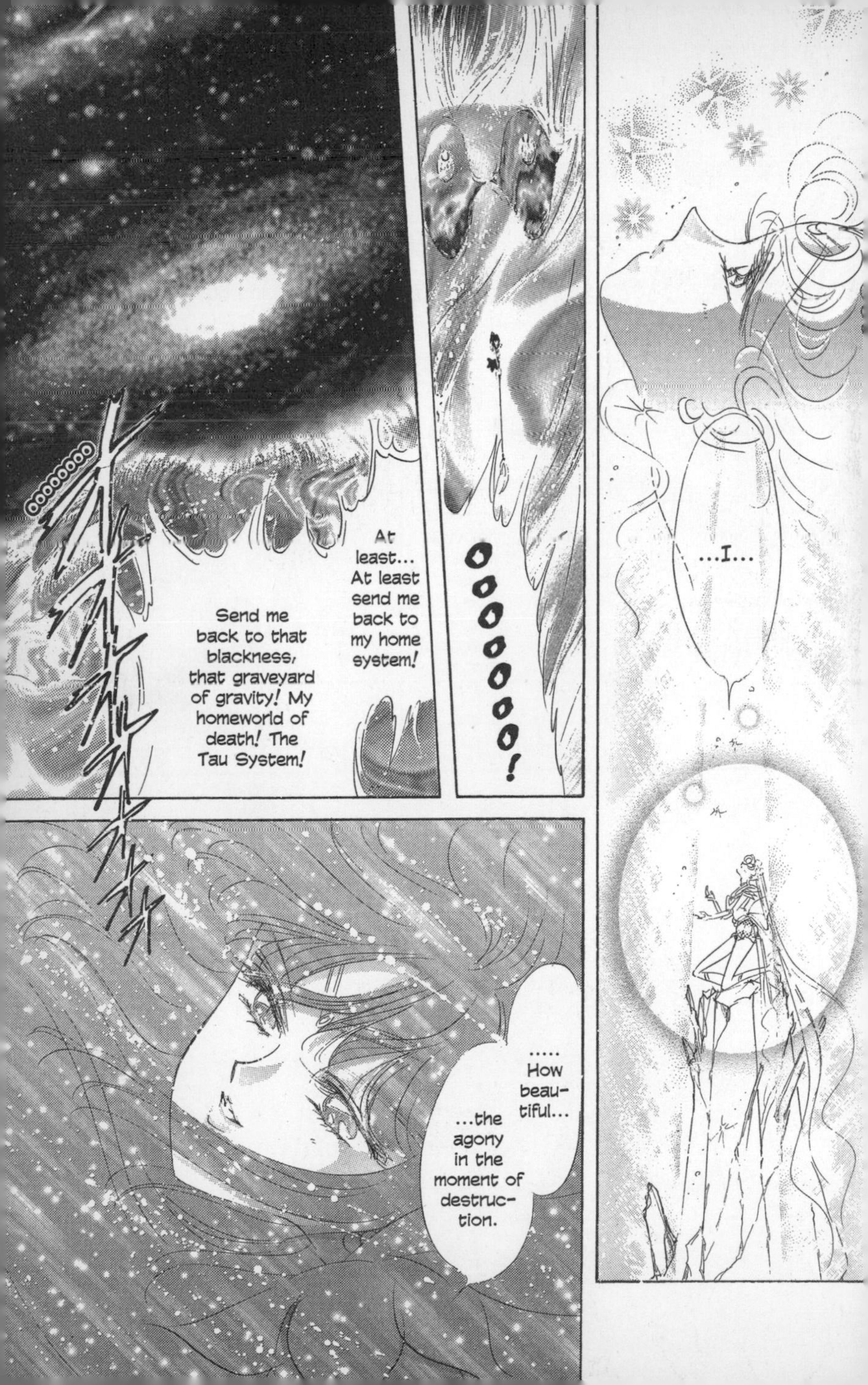
...I...
OOOOOOO!
At least... At least send me back to my home system!
Send me back to that blackness, that graveyard of gravity! My homeworld of death! The Tau System!
OOOOOOOO
..... How beau-tiful...
...the agony in the moment of destruc-tion.

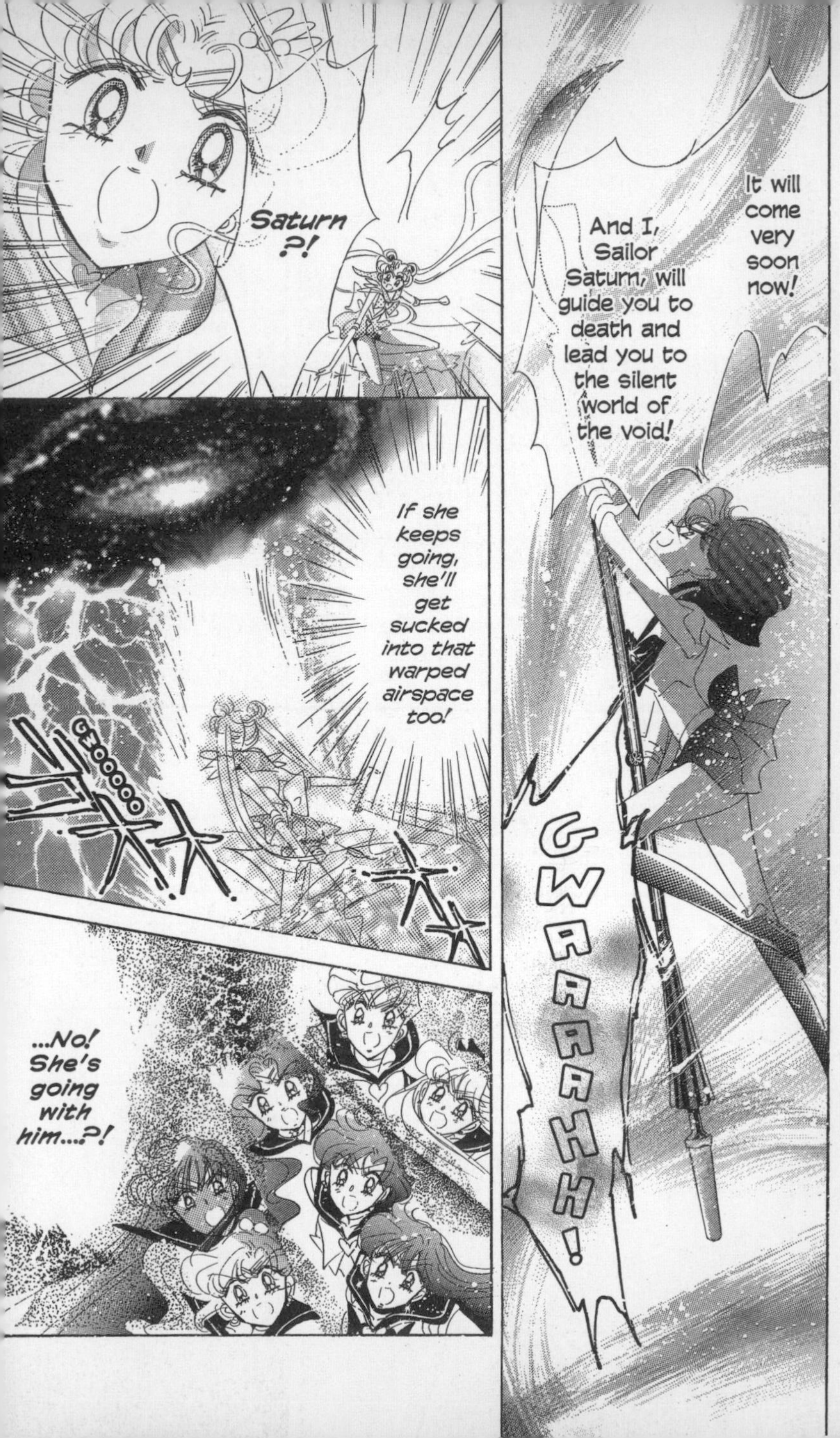
It will come very soon now!
And I, Sailor Saturn, will guide you to death and lead you to the silent world of the void!
GWAAAAAHH!
Saturn ?!
If she keeps going, she'll get sucked into that warped airspace too!
GWOOOOOO
...No! She's going with him...?!

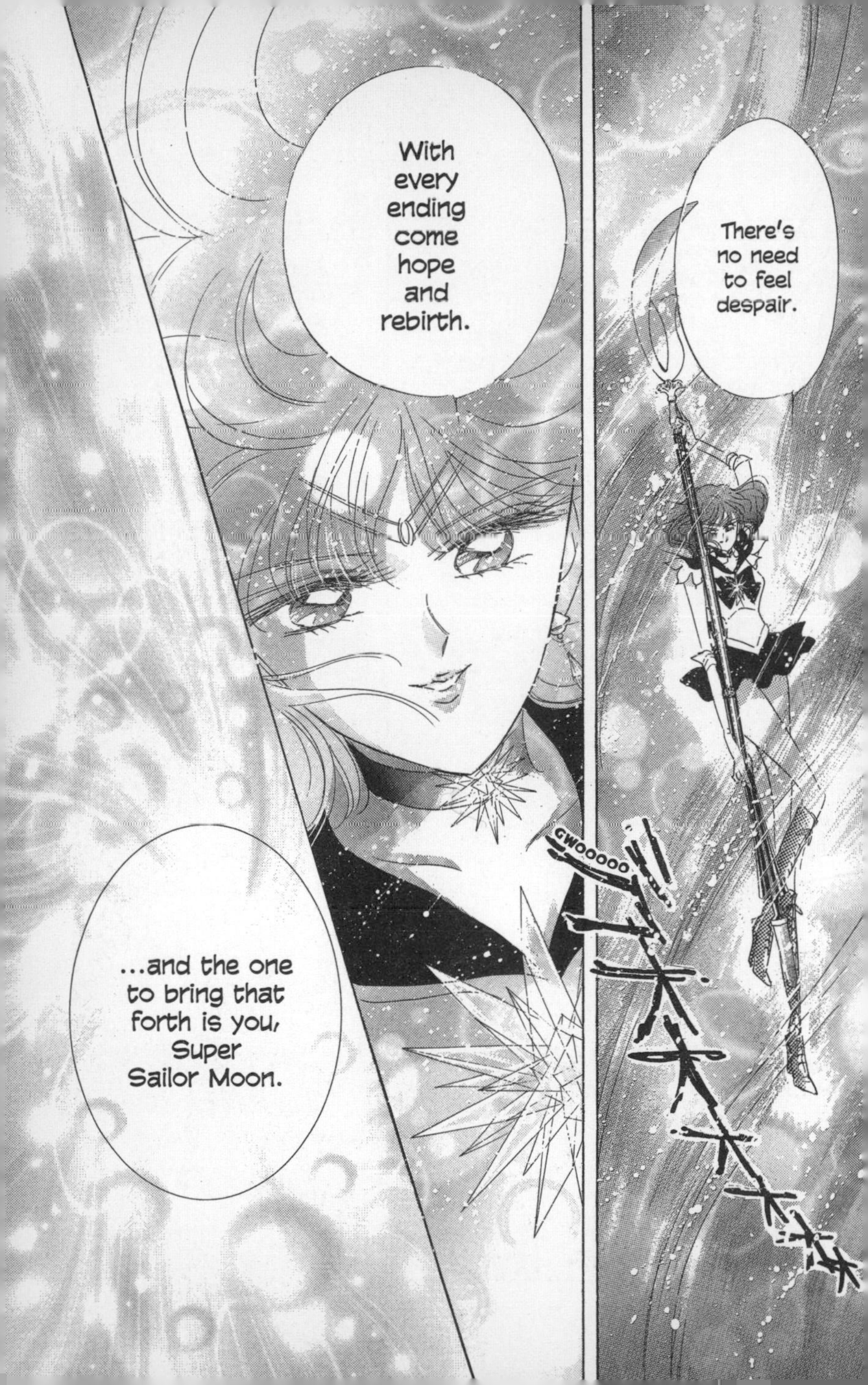
There's no need to feel despair.
GWOOOOO
With every ending come hope and rebirth.
...and the one to bring that forth is you, Super Sailor Moon.

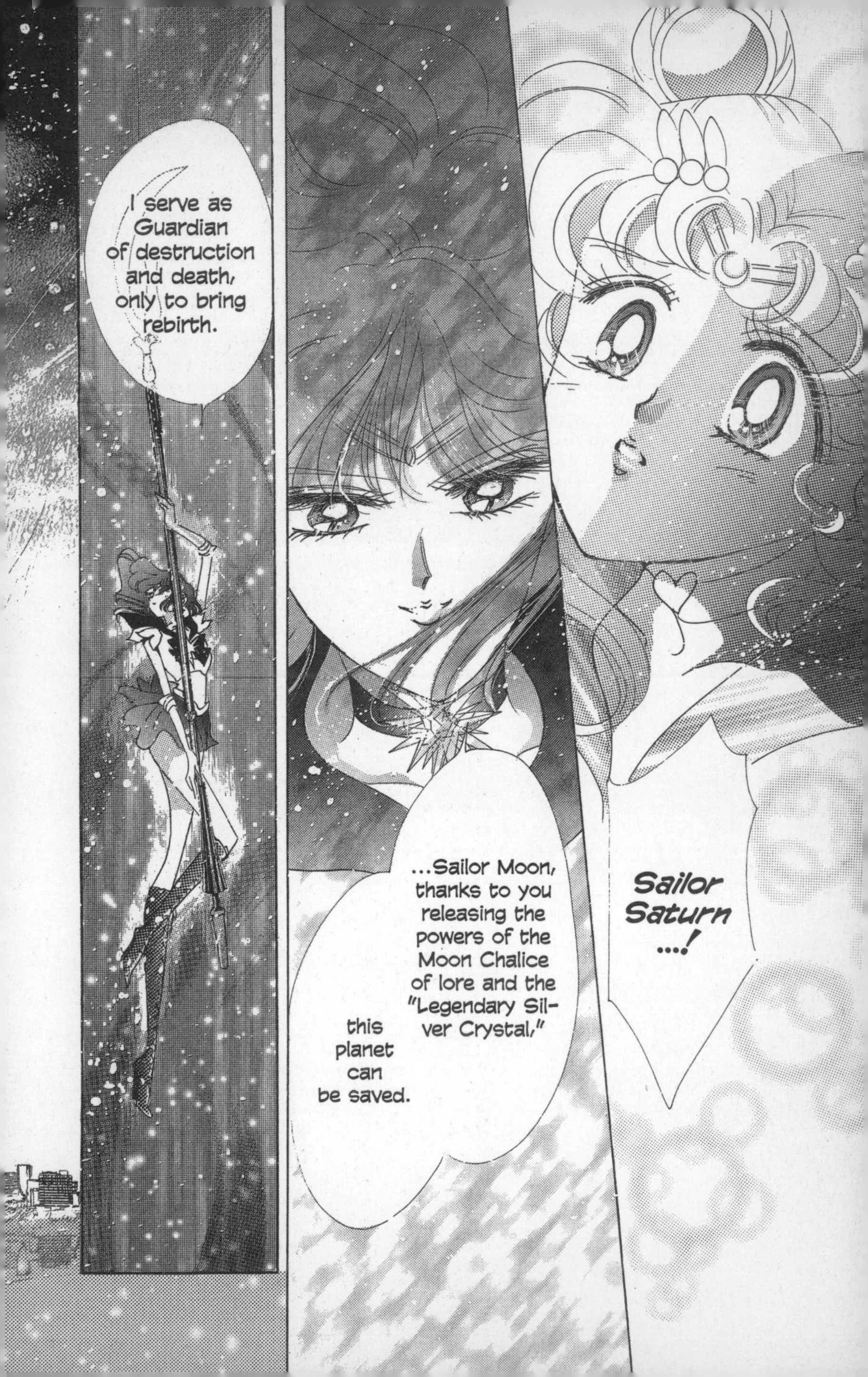
Sailor Saturn ...!
...Sailor Moon, thanks to you releasing the powers of the Moon Chalice of lore and the "Legendary Silver Crystal," this planet can be saved.
I serve as Guardian of destruction and death, only to bring rebirth.

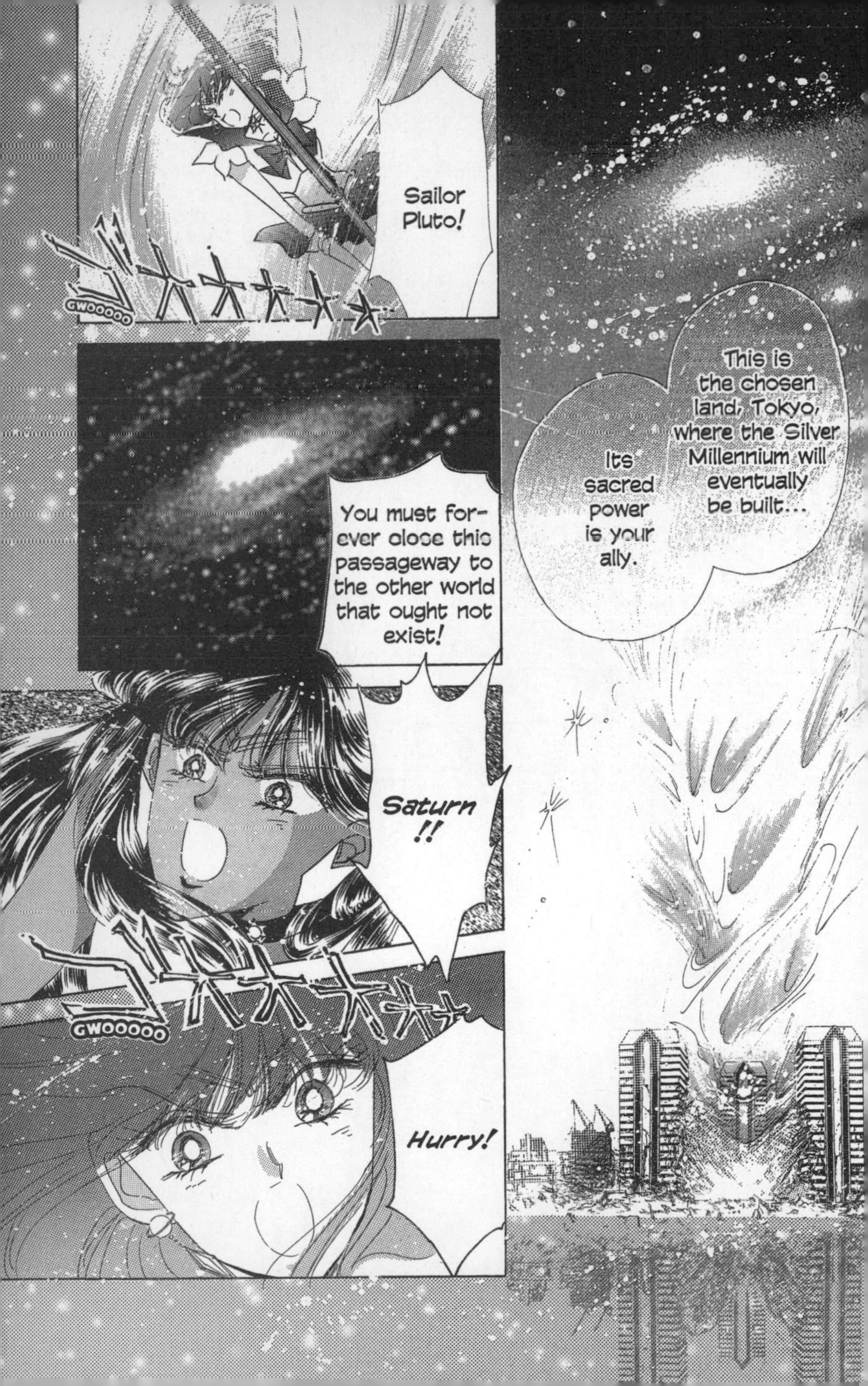
This is the chosen land, Tokyo, where the Silver Millennium will eventually be built...
Its sacred power is your ally.
Sailor Pluto!
GWOOOOO
You must for-ever close this passageway to the other world that ought not exist!
Saturn!!
GWOOOOO
Hurry!

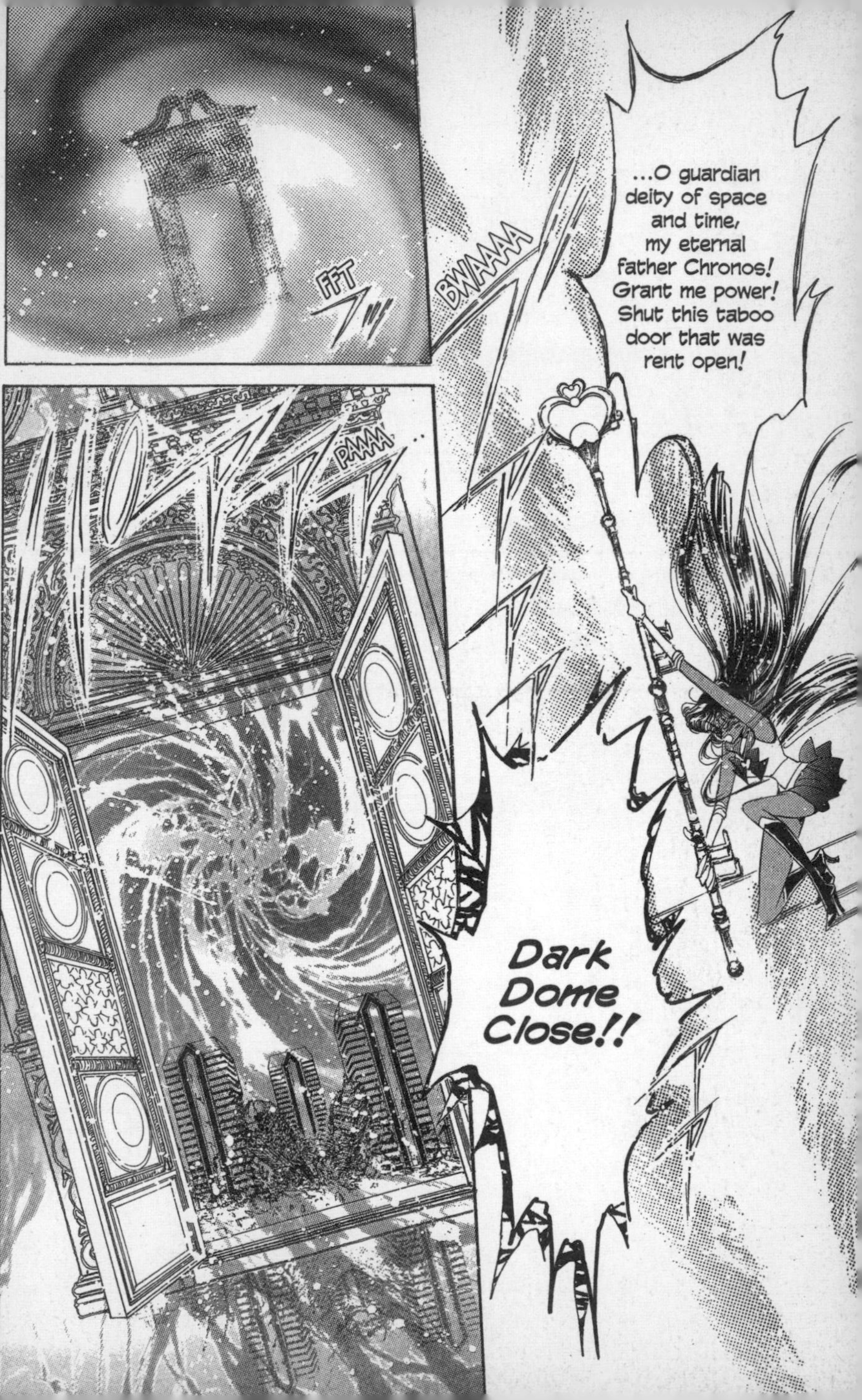
...O guardian deity of space and time, my eternal father Chronos! Grant me power! Shut this taboo door that was rent open!
BWAAAA
Dark Dome Close!!
FFT
PAAAA

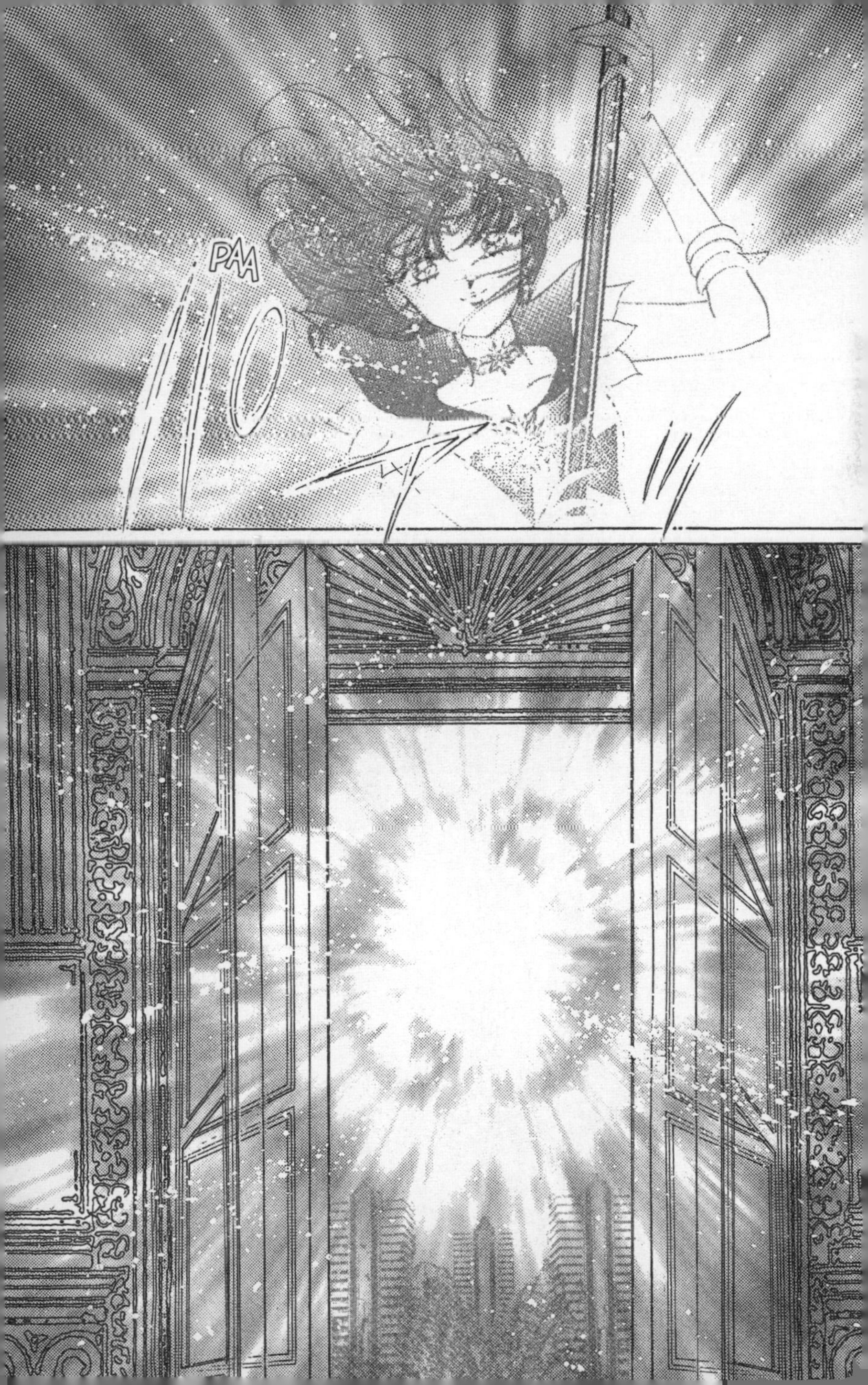
PAA

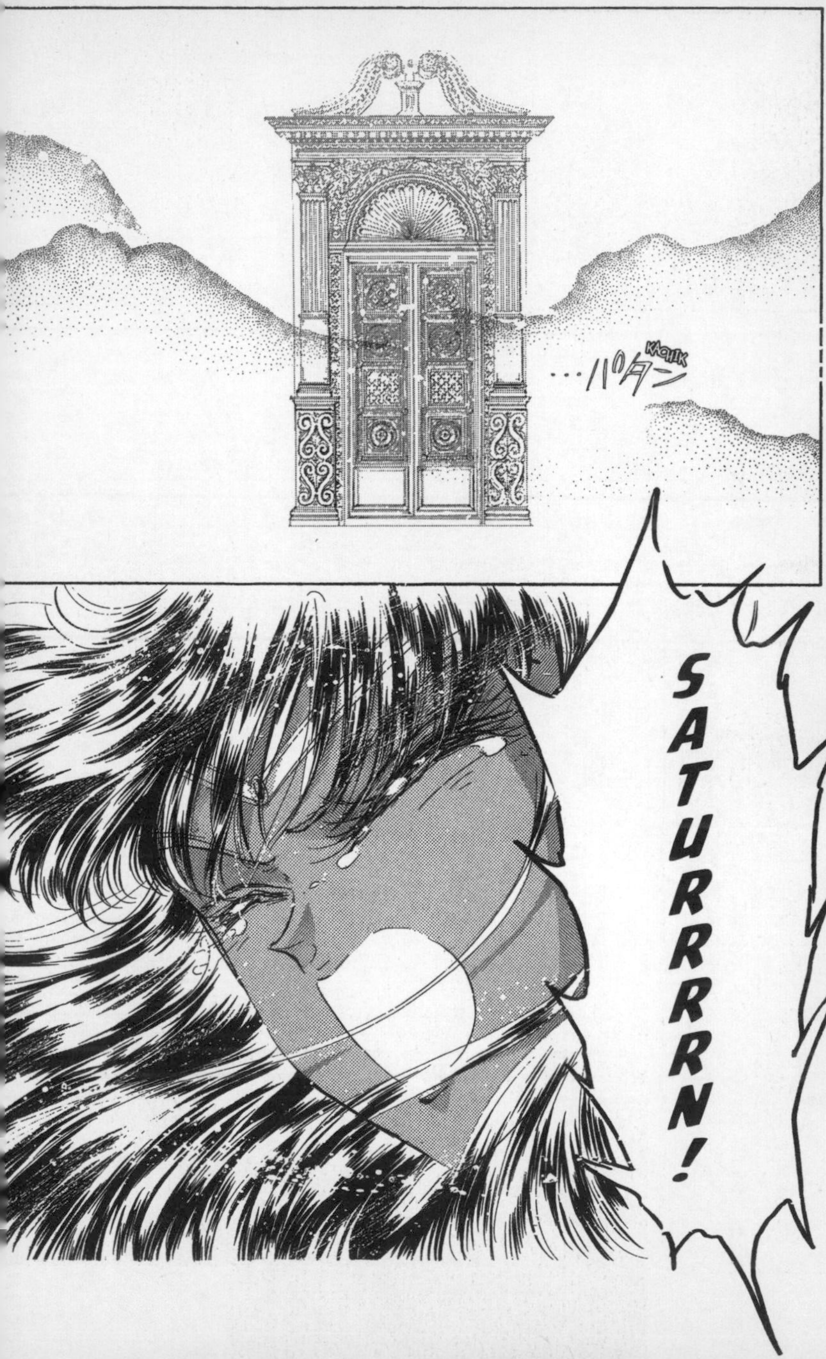
…パタン
KACHIK
SATURRRRN!

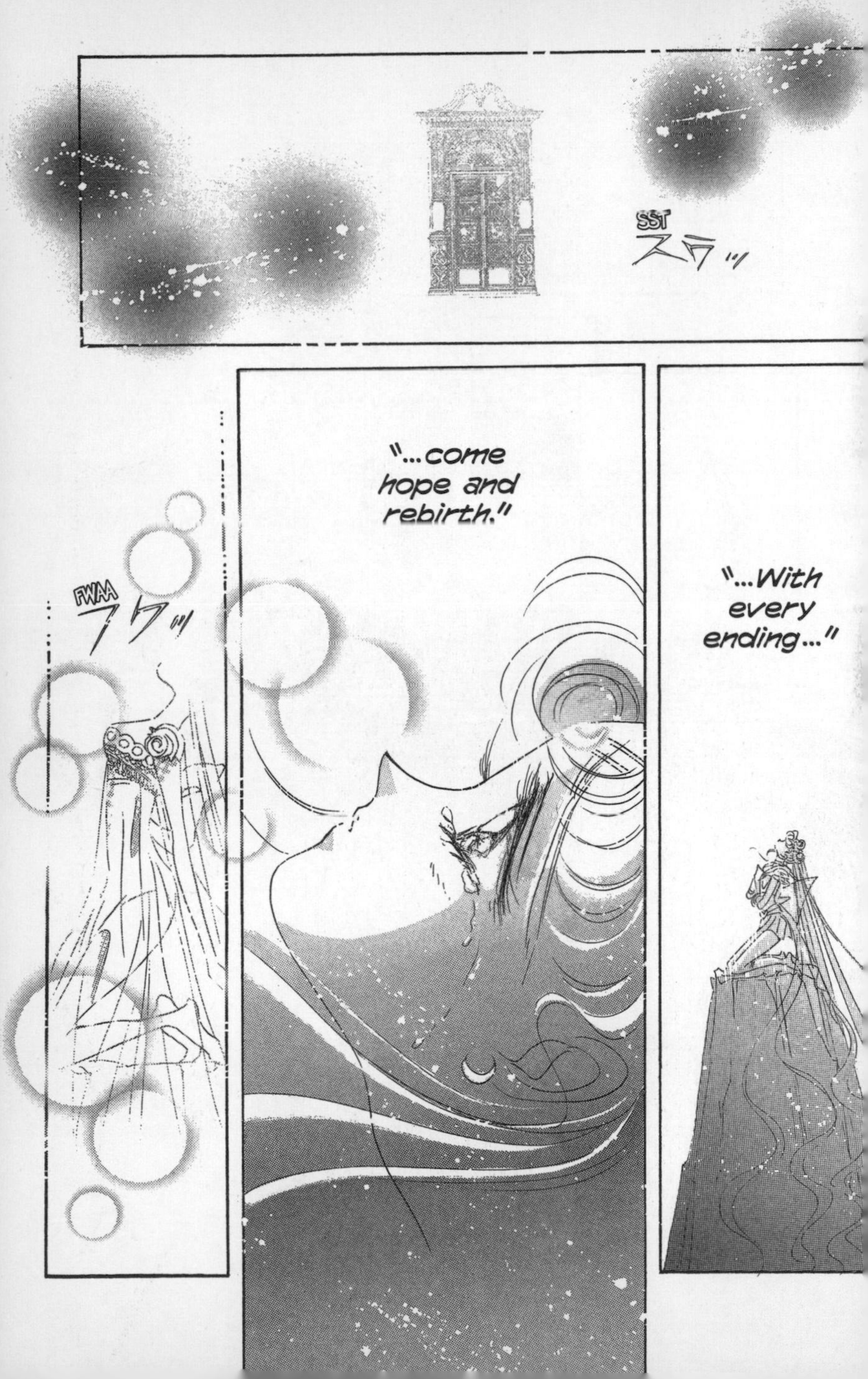
SST
スラッ
"...With every ending..."
"...come hope and rebirth."
FWAA
フワッ

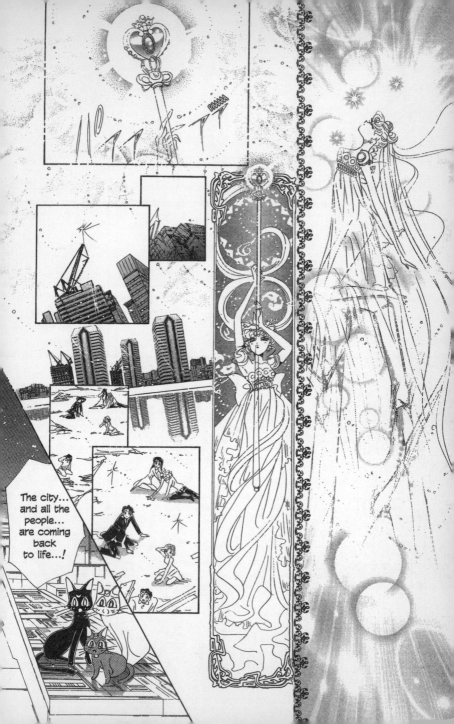

The city... and all the people... are coming back to life...!

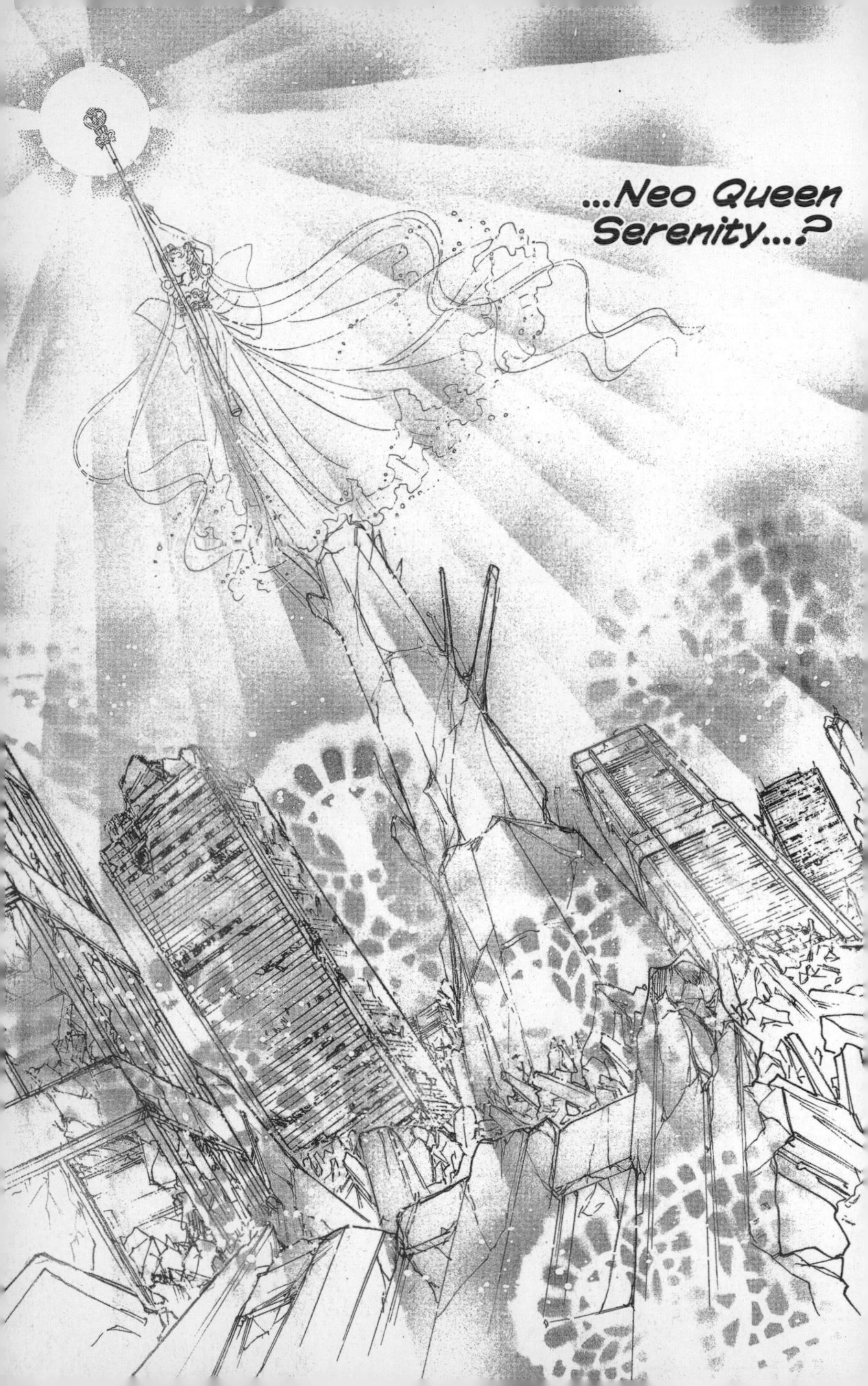
...Neo Queen Serenity...?

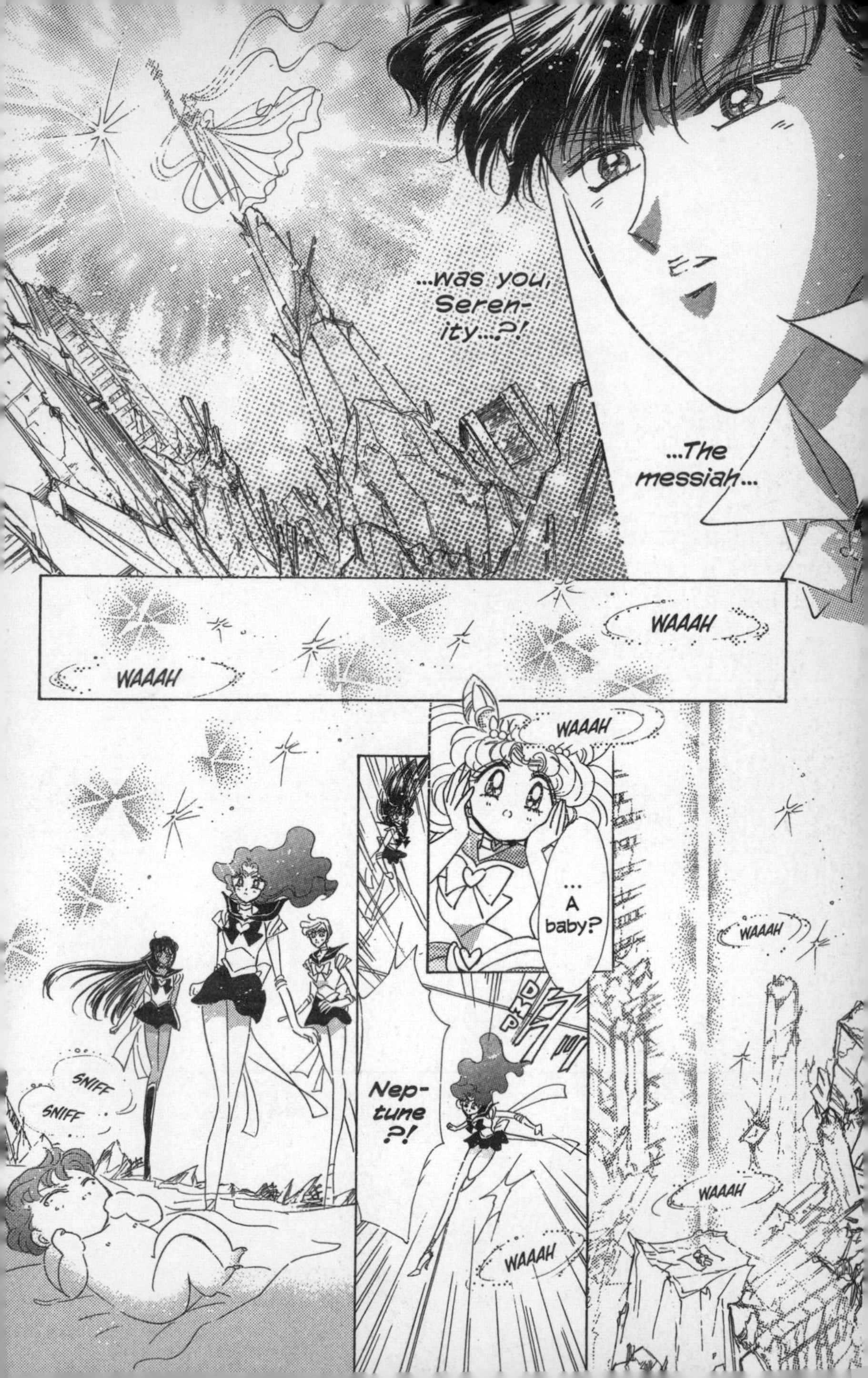

...The messiah...
...was you, Serenity...?!
WAAAH
WAAAH
WAAAH
WAAAH
... A baby?
WAAAH
DMP
Neptune?!
WAAAH
SNIFF
SNIFF

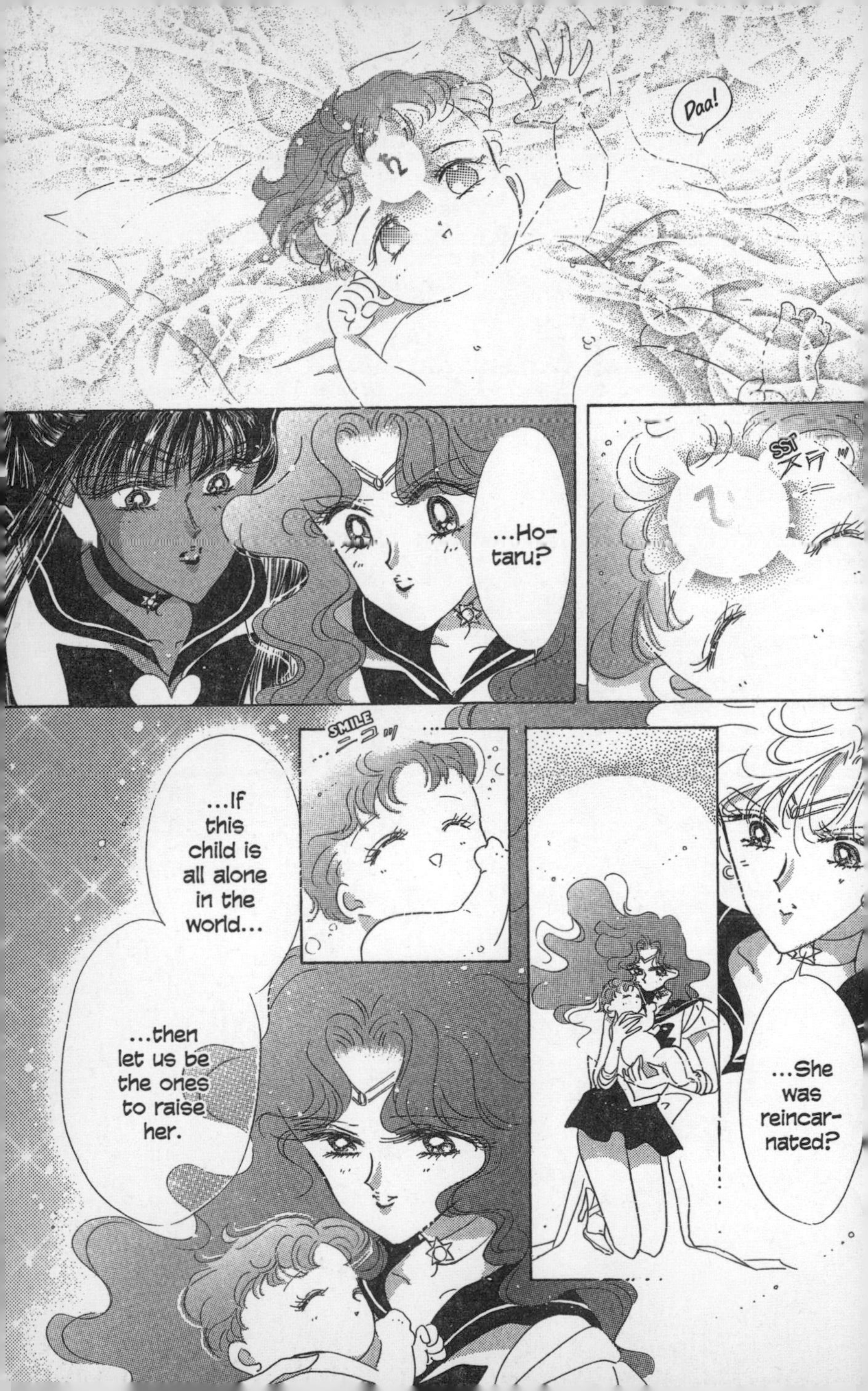
Daa!
SSI
...Ho-taru?
...She was reincar-nated?
SMILE
...If this child is all alone in the world...
...then let us be the ones to raise her.

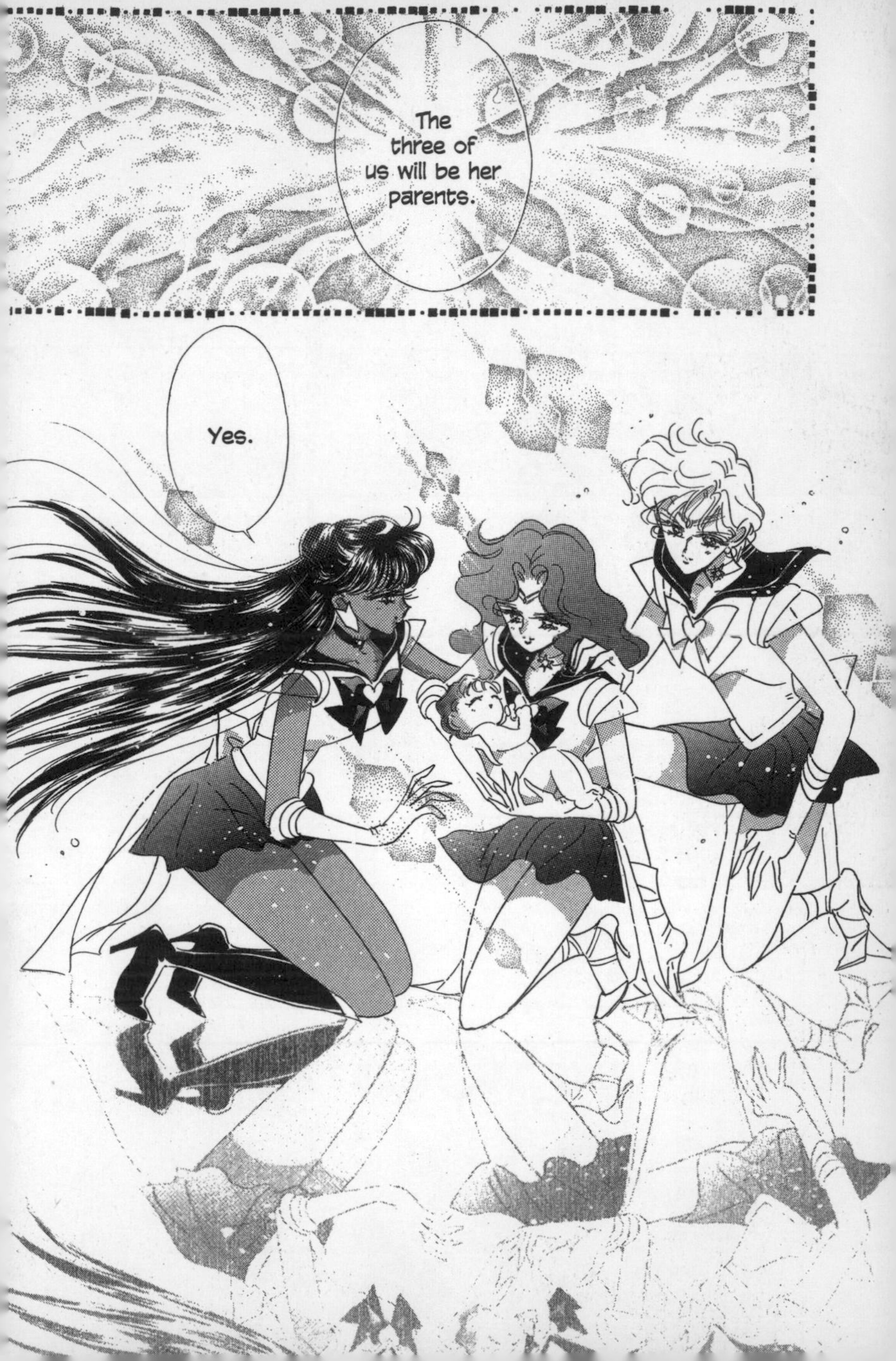
The three of us will be her parents.
Yes.

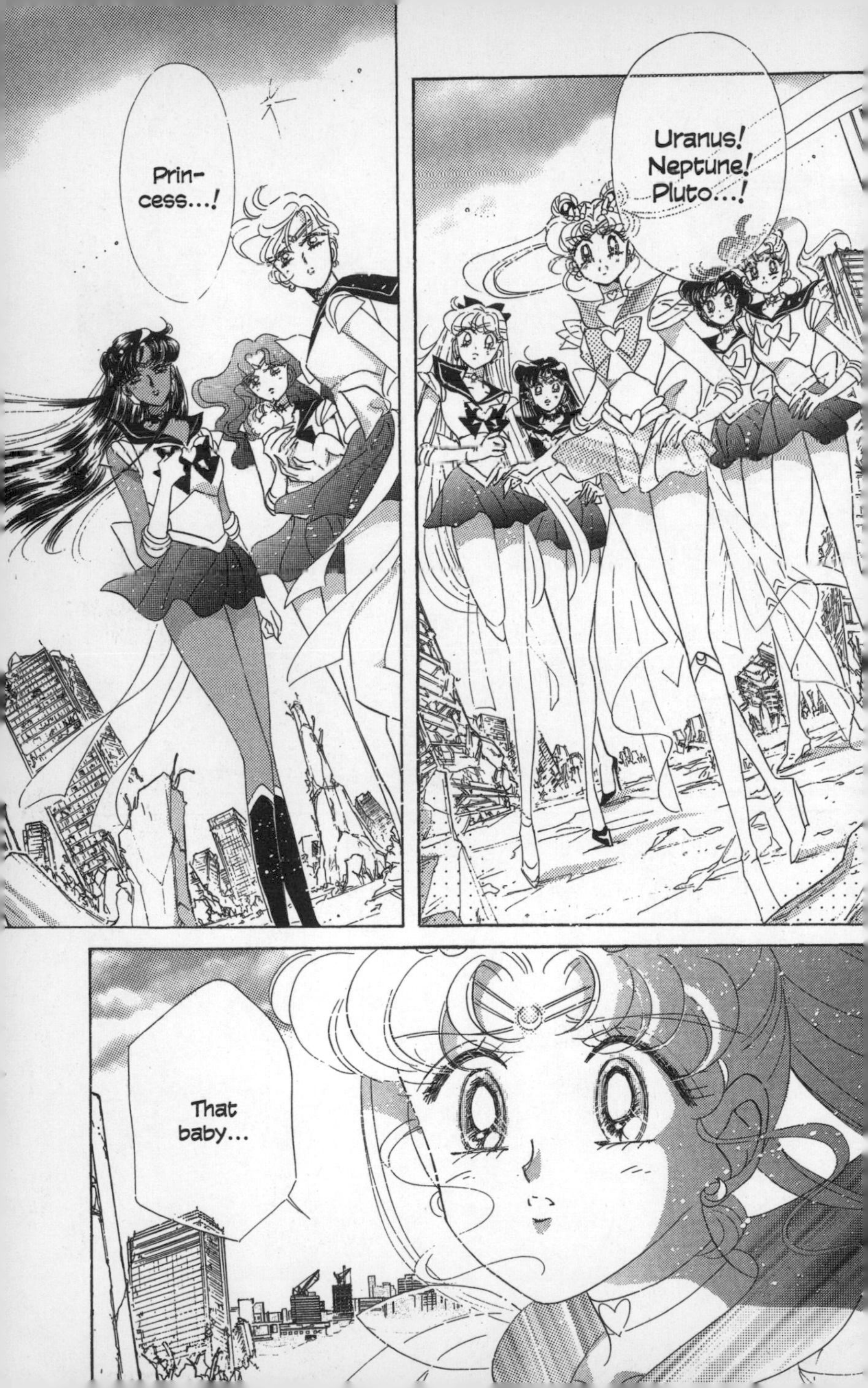
Uranus! Neptune! Pluto...!
Prin-cess...!
That baby...

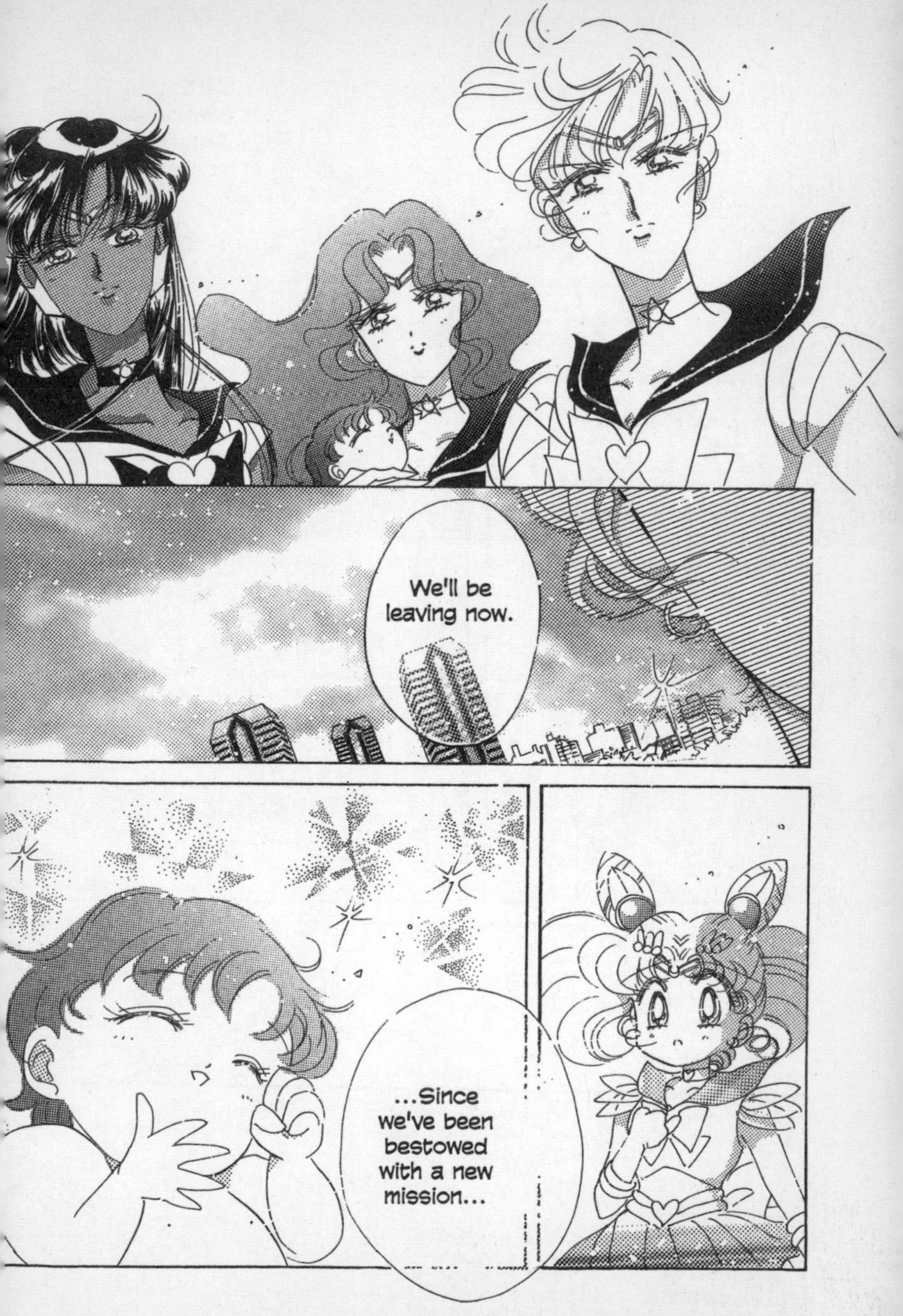
We'll be leaving now.
...Since we've been bestowed with a new mission...

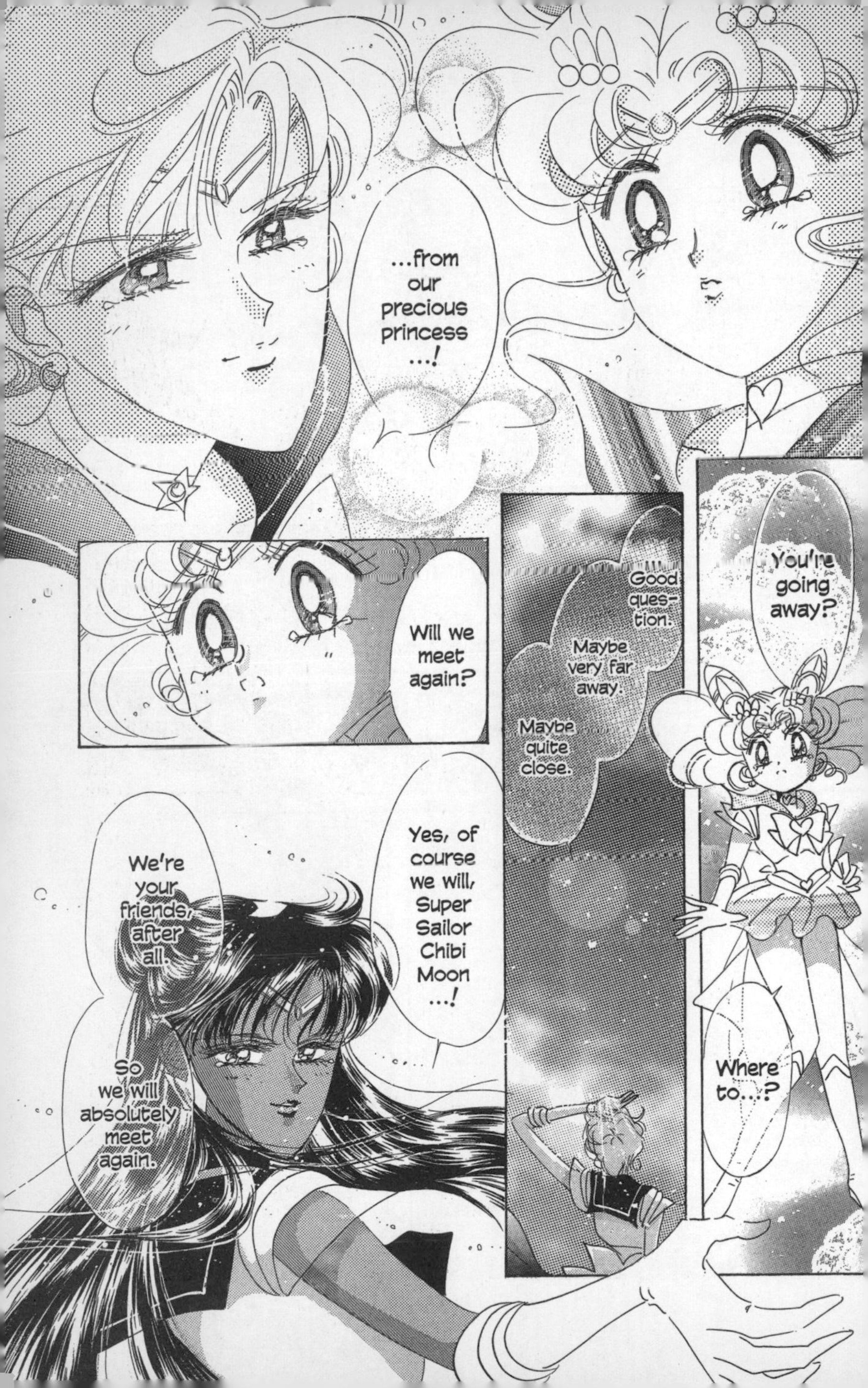
...from our precious princess ...!
You're going away?
Where to...?
Good question.
Maybe very far away.
Maybe quite close.
Will we meet again?
Yes, of course we will, Super Sailor Chibi Moon ...!
We're your friends, after all.
So we will absolutely meet again.

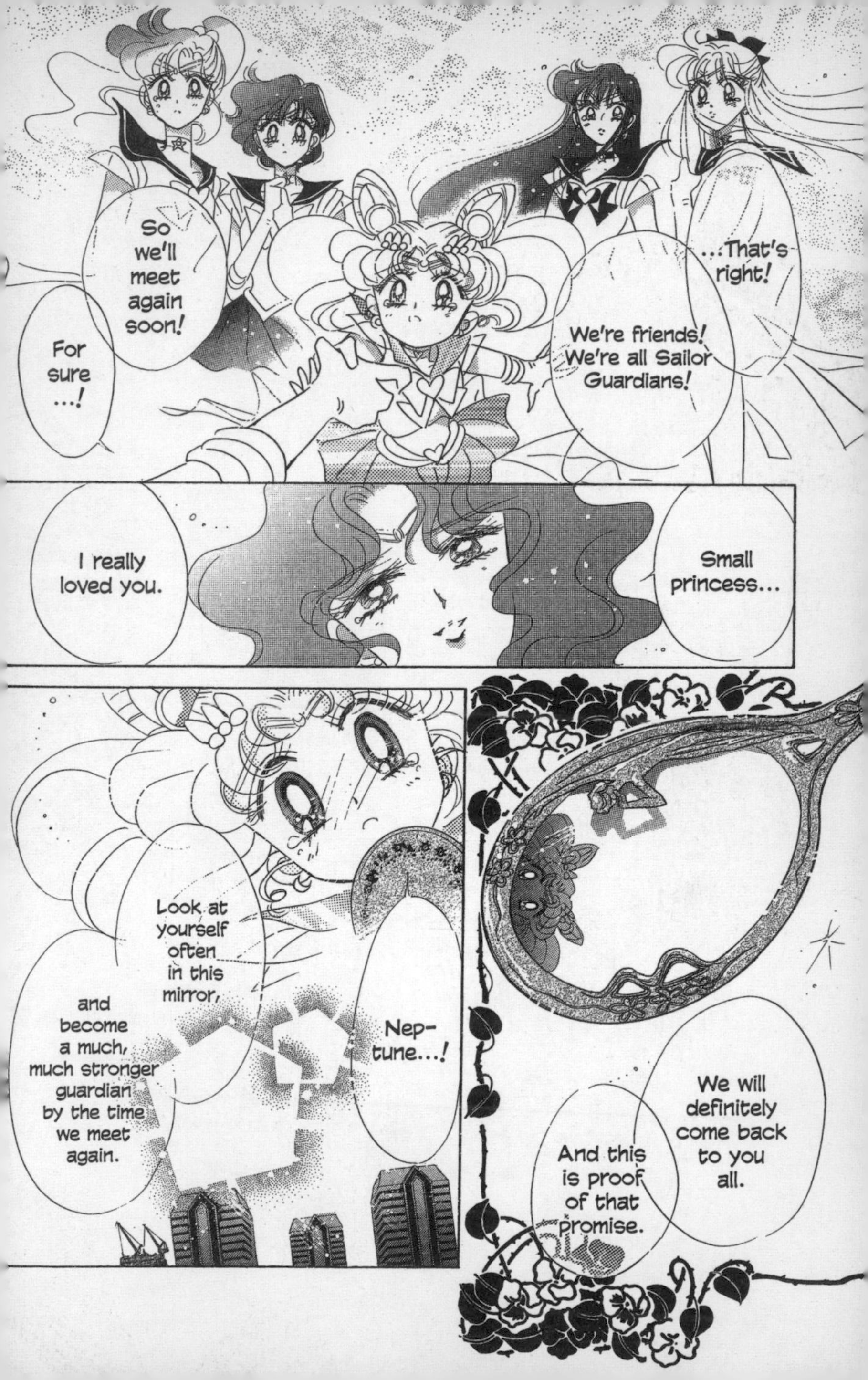
...That's right!
We're friends! We're all Sailor Guardians!
So we'll meet again soon!
For sure ...!
Small princess...
I really loved you.
We will definitely come back to you all.
And this is proof of that promise.
Nep-tune...!
Look at yourself often in this mirror,
and become a much, much stronger guardian by the time we meet again.

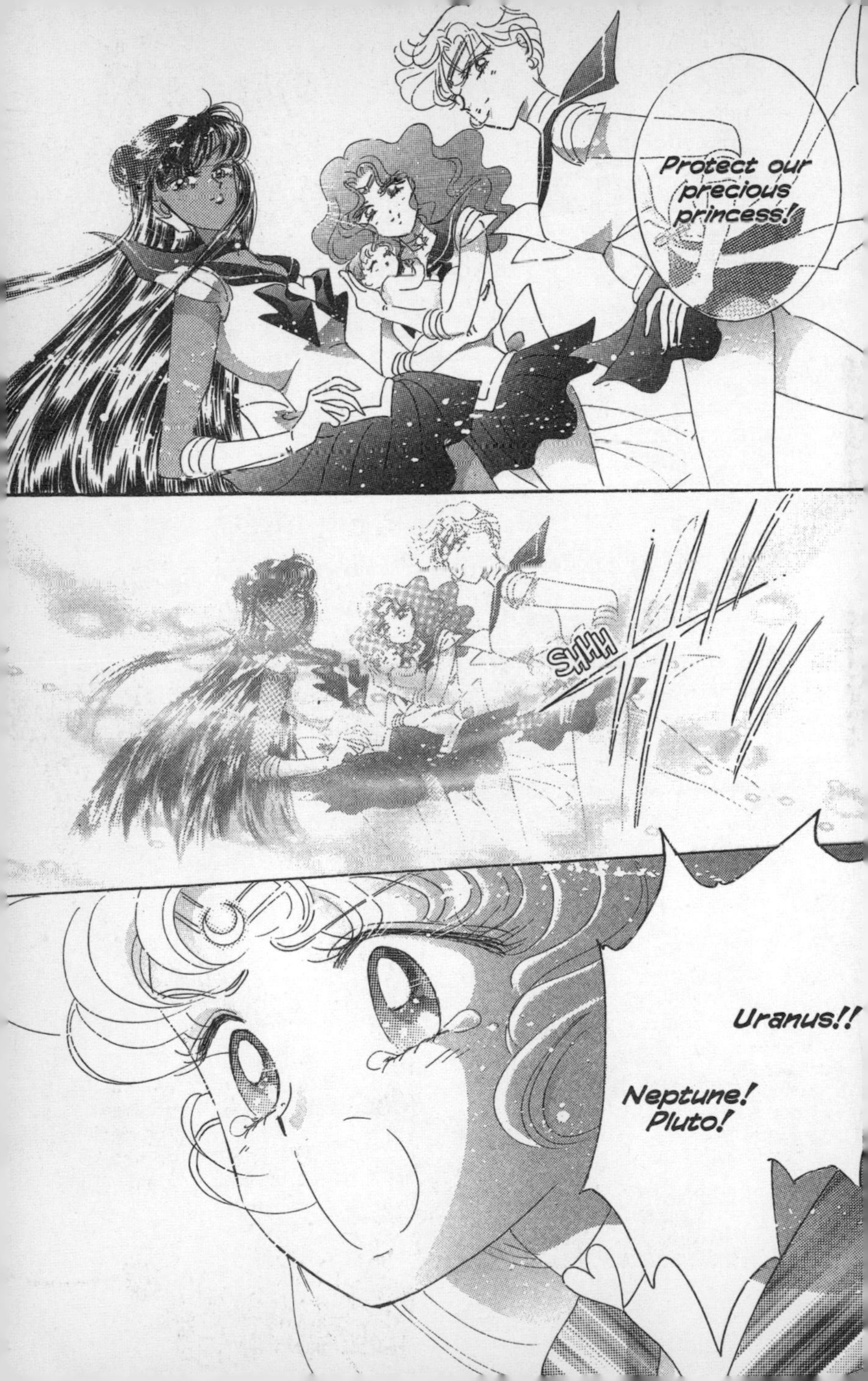
Protect our precious princess!
SHHH
Uranus!!
Neptune! Pluto!

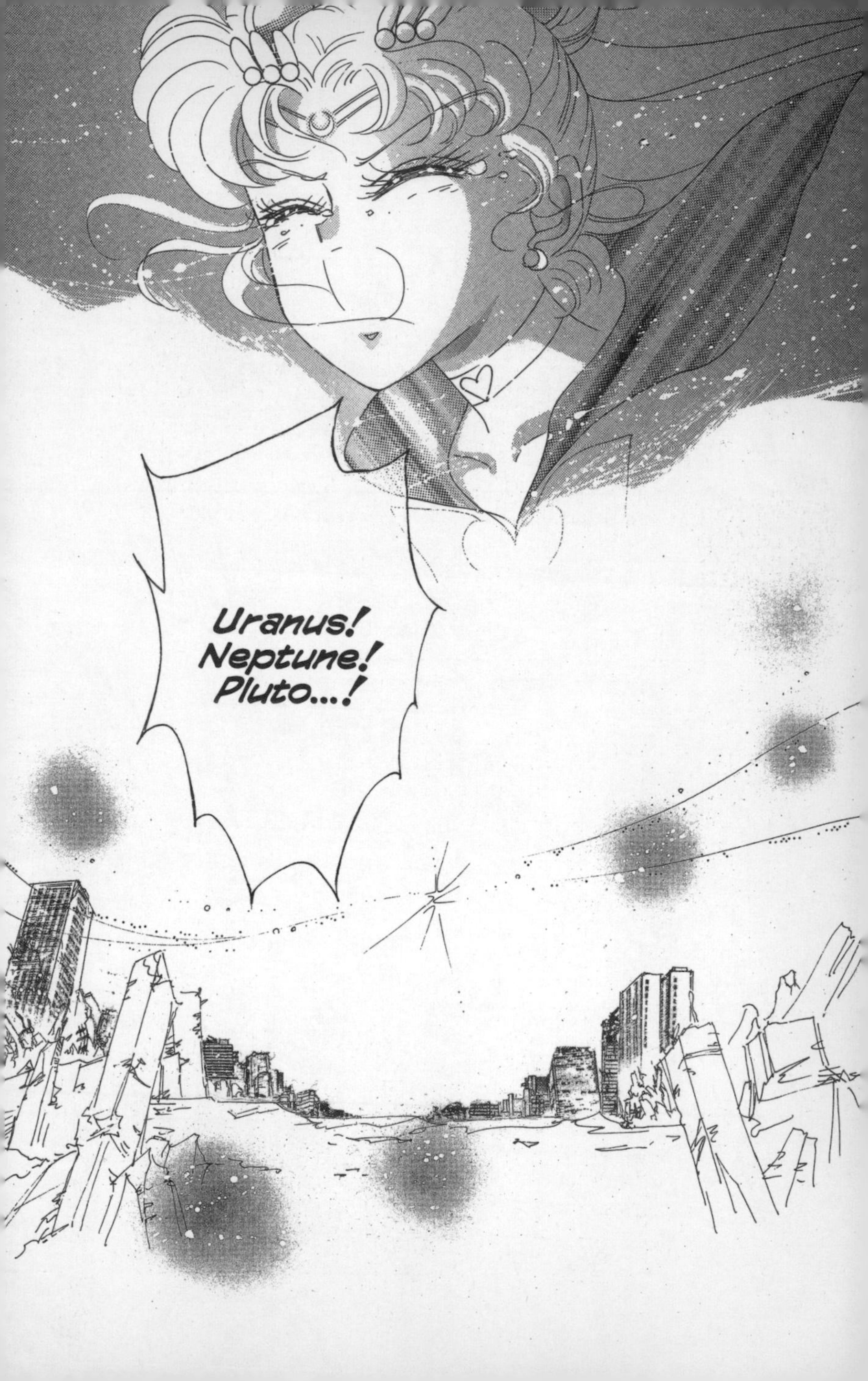
Uranus! Neptune! Pluto...!

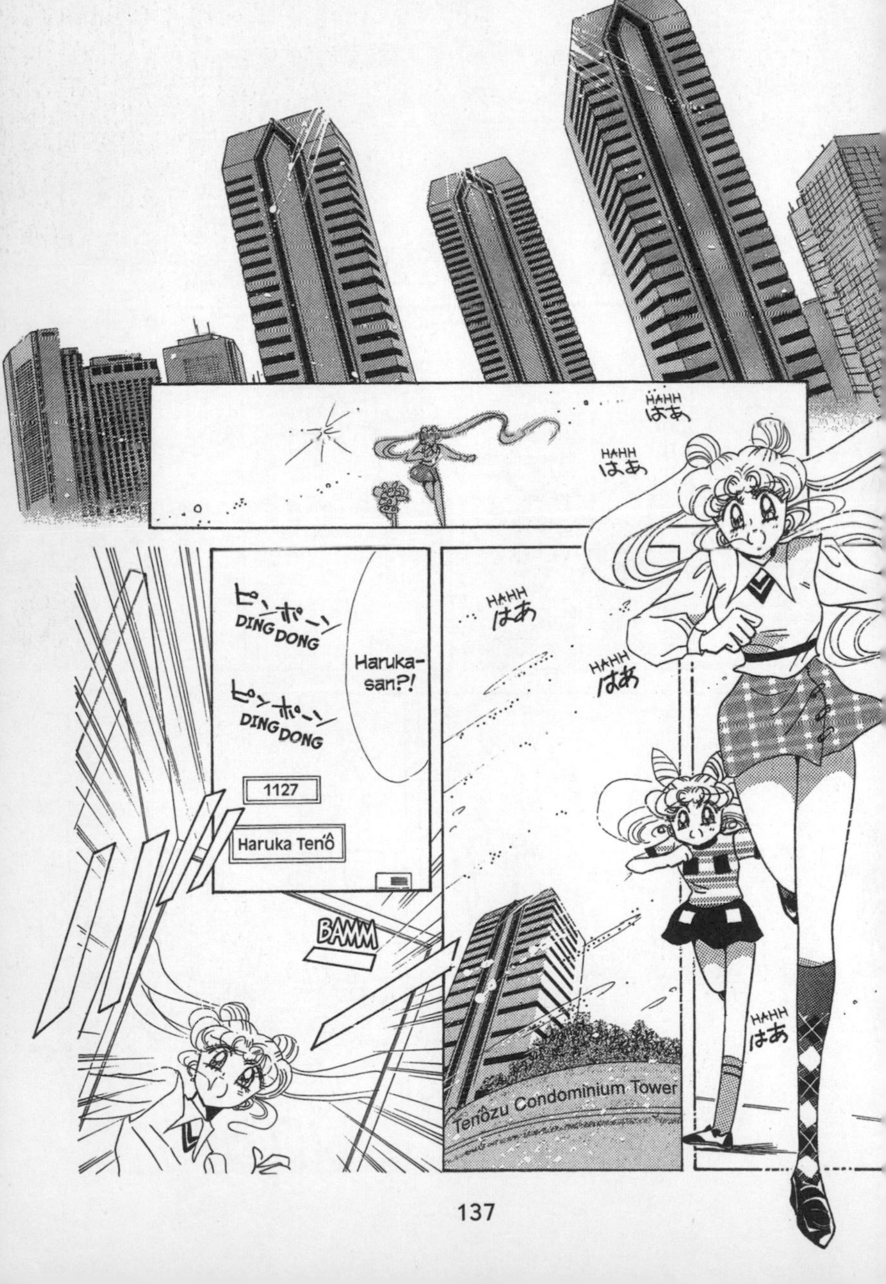

HAHH はあ
HAHH はあ
HAHH はあ
HAHH はあ
Tenôzu Condominium Tower
HAHH はあ
Haruka-san?!
ピンポーン DING DONG
ピンポーン DING DONG
1127
Haruka Tenô
BAMM

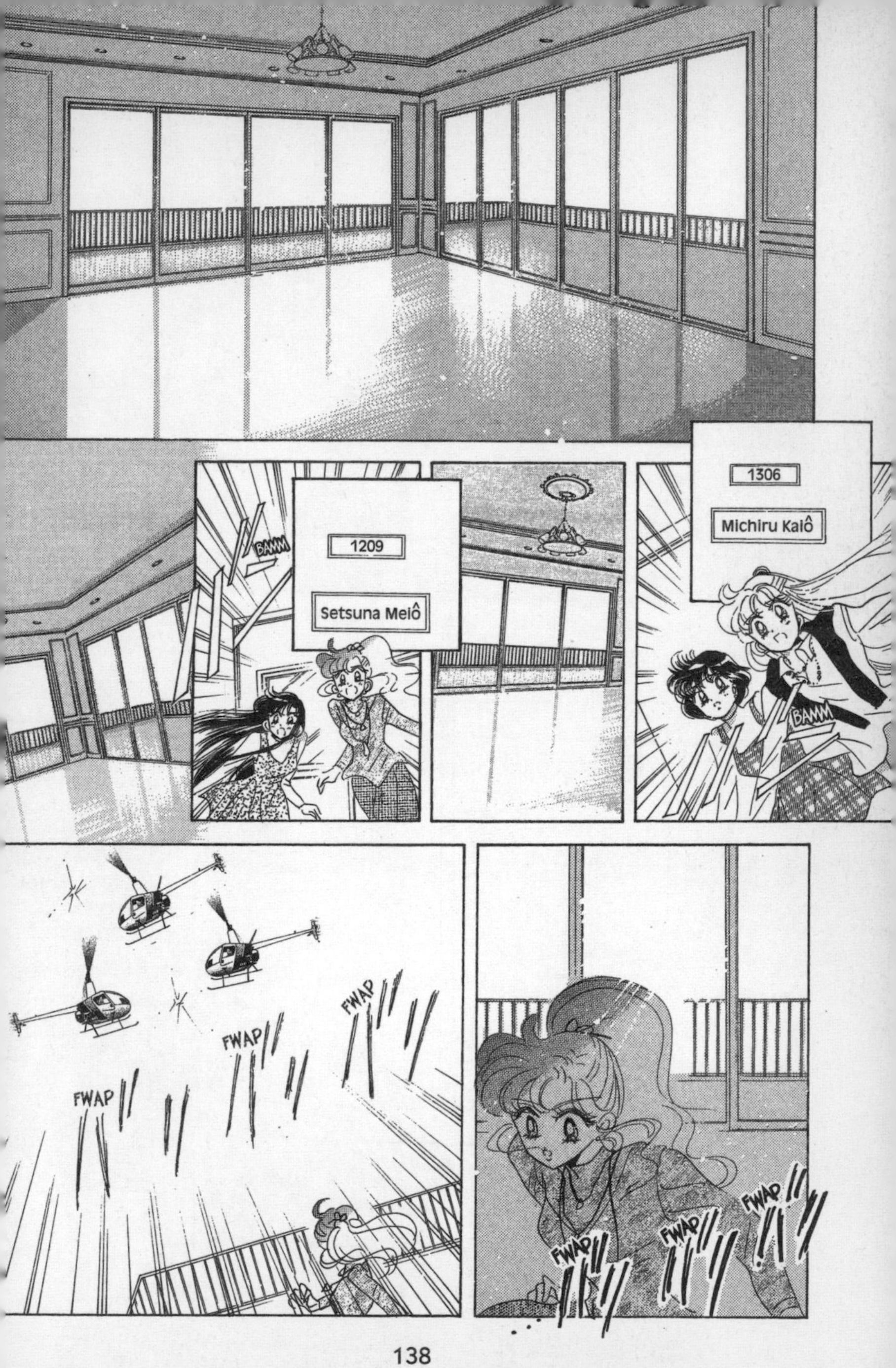

1306
Michiru Kaiô
BAMM
1209
Setsuna Meiô
BAMM
FWAP
FWAP
FWAP
FWAP
FWAP
FWAP

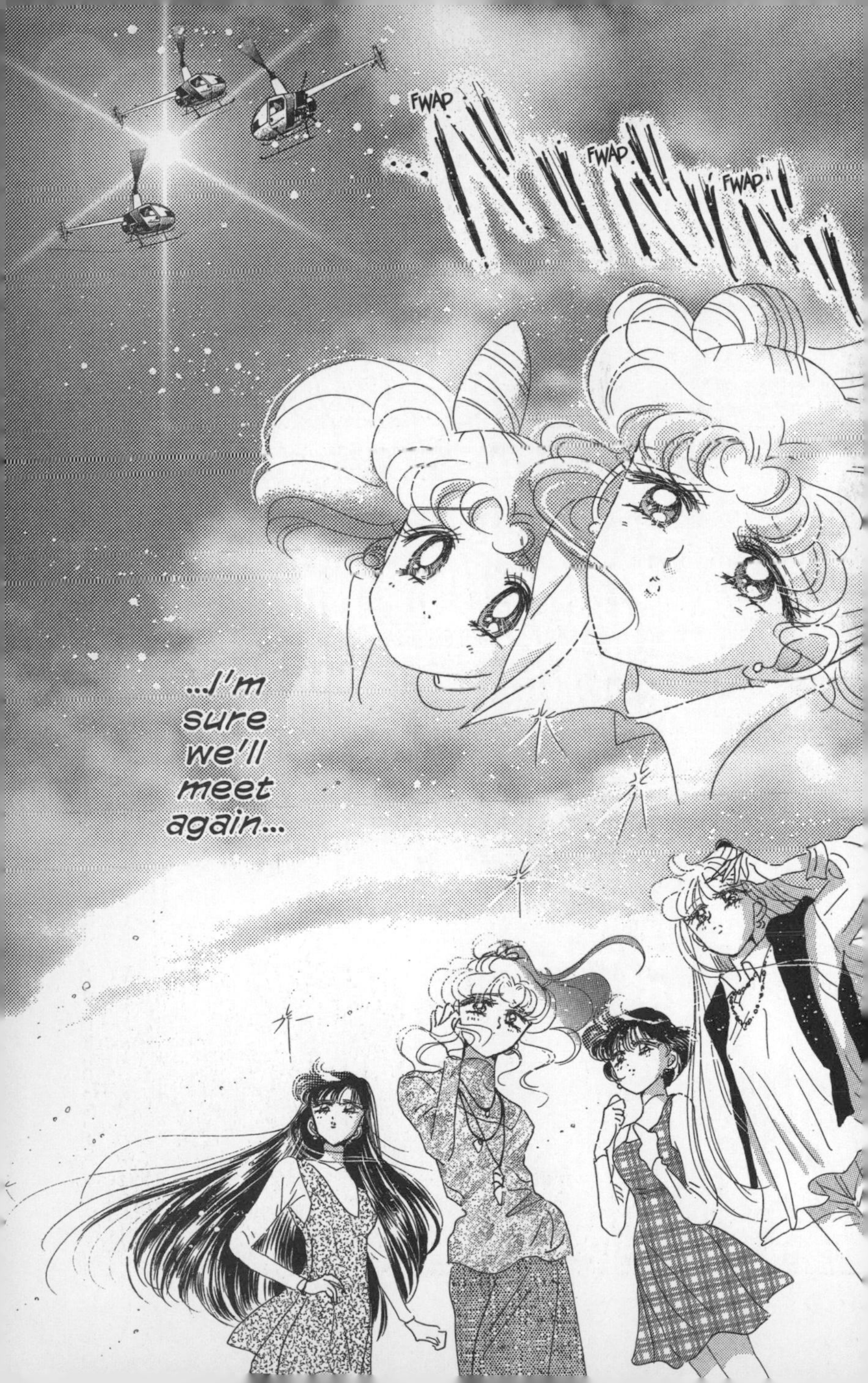
FWAP
FWAP
FWAP
...I'm sure we'll meet again...

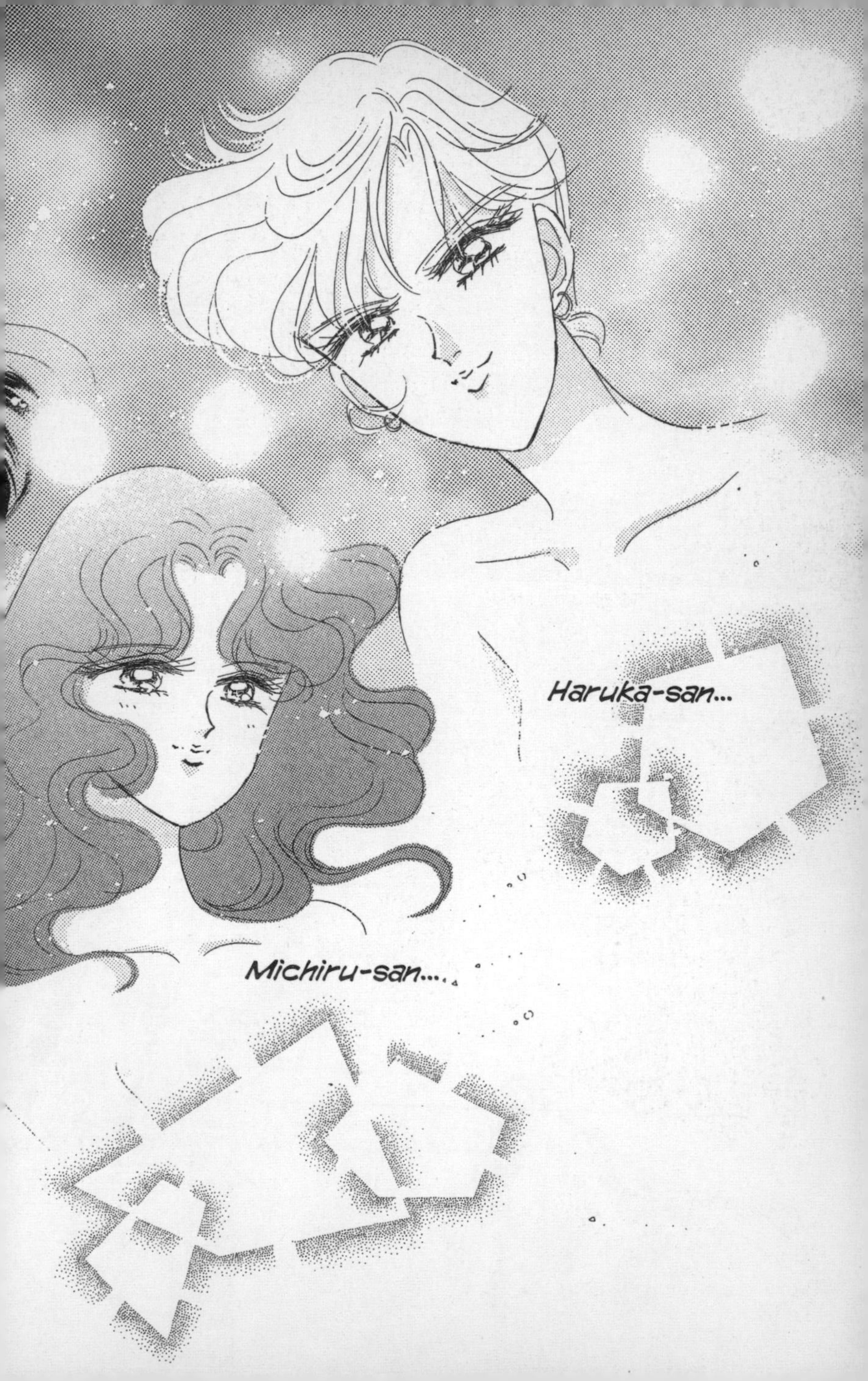
Haruka-san...
Michiru-san....

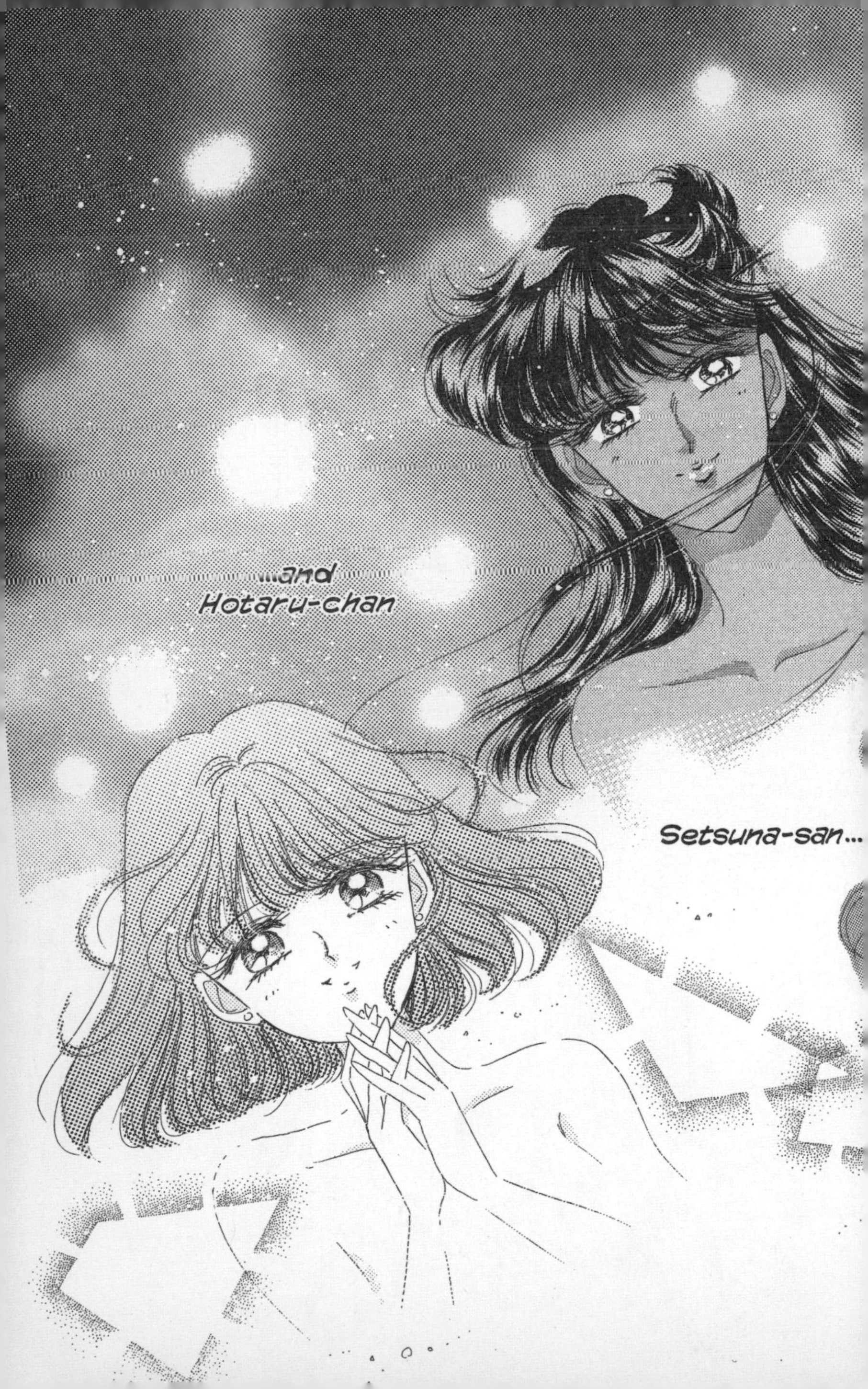
Setsuna-san...
...and Hotaru-chan

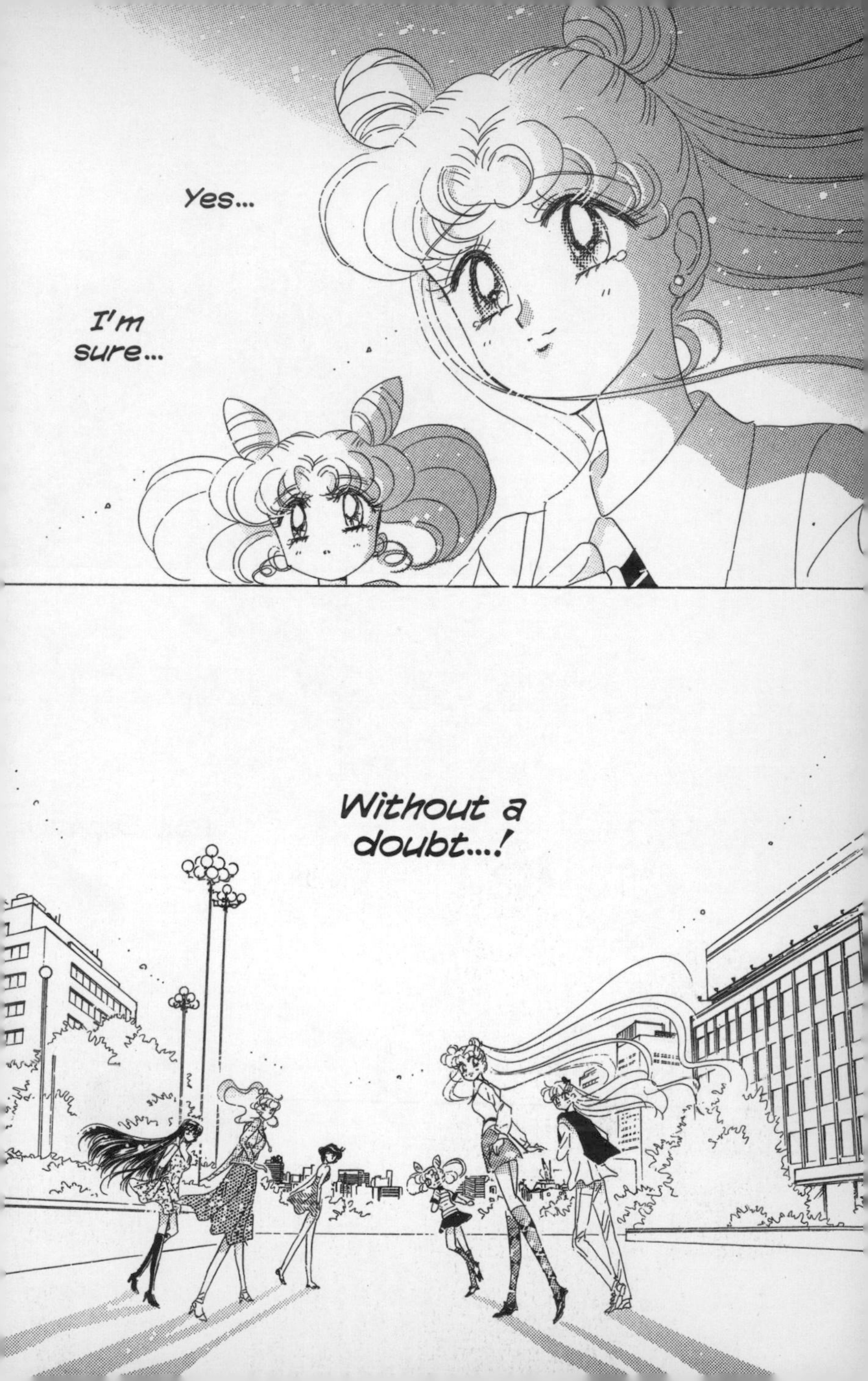
Yes...
I'm sure...
Without a doubt...!

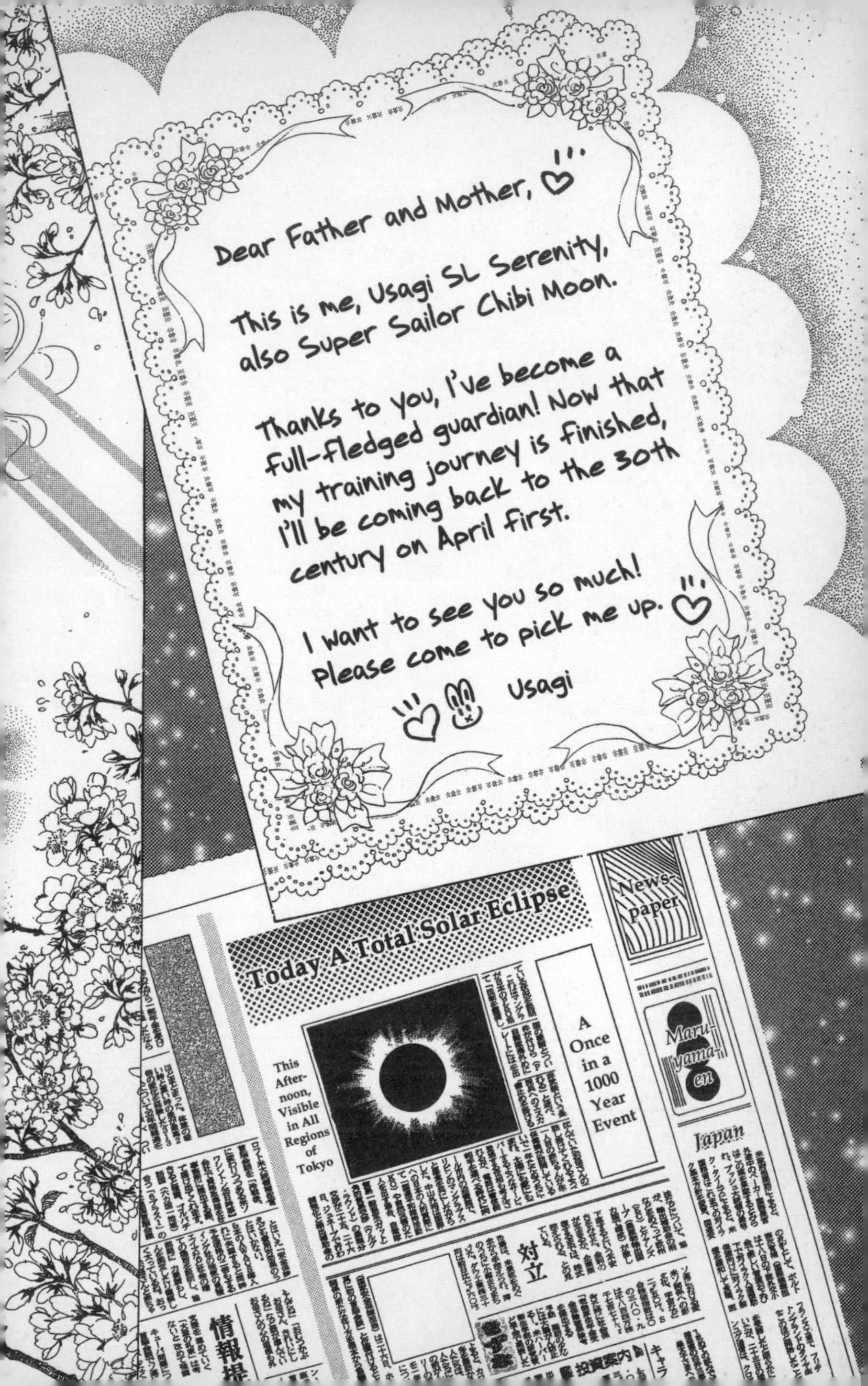
Dear Father and Mother,
This is me, Usagi SL Serenity, also Super Sailor Chibi Moon.
Thanks to you, I've become a full-fledged guardian! Now that my training journey is finished, I'll be coming back to the 30th century on April first.
I want to see you so much! Please come to pick me up.
Usagi
Today A Total Solar Eclipse
News-paper
This Afternoon, Visible in All Regions of Tokyo
A Once in a 1000 Year Event
Maru-yama-en
Japan
対立

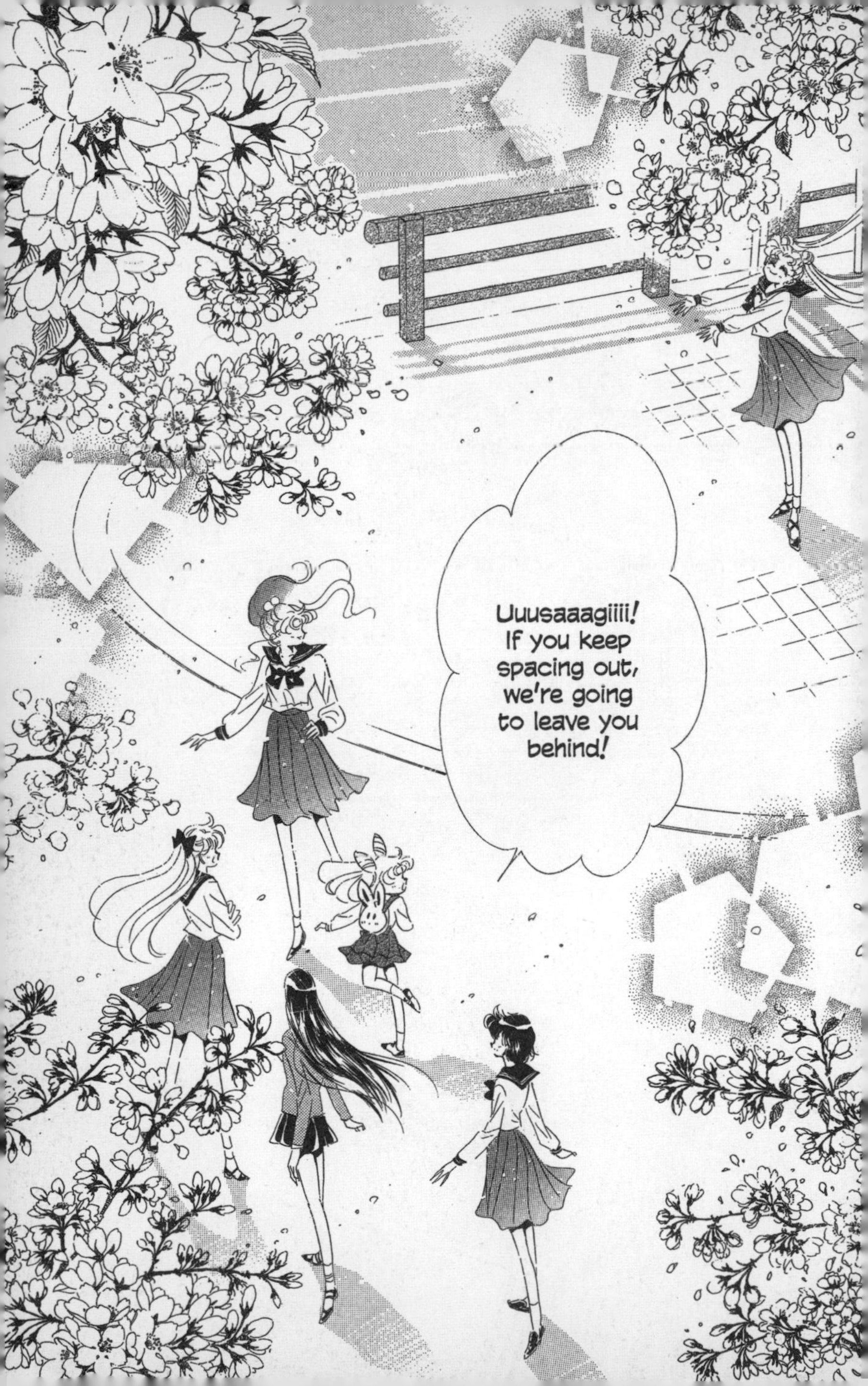
Uuusaaagiiii! If you keep spacing out, we're going to leave you behind!

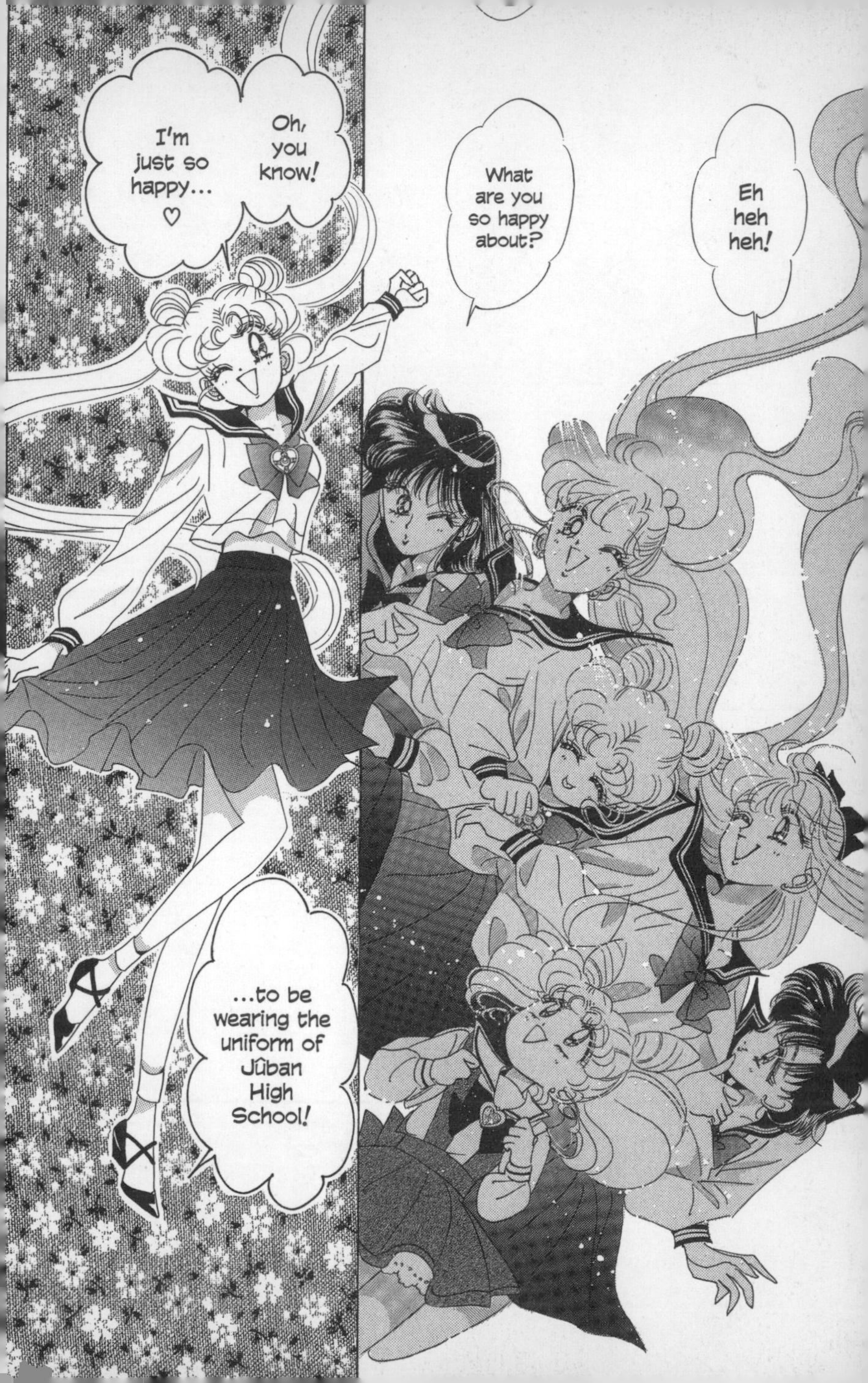
Eh heh heh!
What are you so happy about?
Oh, you know!
I'm just so happy... ♡
...to be wearing the uniform of Jûban High School!

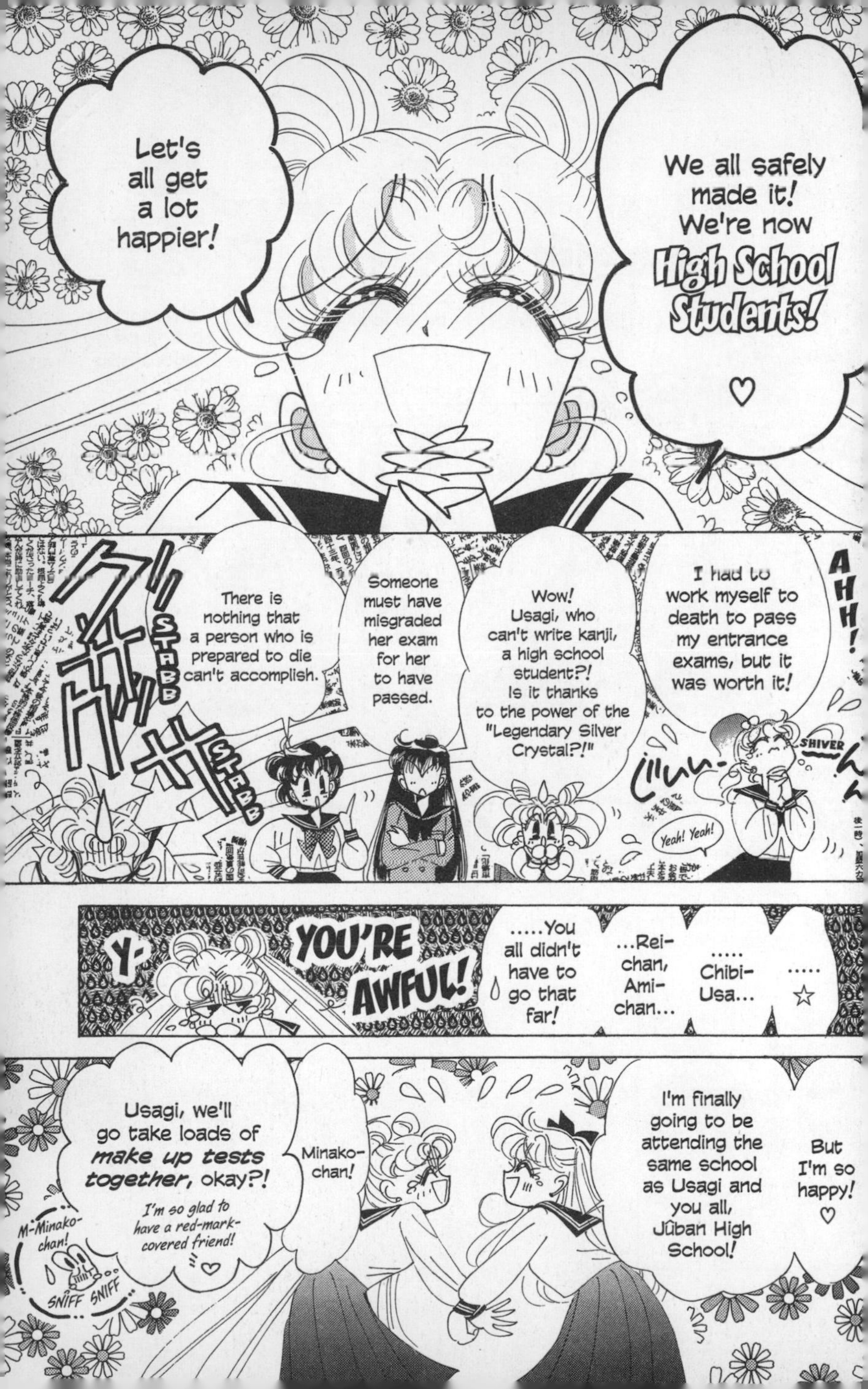
We all safely made it! We're now High School Students! ♡
Let's all get a lot happier!
AHH!
I had to work myself to death to pass my entrance exams, but it was worth it!
SHIVER
Yeah! Yeah!
Wow! Usagi, who can't write kanji, a high school student?! Is it thanks to the power of the "Legendary Silver Crystal?!"
Someone must have misgraded her exam for her to have passed.
There is nothing that a person who is prepared to die can't accomplish.
STABB
STABB
..... ☆
..... Chibi-Usa...
...Rei-chan, Ami-chan...
.....You all didn't have to go that far!
Y- YOU'RE AWFUL!
But I'm so happy! ♡
I'm finally going to be attending the same school as Usagi and you all, Jûban High School!
Minako-chan!
Usagi, we'll go take loads of make up tests together, okay?!
I'm so glad to have a red-mark-covered friend! ♡
M-Minako-chan!
SNIFF SNIFF

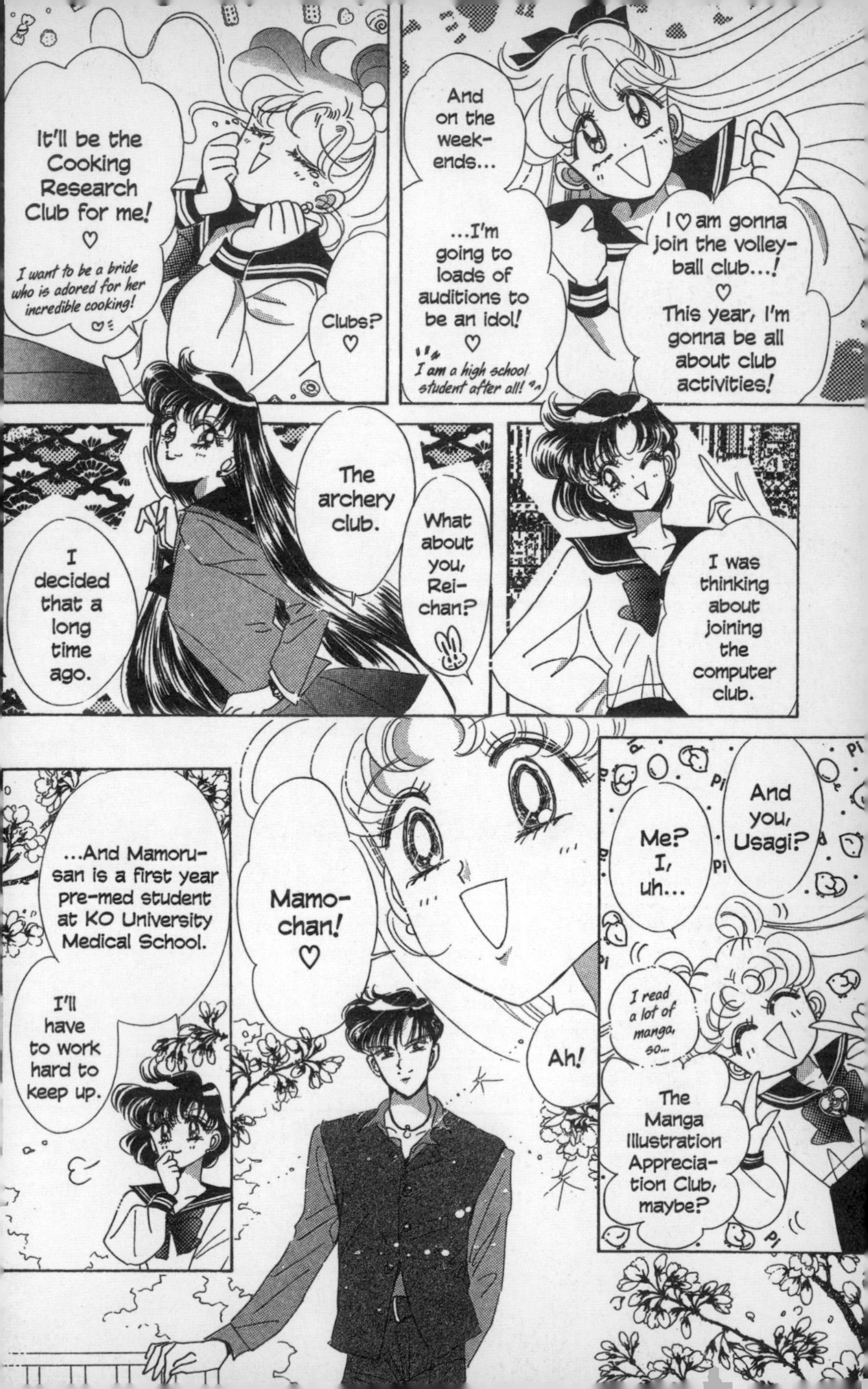
I ♡ am gonna join the volley-ball club...! ♡ This year, I'm gonna be all about club activities!
And on the week-ends...
...I'm going to loads of auditions to be an idol! ♡
I am a high school student after all!
Clubs? ♡
It'll be the Cooking Research Club for me! ♡
I want to be a bride who is adored for her incredible cooking!
I was thinking about joining the computer club.
What about you, Rei-chan?
The archery club.
I decided that a long time ago.
And you, Usagi?
Me? I, uh...
I read a lot of manga, so...
The Manga Illustration Appreciation Club, maybe?
Ah!
Mamo-chan! ♡
...And Mamoru-san is a first year pre-med student at KO University Medical School.
I'll have to work hard to keep up.

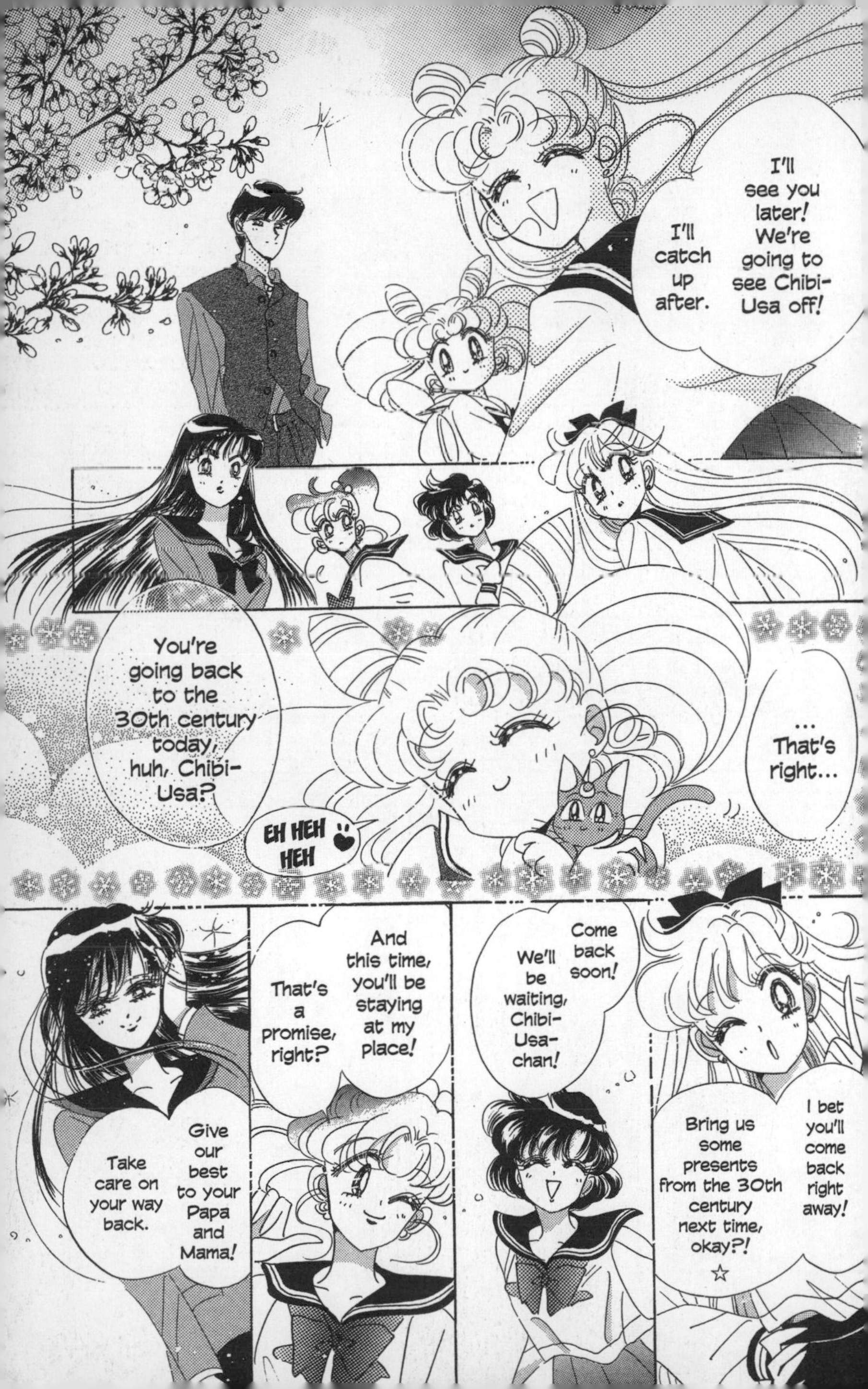
I'll see you later! We're going to see Chibi-Usa off!
I'll catch up after.
You're going back to the 30th century today, huh, Chibi-Usa?
... That's right...
EH HEH HEH
I bet you'll come back right away!
Bring us some presents from the 30th century next time, okay?! ☆
Come back soon!
We'll be waiting, Chibi-Usa-chan!
And this time, you'll be staying at my place!
That's a promise, right?
Give our best to your Papa and Mama!
Take care on your way back.

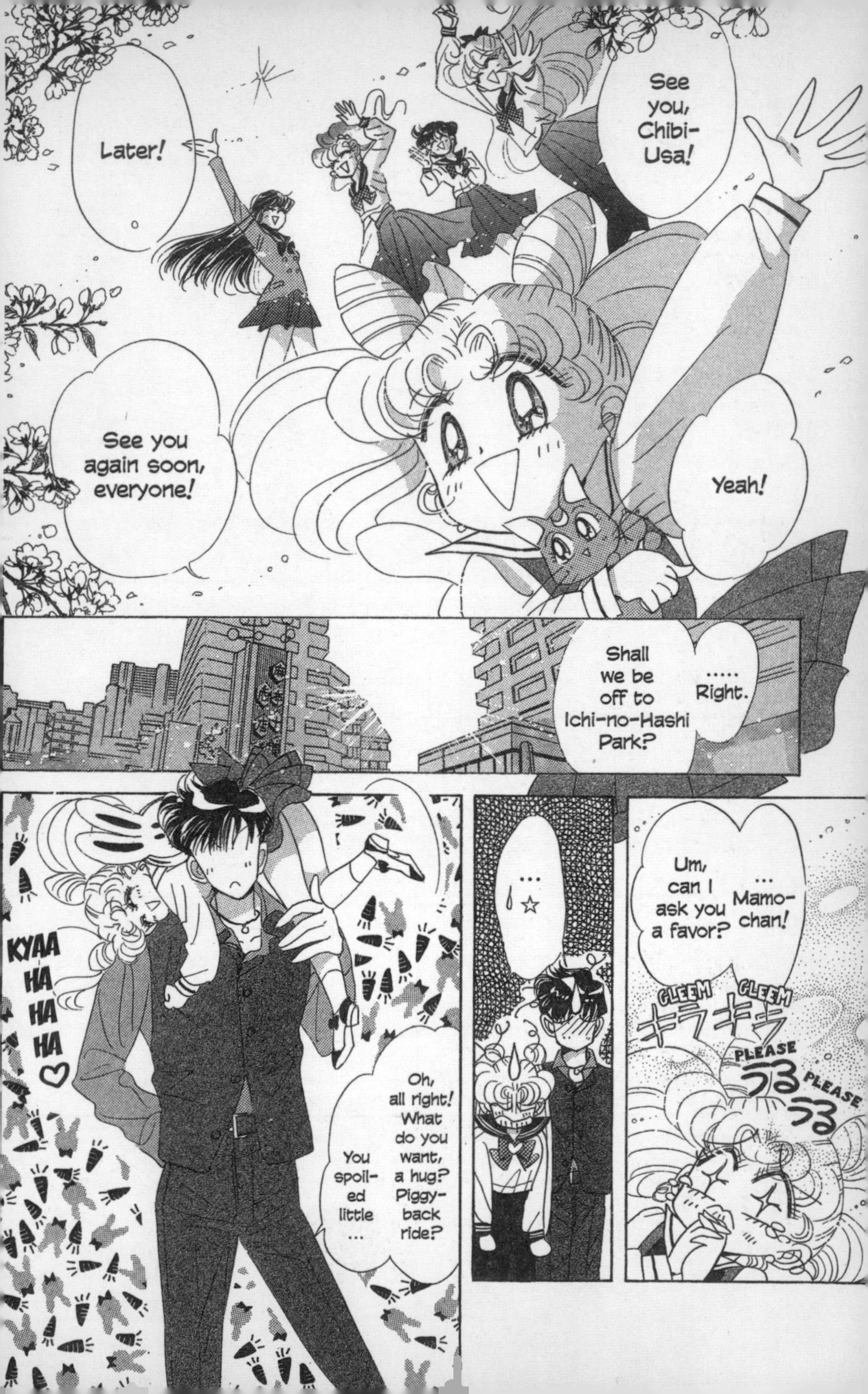
See you, Chibi-Usa!
Later!
Yeah!
See you again soon, everyone!
..... Right.
Shall we be off to Ichi-no-Hashi Park?
... Mamo-chan!
Um, can I ask you a favor?
GLEEM GLEEM
キラキラ
PLEASE PLEASE
うるうる
... ☆
Oh, all right! What do you want, a hug? Piggy-back ride?
You spoil-ed little ...
KYAA HA HA HA ♡

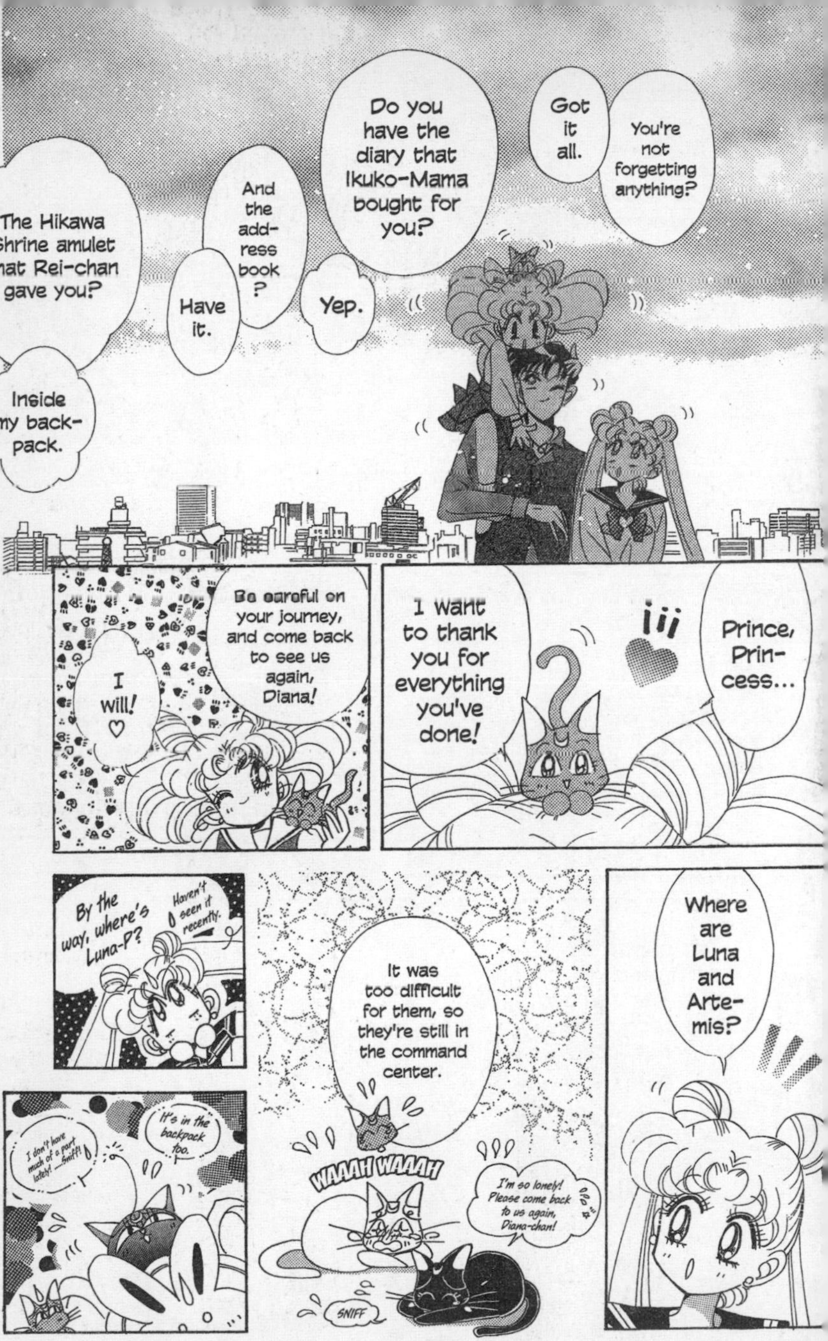
You're not forgetting anything?
Got it all.
Do you have the diary that Ikuko-Mama bought for you?
Yep.
And the address book?
Have it.
The Hikawa Shrine amulet that Rei-chan gave you?
Inside my backpack.
Prince, Princess...
I want to thank you for everything you've done!
Be careful on your journey, and come back to see us again, Diana!
I will! ♡
Where are Luna and Artemis?
It was too difficult for them, so they're still in the command center.
WAAAH WAAAH
I'm so lonely! Please come back to us again, Diana-chan!
SNIFF
By the way, where's Luna-P?
Haven't seen it recently.
It's in the backpack too.
I don't have much of a part lately! ...Sniff!

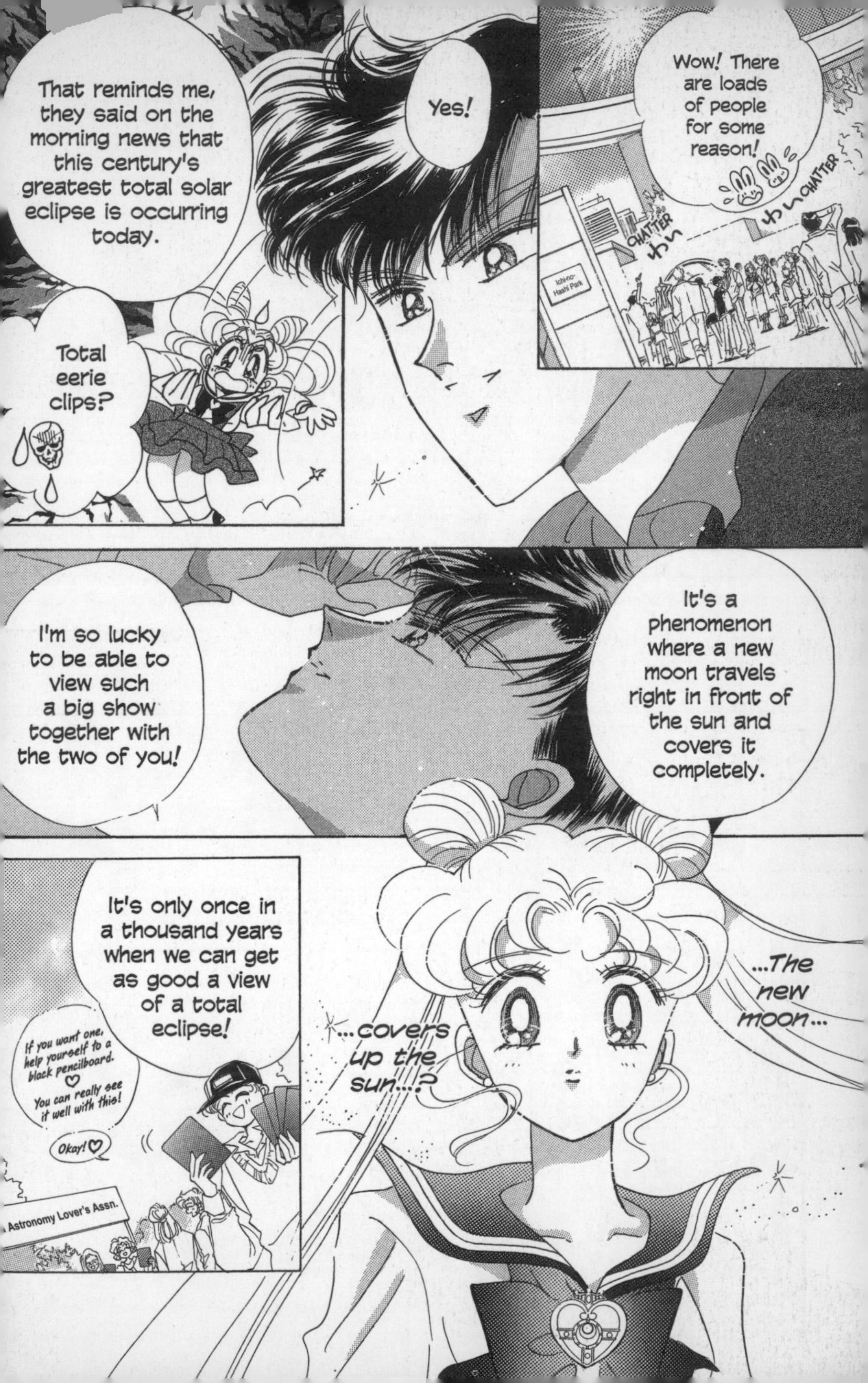
Wow! There are loads of people for some reason!
CHATTER
CHATTER
Ichi-no-Hashi Park
Yes!
That reminds me, they said on the morning news that this century's greatest total solar eclipse is occurring today.
Total eerie clips?
It's a phenomenon where a new moon travels right in front of the sun and covers it completely.
I'm so lucky to be able to view such a big show together with the two of you!
...The new moon...
...covers up the sun...?
It's only once in a thousand years when we can get as good a view of a total eclipse!
If you want one, help yourself to a black pencilboard. ♡ You can really see it well with this!
Okay! ♡
Astronomy Lover's Assn.

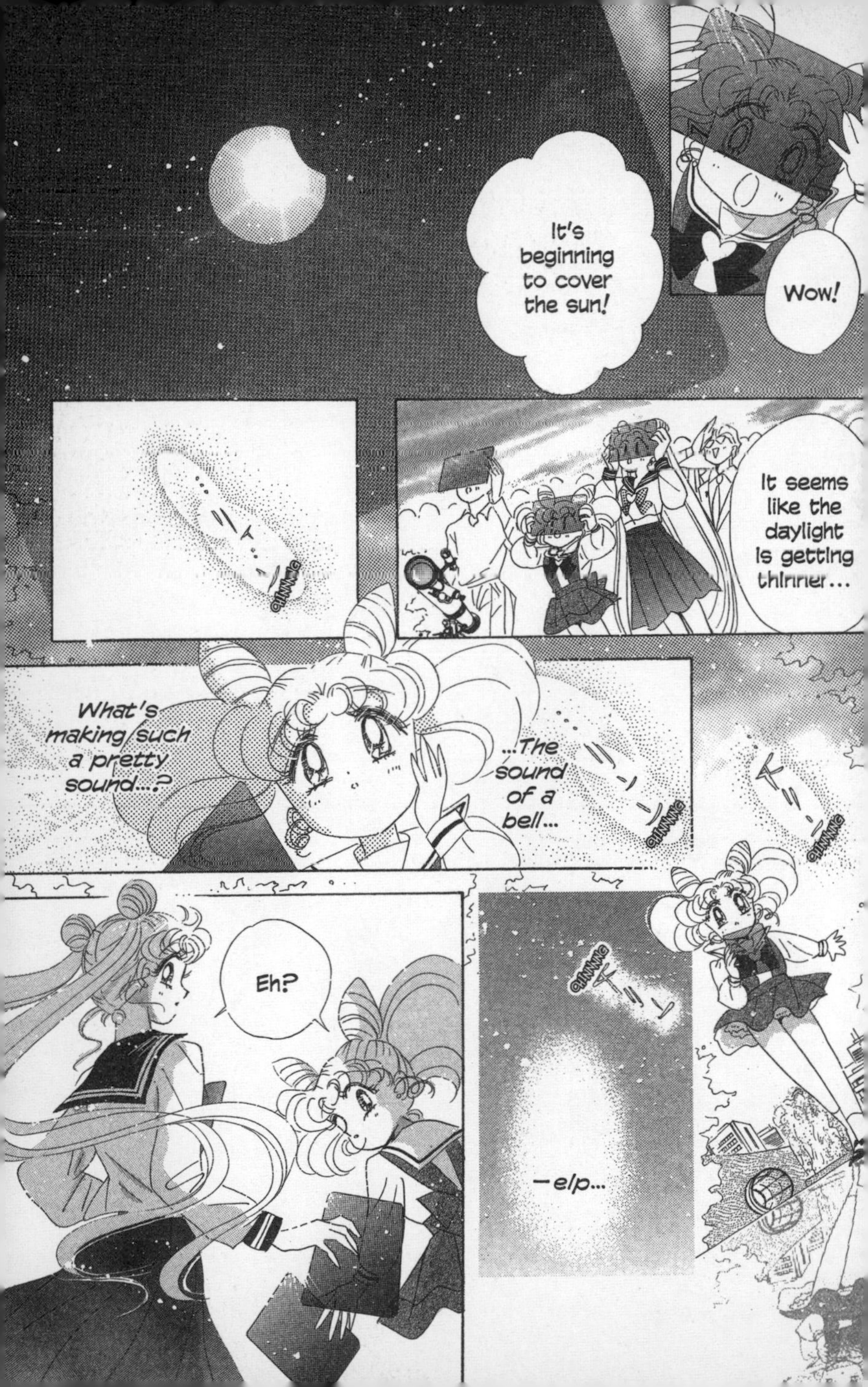
Wow!
It's beginning to cover the sun!
It seems like the daylight is getting thinner...
CHINNNG
CHINNNG
...The sound of a bell...
What's making such a pretty sound...?
CHINNNG
CHINNNG
—elp...
Eh?

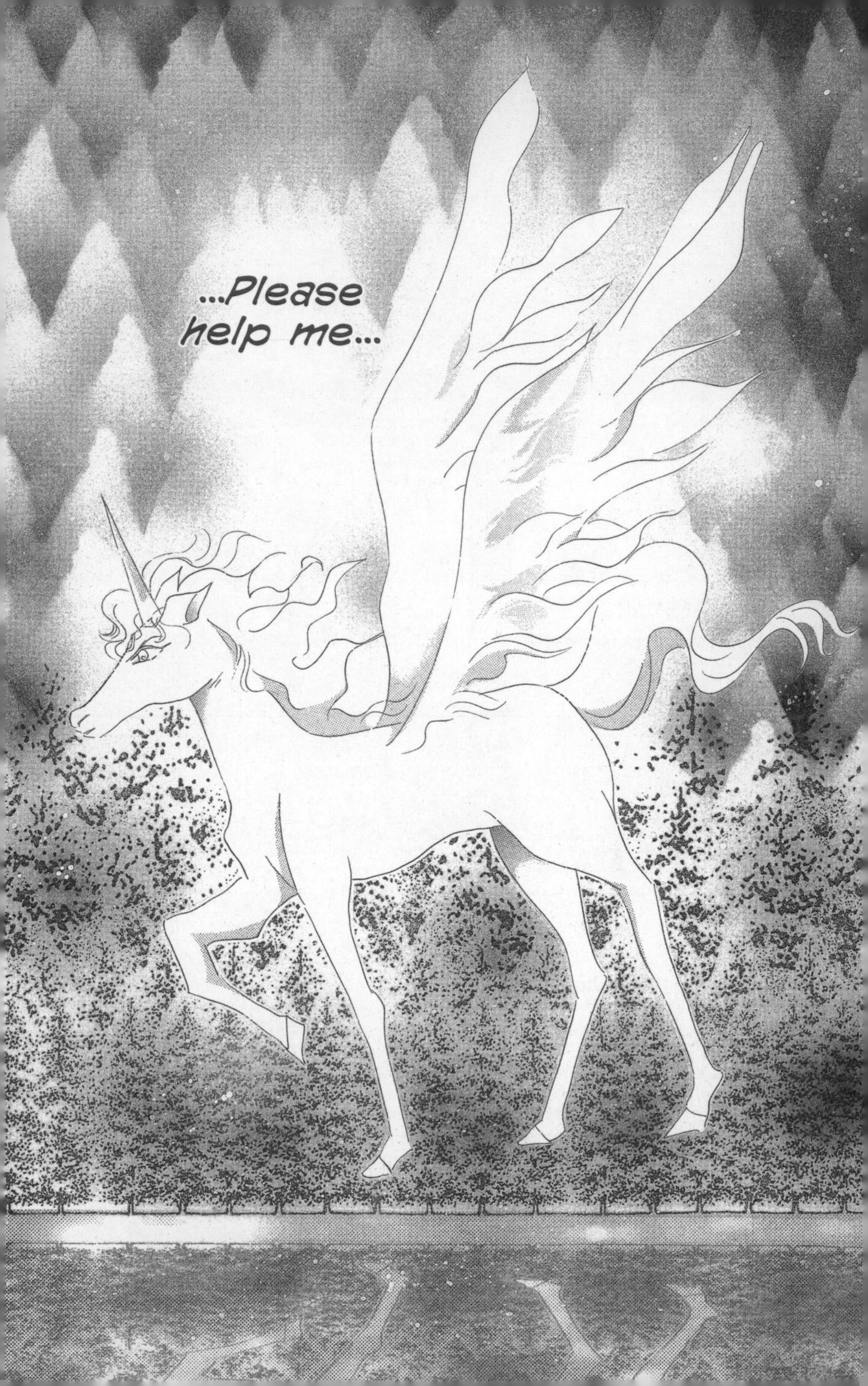
...Please help me...

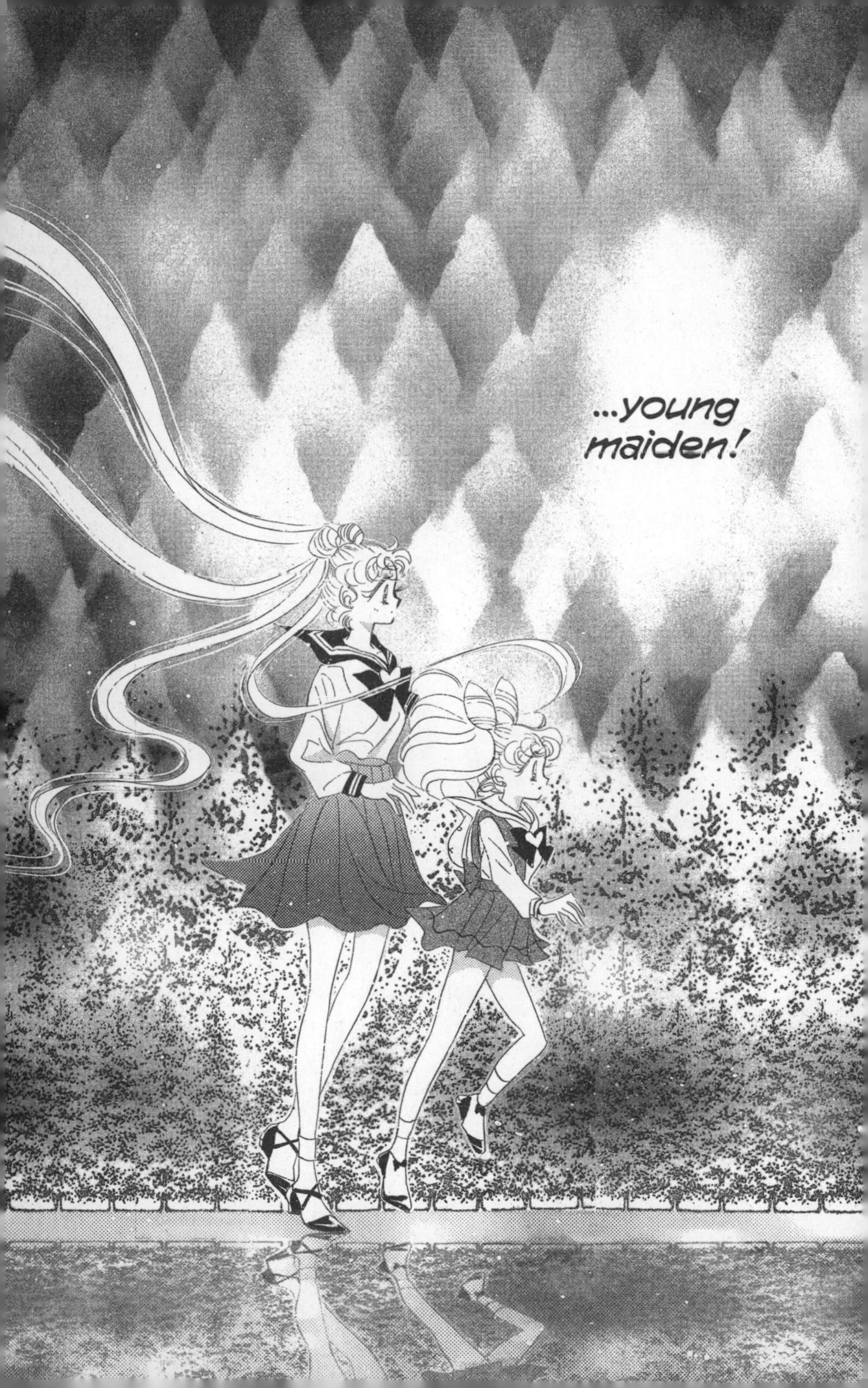
...young maiden!

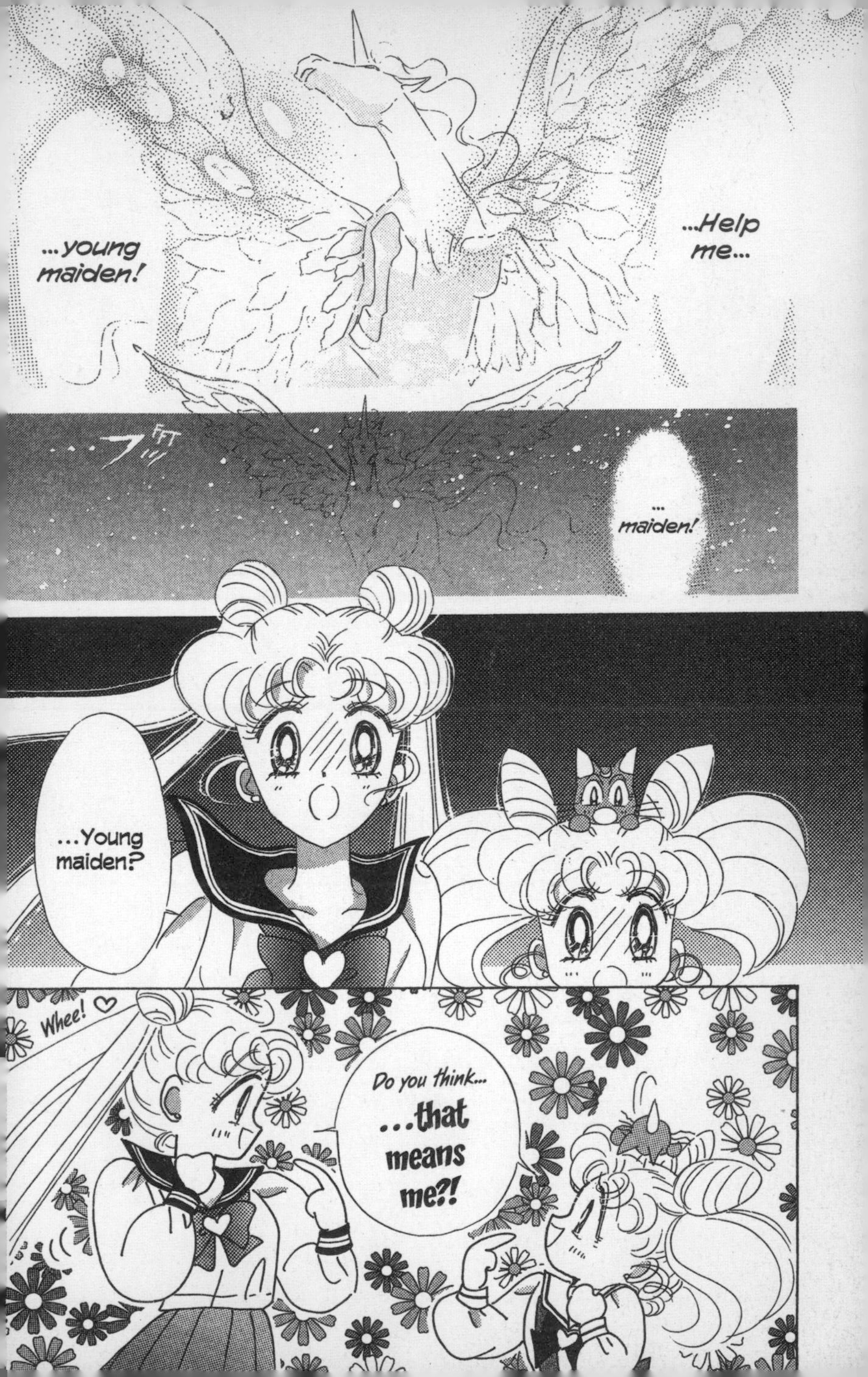
...Help me...
...young maiden!
... maiden!
FFT
...Young maiden?
Do you think... ...that means me?!
Whee! ♡

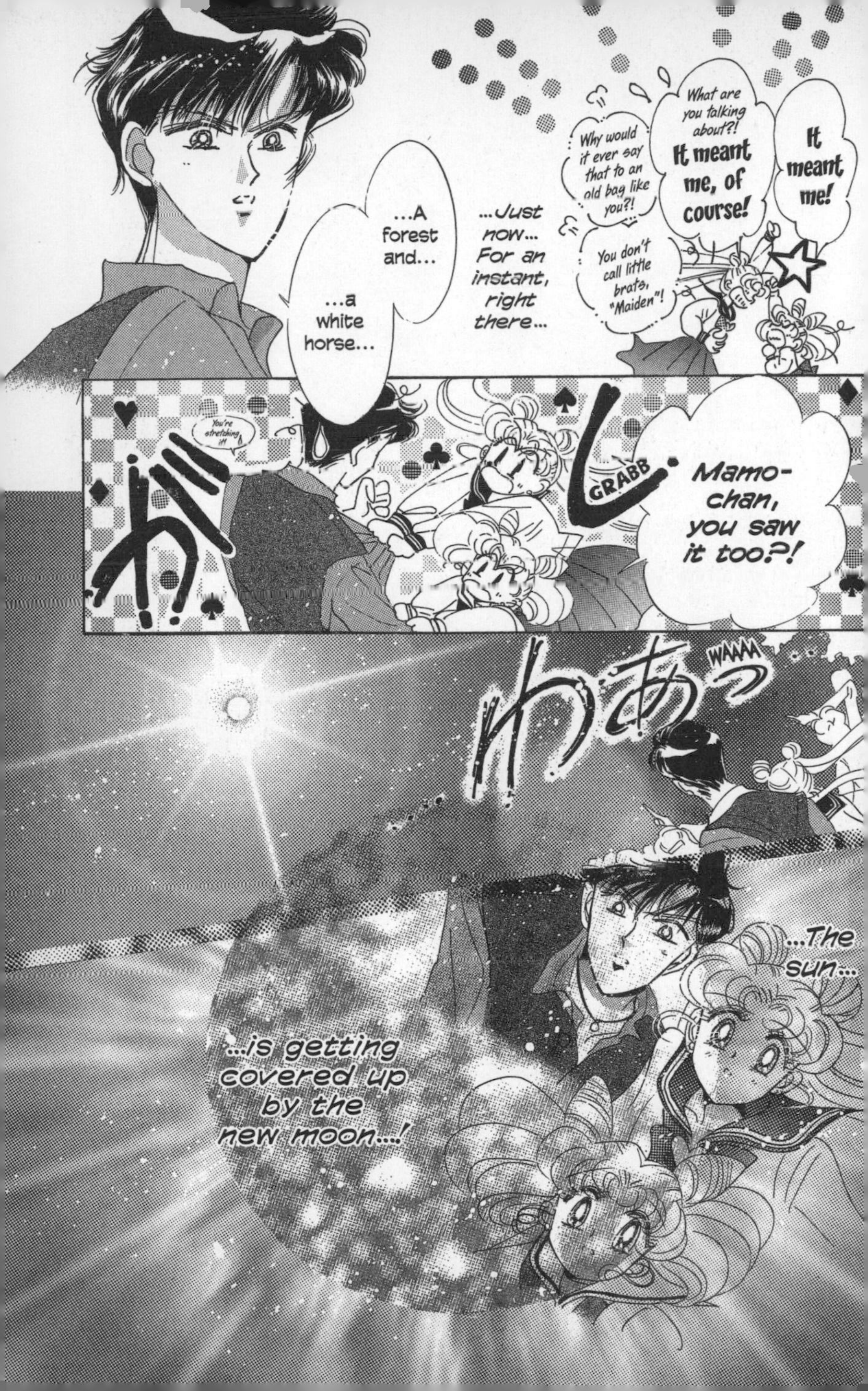
It meant me!
What are you talking about?! It meant me, of course!
Why would it ever say that to an old bag like you?!
You don't call little brats, "Maiden"!
...Just now... For an instant, right there...
...A forest and...
...a white horse...
Mamo-chan, you saw it too?!
GRABB
You're stretching it!
WAAAA
...The sun...
...is getting covered up by the new moon...!

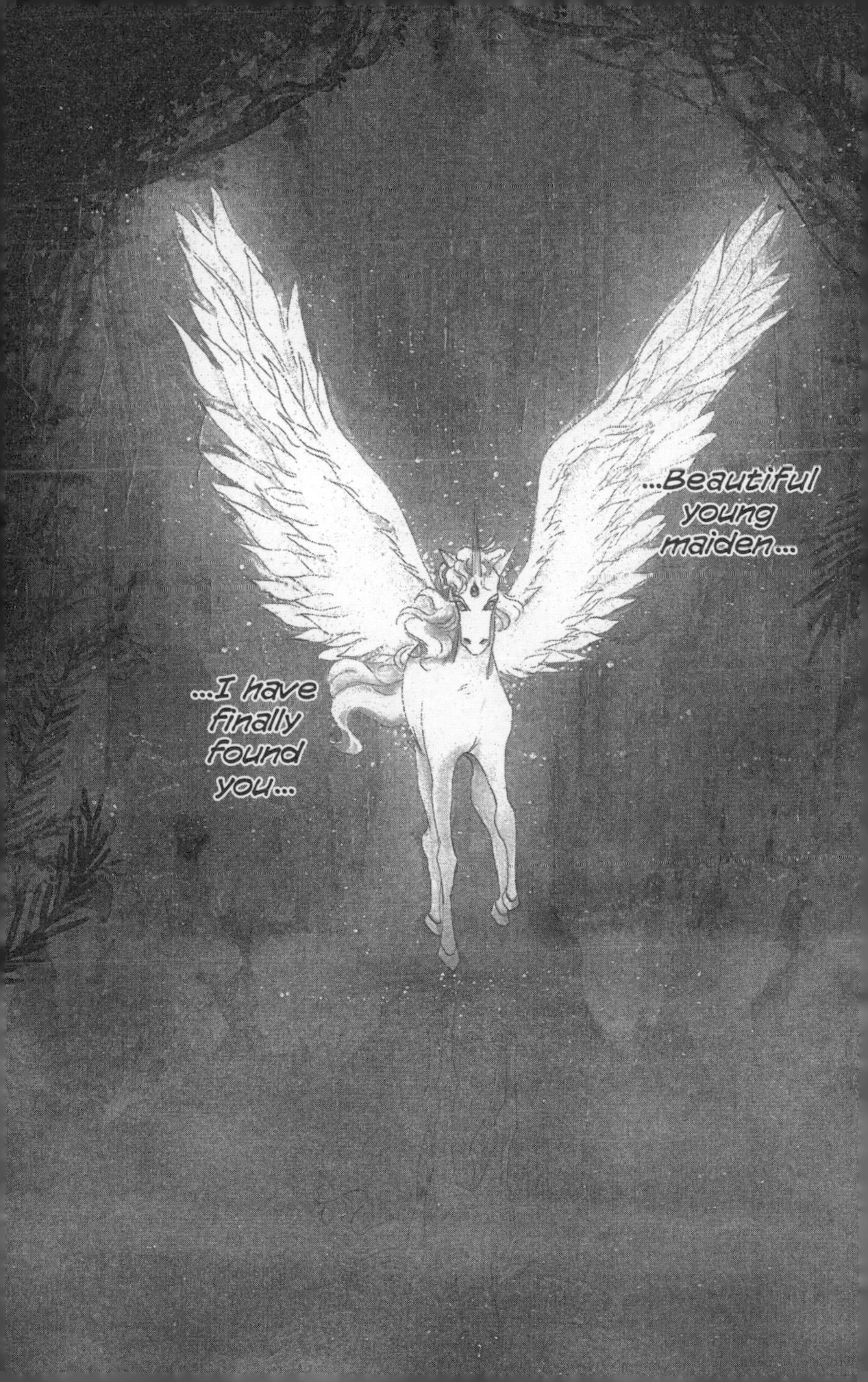
...Beautiful young maiden...
...I have finally found you...

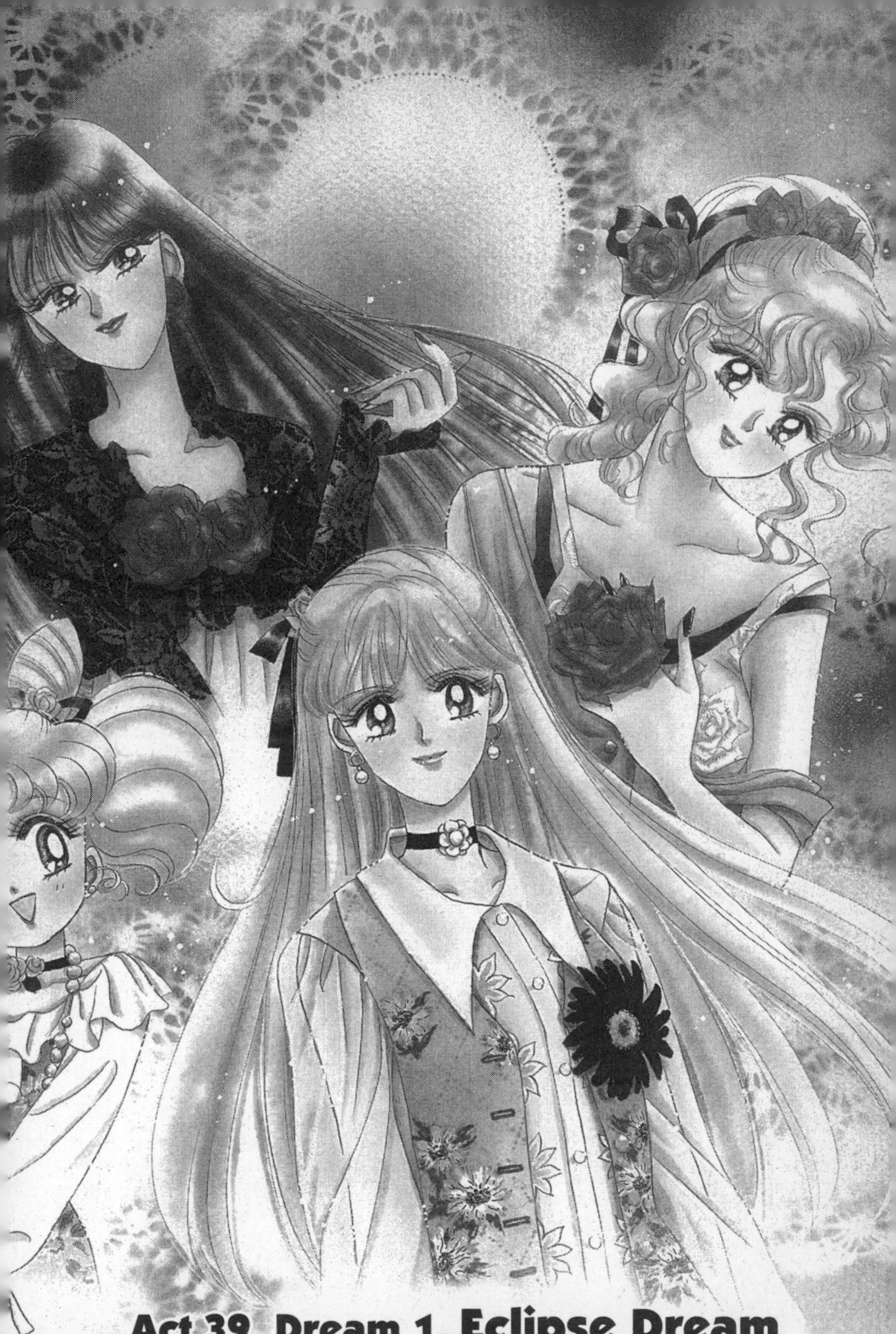

Act 39 Dream 1, Eclipse Dream

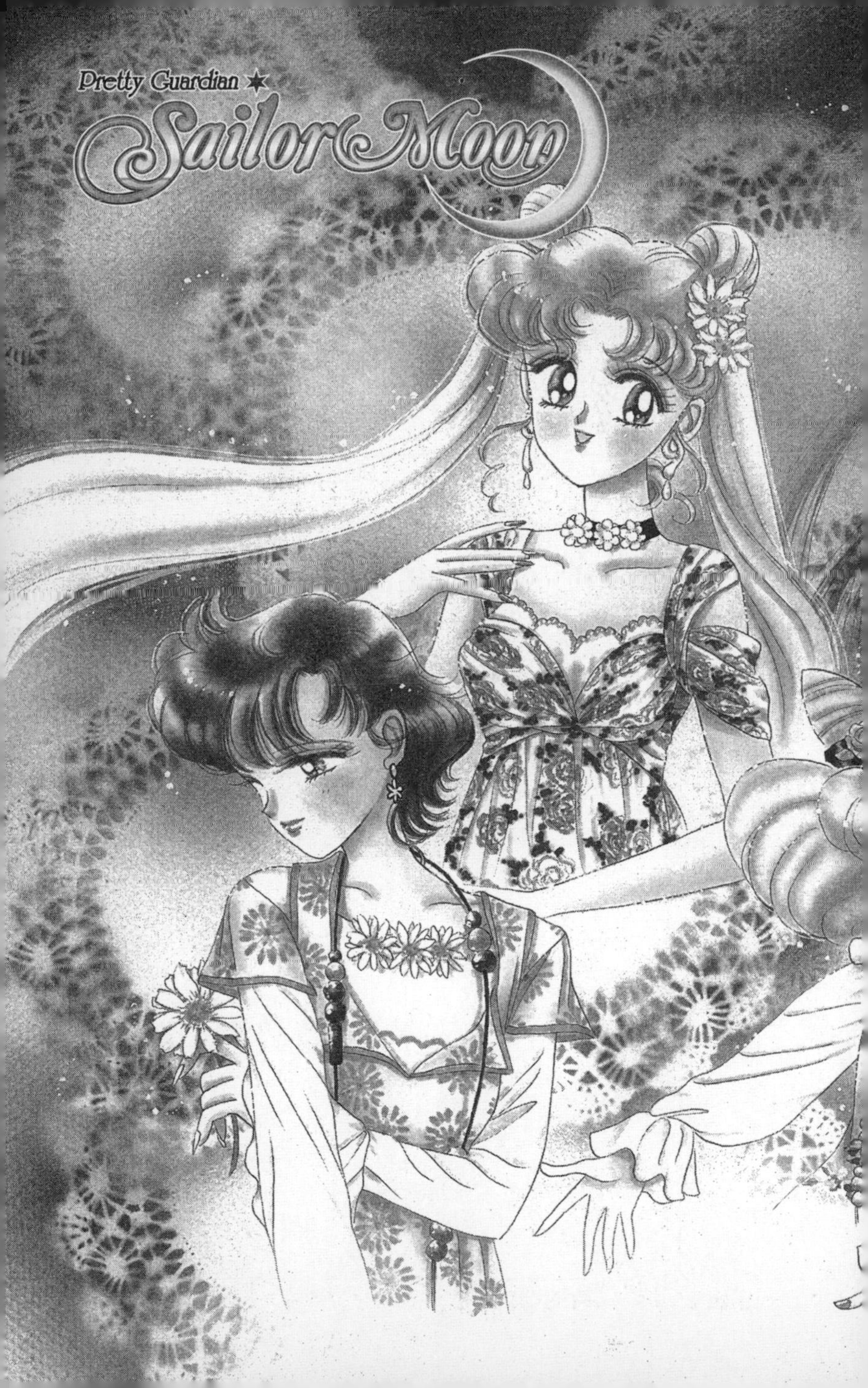
Pretty Guardian
Sailor Moon

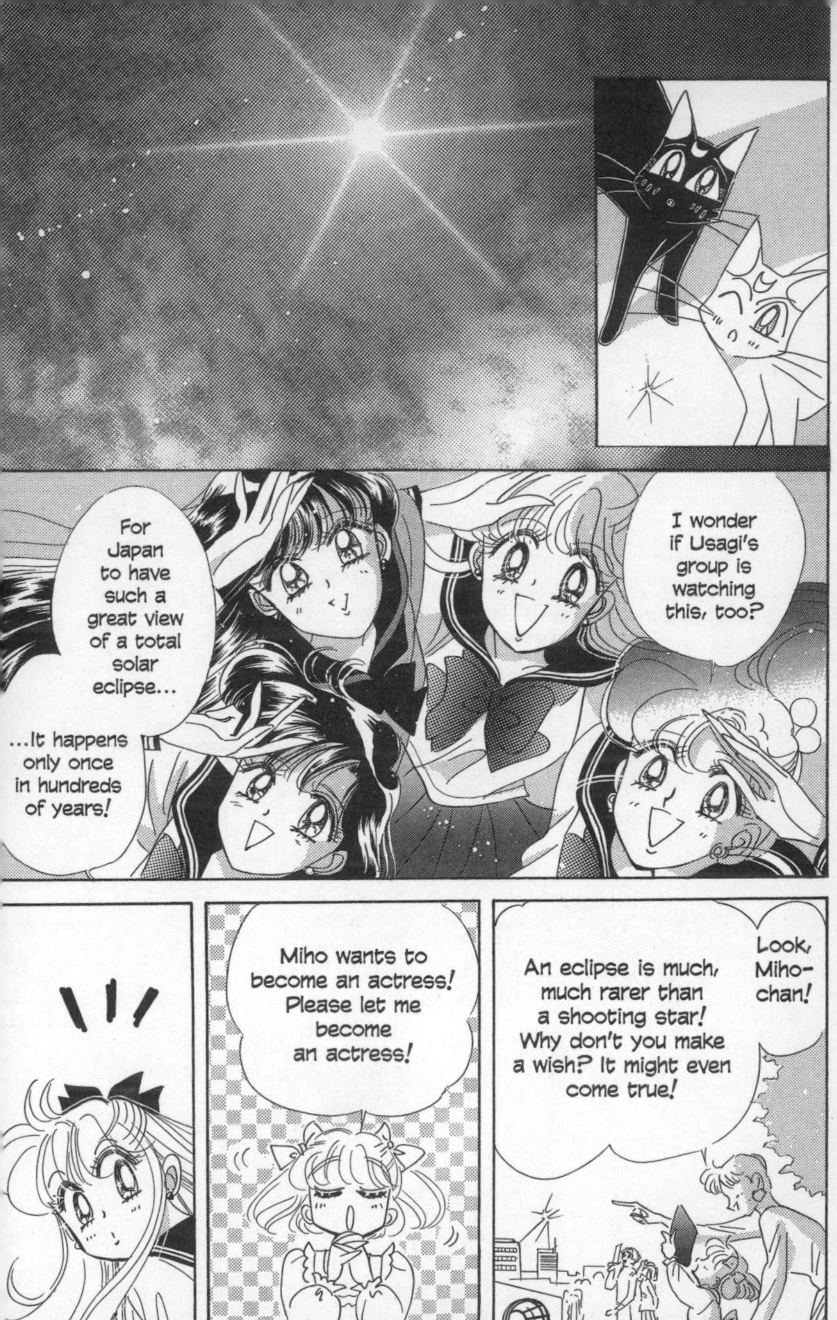
I wonder if Usagi's group is watching this, too?
For Japan to have such a great view of a total solar eclipse...
...It happens only once in hundreds of years!
Look, Miho-chan!
An eclipse is much, much rarer than a shooting star! Why don't you make a wish? It might even come true!
Miho wants to become an actress! Please let me become an actress!

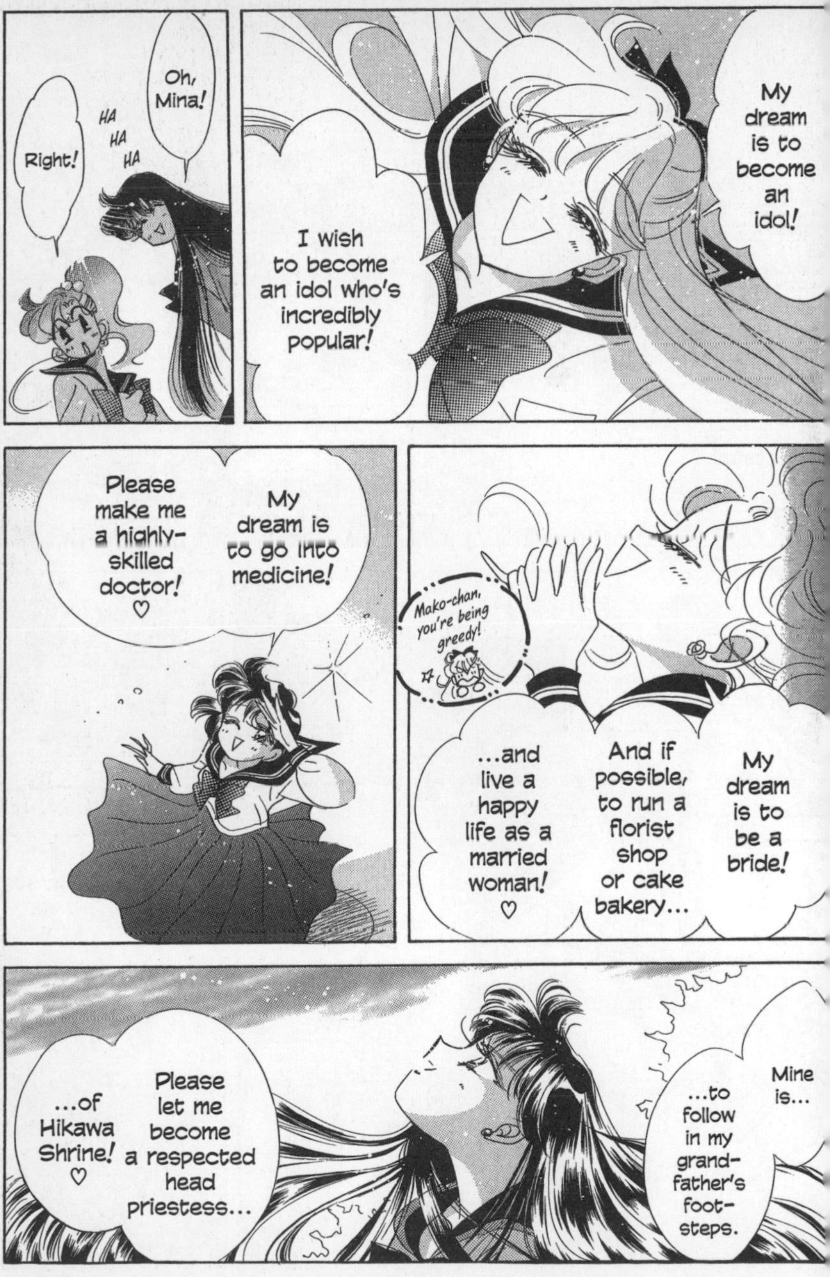
My dream is to become an idol!
I wish to become an idol who's incredibly popular!
Oh, Mina!
HA HA HA
Right!
My dream is to be a bride!
And if possible, to run a florist shop or cake bakery...
...and live a happy life as a married woman! ♡
Mako-chan, you're being greedy!
My dream is to go into medicine!
Please make me a highly-skilled doctor! ♡
Mine is...
...to follow in my grandfather's foot-steps.
Please let me become a respected head priestess...
...of Hikawa Shrine! ♡

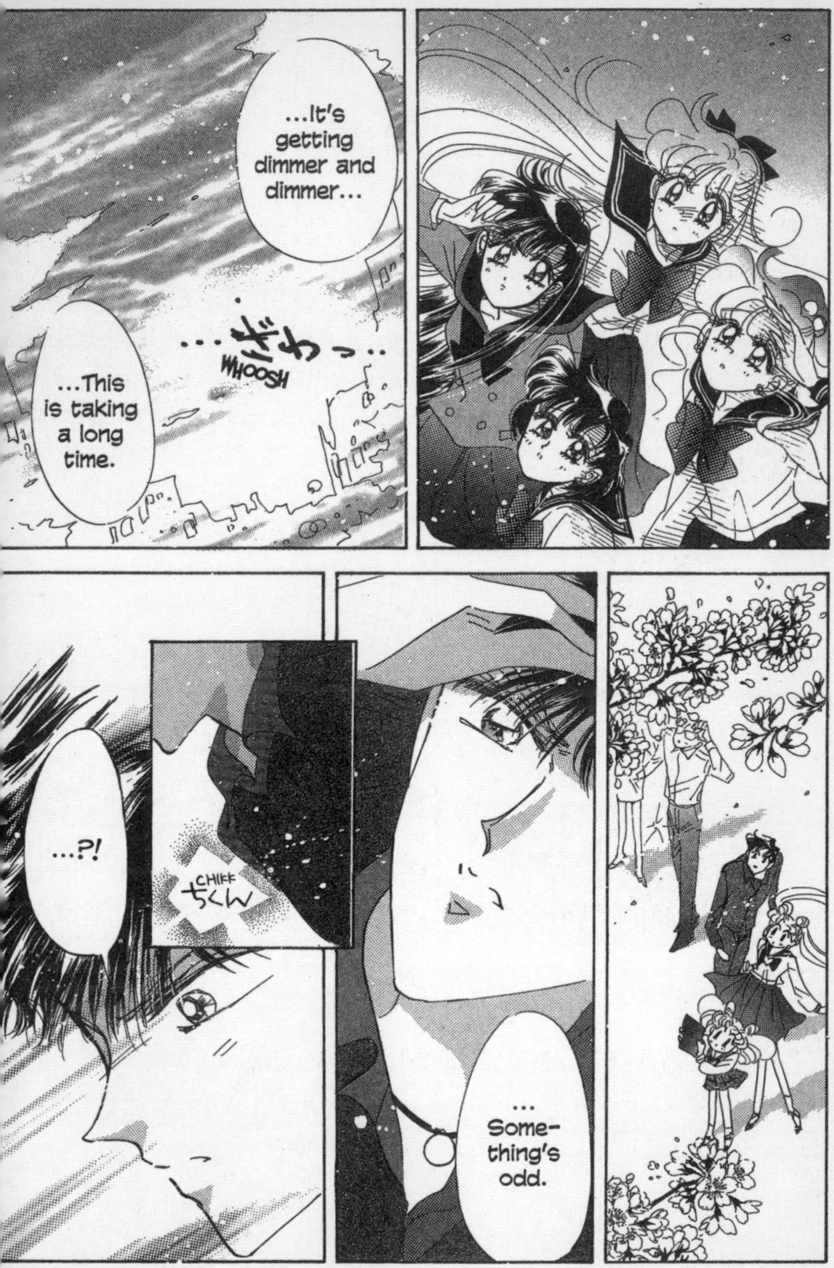
...It's getting dimmer and dimmer...
...ざわっ...
WHOOSH
...This is taking a long time.
... Some-thing's odd.
CHIFF
ちくん
...?!

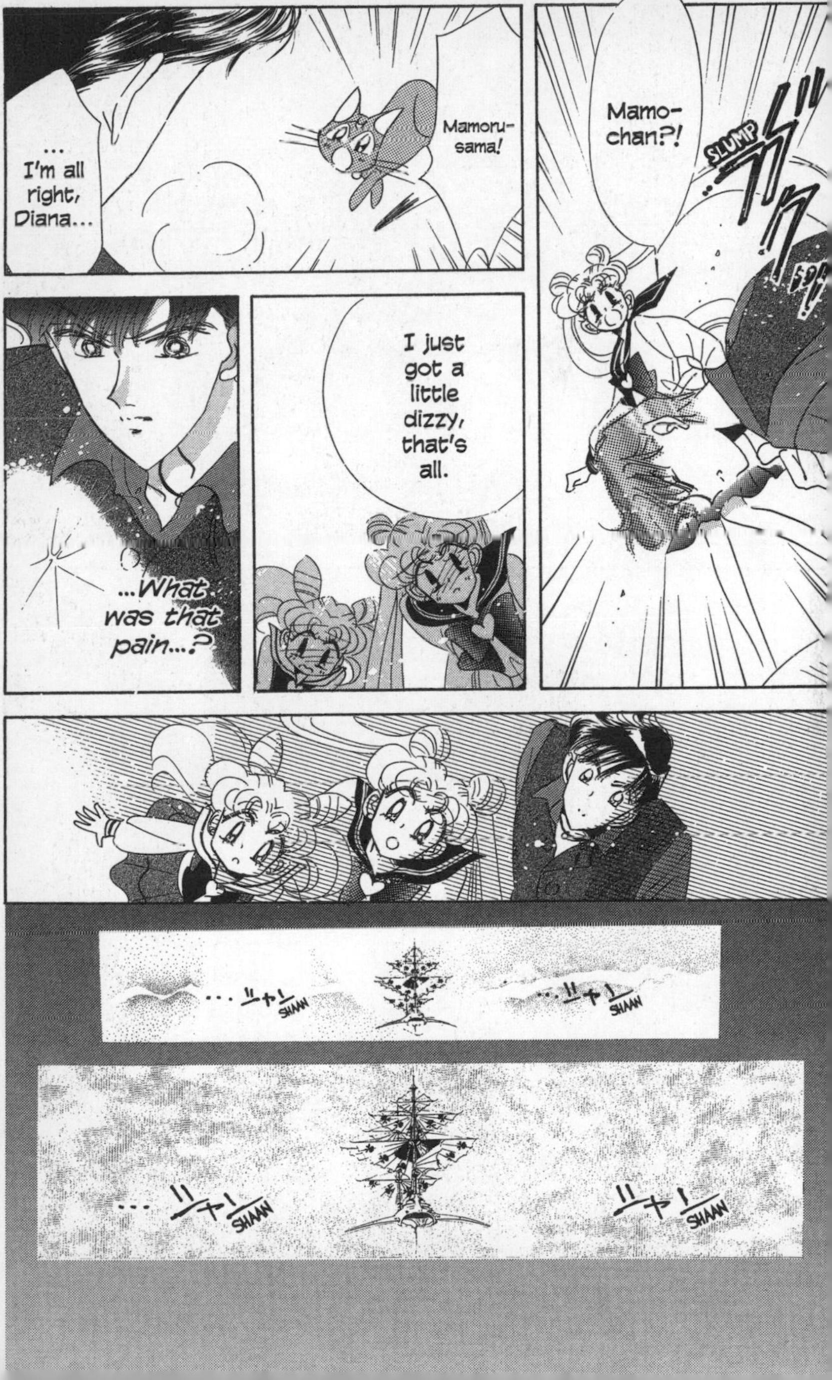
Mamo-chan?!
...SLUMP
Mamoru-sama!
... I'm all right, Diana...
I just got a little dizzy, that's all.
...What was that pain...?
...SHAAN
...SHAAN
...SHAAN
SHAAN

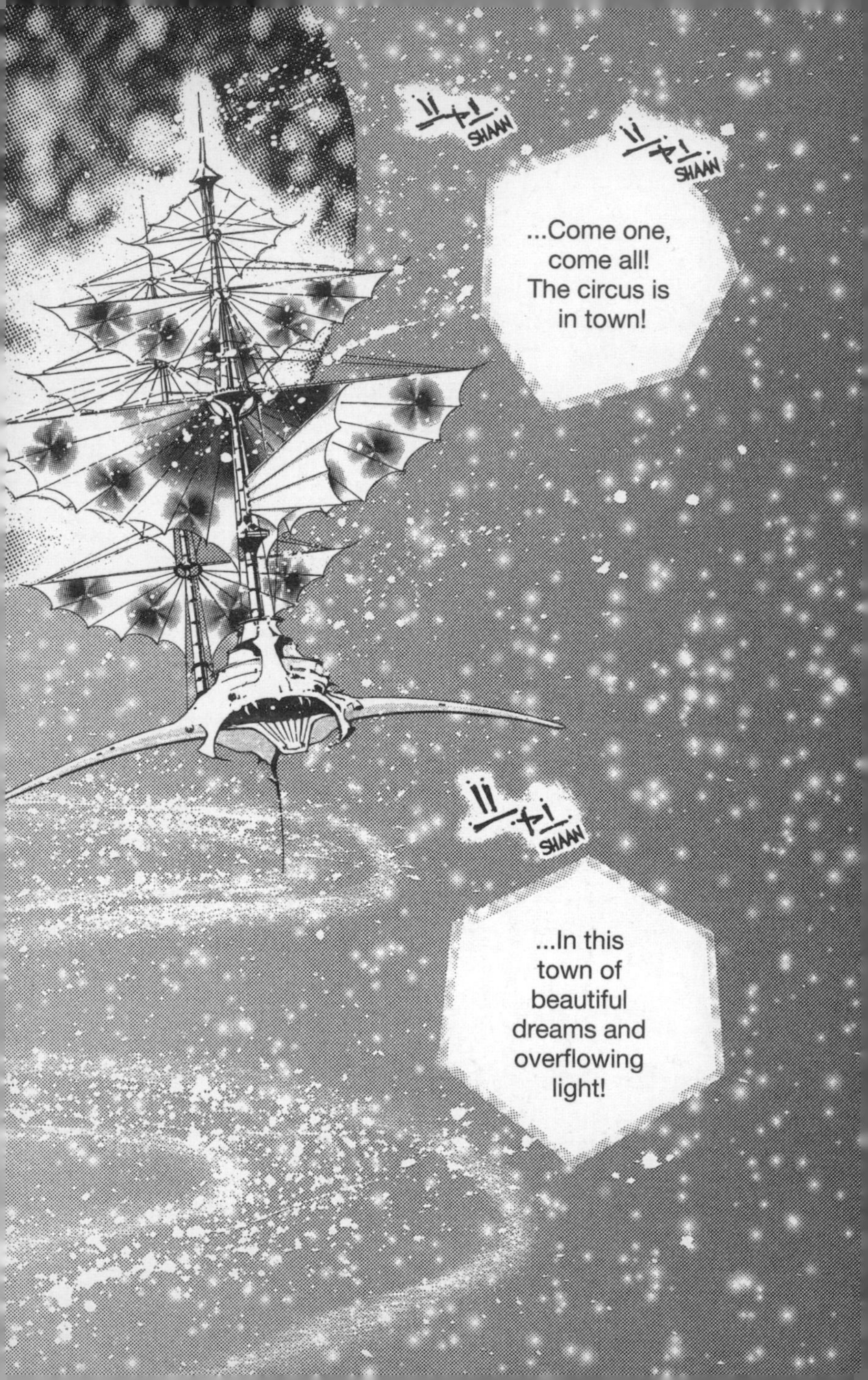
SHAAN
SHAAN
...Come one, come all! The circus is in town!
SHAAN
...In this town of beautiful dreams and overflowing light!

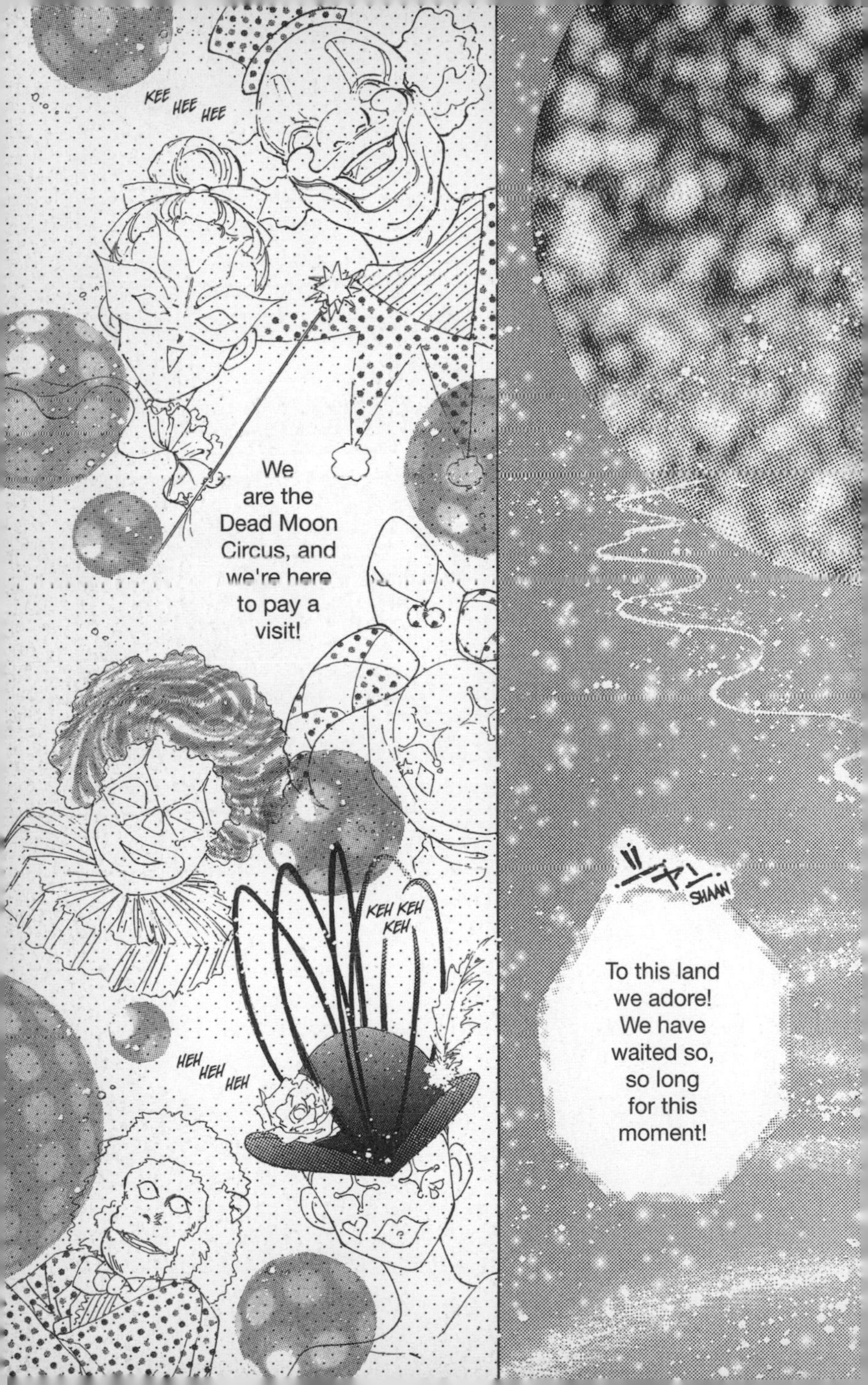
SHAAN
To this land we adore! We have waited so, so long for this moment!
KEE HEE HEE
We are the Dead Moon Circus, and we're here to pay a visit!
KEH KEH KEH
HEH HEH HEH

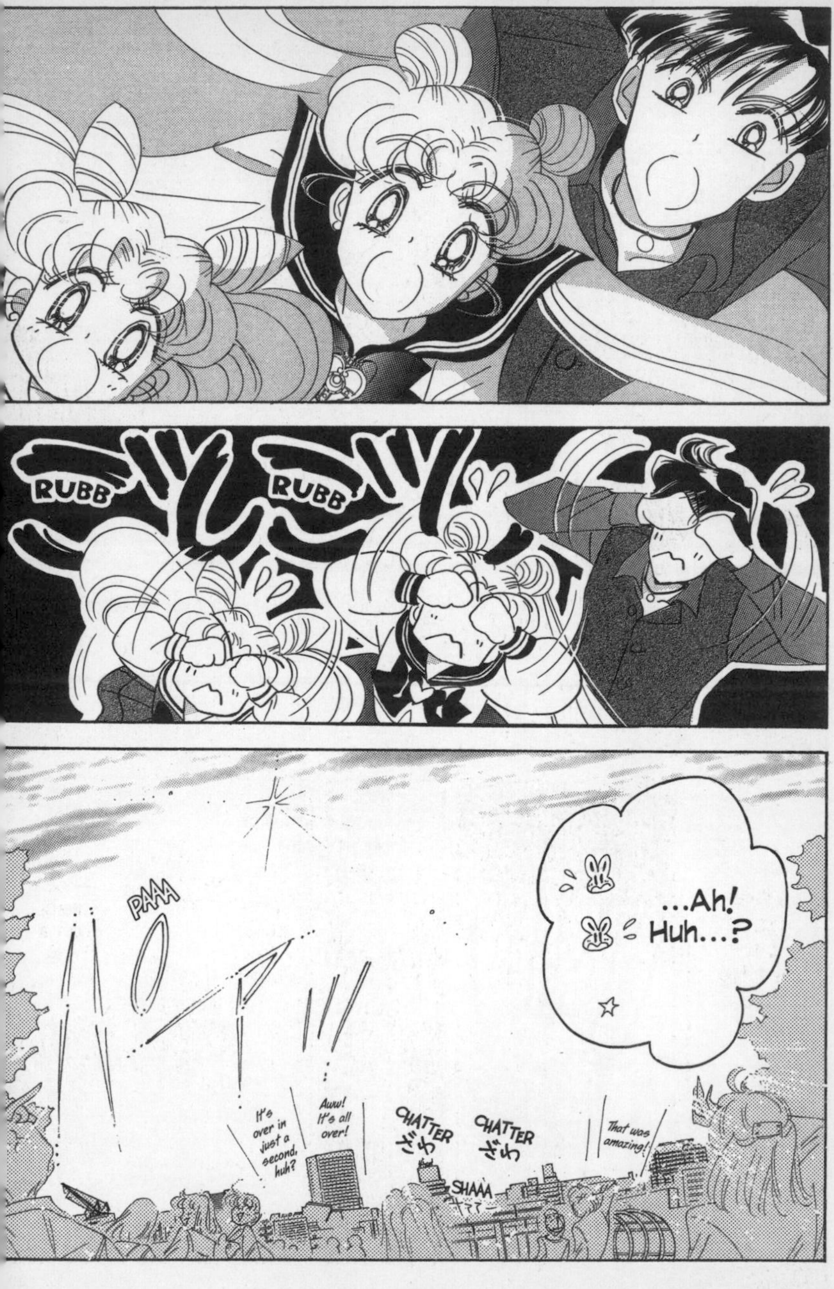
RUBB
RUBB
...Ah!
Huh...?
That was amazing!
CHATTER ざわ
CHATTER ざわ
Aww! It's all over!
It's over in just a second, huh?
SHAAA
PAAA

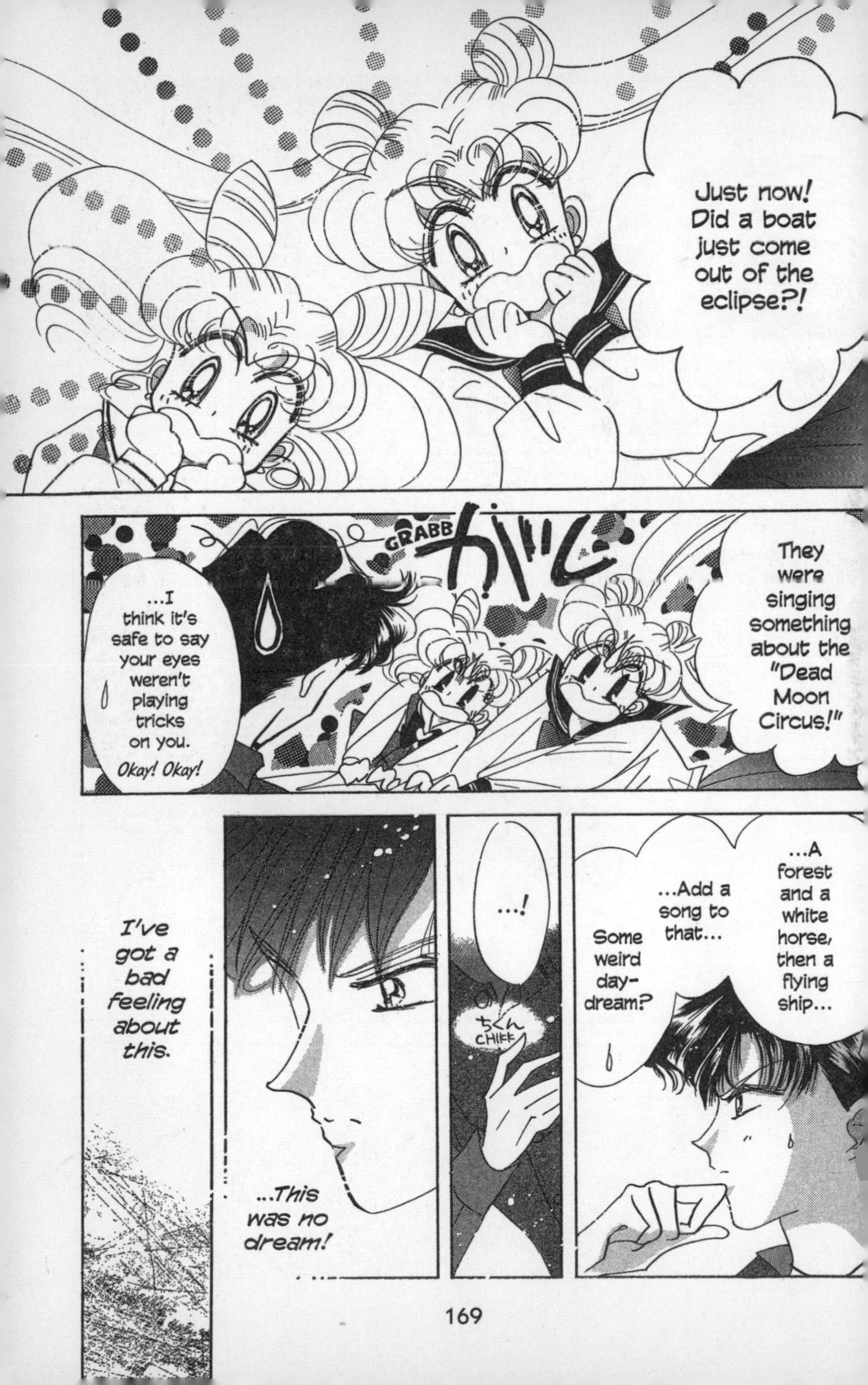
Just now! Did a boat just come out of the eclipse?!
They were singing something about the "Dead Moon Circus!"
GRABB
...I think it's safe to say your eyes weren't playing tricks on you.
Okay! Okay!
...A forest and a white horse, then a flying ship...
...Add a song to that...
Some weird day-dream?
...!
CHIFF
...This was no dream!
I've got a bad feeling about this.

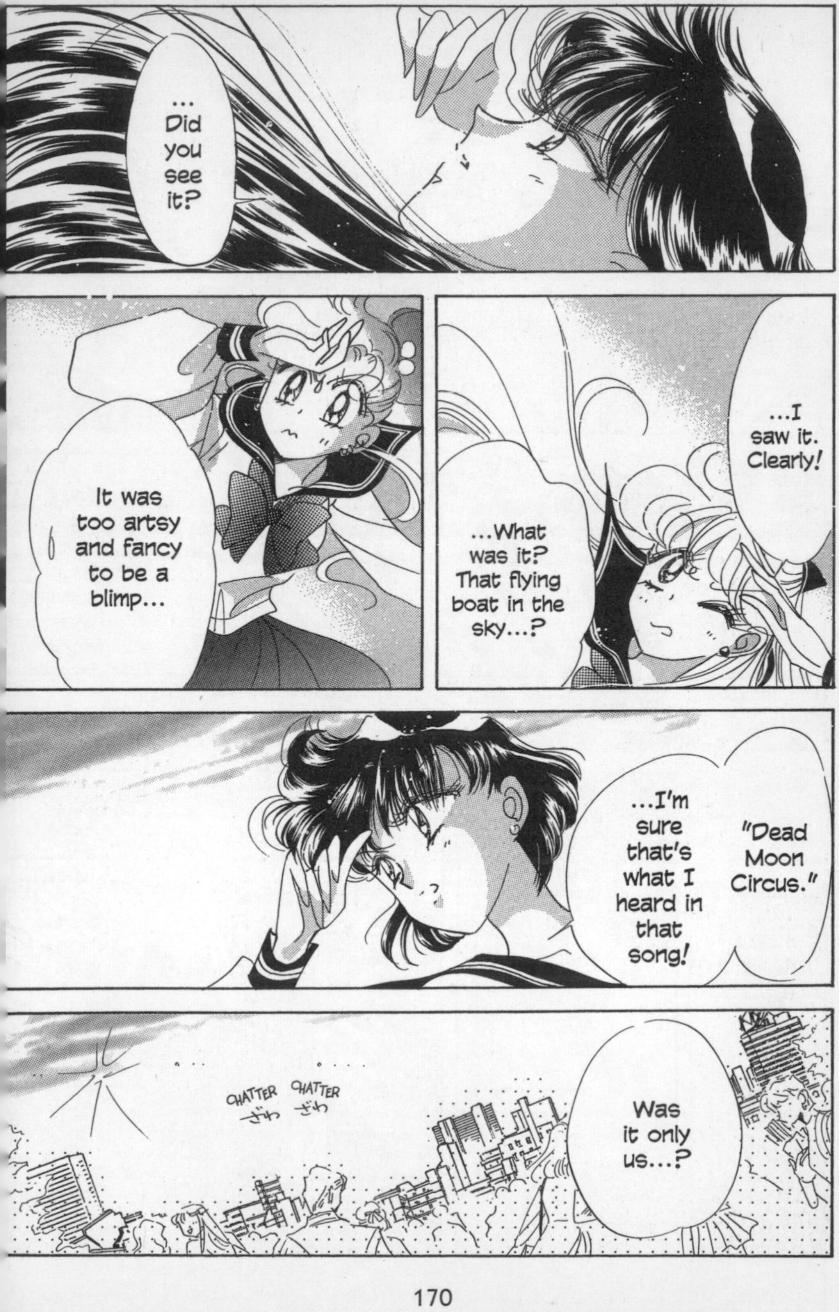
... Did you see it?
...I saw it. Clearly!
...What was it? That flying boat in the sky...?
It was too artsy and fancy to be a blimp...
"Dead Moon Circus."
...I'm sure that's what I heard in that song!
Was it only us...?
CHATTER CHATTER
ざわ ざわ

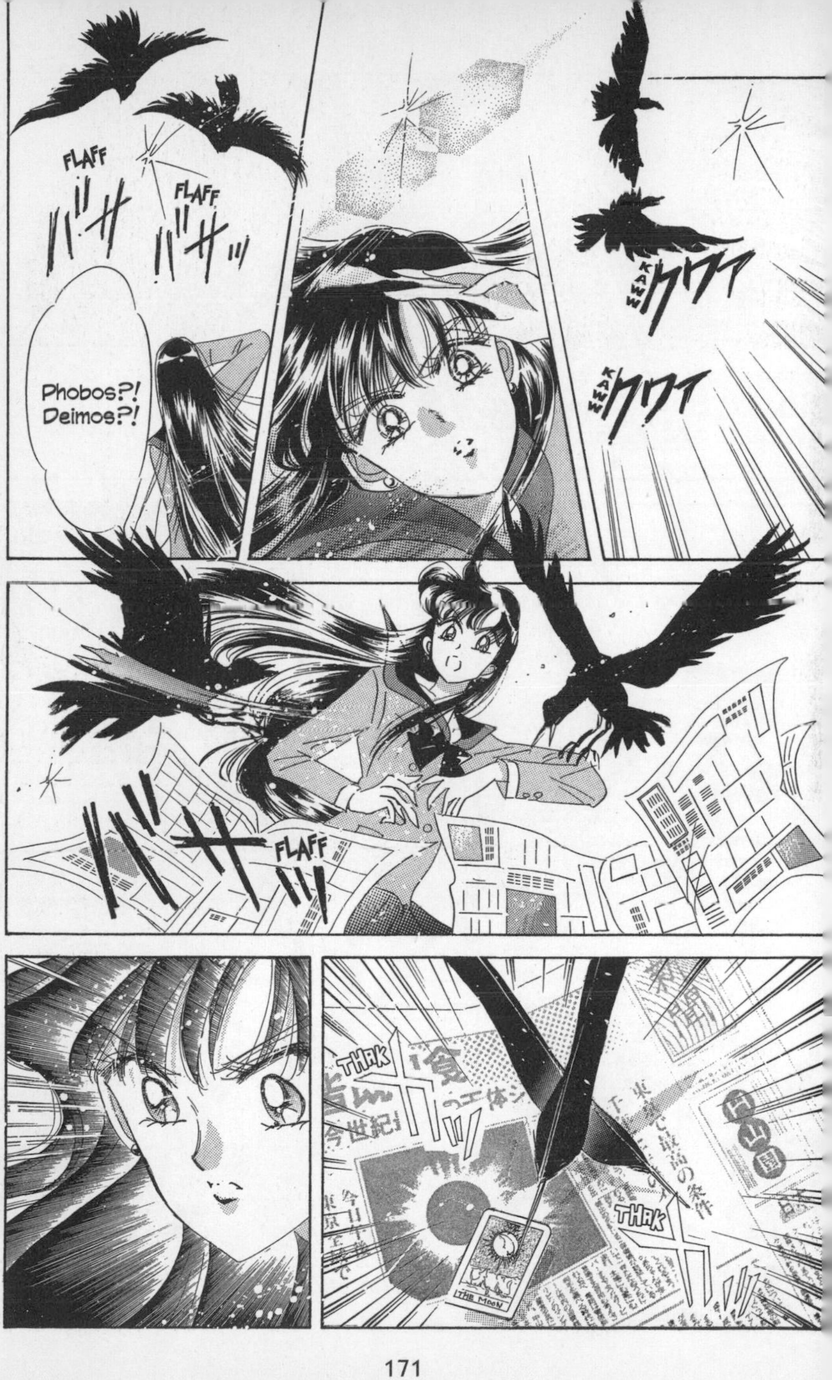
KAWW クワァ
KAWW クワァ
FLAFF
FLAFF
Phobos?! Deimos?!
FLAFF
THAK
THAK
THE MOON

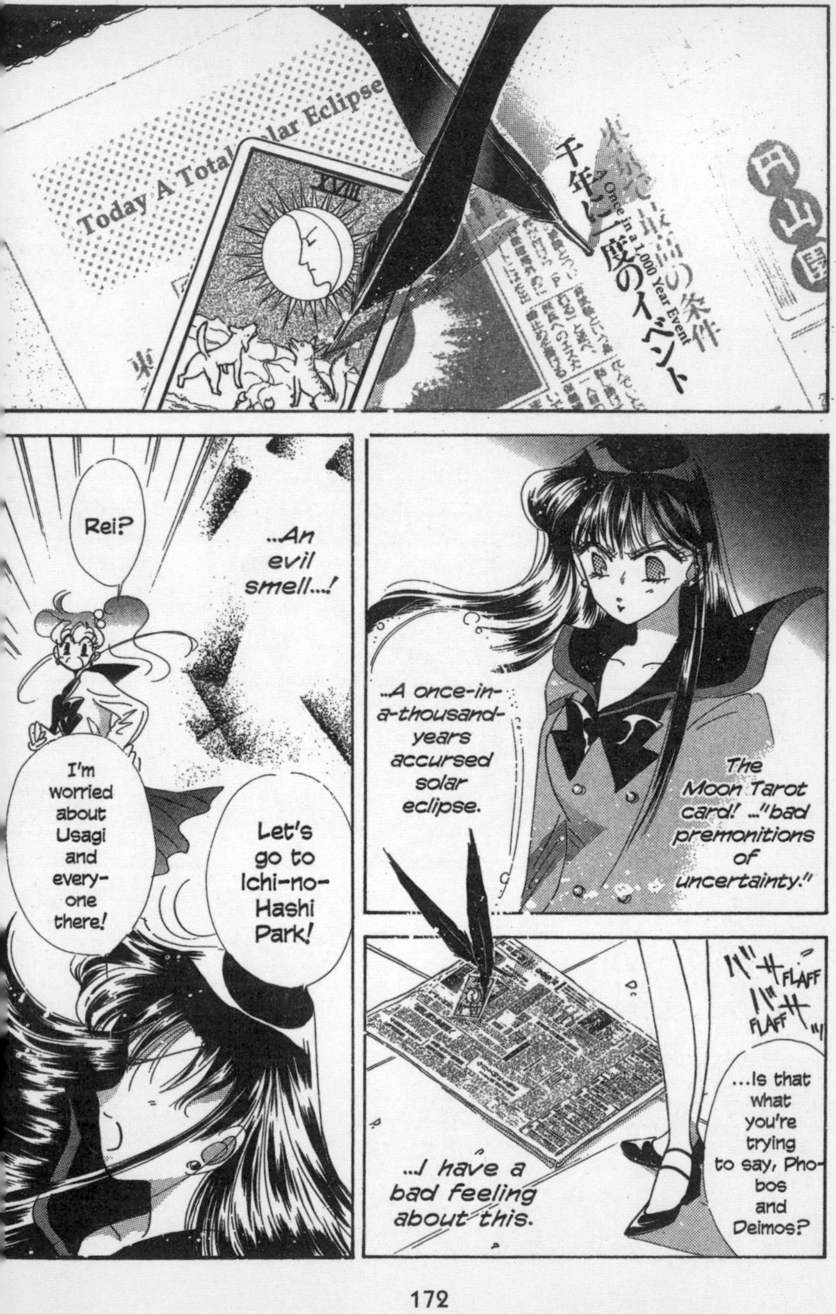
Today A Total
lar Eclipse
千年に一度のイベント
Once in a 1,000 Year Event
The Moon Tarot card! ..."bad premonitions of uncertainty."
...A once-in-a-thousand-years accursed solar eclipse.
FLAFF
FLAFF
...Is that what you're trying to say, Phobos and Deimos?
...I have a bad feeling about this.
...An evil smell...!
Rei?
Let's go to Ichi-no-Hashi Park!
I'm worried about Usagi and everyone there!

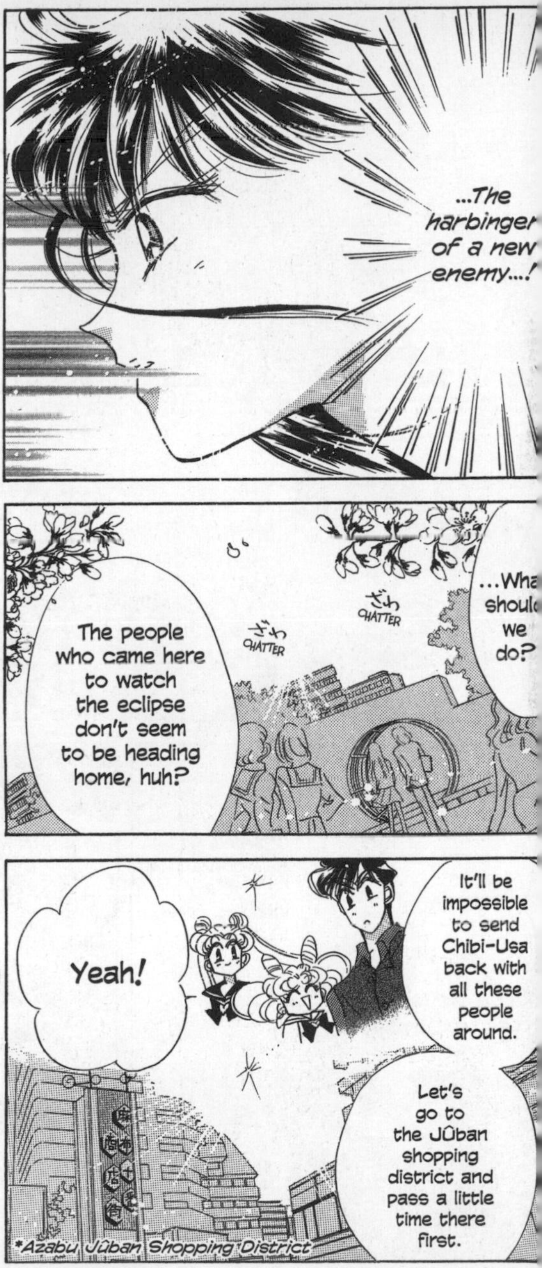
...The harbinger of a new enemy...!
...Wha shoul we do?
ざわ CHATTER
ざわ CHATTER
The people who came here to watch the eclipse don't seem to be heading home, huh?
It'll be impossible to send Chibi-Usa back with all these people around.
Let's go to the Jûban shopping district and pass a little time there first.
Yeah!
*Azabu Jûban Shopping District
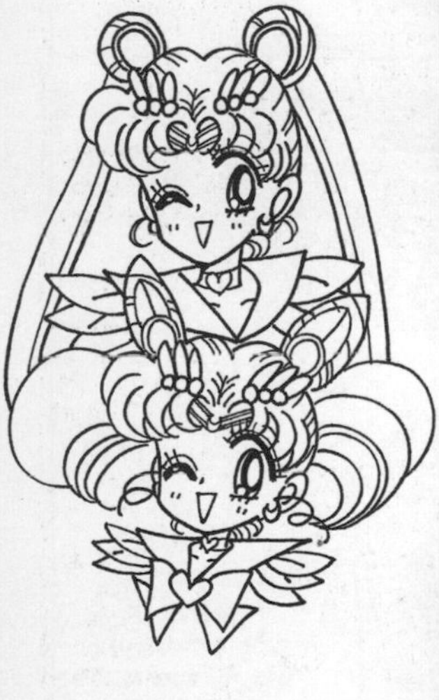

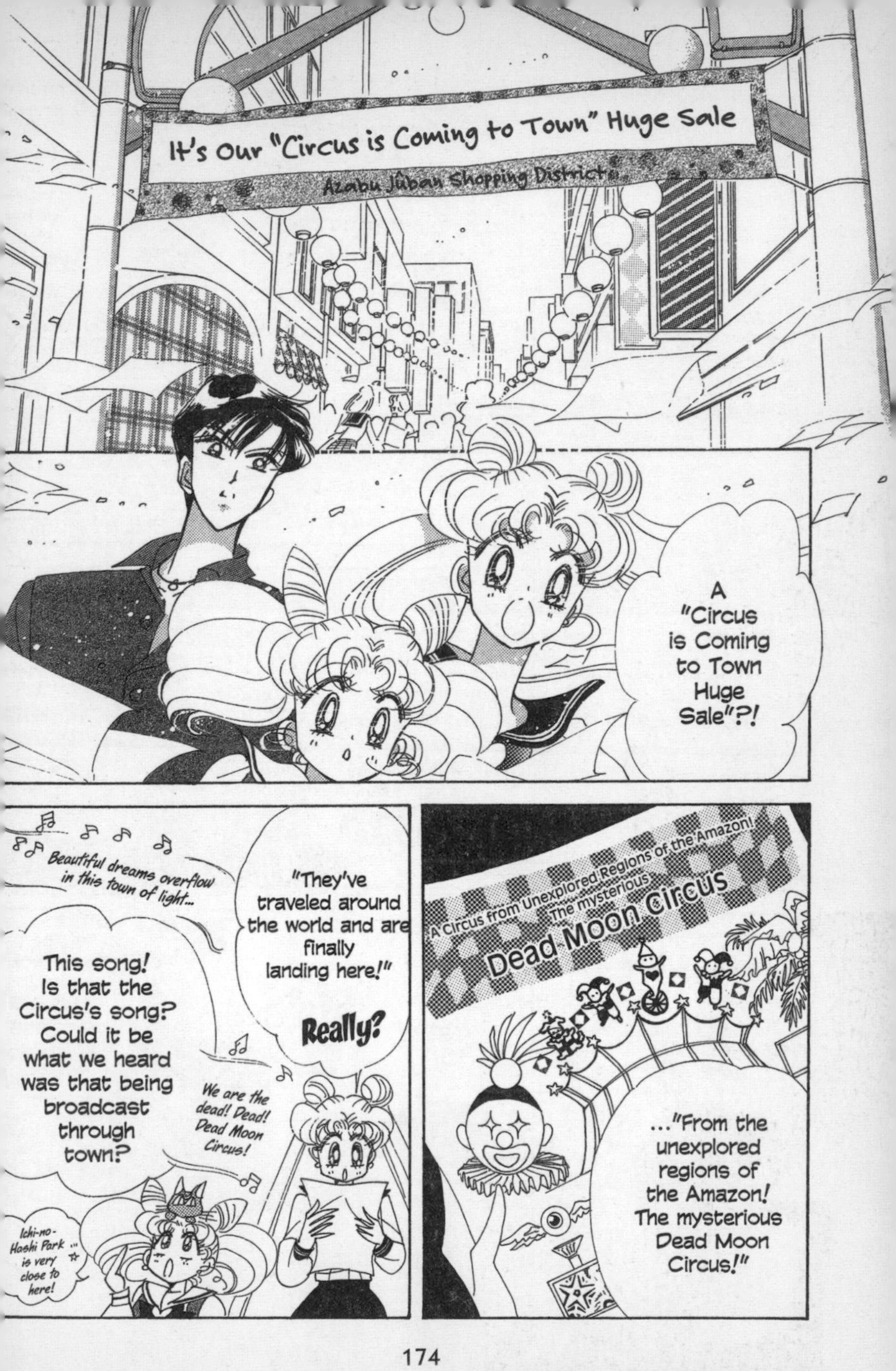
It's Our "Circus is Coming to Town" Huge Sale
Azabu Jûban Shopping District
A "Circus is Coming to Town Huge Sale"?!
A Circus from Unexplored Regions of the Amazon!
The mysterious
Dead Moon Circus
..."From the unexplored regions of the Amazon! The mysterious Dead Moon Circus!"
"They've traveled around the world and are finally landing here!"
Really?
Beautiful dreams overflow in this town of light...
This song! Is that the Circus's song? Could it be what we heard was that being broadcast through town?
We are the dead! Dead! Dead Moon Circus!
Ichi-no-Hashi Park ... is very close to here!

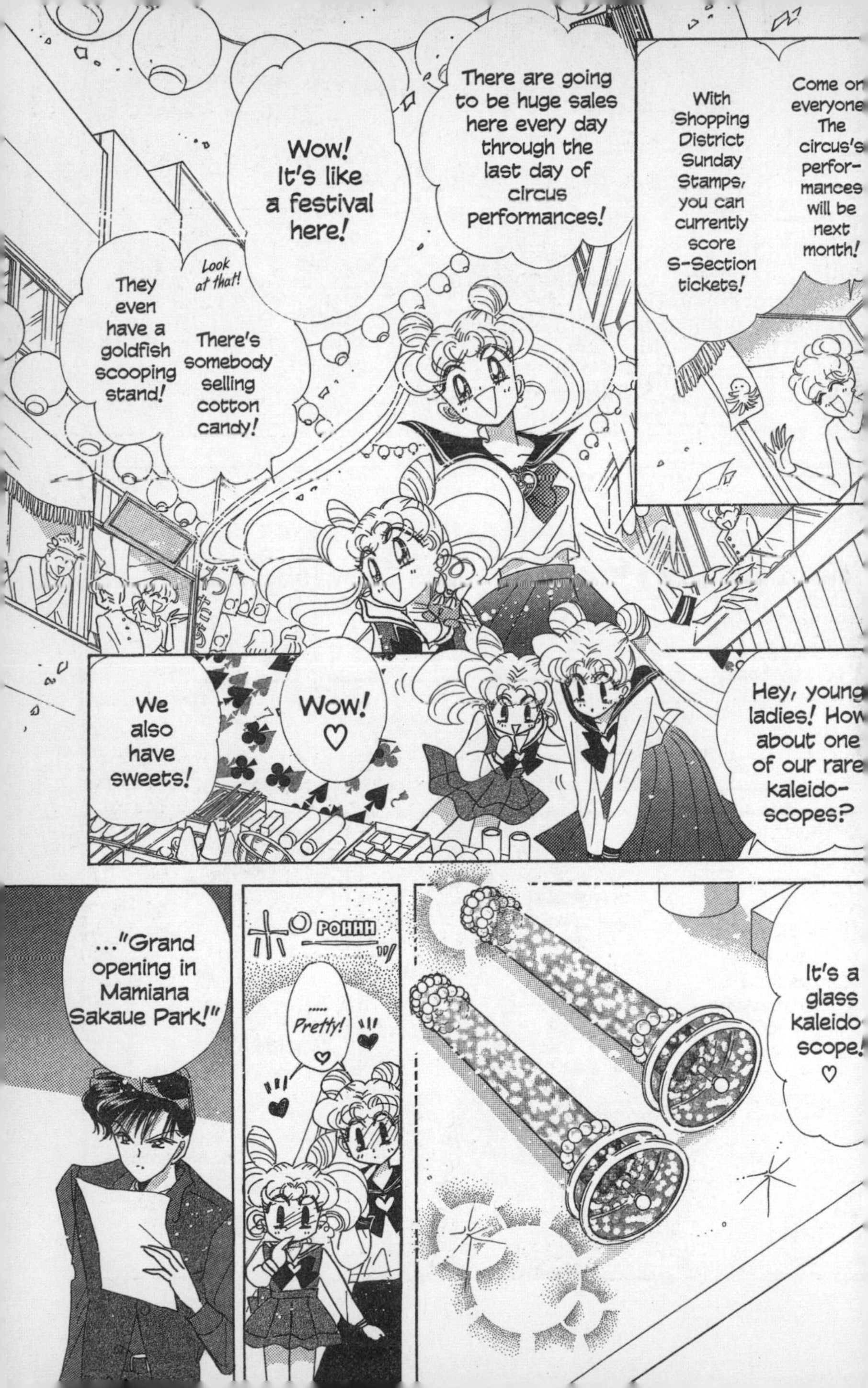

Come on everyone! The circus's performances will be next month!
With Shopping District Sunday Stamps, you can currently score S-Section tickets!
There are going to be huge sales here every day through the last day of circus performances!
Wow! It's like a festival here!
Look at that!
There's somebody selling cotton candy!
They even have a goldfish scooping stand!
Hey, young ladies! How about one of our rare kaleido-scopes?
Wow! ♡
We also have sweets!
It's a glass kaleido scope! ♡
POHHH
...... Pretty! ♡
..."Grand opening in Mamiana Sakaue Park!"

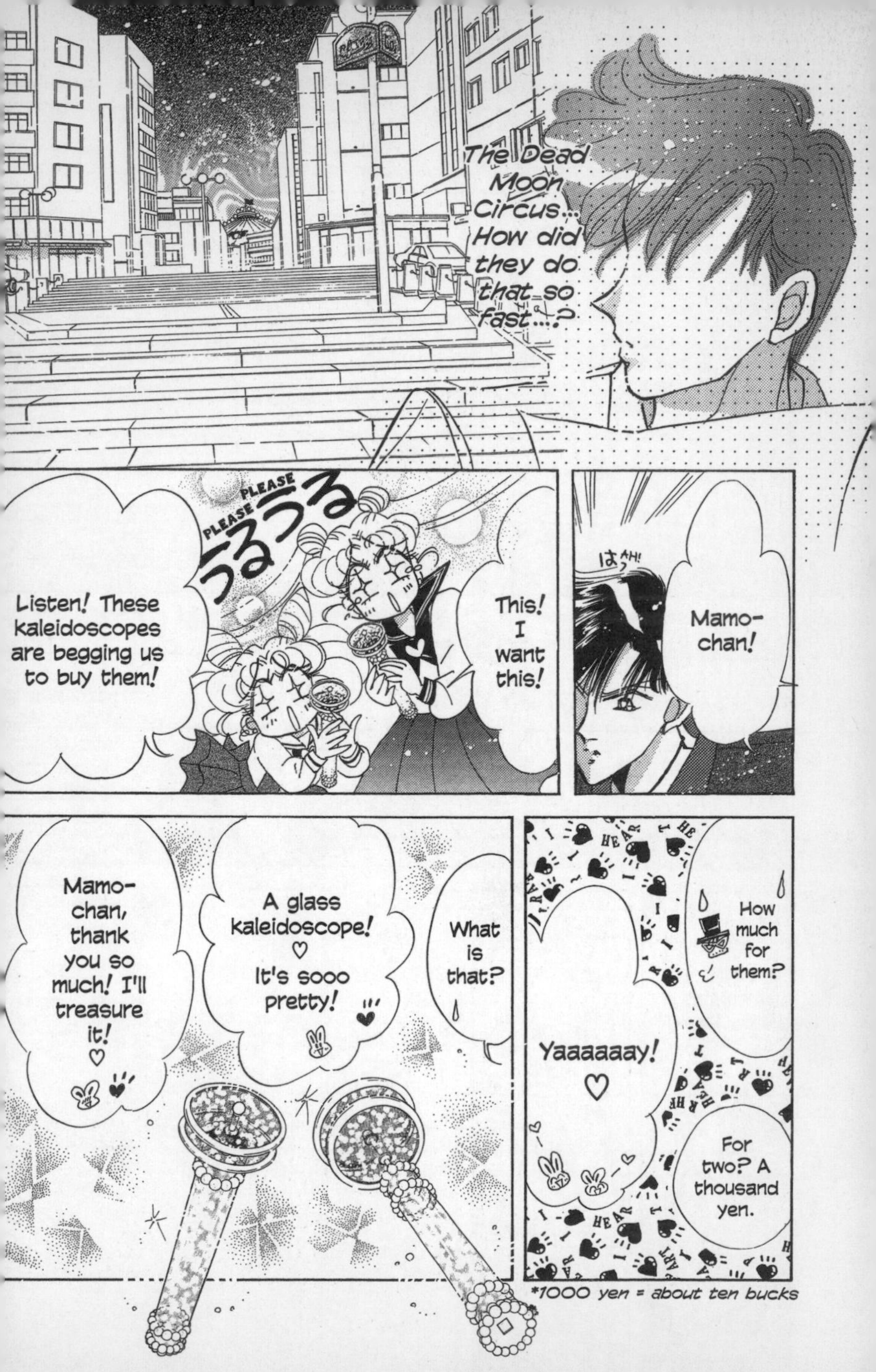
The Dead Moon Circus... How did they do that so fast...?
は AH!
Mamo-chan!
うるうる PLEASE PLEASE
This! I want this!
Listen! These kaleidoscopes are begging us to buy them!
How much for them?
For two? A thousand yen.
Yaaaaaay! ♡
What is that?
A glass kaleidoscope! ♡ It's sooo pretty!
Mamo-chan, thank you so much! I'll treasure it! ♡

*1000 yen = about ten bucks

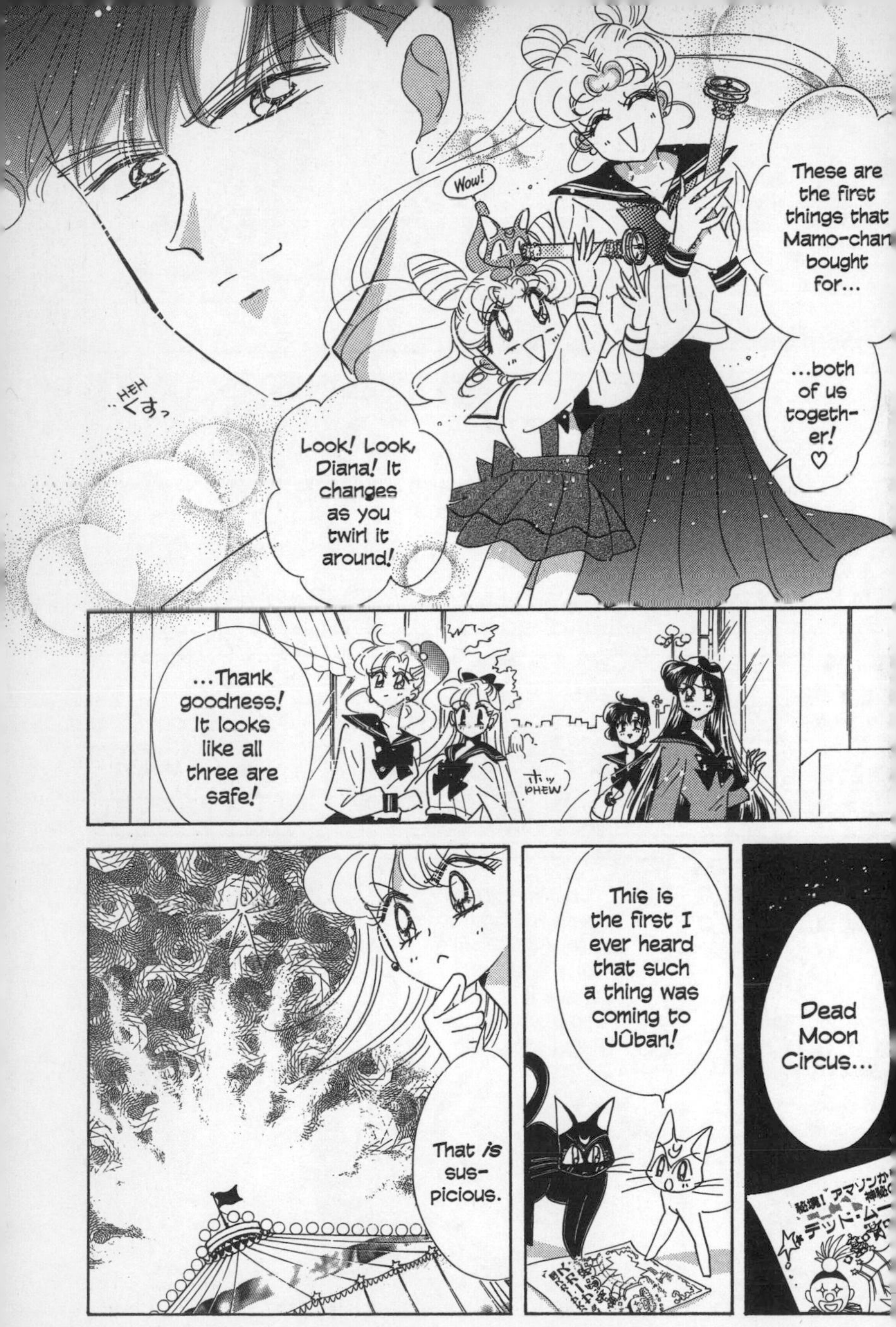
These are the first things that Mamo-chan bought for...
...both of us togeth-er! ♡
Wow!
Look! Look, Diana! It changes as you twirl it around!
HEH
くすっ
...Thank goodness! It looks like all three are safe!
ホッ
PHEW
Dead Moon Circus...
This is the first I ever heard that such a thing was coming to Jûban!
That *is* sus-picious.

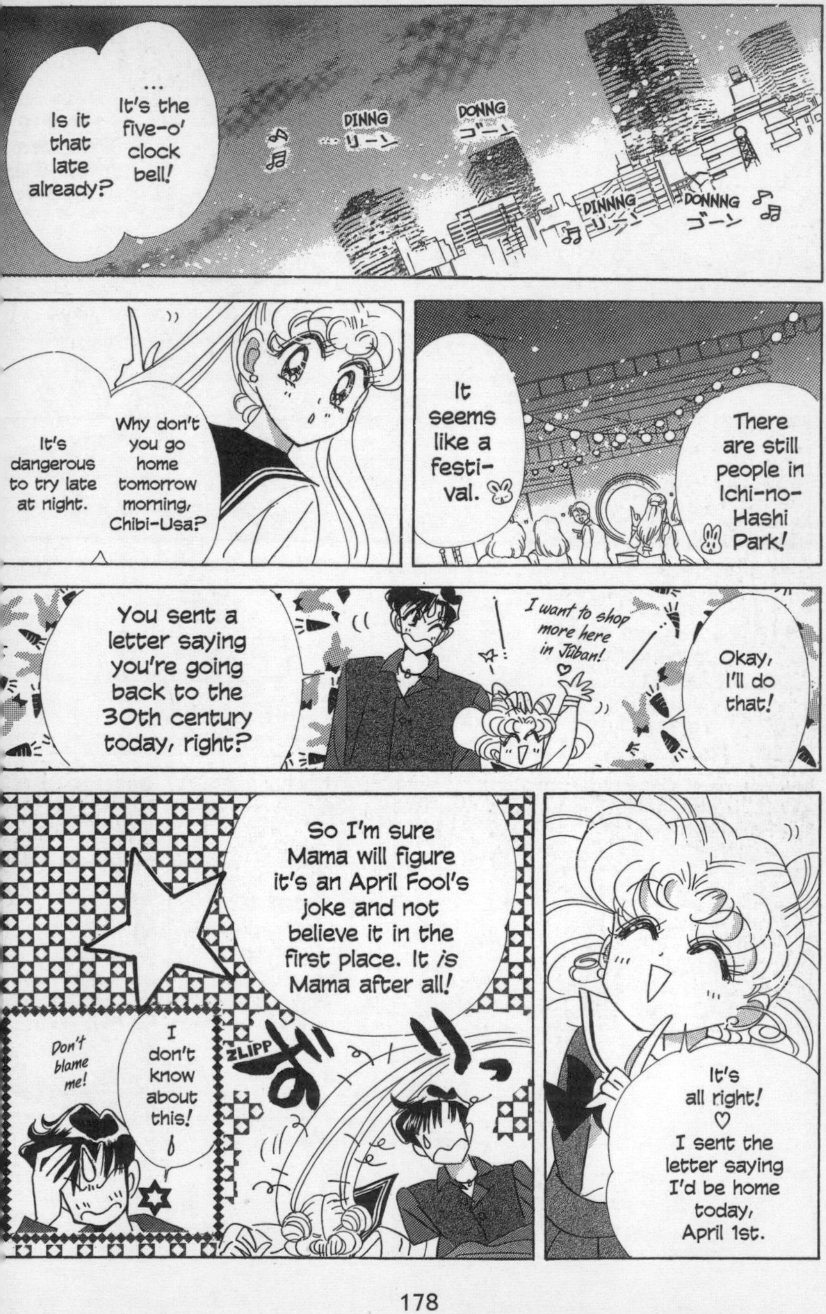
DONNG ゴーン
DINNG リーン
DONNNG ゴーン
DINNNG リーン
... It's the five-o' clock bell!
Is it that late already?
There are still people in Ichi-no-Hashi Park!
It seems like a festival.
Why don't you go home tomorrow morning, Chibi-Usa?
It's dangerous to try late at night.
Okay, I'll do that!
I want to shop more here in Jūban! ♡
You sent a letter saying you're going back to the 30th century today, right?
It's all right! ♡ I sent the letter saying I'd be home today, April 1st.
So I'm sure Mama will figure it's an April Fool's joke and not believe it in the first place. It *is* Mama after all!
ZLIPP
I don't know about this!
Don't blame me!

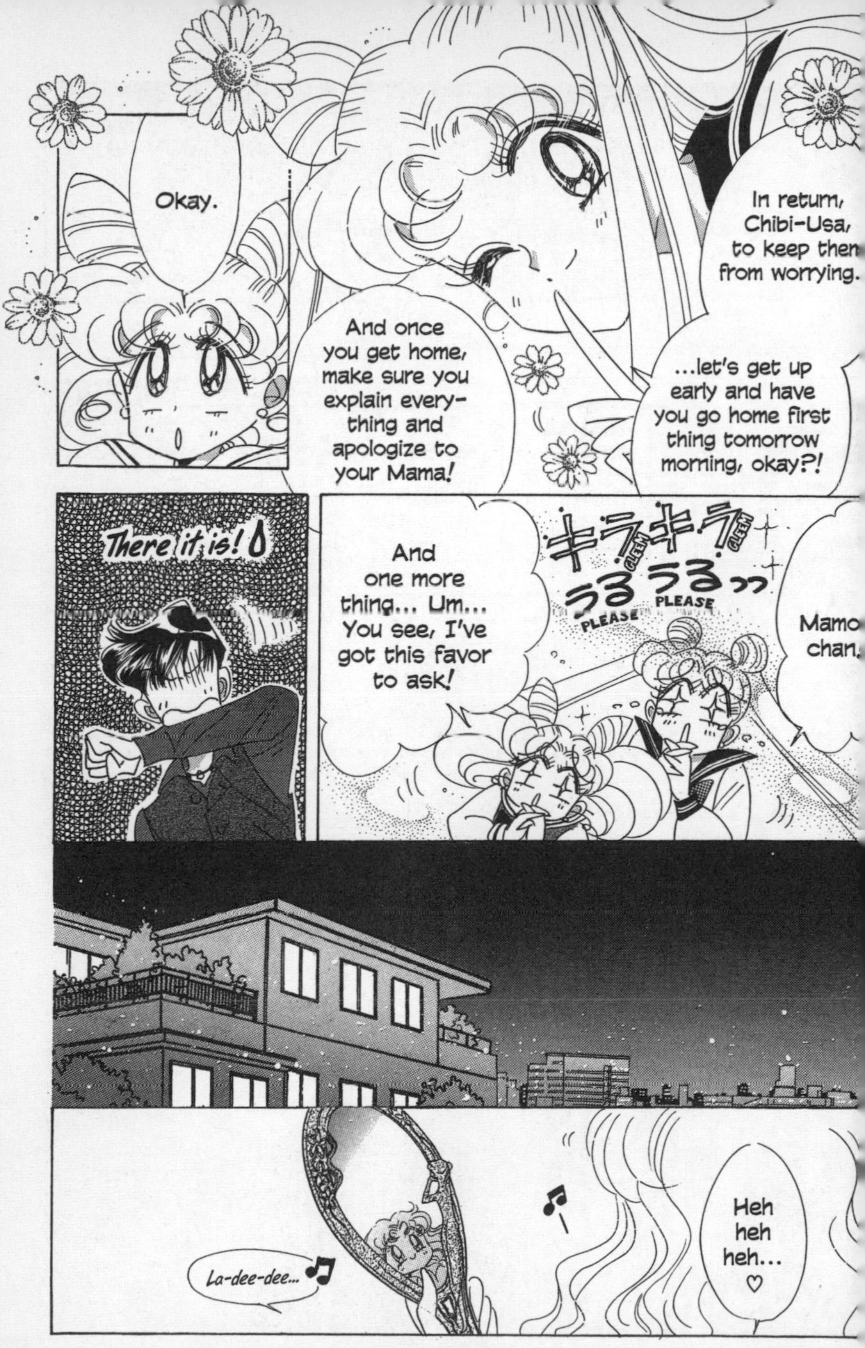

In return, Chibi-Usa, to keep them from worrying.
...let's get up early and have you go home first thing tomorrow morning, okay?!
And once you get home, make sure you explain everything and apologize to your Mama!
Okay.
Mamo chan,
キラキラ
GLEEM GLEEM
うるうる
PLEASE PLEASE
And one more thing... Um... You see, I've got this favor to ask!
There it is!
Heh heh heh... ♡
La-dee-dee...

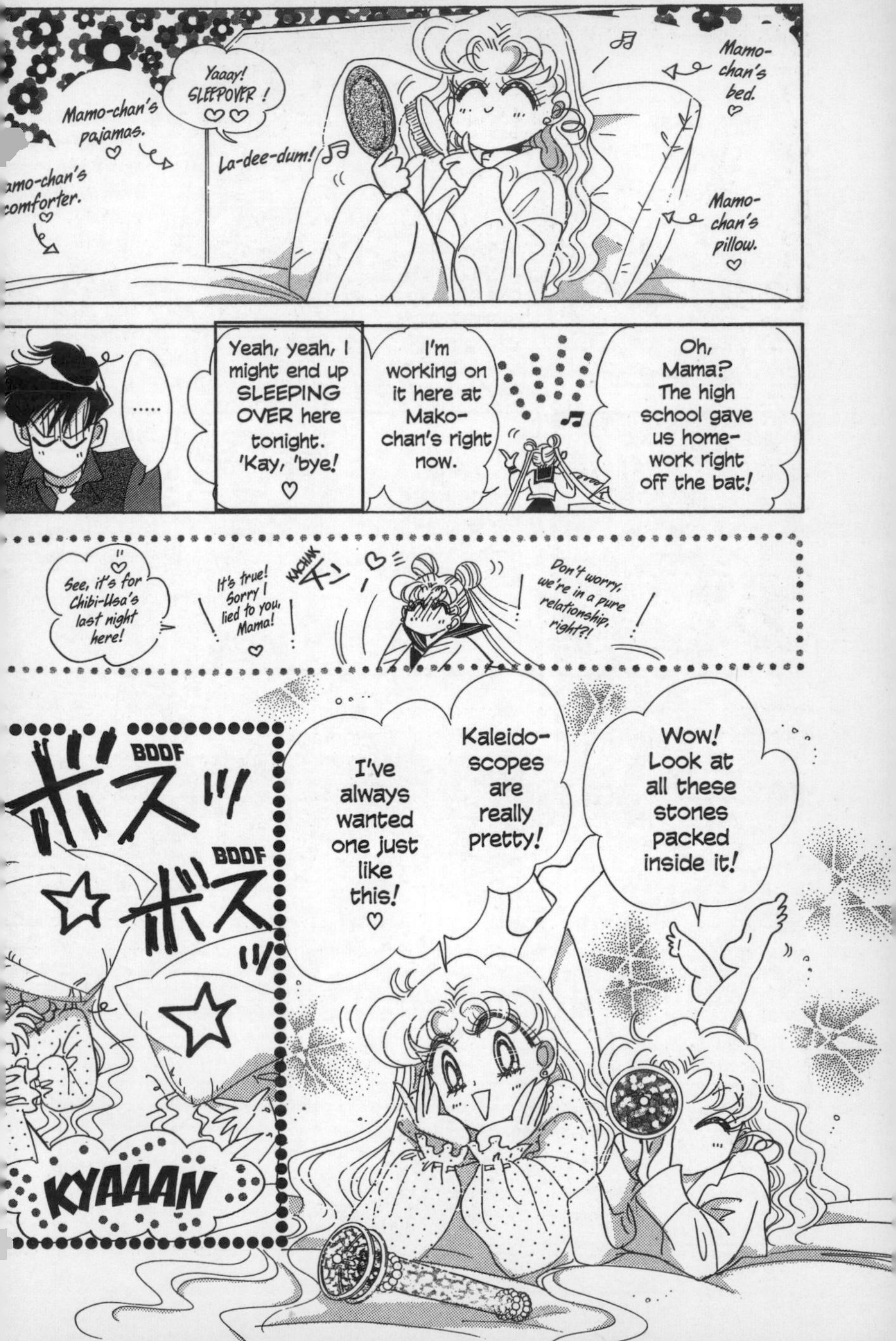
Mamo-chan's bed.
Mamo-chan's pillow.
Yaaay! SLEEPOVER!
La-dee-dum!
Mamo-chan's pajamas.
amo-chan's comforter.
Oh, Mama? The high school gave us home-work right off the bat!
I'm working on it here at Mako-chan's right now.
Yeah, yeah, I might end up SLEEPING OVER here tonight. 'Kay, 'bye!
.....
Don't worry, we're in a pure relationship, right?!
KACHAK
It's true! Sorry I lied to you, Mama!
See, it's for Chibi-Usa's last night here!
Wow! Look at all these stones packed inside it!
Kaleido-scopes are really pretty!
I've always wanted one just like this!
BOOF
BOOF
KYAAAN

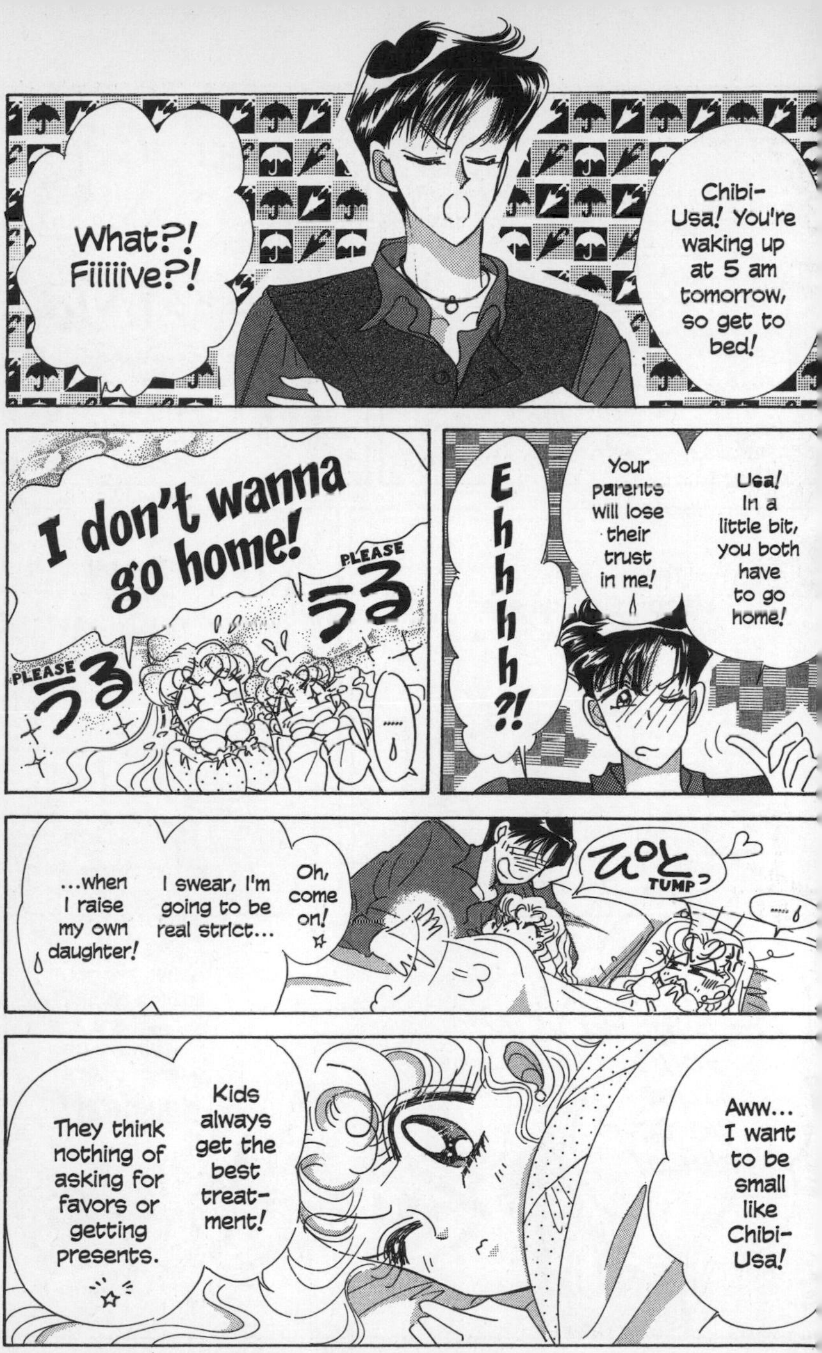
Chibi-Usa! You're waking up at 5 am tomorrow, so get to bed!
What?! Fiiiiive?!
Usa! In a little bit, you both have to go home!
Your parents will lose their trust in me!
Ehhhh?!
I don't wanna go home!
PLEASE うる
PLEASE うる
......
ぴと TUMP
......
Oh, come on! ☆
I swear, I'm going to be real strict...
...when I raise my own daughter!
Aww... I want to be small like Chibi-Usa!
Kids always get the best treatment!
They think nothing of asking for favors or getting presents.

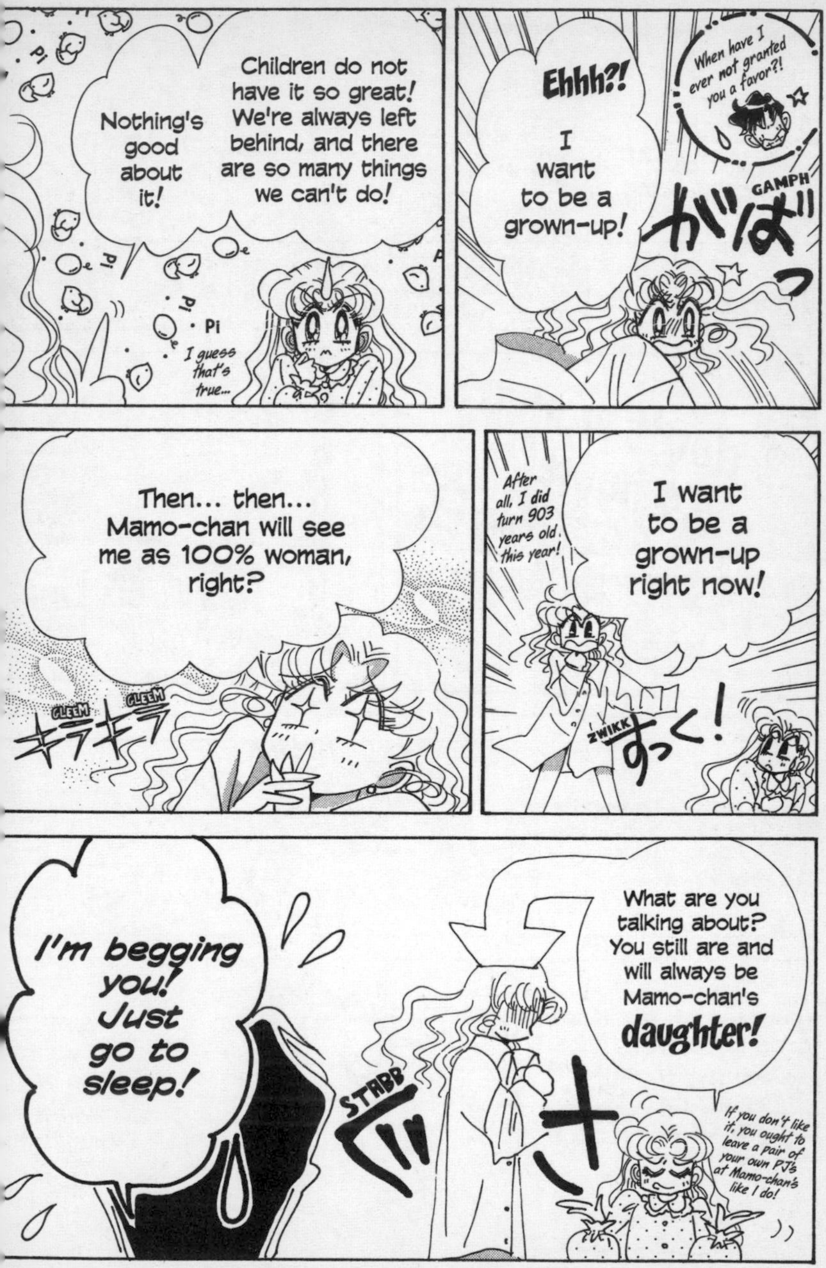
Ehhh?!
I want to be a grown-up!
When have I ever not granted you a favor?!
GAMPH
Children do not have it so great! We're always left behind, and there are so many things we can't do!
Nothing's good about it!
Pi
Pi
Pi
I guess that's true...
After all, I did turn 903 years old this year!
I want to be a grown-up right now!
ZWIKK
Then... then... Mamo-chan will see me as 100% woman, right?
GLEEM GLEEM
What are you talking about? You still are and will always be Mamo-chan's **daughter!**
If you don't like it, you ought to leave a pair of your own PJ's at Mamo-chan's like I do!
STABB
I'm begging you! Just go to sleep!

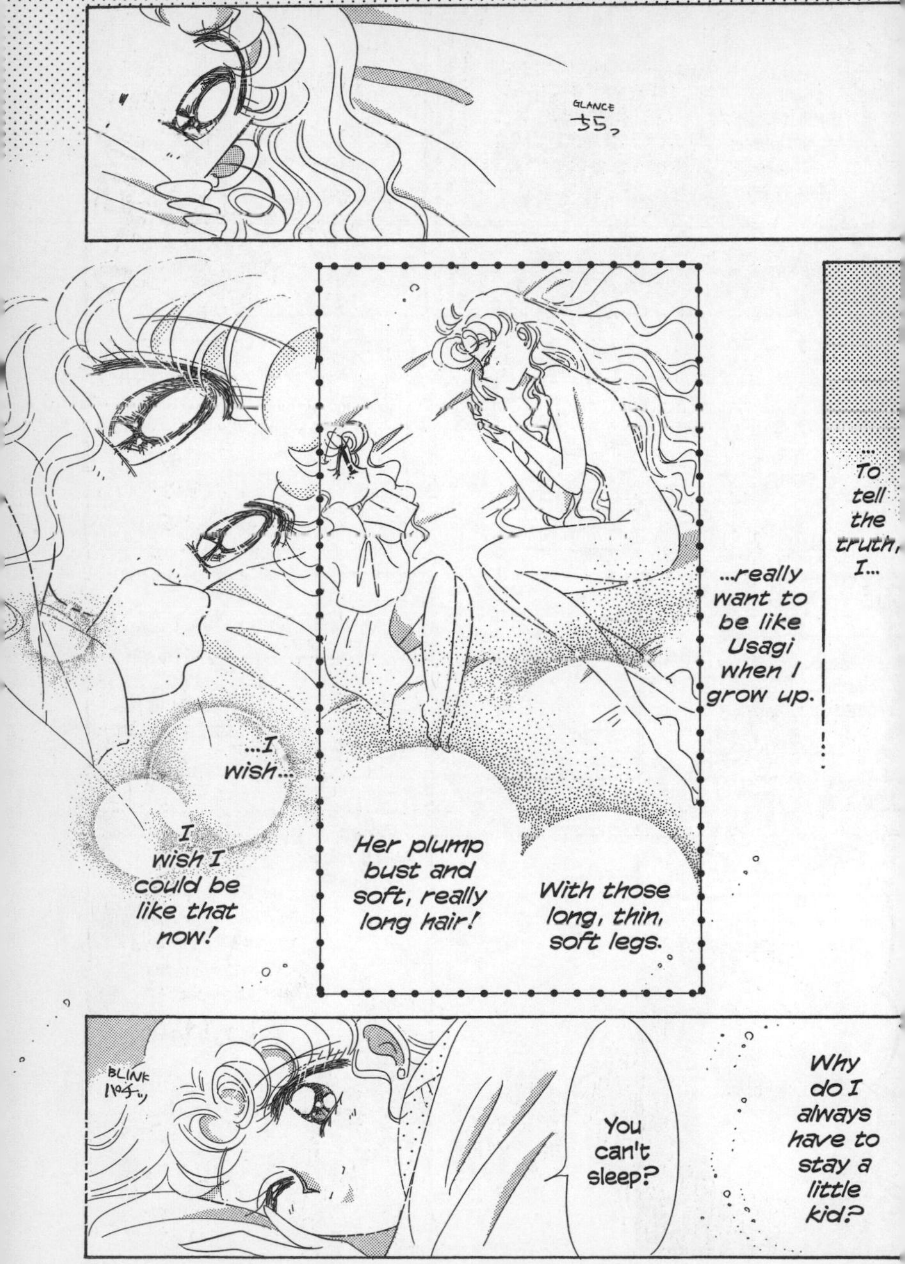
GLANCE
ちらっ
... To tell the truth, I...
...really want to be like Usagi when I grow up.
With those long, thin, soft legs.
Her plump bust and soft, really long hair!
...I wish...
I wish I could be like that now!
Why do I always have to stay a little kid?
You can't sleep?
BLINK
パチッ

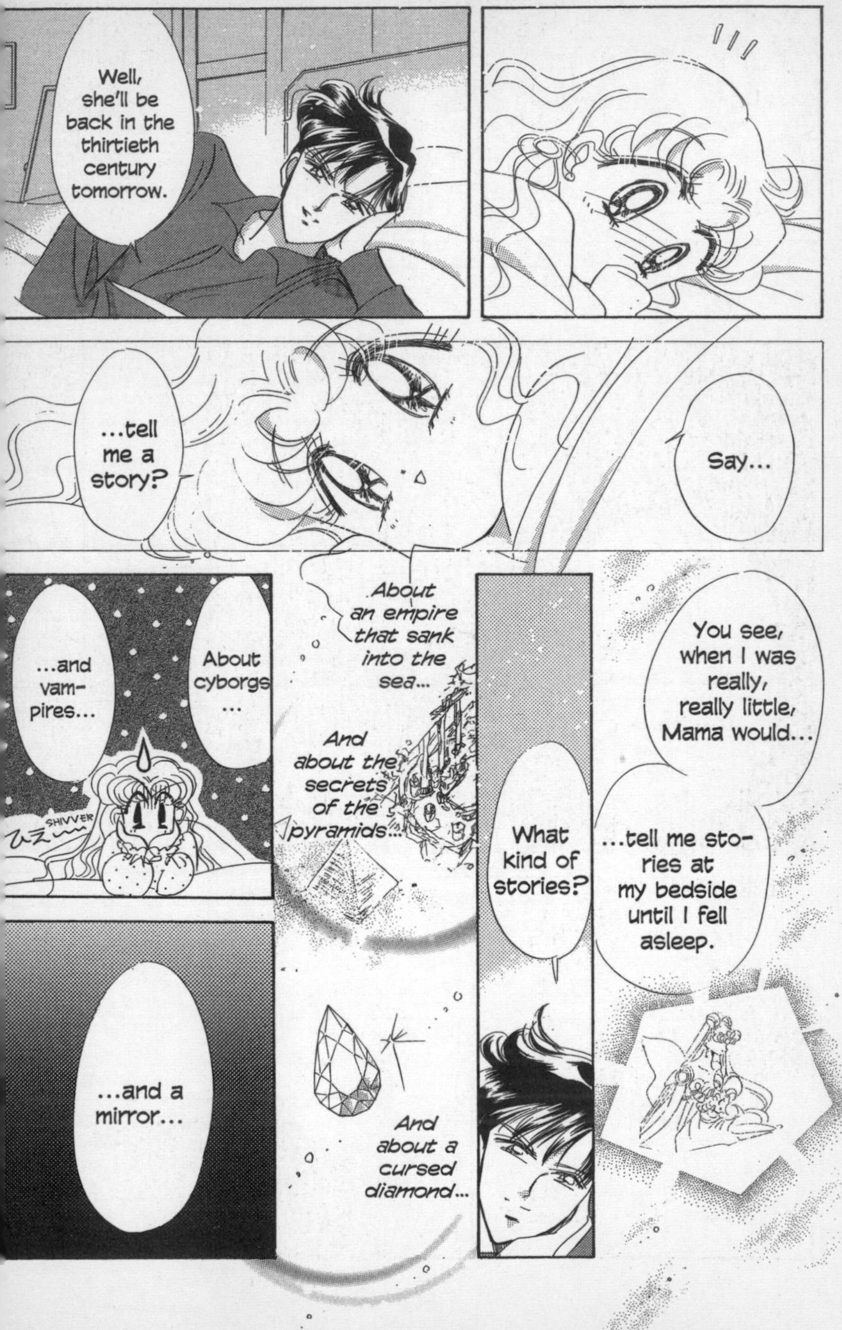
Well, she'll be back in the thirtieth century tomorrow.
Say...
...tell me a story?
You see, when I was really, really little, Mama would...
...tell me sto-ries at my bedside until I fell asleep.
What kind of stories?
About an empire that sank into the sea...
About cyborgs...
...and vam-pires...
SHIVVER
And about the secrets of the pyramids...
And about a cursed diamond...
...and a mirror...

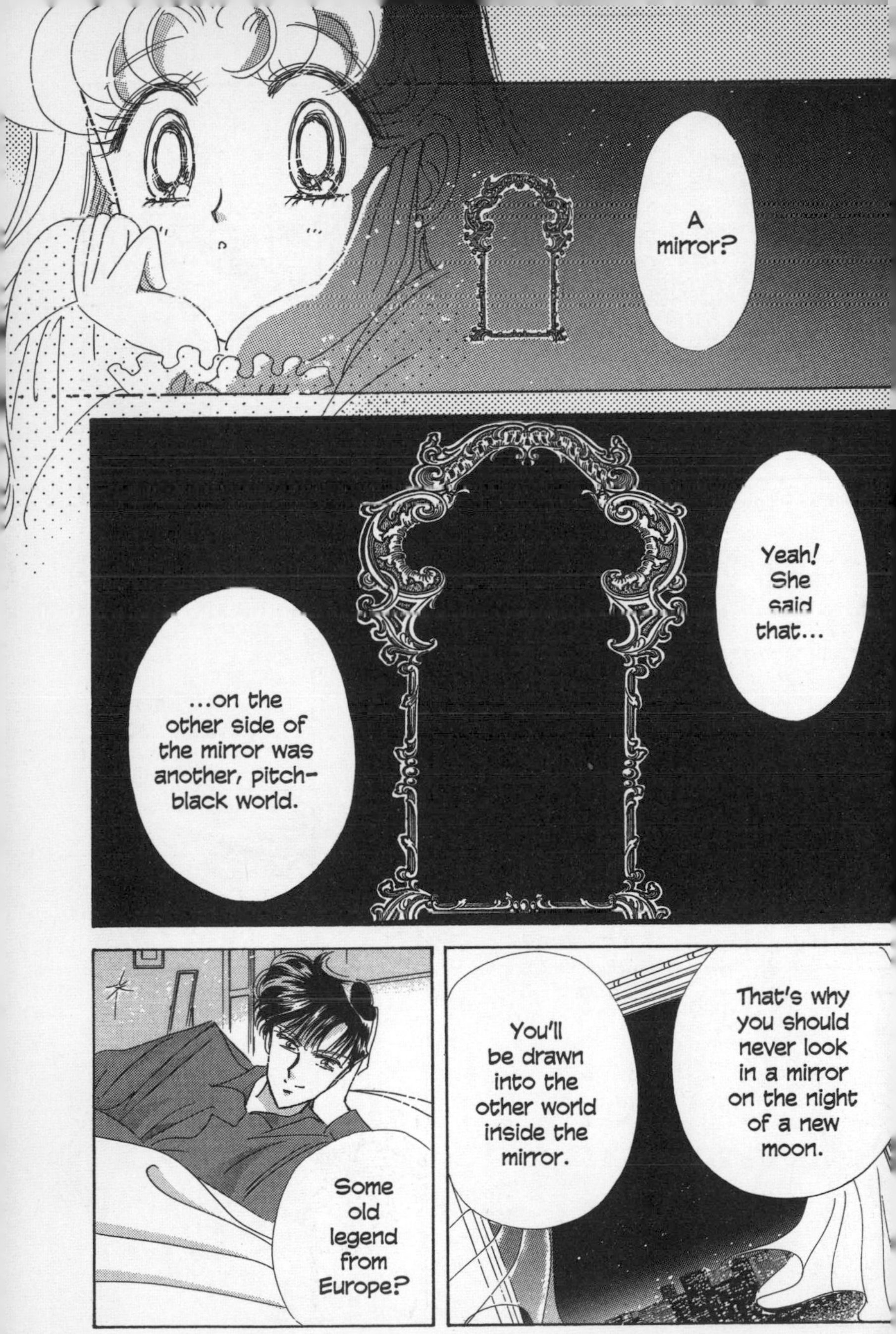
A mirror?
Yeah! She said that...
...on the other side of the mirror was another, pitch-black world.
That's why you should never look in a mirror on the night of a new moon.
You'll be drawn into the other world inside the mirror.
Some old legend from Europe?

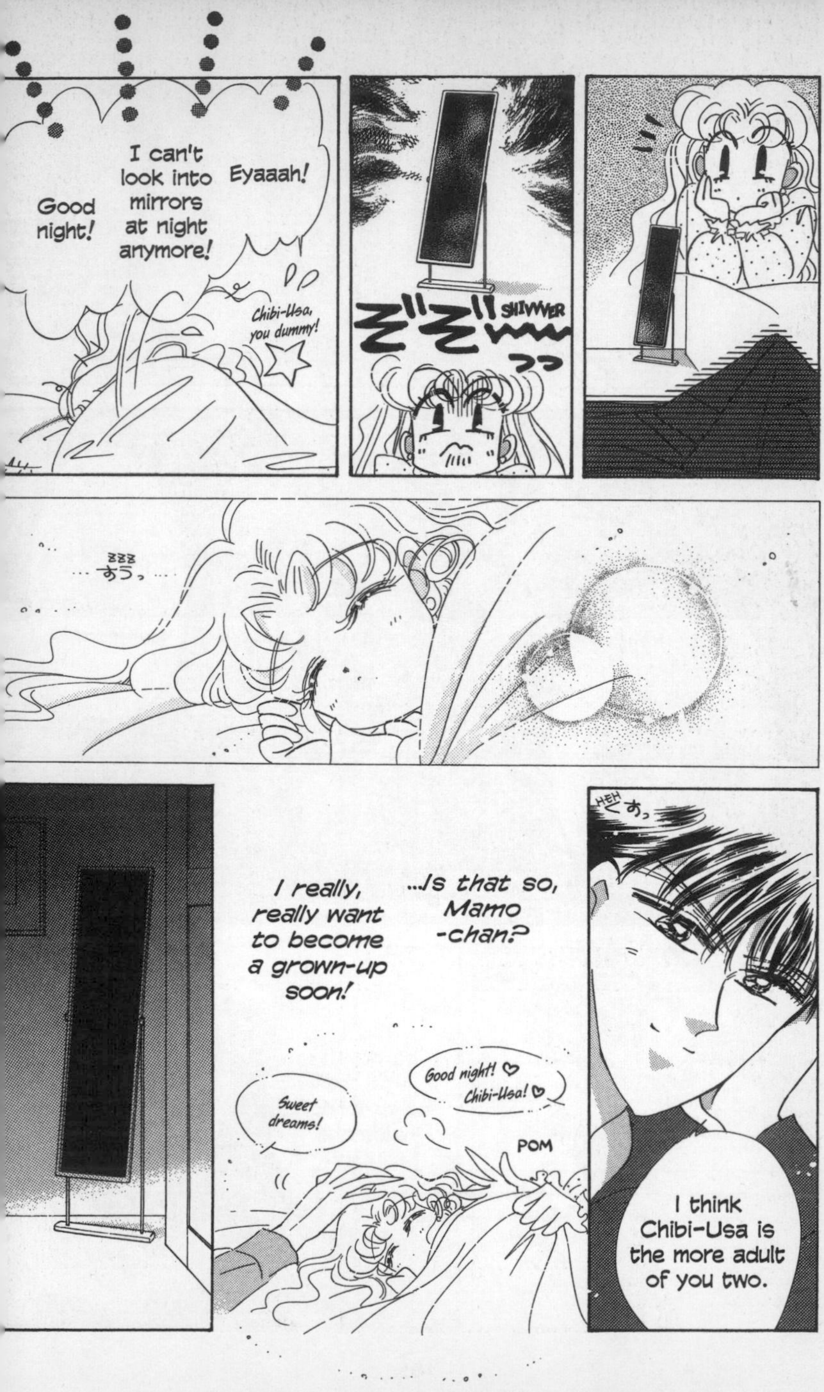
ぞぞ SHIVVVER
Eyaaah!
I can't look into mirrors at night anymore!
Good night!
Chibi-Usa, you dummy!
zzz すうっ
HEH くすっ
I think Chibi-Usa is the more adult of you two.
...Is that so, Mamo-chan?
I really, really want to become a grown-up soon!
Good night! ♡ Chibi-Usa! ♡
POM
Sweet dreams!

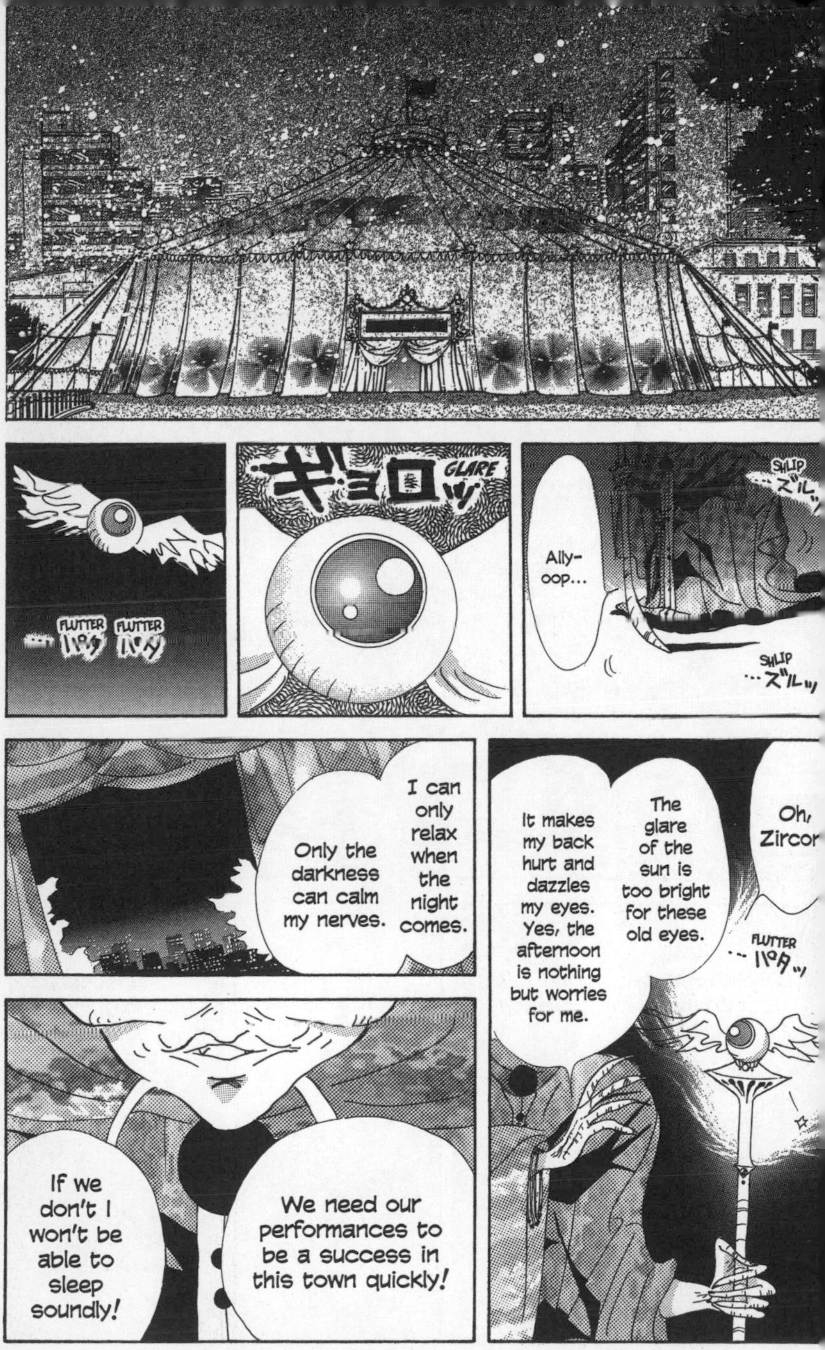
SHLIP
ズルッ
Ally-oop...
SHLIP
ズルッ
GLARE
ギョロッ
FLUTTER
FLUTTER
Oh, Zircor
The glare of the sun is too bright for these old eyes.
It makes my back hurt and dazzles my eyes. Yes, the afternoon is nothing but worries for me.
FLUTTER
パタッ
I can only relax when the night comes.
Only the darkness can calm my nerves.
We need our performances to be a success in this town quickly!
If we don't I won't be able to sleep soundly!

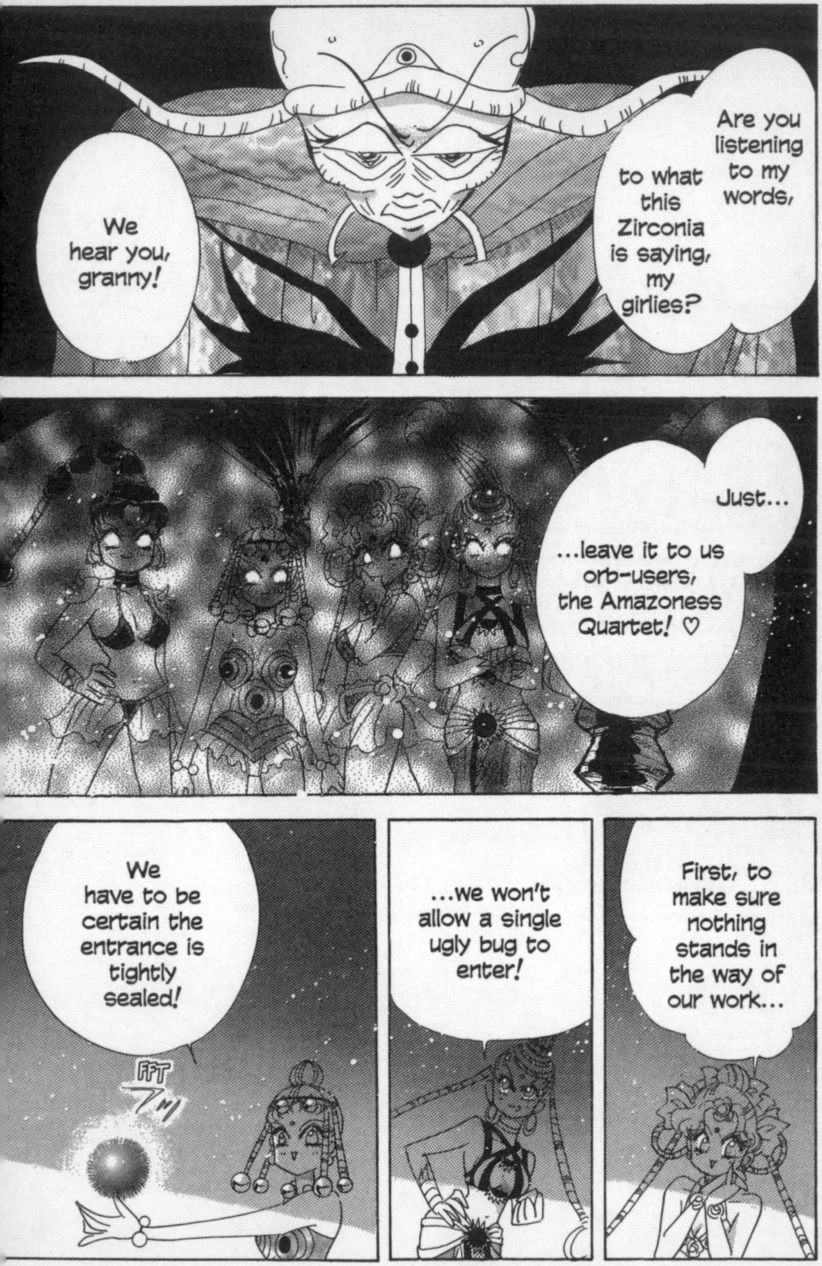
Are you listening to my words,
to what this Zirconia is saying, my girlies?
We hear you, granny!
Just...
...leave it to us orb-users, the Amazoness Quartet! ♡
First, to make sure nothing stands in the way of our work...
...we won't allow a single ugly bug to enter!
We have to be certain the entrance is tightly sealed!
FFT

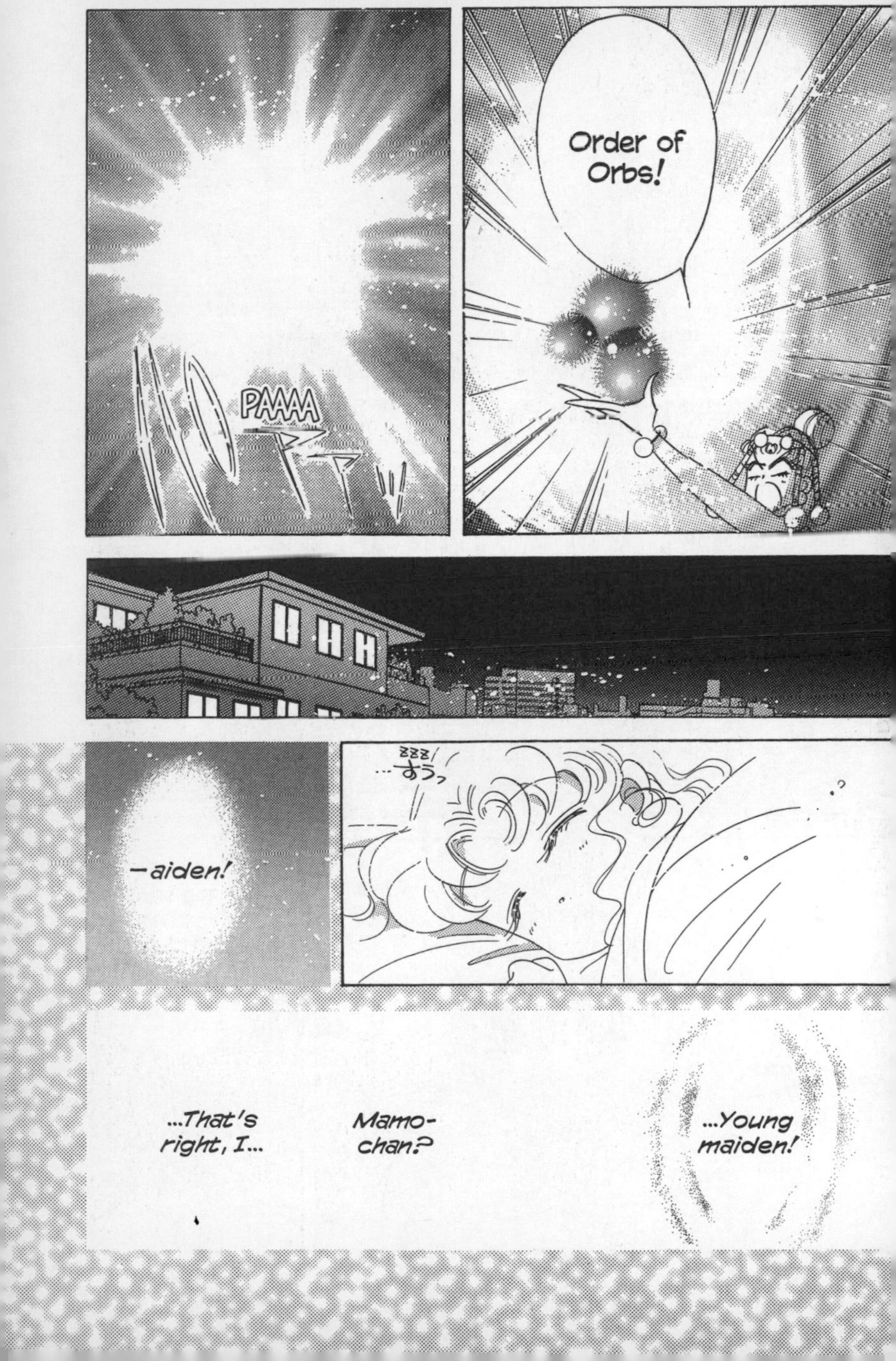
Order of Orbs!
PAAAA
zzz
...すうっ
—aiden!
...Young maiden!
Mamo-chan?
...That's right, I...

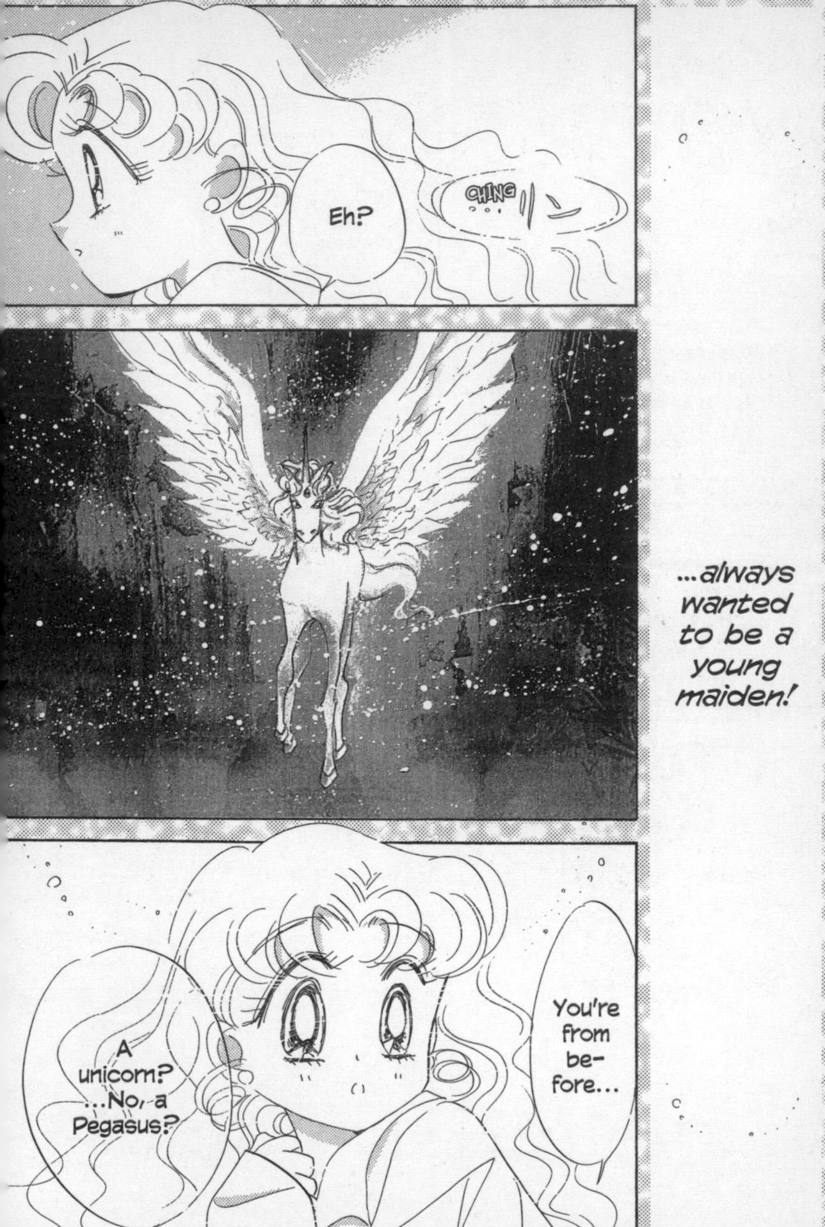
...always wanted to be a young maiden!
Eh?
CHING
You're from be- fore...
A unicorn? ...No, a Pegasus?

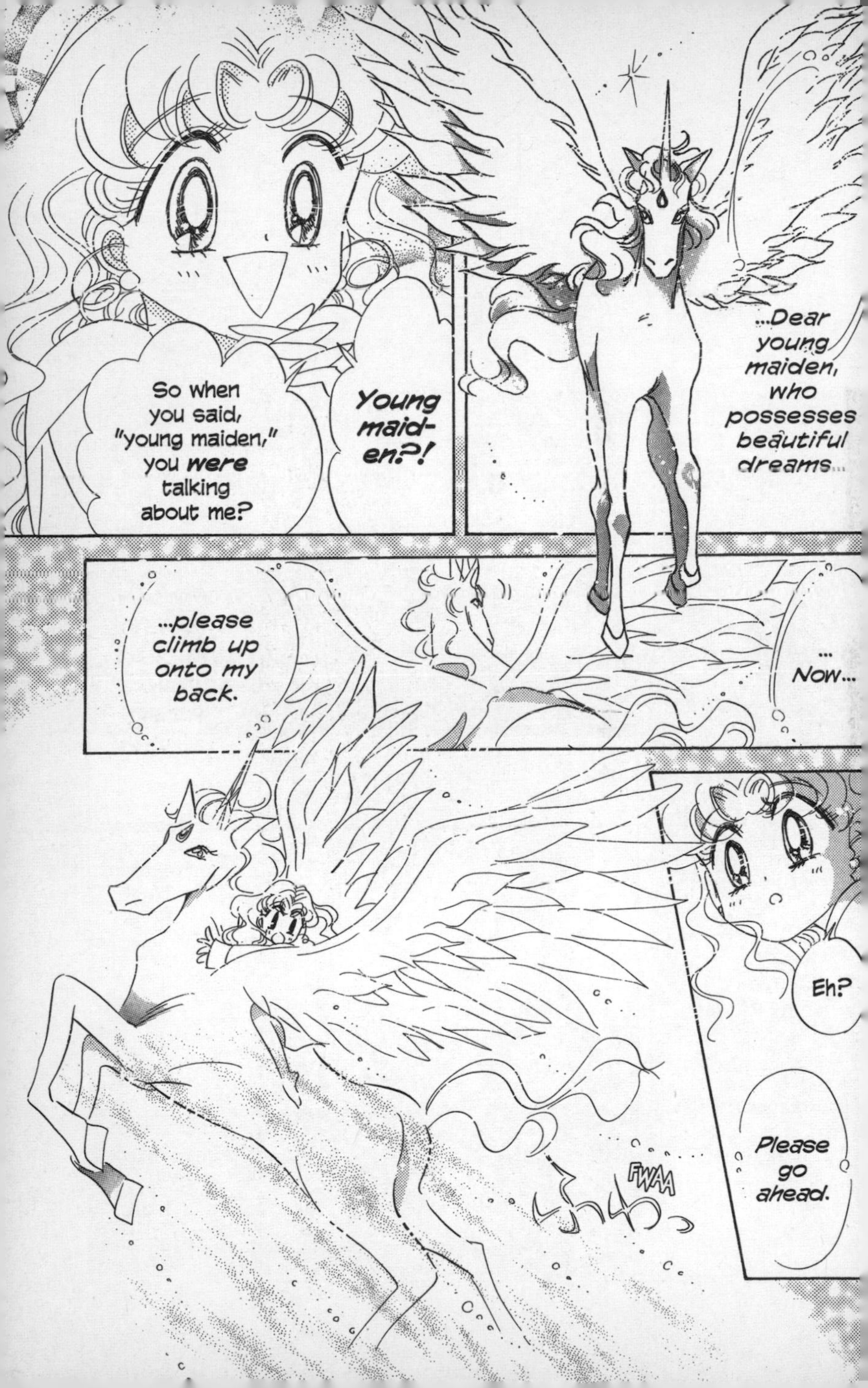
...Dear young maiden, who possesses beautiful dreams...
Young maid-en?!
So when you said, "young maiden," you *were* talking about me?
... Now...
...please climb up onto my back.
Eh?
Please go ahead.
FWAA

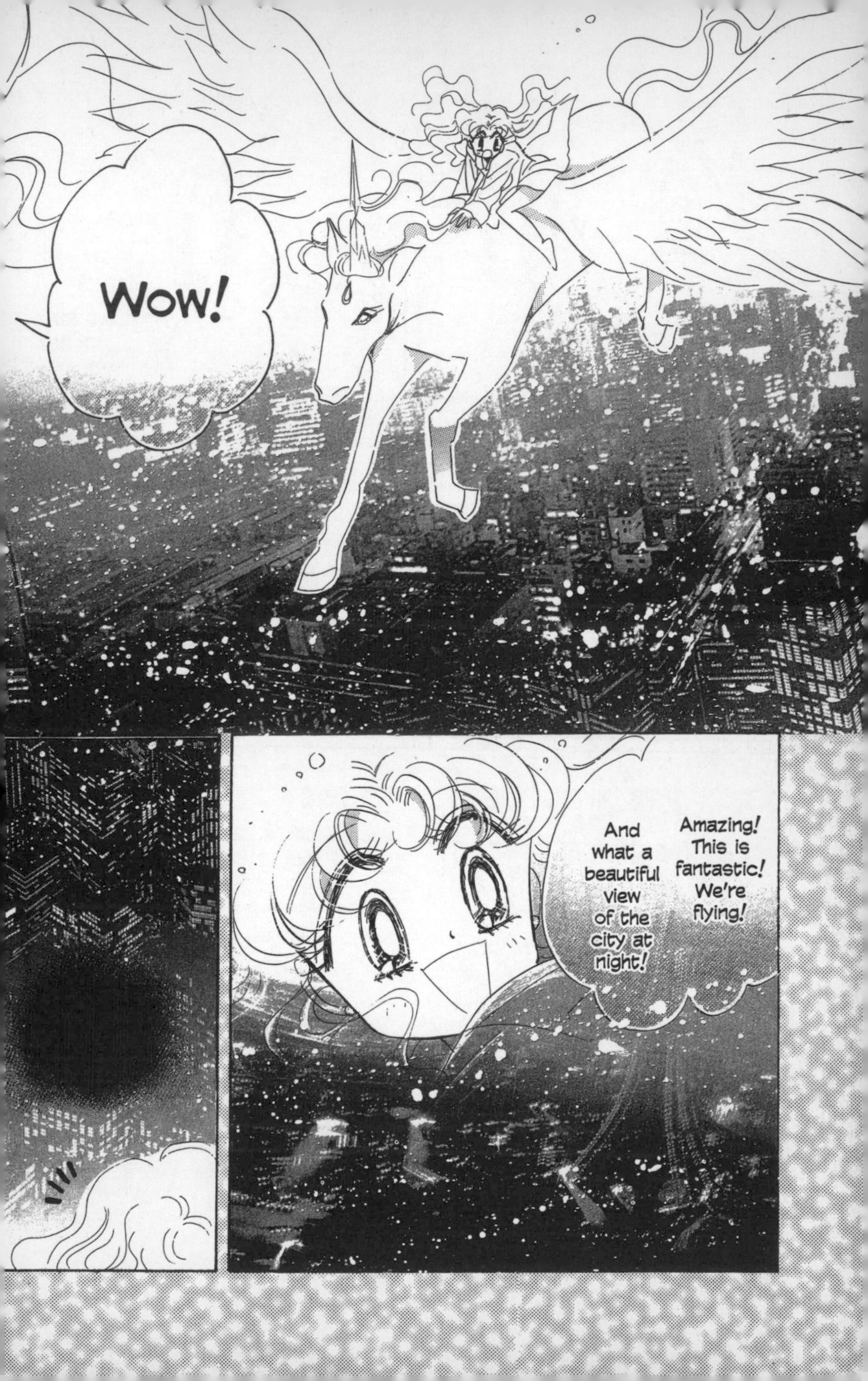
Wow!
Amazing! This is fantastic! We're flying!
And what a beautiful view of the city at night!

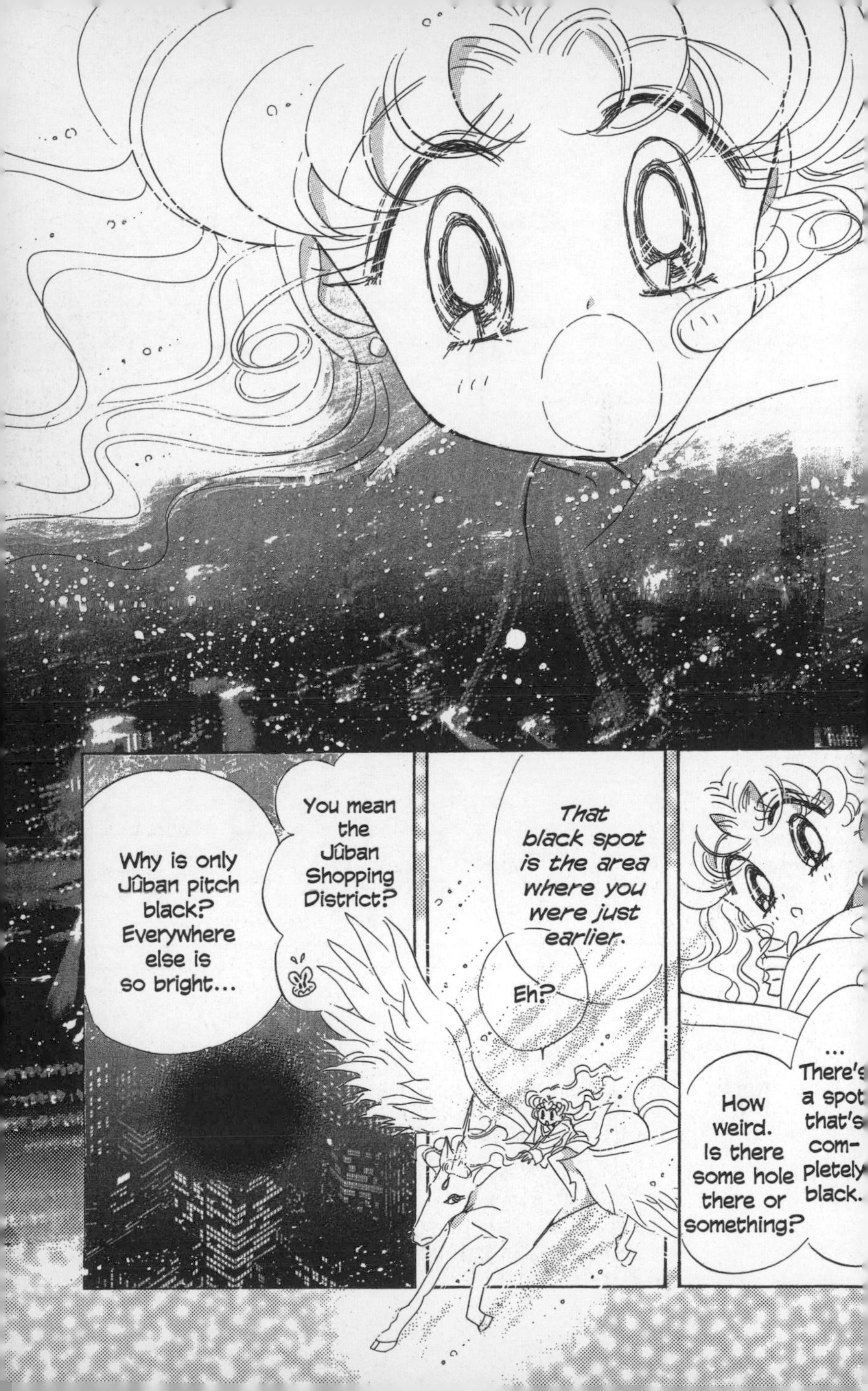

... There's a spot that's completely black.
How weird. Is there some hole there or something?
That black spot is the area where you were just earlier.
Eh?
You mean the Jûban Shopping District?
Why is only Jûban pitch black? Everywhere else is so bright...

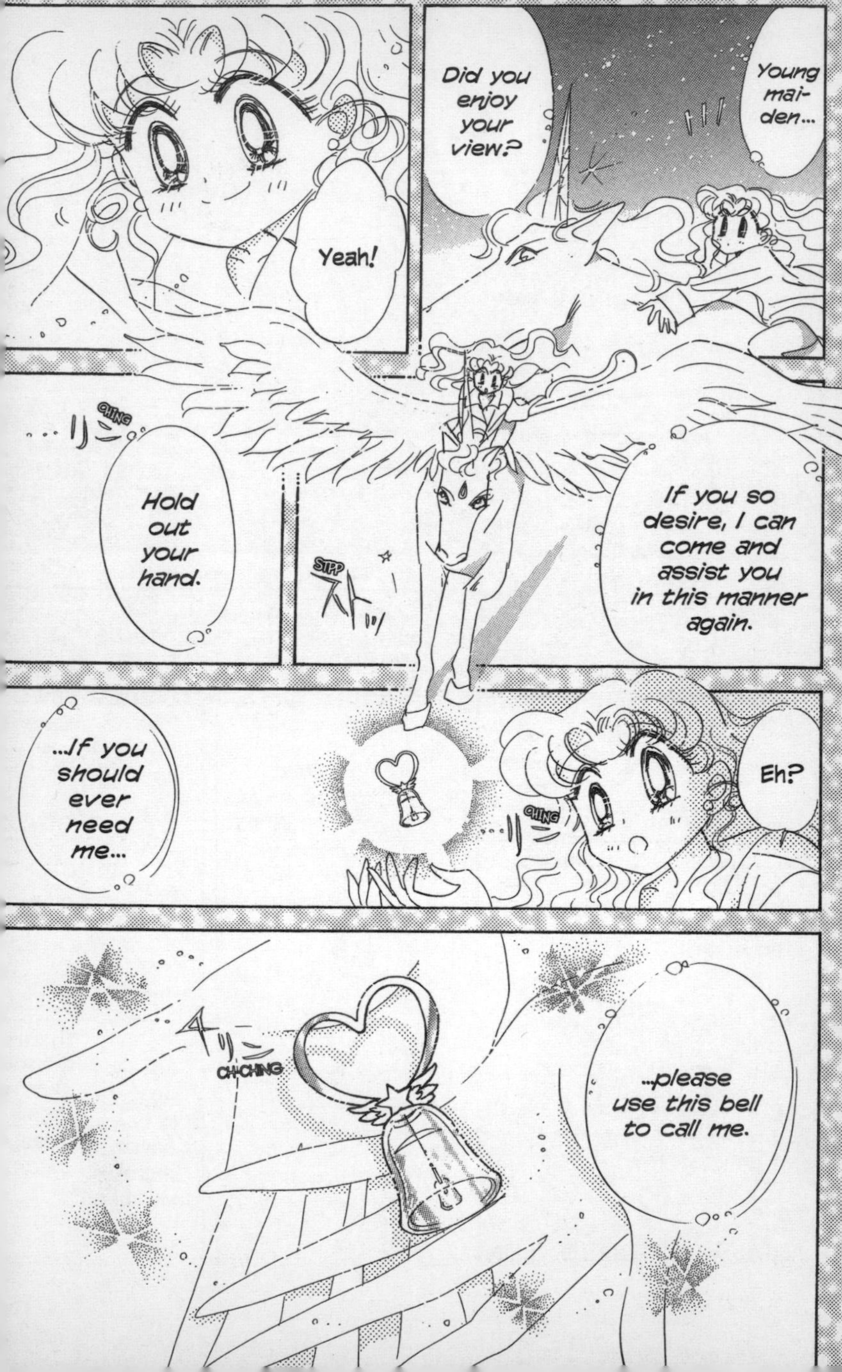
Young maiden...
Did you enjoy your view?
Yeah!
If you so desire, I can come and assist you in this manner again.
STPP
CHING
Hold out your hand.
Eh?
CHING
...If you should ever need me...
...please use this bell to call me.
CHI-CHING

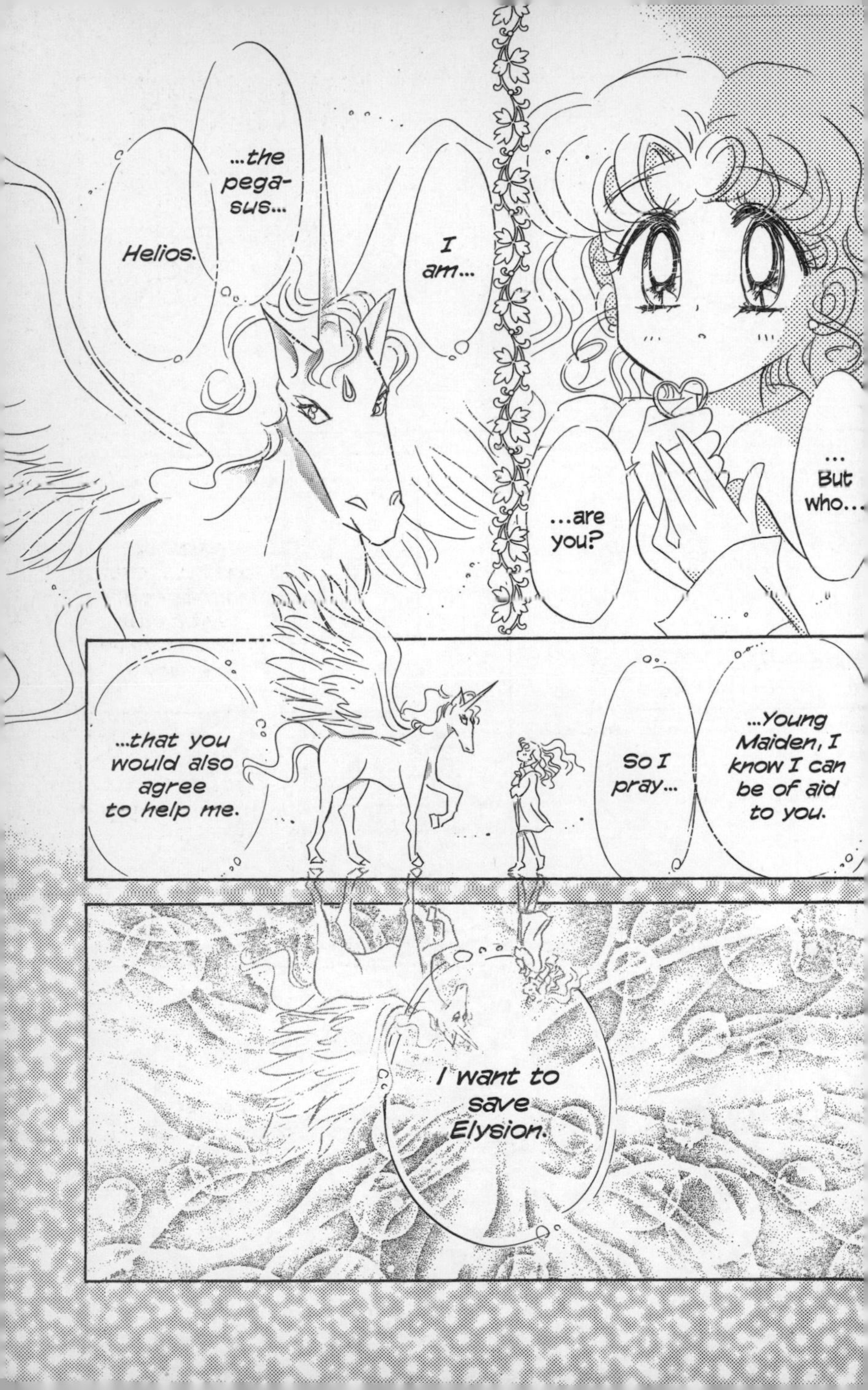

... But who...
...are you?
I am...
...the pega-sus...
Helios.
...Young Maiden, I know I can be of aid to you.
So I pray...
...that you would also agree to help me.
I want to save Elysion.

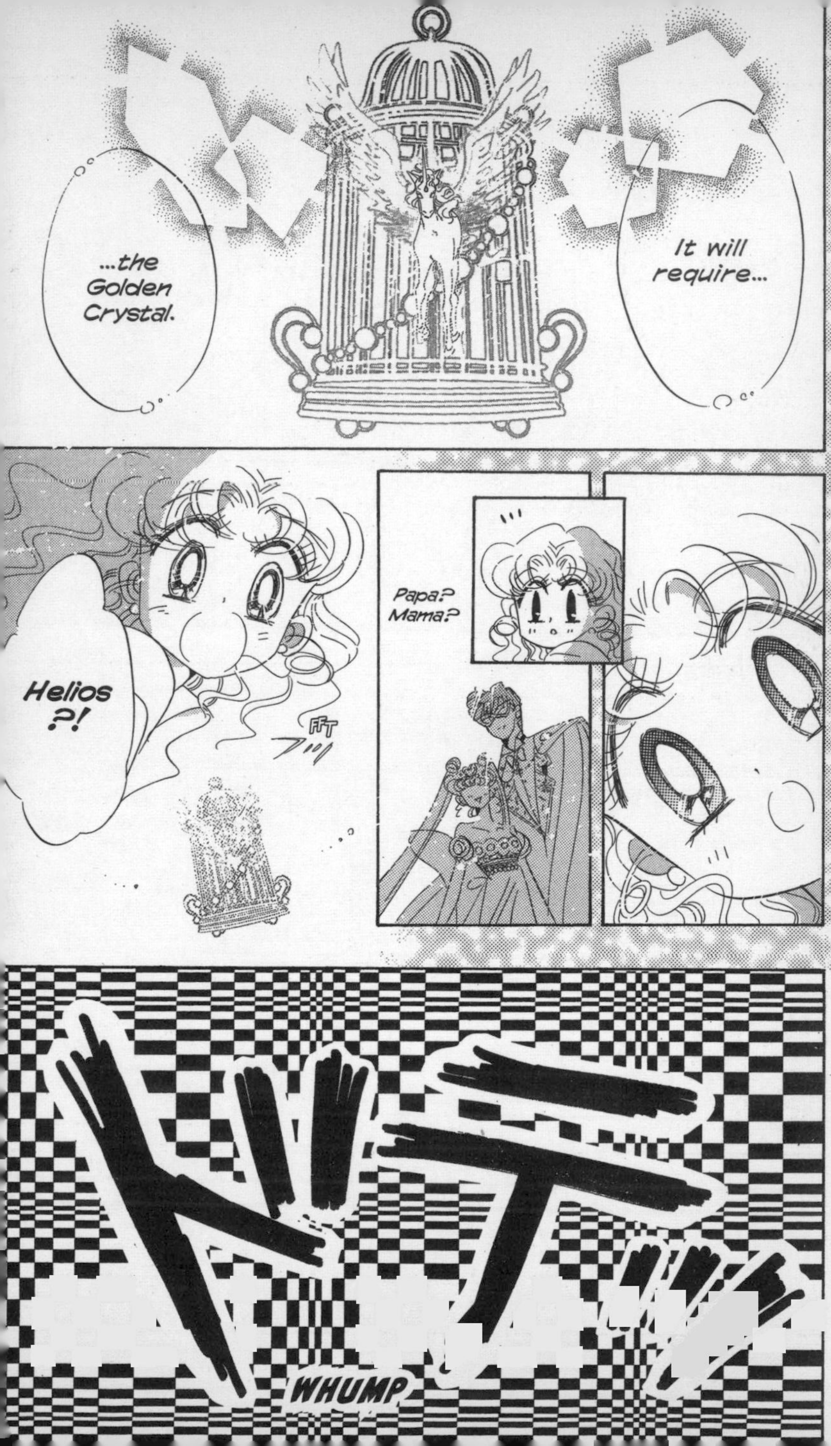
It will require...
...the Golden Crystal.
Papa? Mama?
Helios ?!
FFT
WHUMP

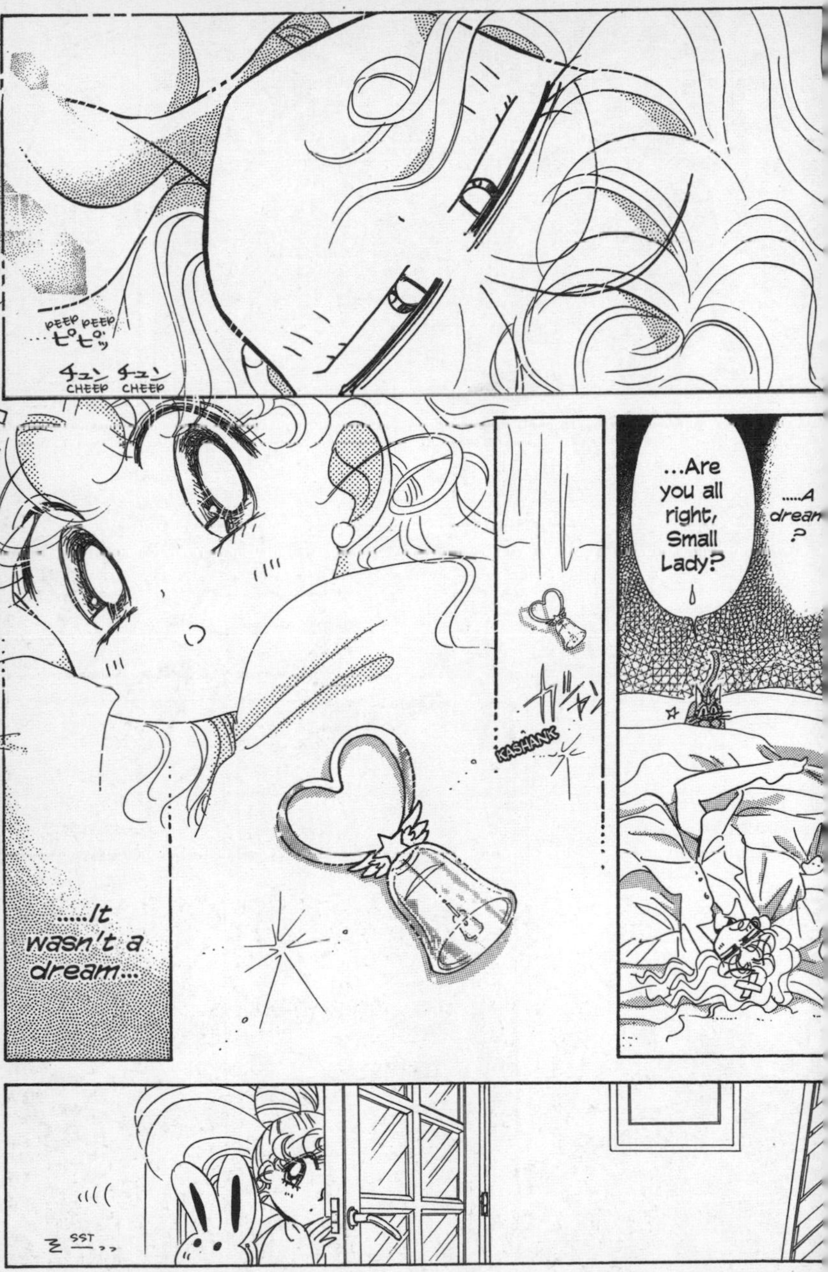
PEEP PEEP
ピピッ
チュン チュン
CHEEP CHEEP
.....A dream?
...Are you all right, Small Lady?
ガチャン
KASHANK
.....It wasn't a dream...
SST

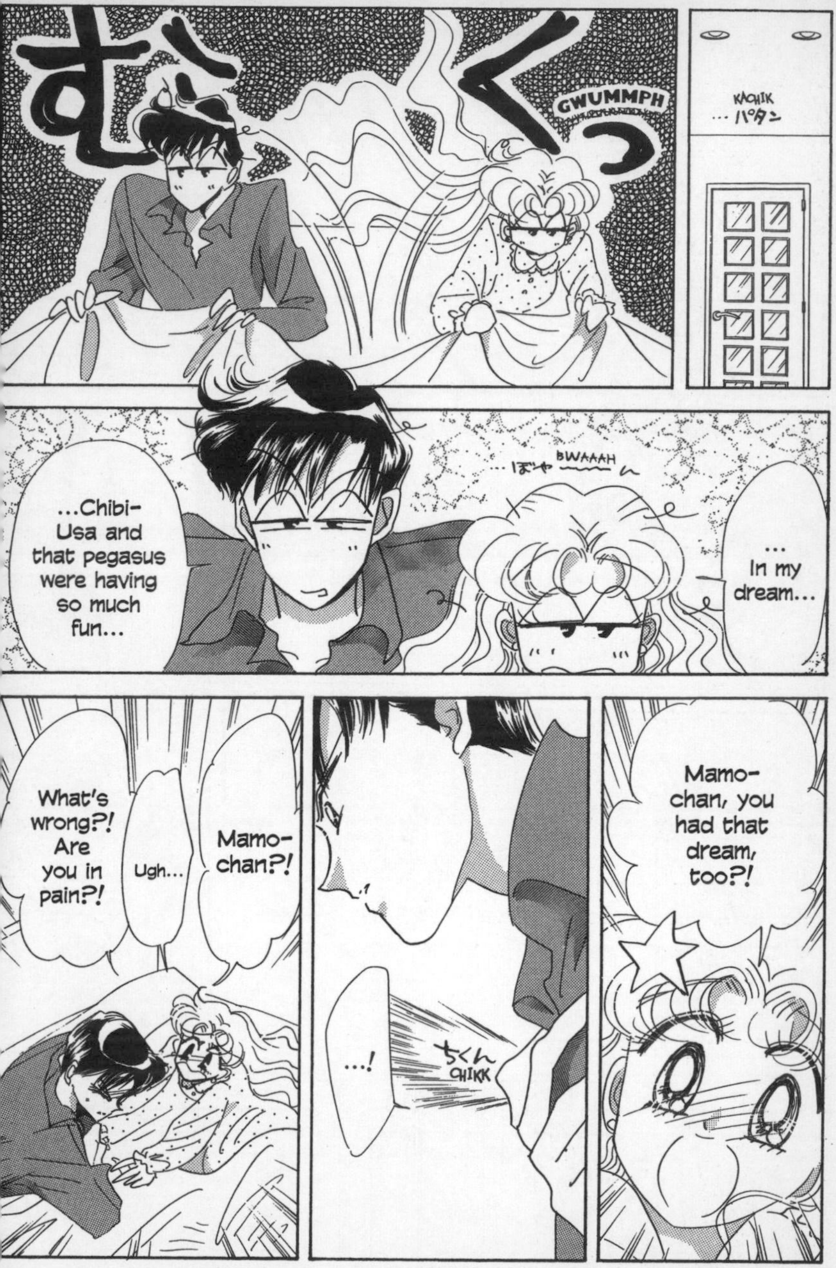
KACHIK
...パタン
すくっ
GWUMMPH
... In my dream...
...ぼや BWAAAH ん
...Chibi-Usa and that pegasus were having so much fun...
Mamo-chan, you had that dream, too?!
...!
ちくん
CHIKK
Mamo-chan?!
Ugh...
What's wrong?! Are you in pain?!

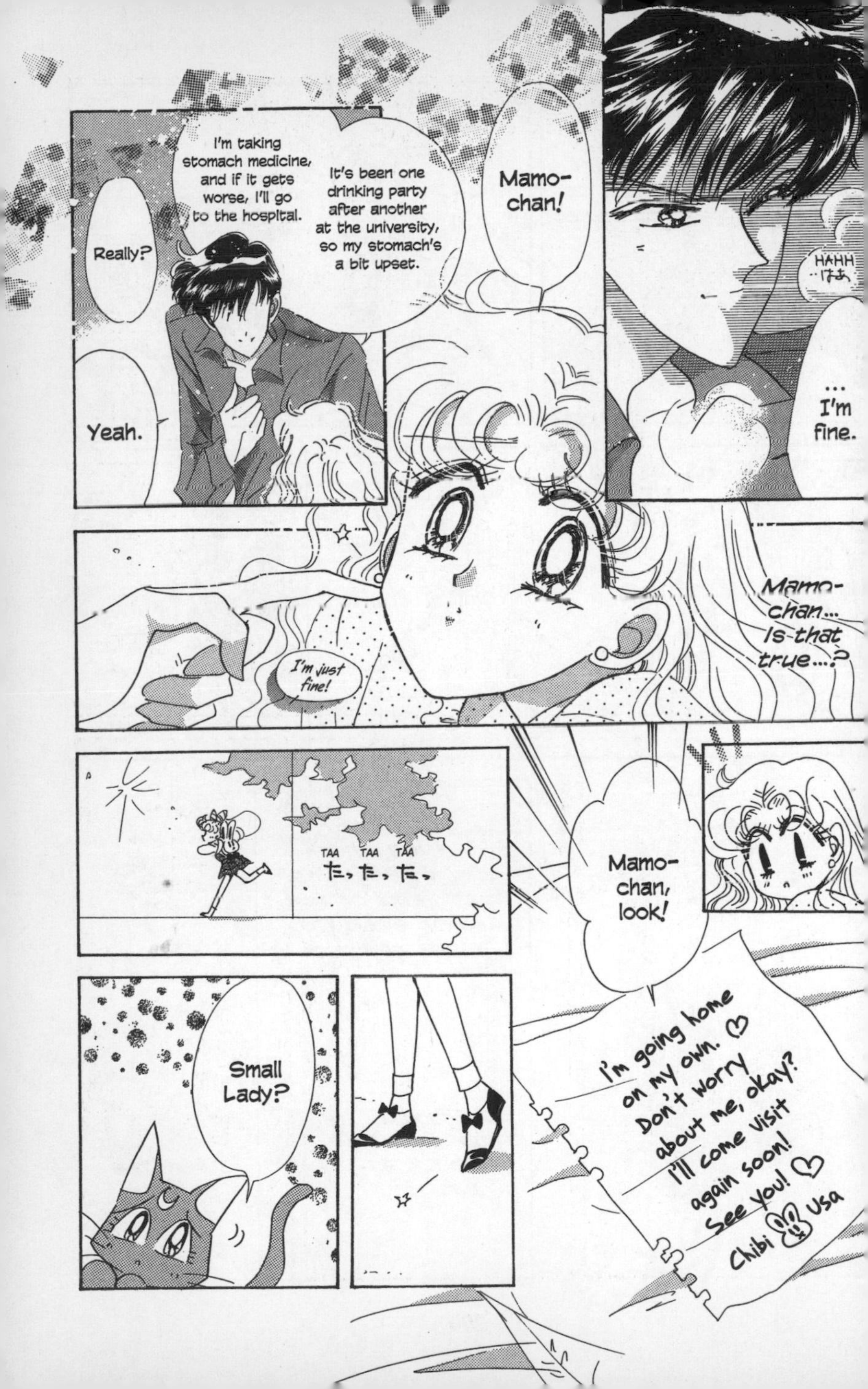
Mamo-chan!
HAHH
…はあ
... I'm fine.
It's been one drinking party after another at the university, so my stomach's a bit upset.
I'm taking stomach medicine, and if it gets worse, I'll go to the hospital.
Really?
Yeah.
Mamo-chan... Is that true...?
I'm just fine!
Mamo-chan, look!
TAA TAA TAA
たっ たっ たっ
I'm going home on my own. Don't worry about me, okay? I'll come visit again soon! See you! Chibi Usa
Small Lady?

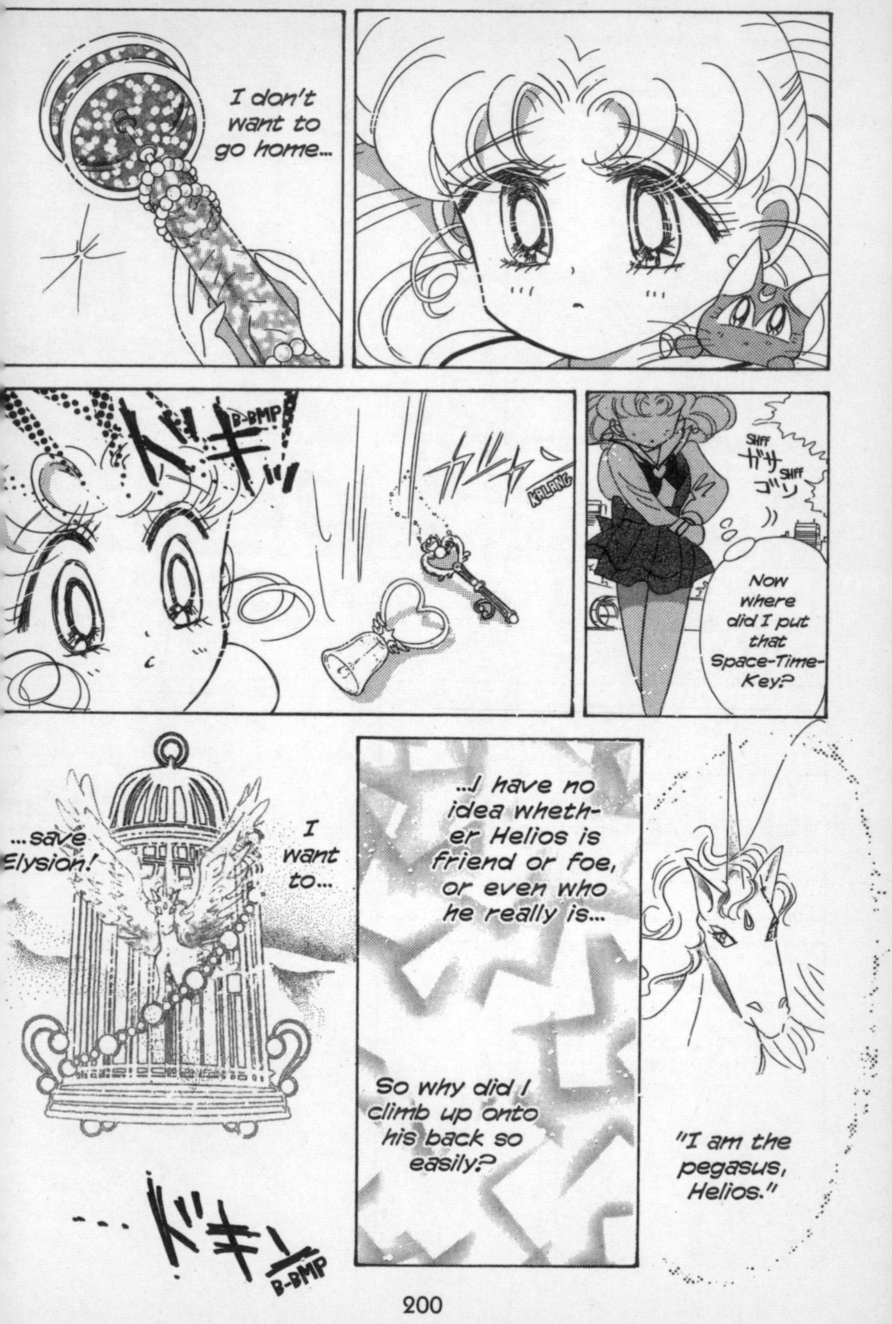
I don't want to go home...
SHFF
SHFF
Now where did I put that Space-Time-Key?
KALANG
B-BMP
"I am the pegasus, Helios."
...I have no idea whether Helios is friend or foe, or even who he really is...
So why did I climb up onto his back so easily?
I want to...
...save Elysion!
B-BMP

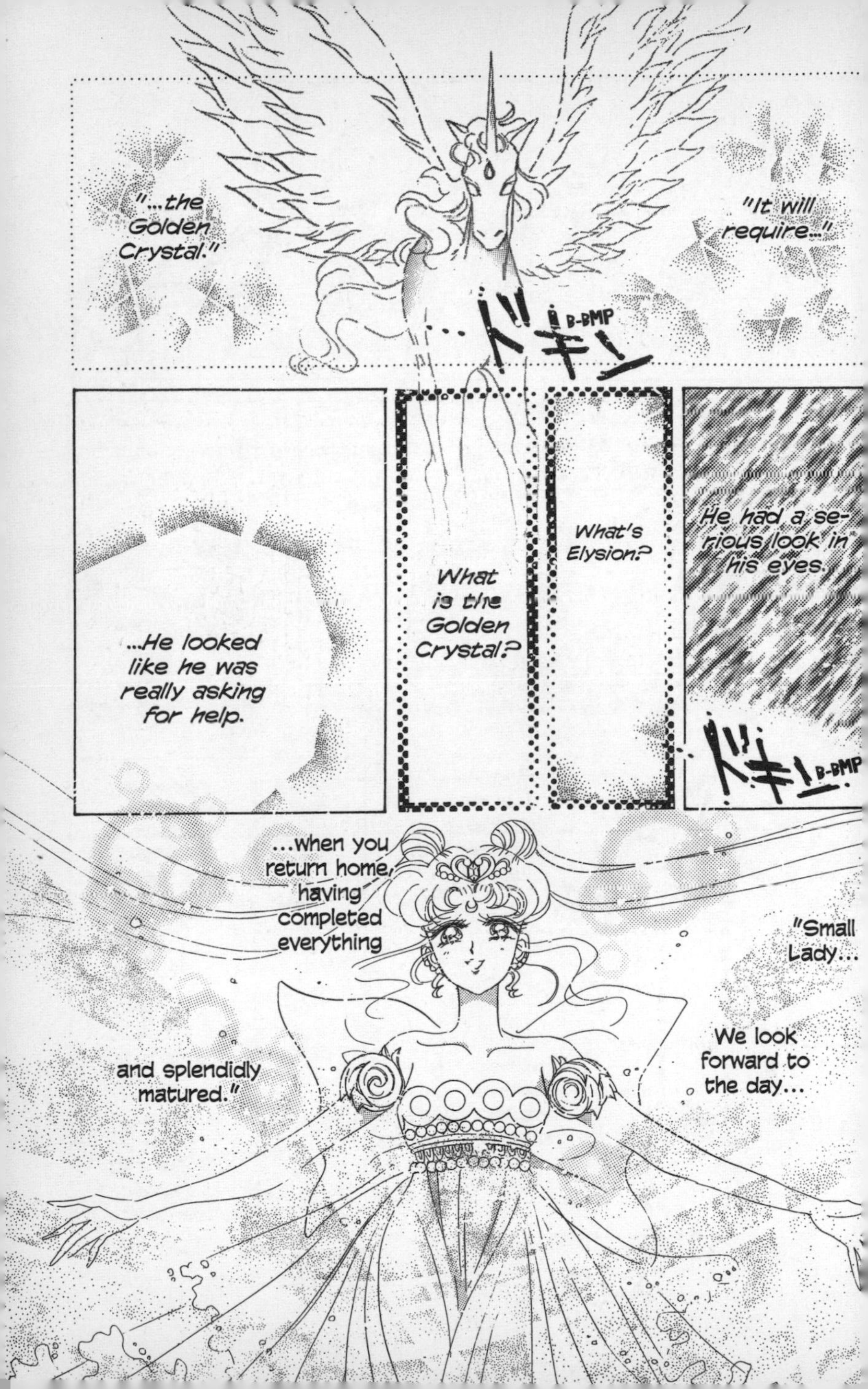
"It will require..."
"...the Golden Crystal."
ドキン
B-BMP
He had a serious look in his eyes.
ドキン
B-BMP
What's Elysion?
What is the Golden Crystal?
...He looked like he was really asking for help.
"Small Lady...
We look forward to the day...
...when you return home, having completed everything
and splendidly matured."

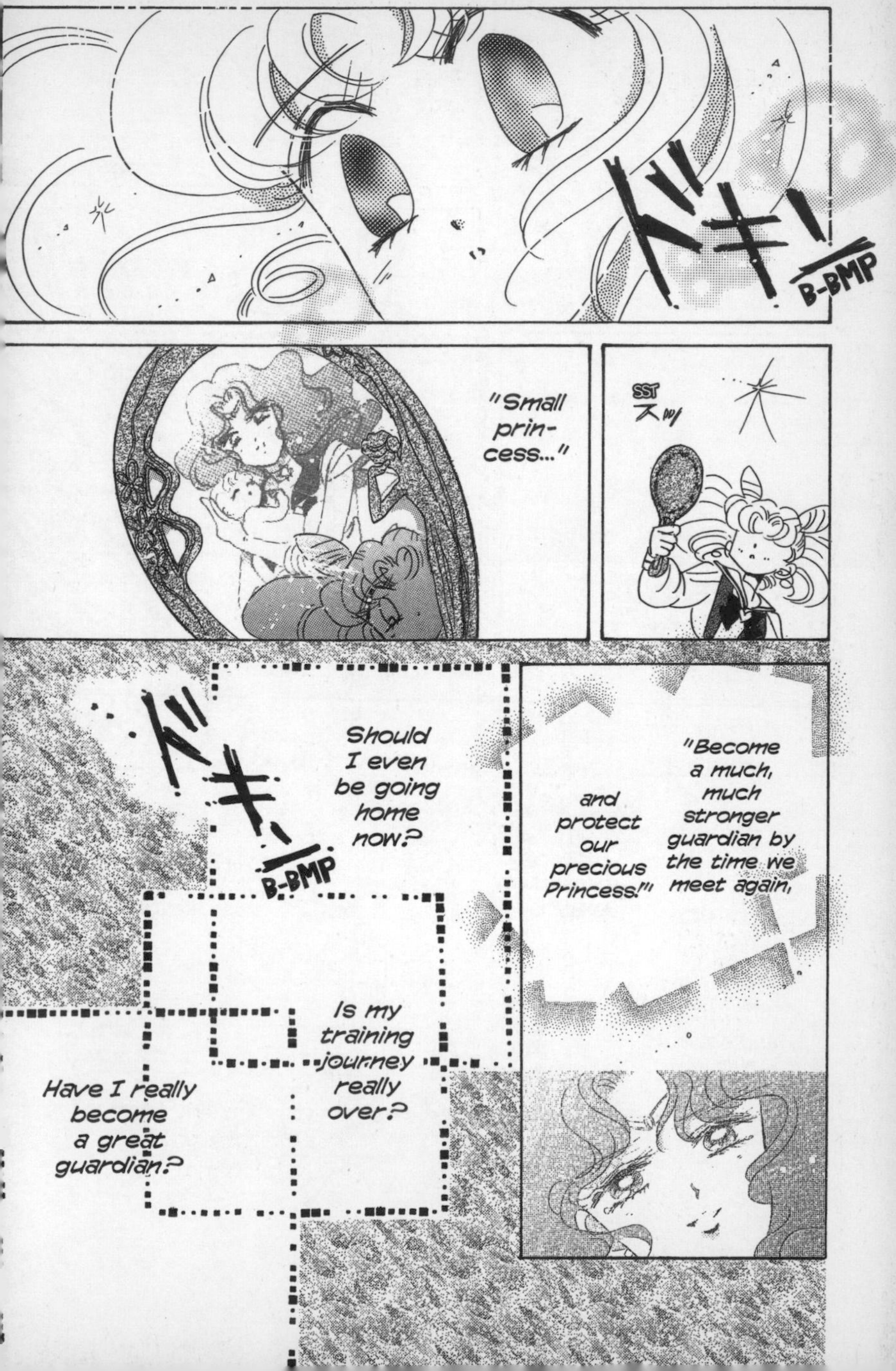
B-BMP
SST
"Small prin-cess..."
"Become a much, much stronger guardian by the time we meet again,
and protect our precious Princess!"
B-BMP
Should I even be going home now?
Is my training journey really over?
Have I really become a great guardian?

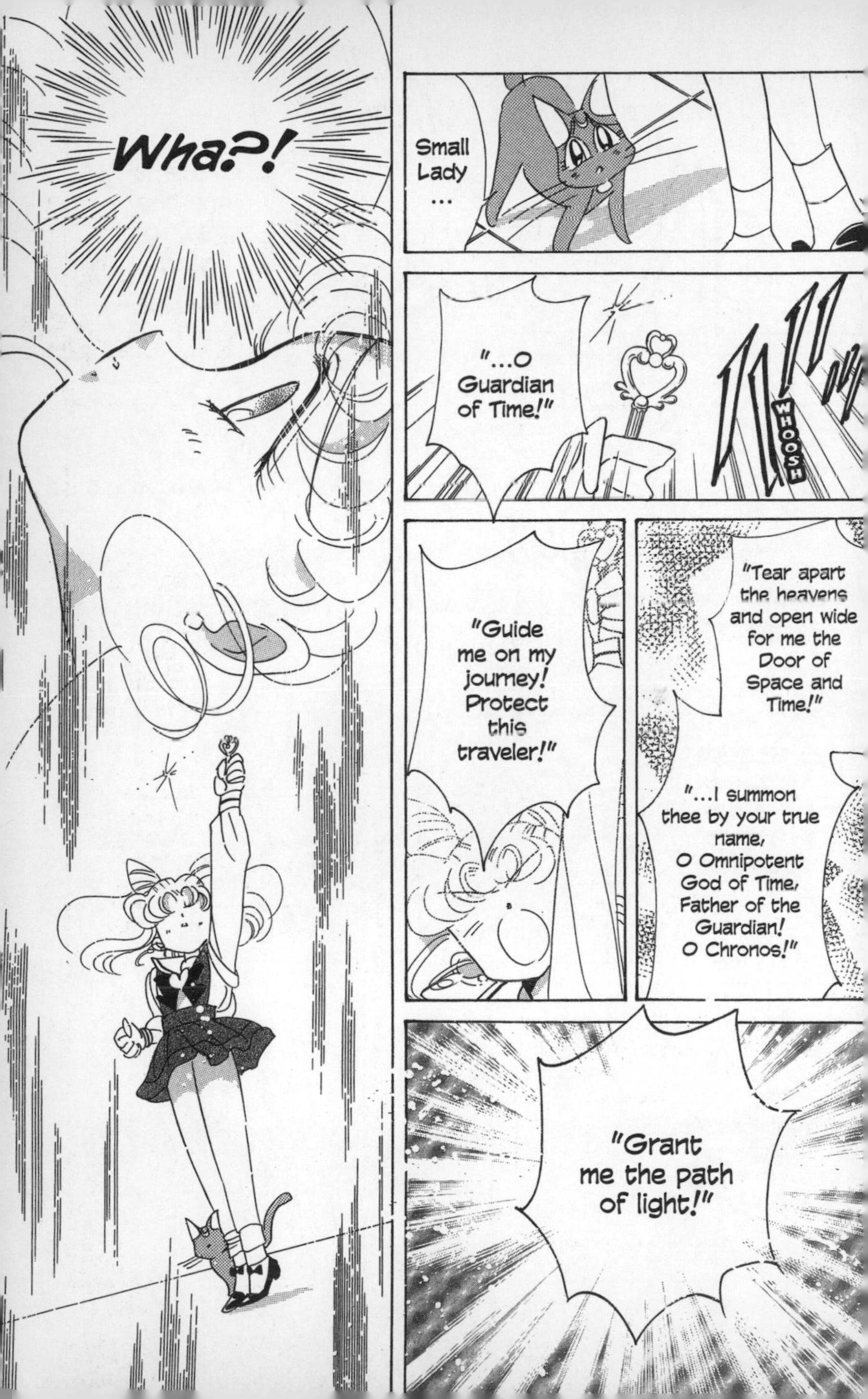
Small Lady ...
WHOOSH
"...O Guardian of Time!"
"Tear apart the heavens and open wide for me the Door of Space and Time!"
"...I summon thee by your true name, O Omnipotent God of Time, Father of the Guardian! O Chronos!"
"Guide me on my journey! Protect this traveler!"
"Grant me the path of light!"
Wha?!

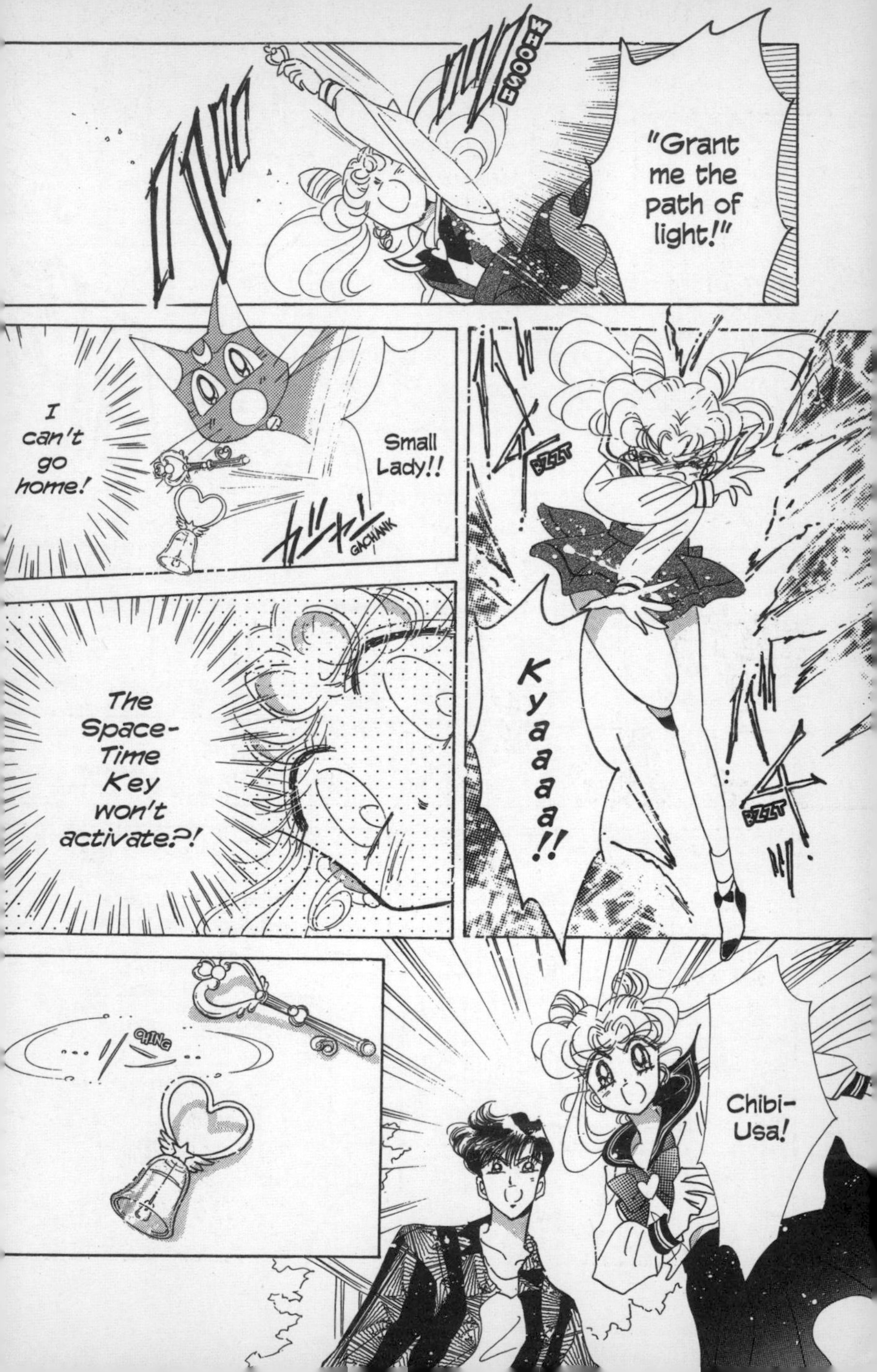
WHOOSH
"Grant me the path of light!"
BZZT
Kyaaaa!!
BZZT
Small Lady!!
I can't go home!
GACHANK
The Space-Time Key won't activate?!
Chibi-Usa!
QING
... ...

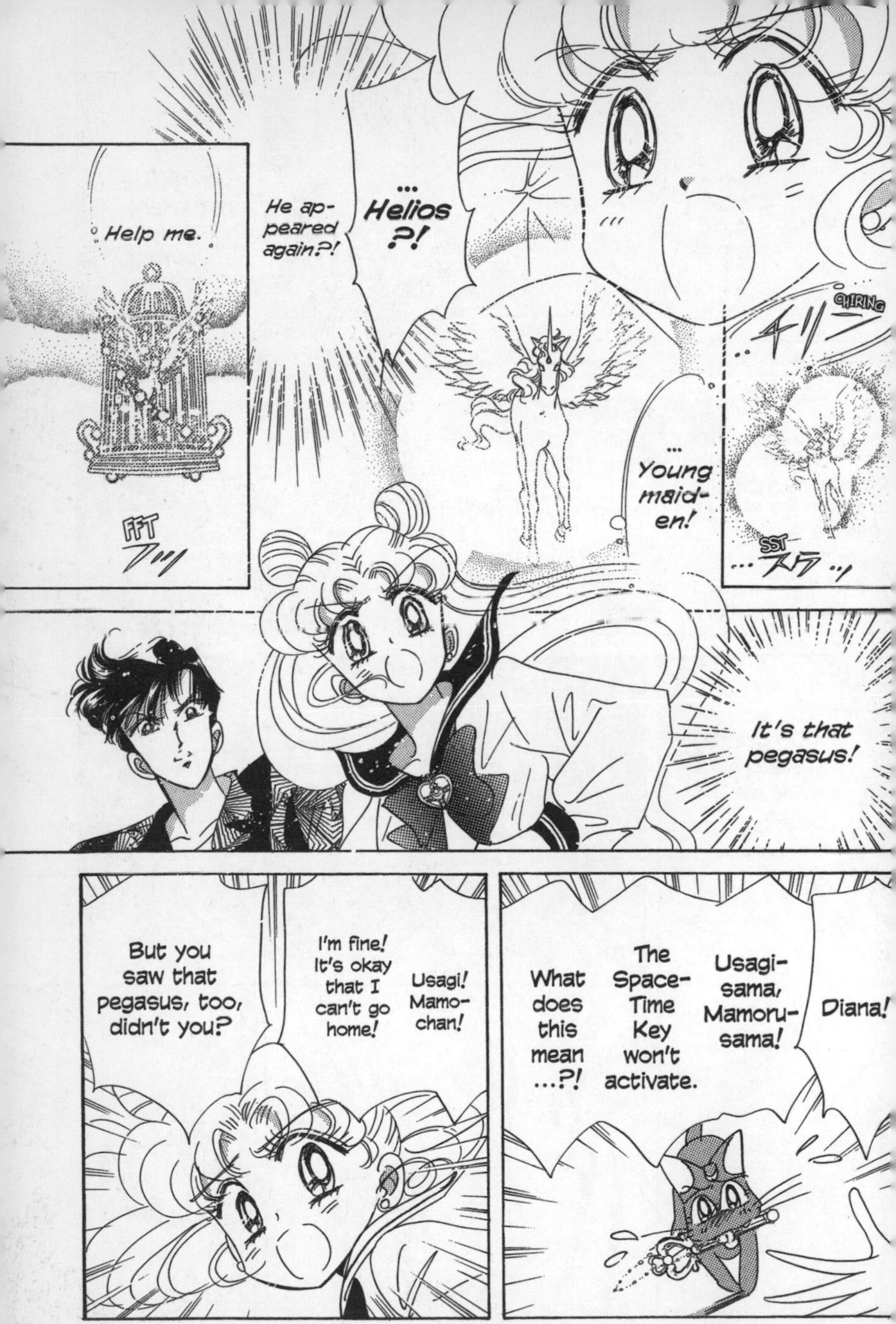
CHIRING
チリン
SST
スッ
... Helios ?!
He appeared again?!
... Young maiden!
Help me.
FFT
フッ
It's that pegasus!
Diana!
Usagi-sama, Mamoru-sama!
The Space-Time Key won't activate.
What does this mean ...?!
Usagi! Mamo-chan!
I'm fine! It's okay that I can't go home!
But you saw that pegasus, too, didn't you?

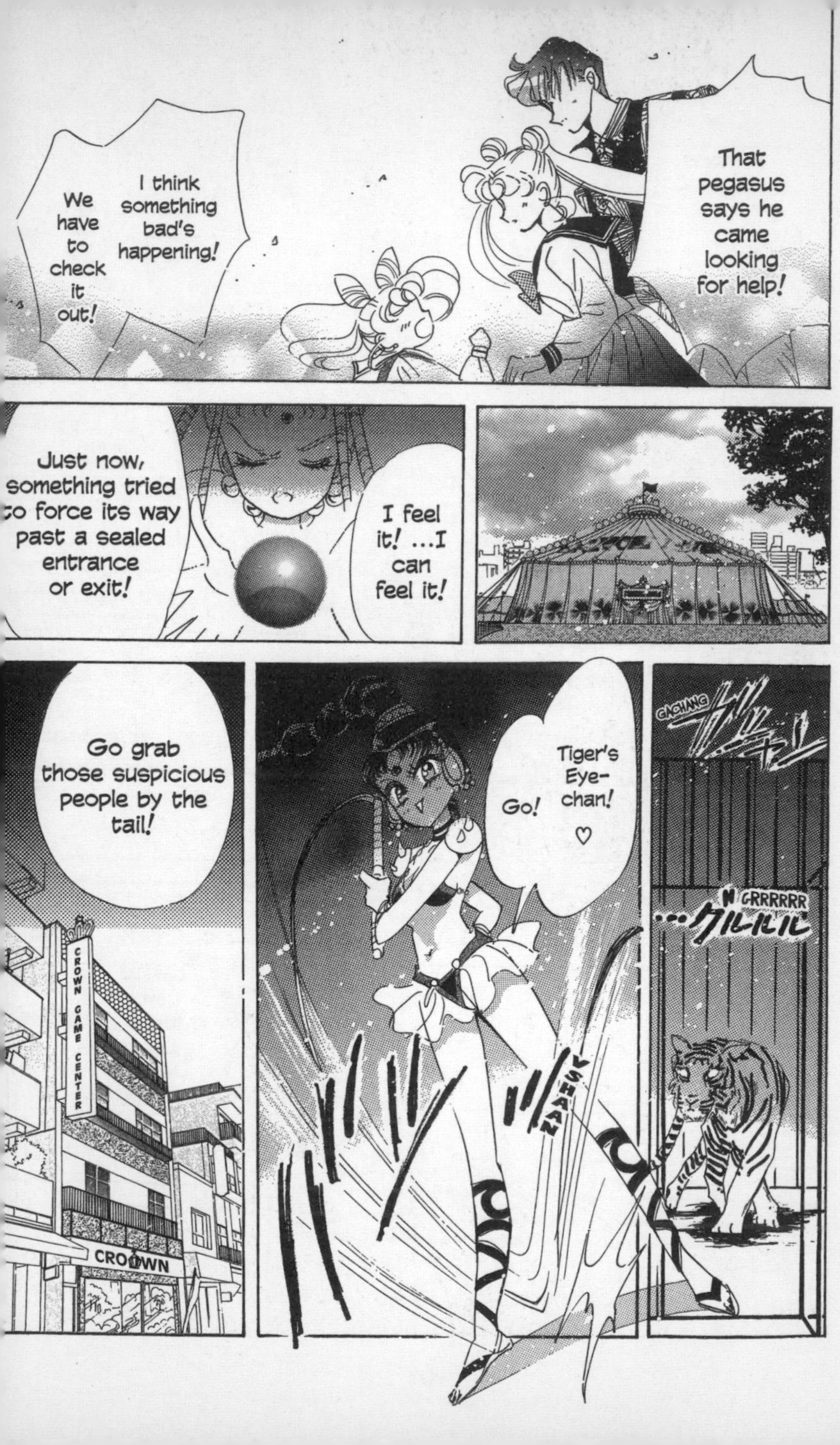
That pegasus says he came looking for help!
I think something bad's happening!
We have to check it out!
I feel it! ...I can feel it!
Just now, something tried to force its way past a sealed entrance or exit!
GACHANG
N GRRRRRR
Tiger's Eye-chan! ♡
Go!
VSHAAN
Go grab those suspicious people by the tail!
CROWN GAME CENTER
CROWN

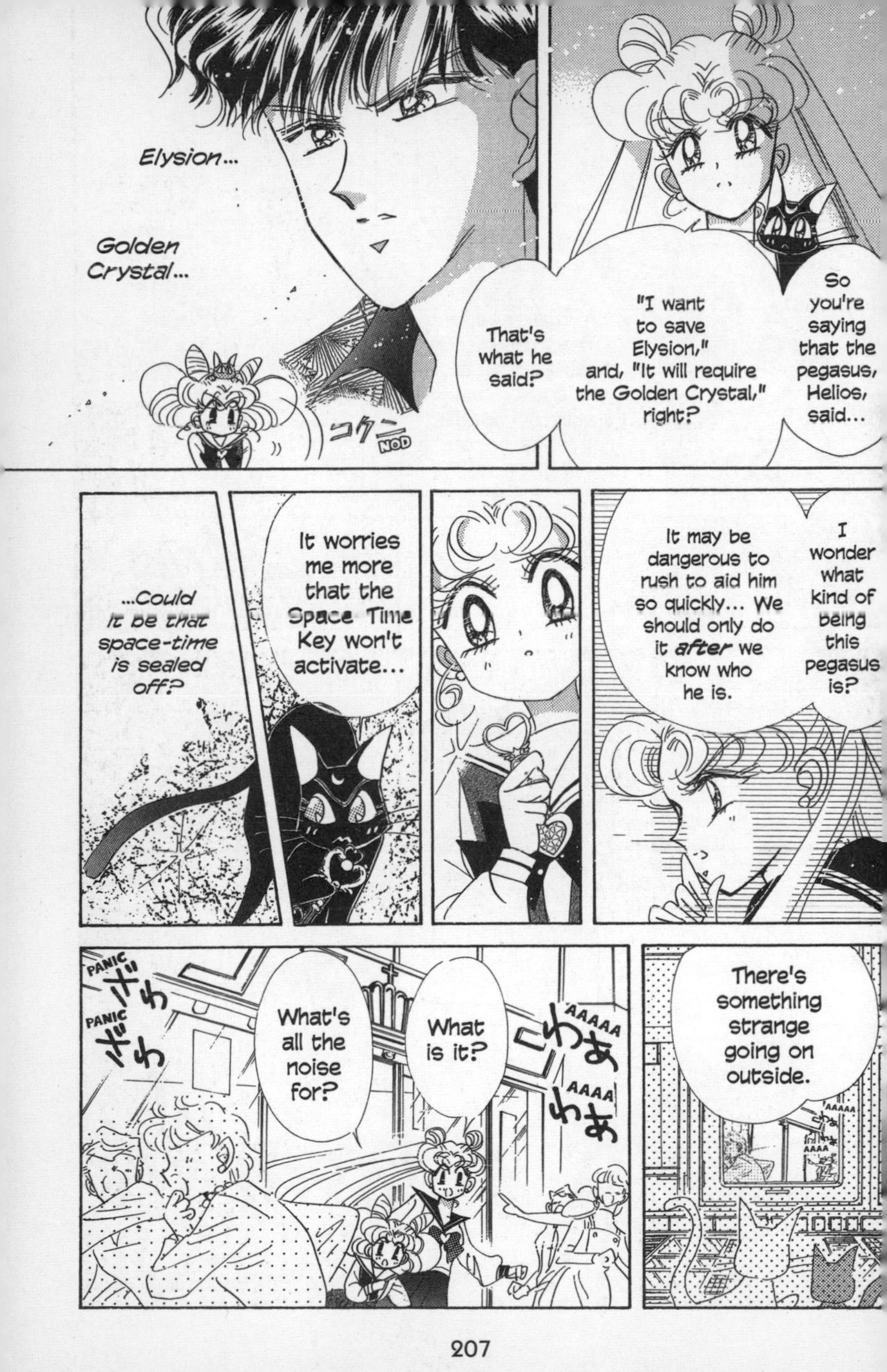

So you're saying that the pegasus, Helios, said...
"I want to save Elysion," and, "It will require the Golden Crystal," right?
That's what he said?
Elysion...
Golden Crystal...
コクン
NOD
I wonder what kind of being this pegasus is?
It may be dangerous to rush to aid him so quickly... We should only do it *after* we know who he is.
It worries me more that the Space Time Key won't activate...
...Could it be that space-time is sealed off?
There's something strange going on outside.
わあ
AAAAA
わあ
AAAA
What is it?
What's all the noise for?
ざわ
PANIC
ざわ
PANIC

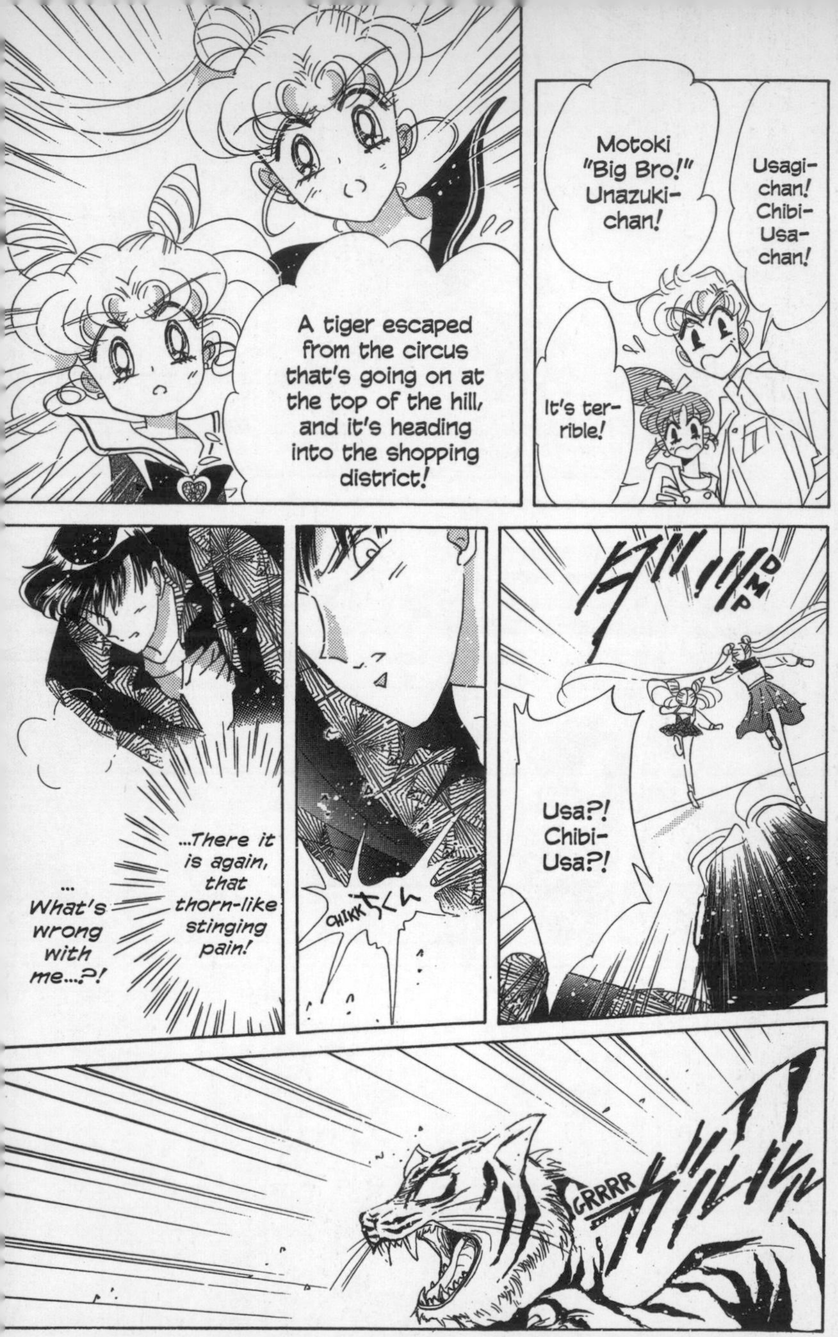
Usagi-chan! Chibi-Usa-chan!
Motoki "Big Bro!" Unazuki-chan!
It's terrible!
A tiger escaped from the circus that's going on at the top of the hill, and it's heading into the shopping district!
DMP
Usa?! Chibi-Usa?!
CHIKK ちくん
...There it is again, that thorn-like stinging pain!
... What's wrong with me...?!
GRRRR

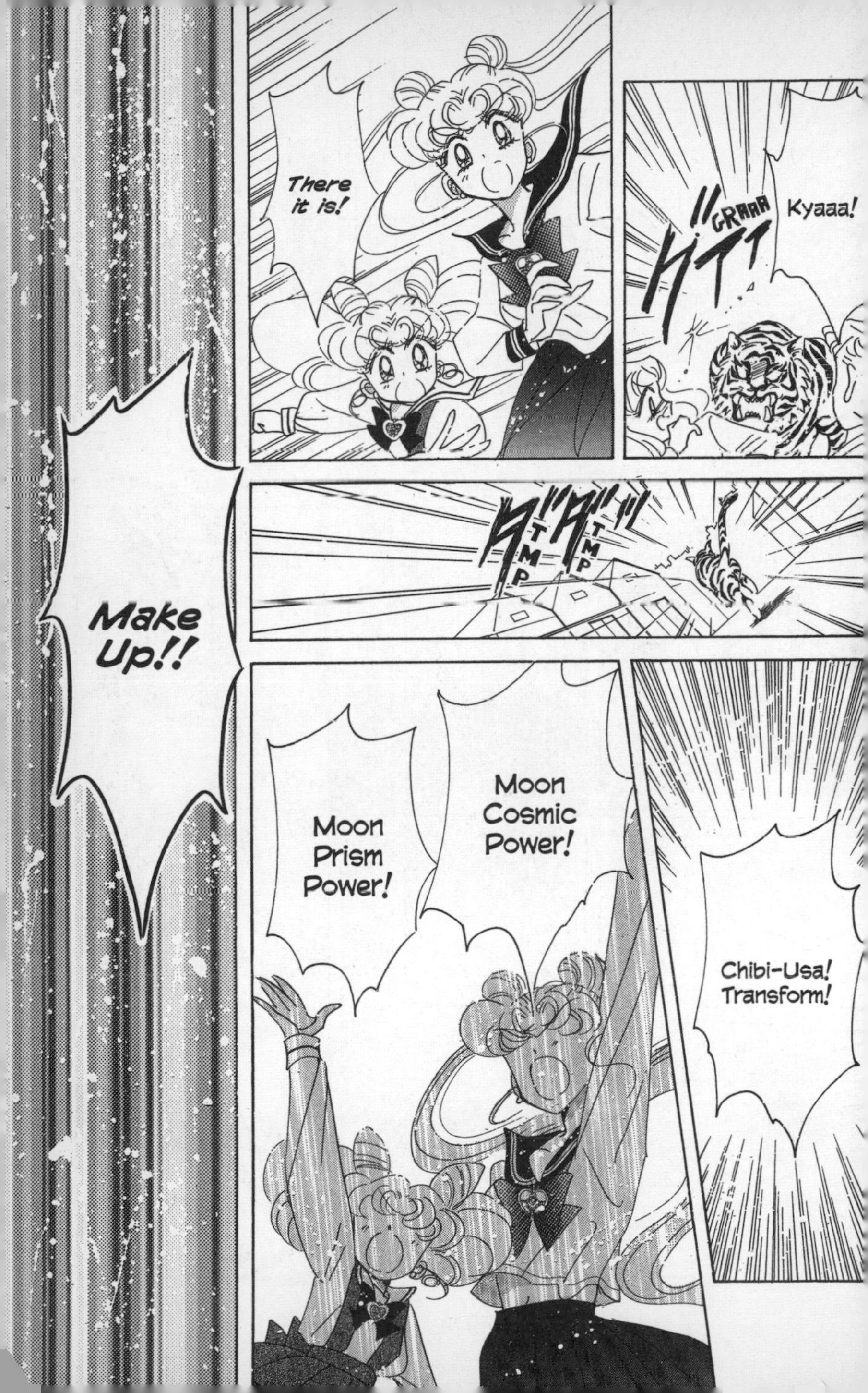
Kyaaa!
GRAAA
There it is!
TMP TMP
Chibi-Usa! Transform!
Moon Cosmic Power!
Moon Prism Power!
Make Up!!

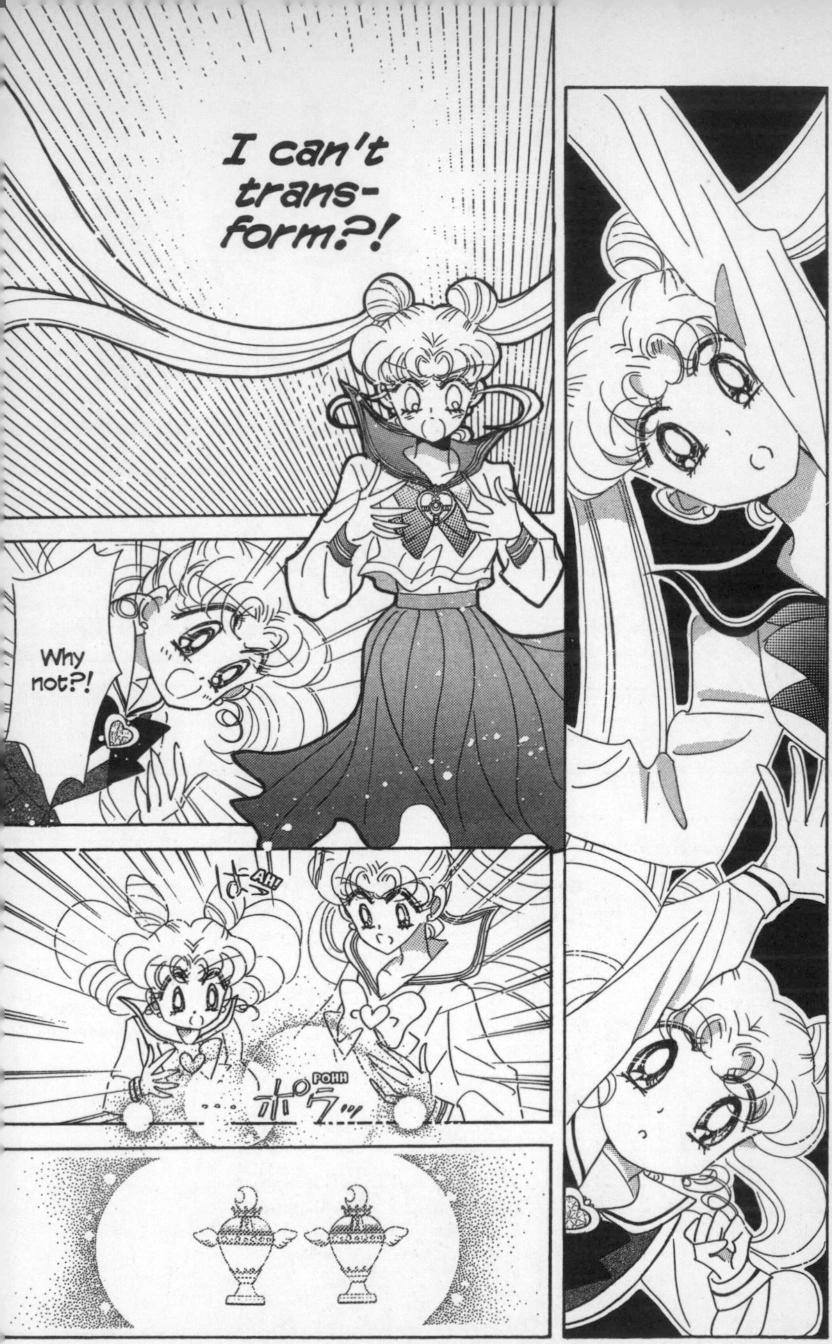
I can't trans- form?!
Why not?!
はっ
AH!
ポワッ
POHH

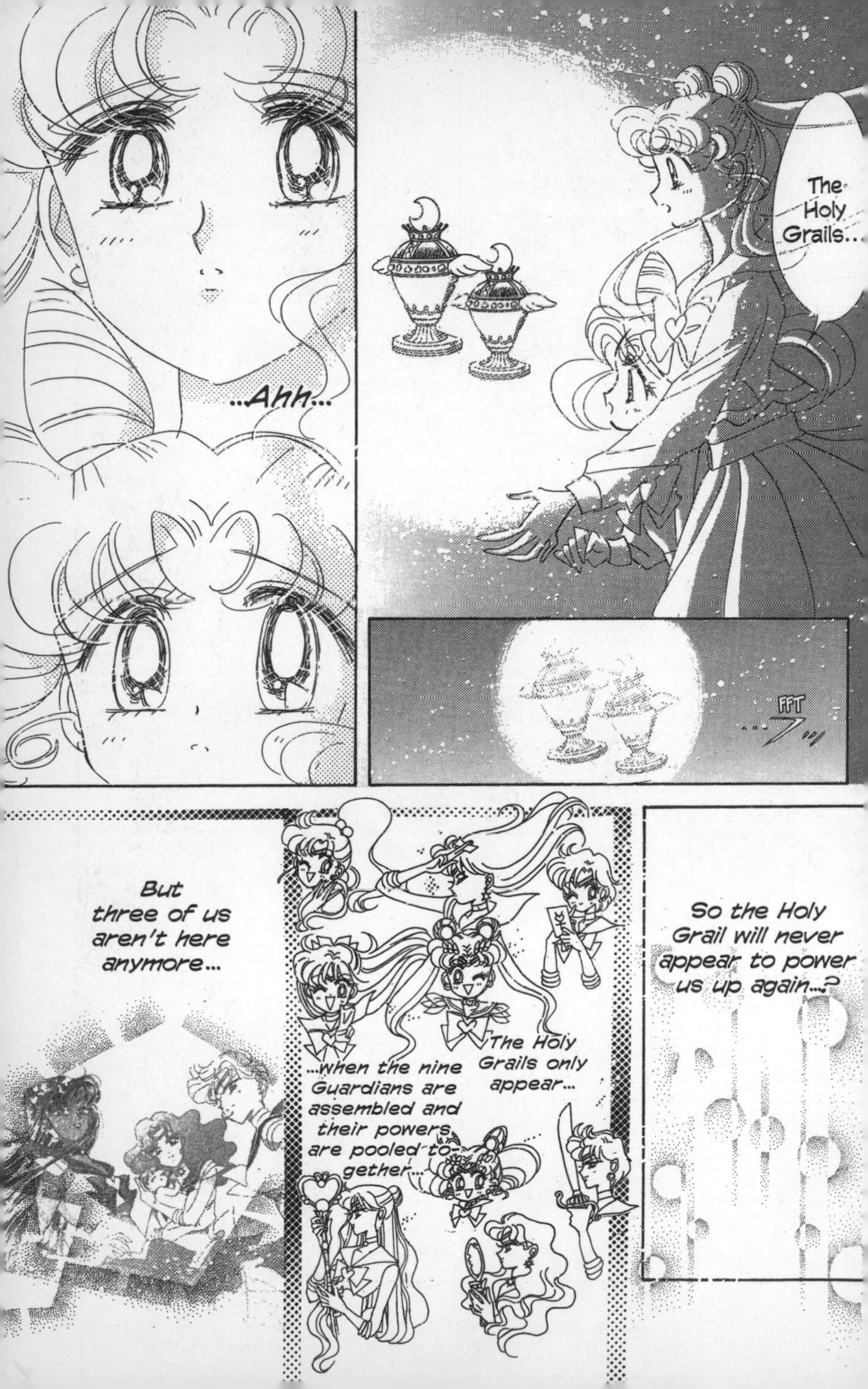

The Holy Grails...
...Ahh...
FFT
So the Holy Grail will never appear to power us up again...?
The Holy Grails only appear...
...when the nine Guardians are assembled and their powers are pooled together...
But three of us aren't here anymore...

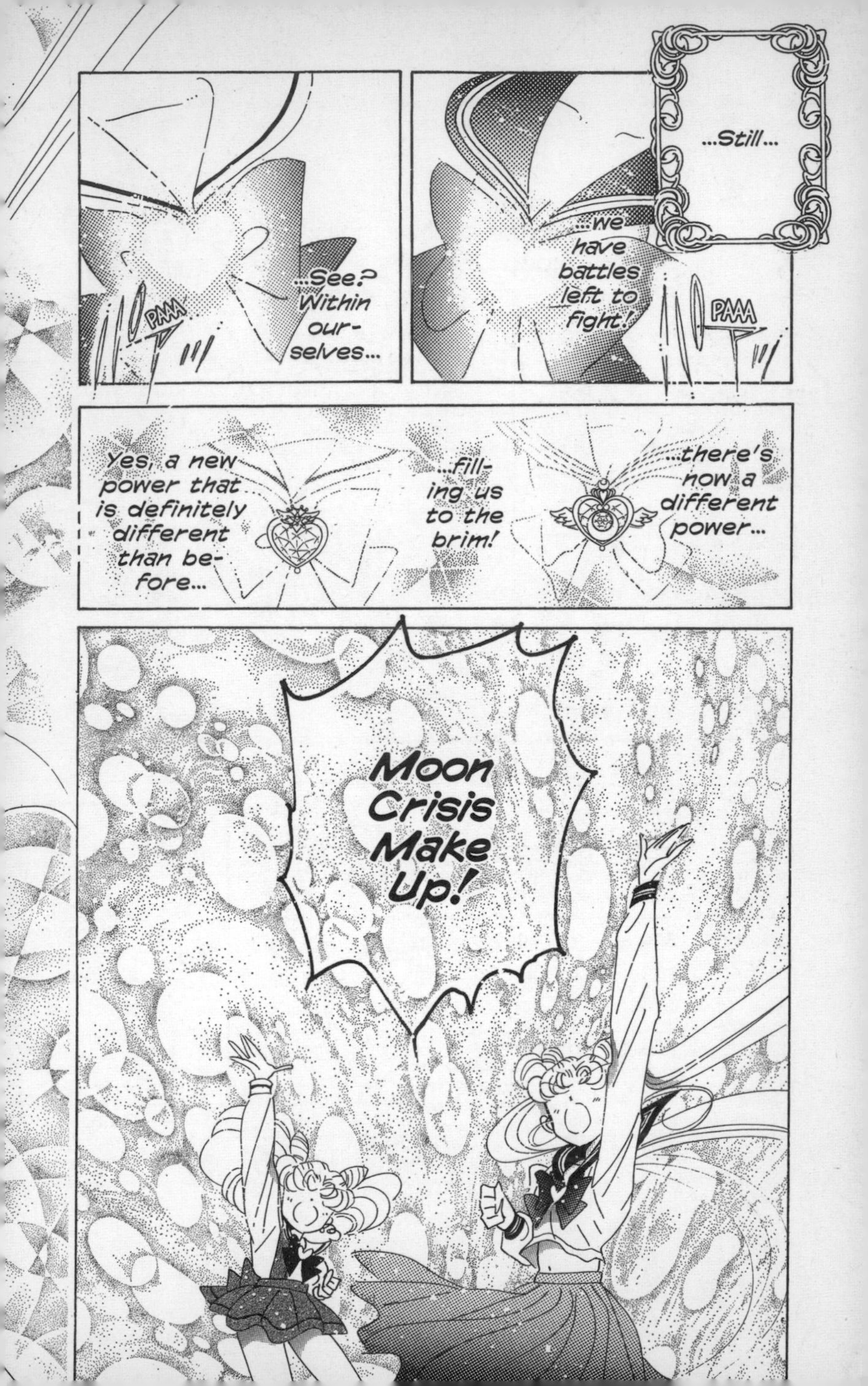
...Still...
...we have battles left to fight!
PAAA
...See? Within ourselves...
PAAA
...there's now a different power...
...filling us to the brim!
Yes, a new power that is definitely different than before...
Moon Crisis Make Up!

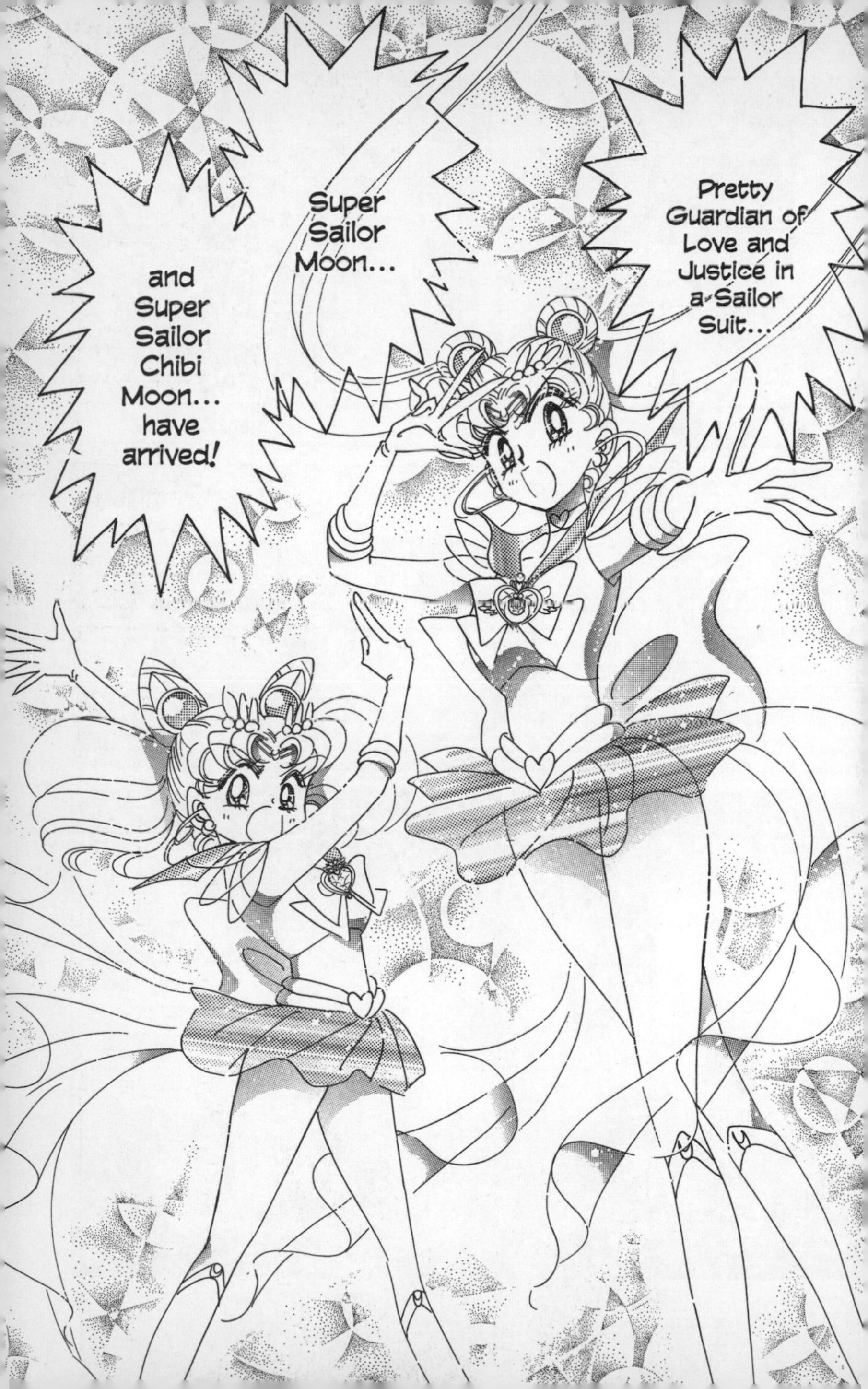
Pretty Guardian of Love and Justice in a Sailor Suit...
Super Sailor Moon...
and Super Sailor Chibi Moon... have arrived!

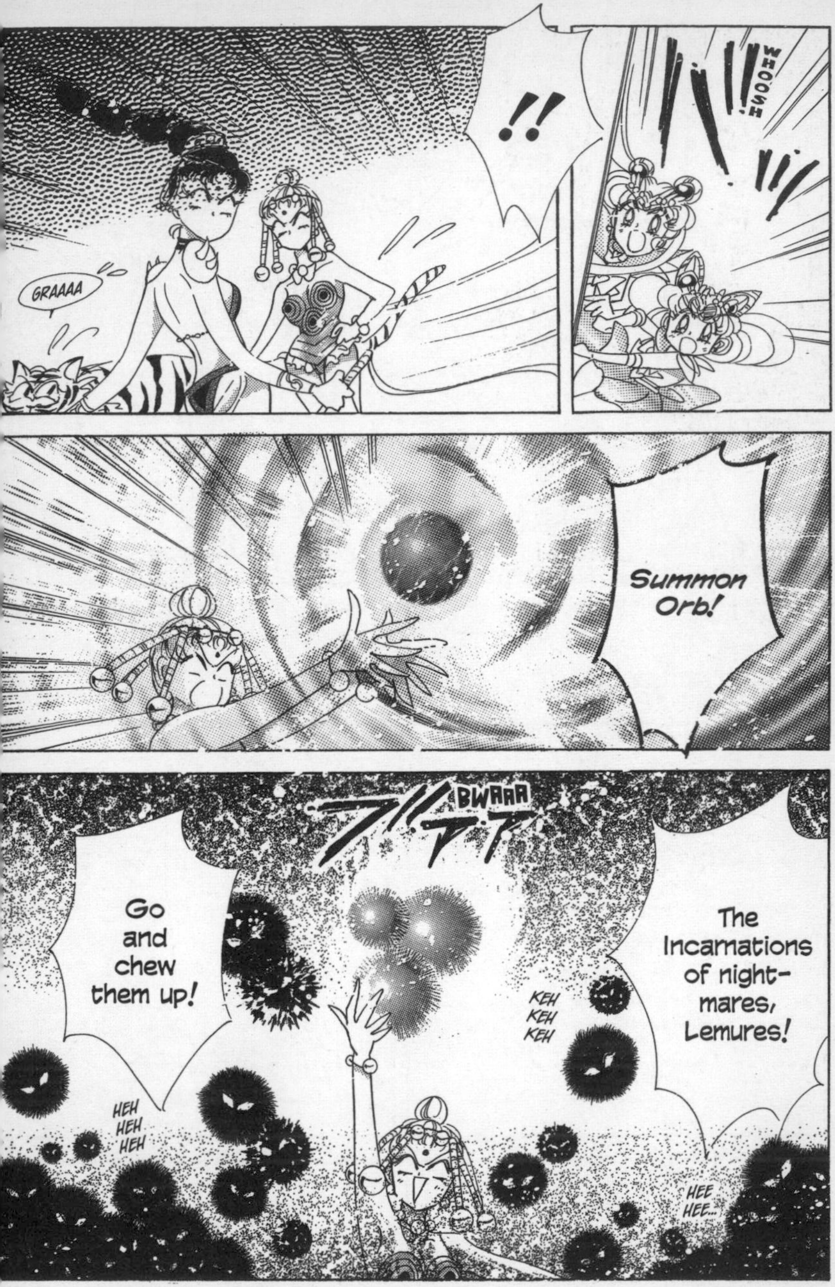
WHOOSH
!!
GRAAAA
Summon Orb!
BWAAA
The Incarnations of night-mares, Lemures!
KEH KEH KEH
Go and chew them up!
HEE HEE...
HEH HEH HEH

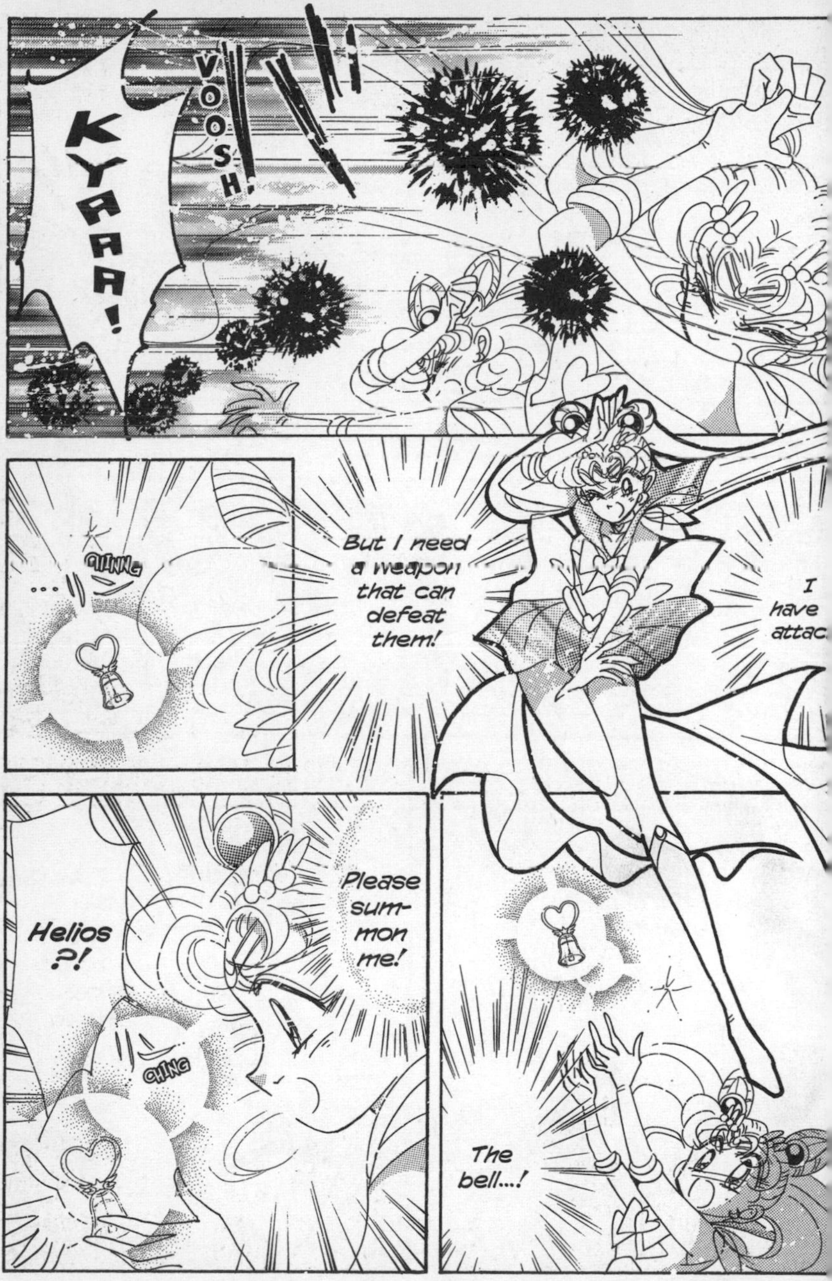
VOOSH!
KYAAA!
I have attac
But I need a weapon that can defeat them!
...
The bell...!
Please summon me!
CHING
Helios ?!

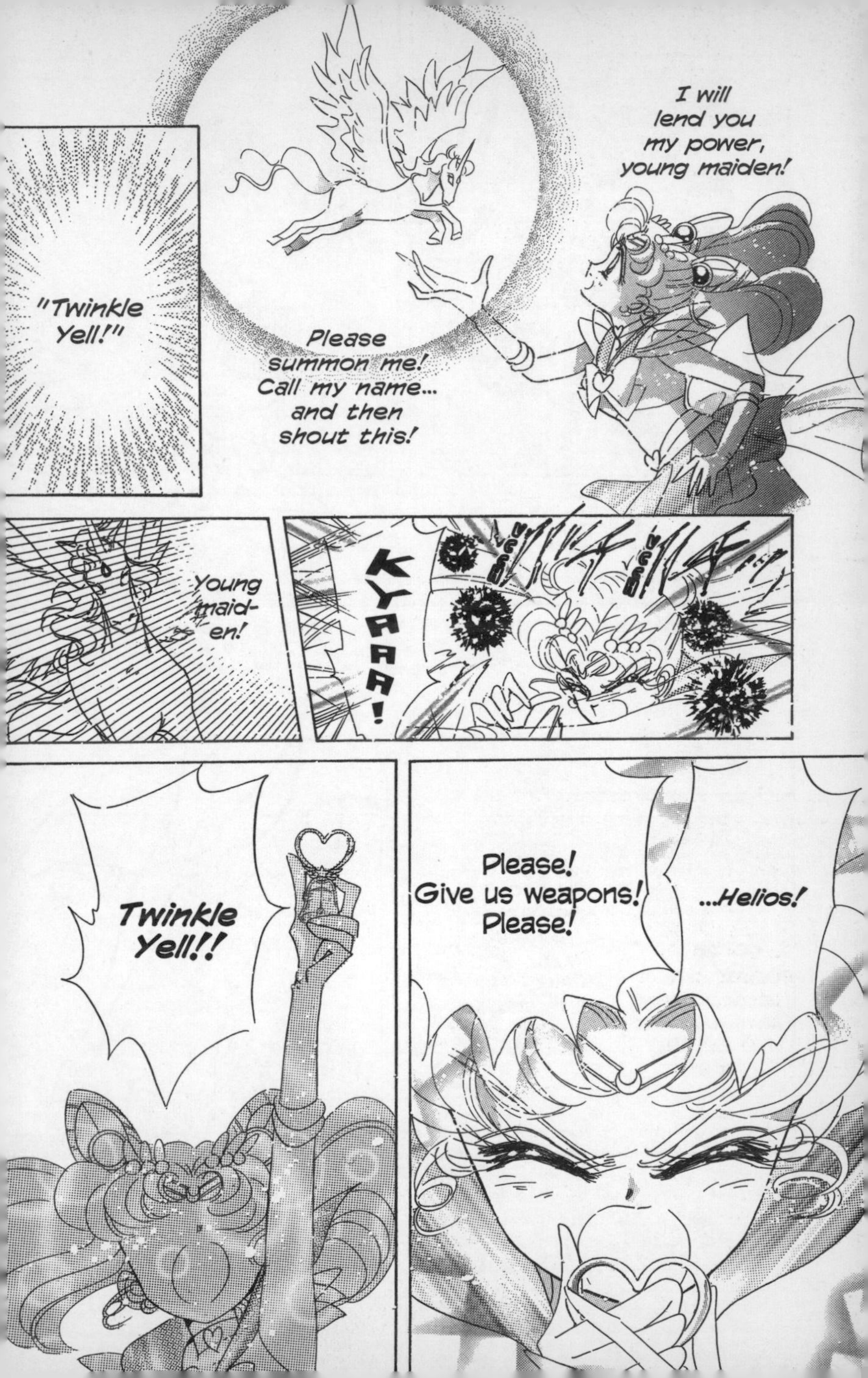
I will lend you my power, young maiden!
Please summon me! Call my name... and then shout this!
"Twinkle Yell!"
KYAAAA!
Young maid-en!
...Helios!
Please! Give us weapons! Please!
Twinkle Yell!!

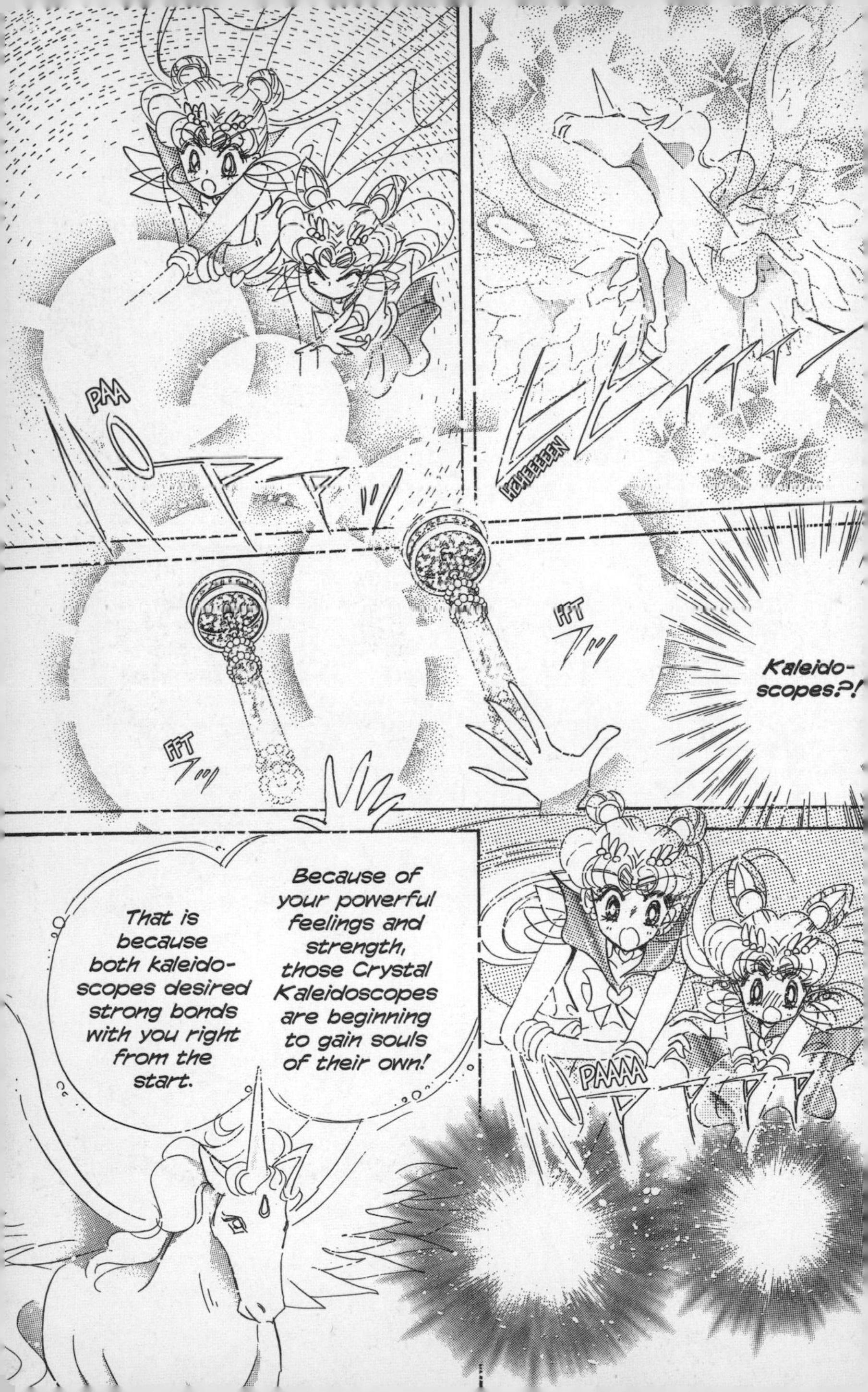
KCHEEEEEN
PAA
Kaleido-scopes?!
FFT
FFT
PAAAA
Because of your powerful feelings and strength, those Crystal Kaleidoscopes are beginning to gain souls of their own!
That is because both kaleido-scopes desired strong bonds with you right from the start.

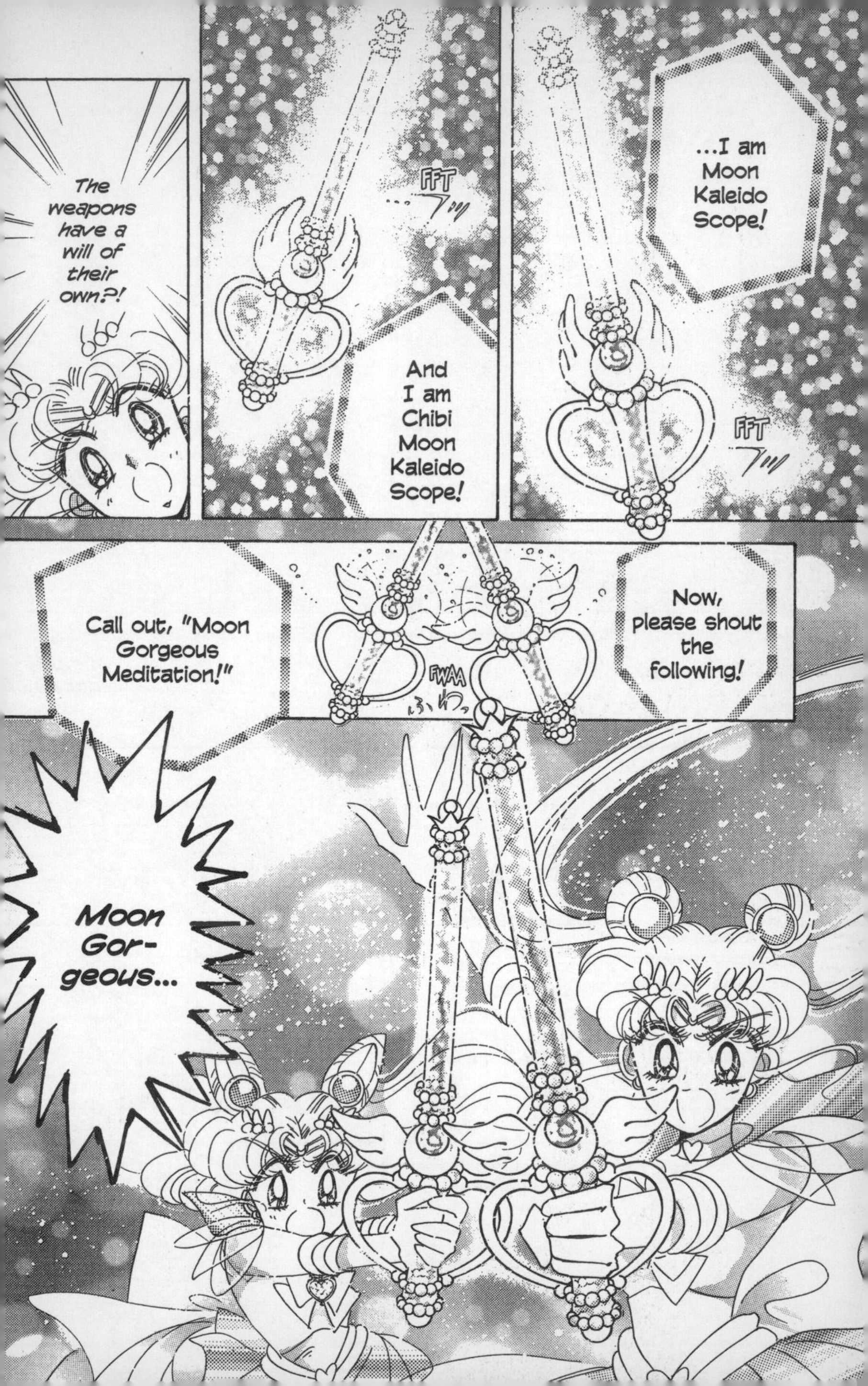
...I am Moon Kaleido Scope!
FFT
And I am Chibi Moon Kaleido Scope!
FFT
The weapons have a will of their own?!
Now, please shout the following!
FWAA
Call out, "Moon Gorgeous Meditation!"
Moon Gor-geous...

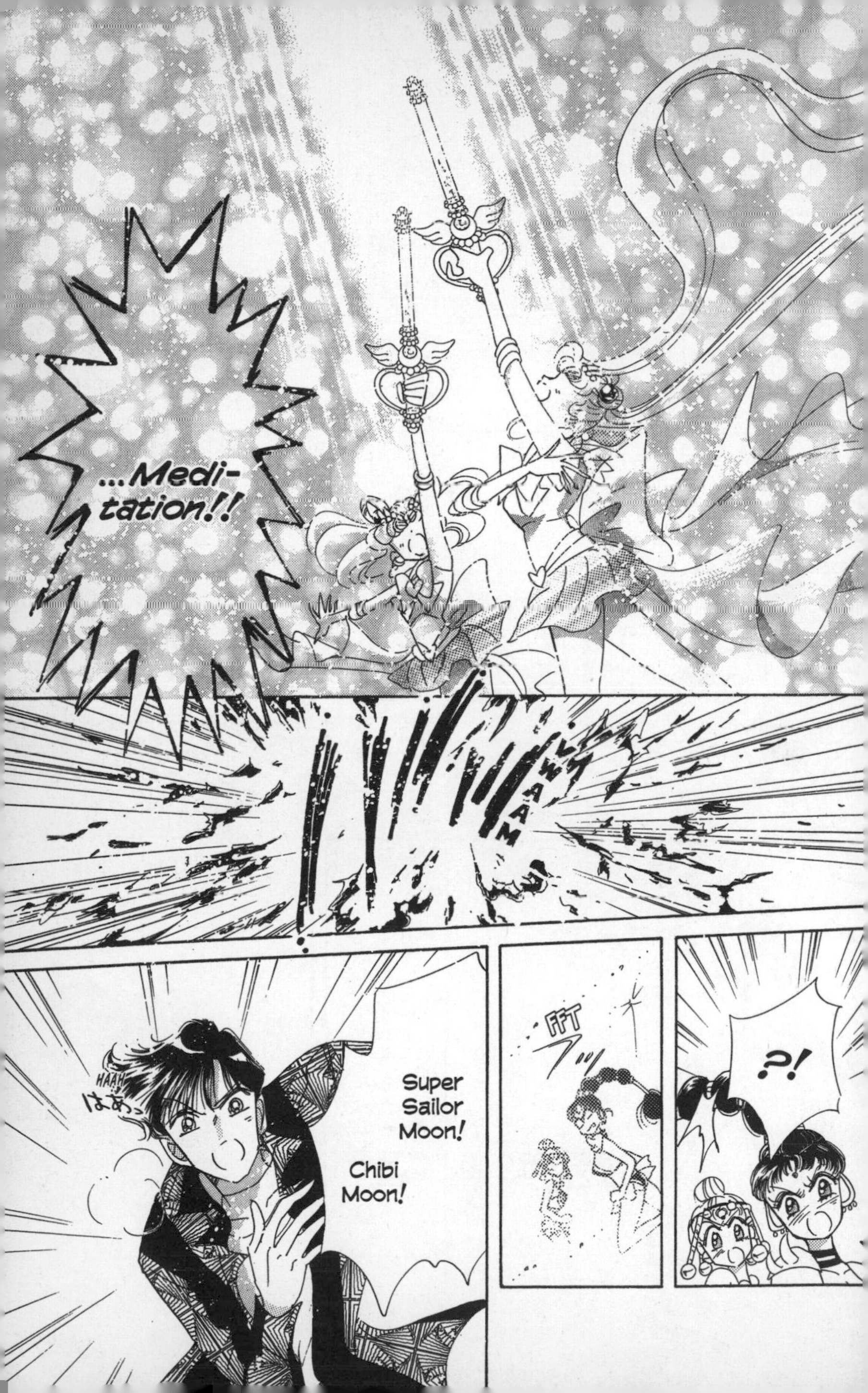
...Medi-
tation!!
VWAAAM
?!
FFT
フッ
Super Sailor Moon!
Chibi Moon!
HAAH
はあっ

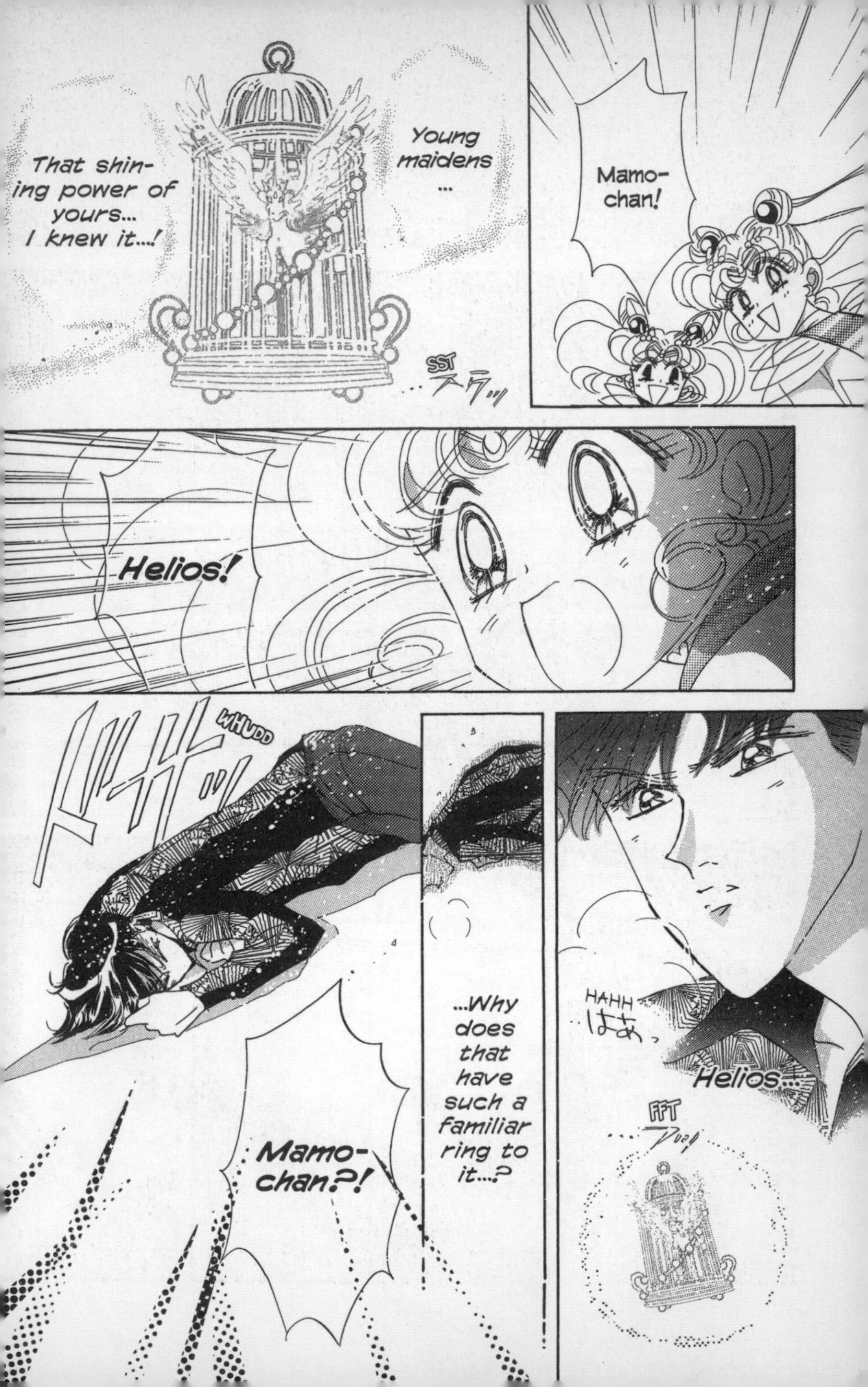

Mamo-chan!
Young maidens ...
That shin-ing power of yours... I knew it...!
SST
スラッ
Helios!
HAHH
はあっ
Helios...
FFT
ブワッ
...Why does that have such a familiar ring to it...?
WHUDD
ドサッ
Mamo-chan?!

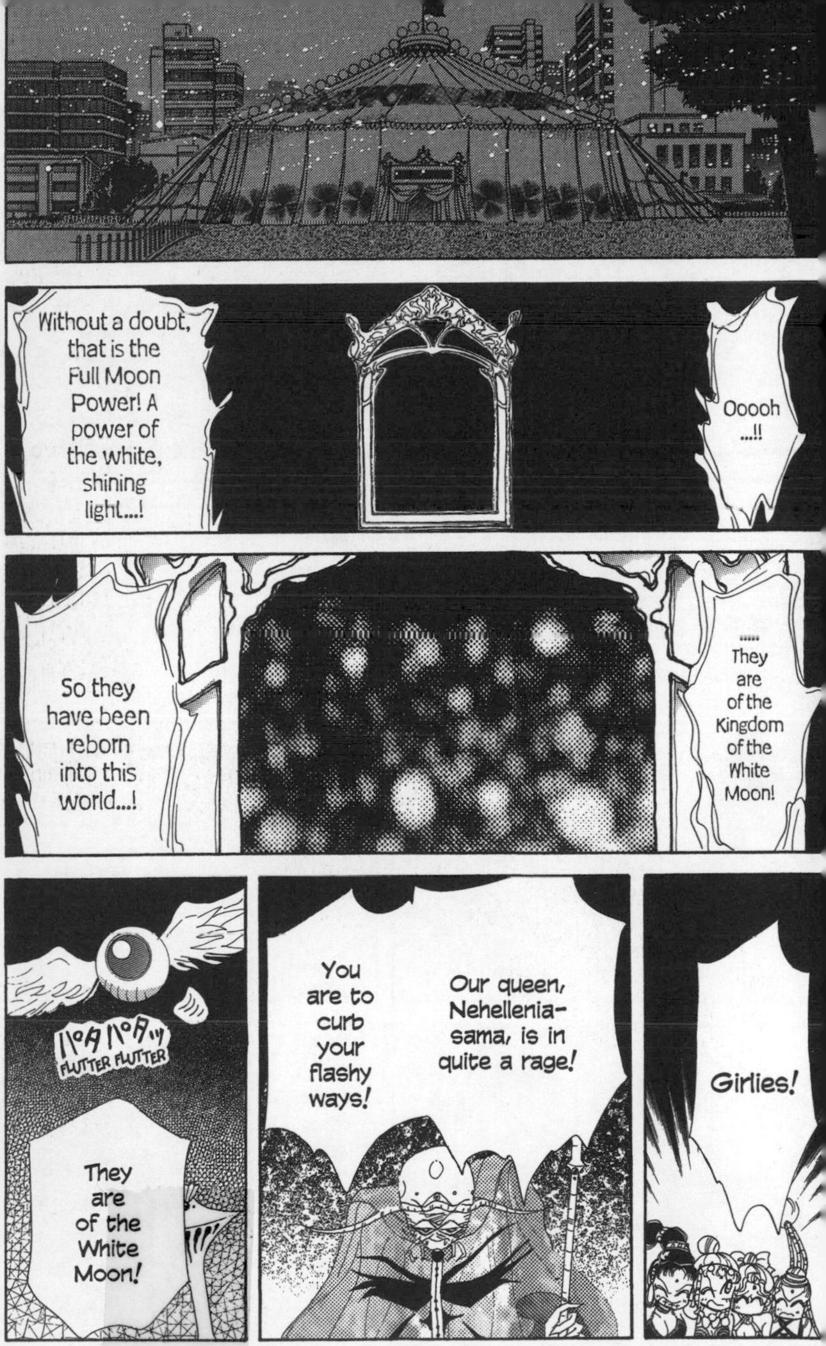
Ooooh ...!!
Without a doubt, that is the Full Moon Power! A power of the white, shining light...!
...... They are of the Kingdom of the White Moon!
So they have been reborn into this world...!
Girlies!
Our queen, Nehellenia-sama, is in quite a rage!
You are to curb your flashy ways!
パタパタッ
FLUTTER FLUTTER
They are of the White Moon!

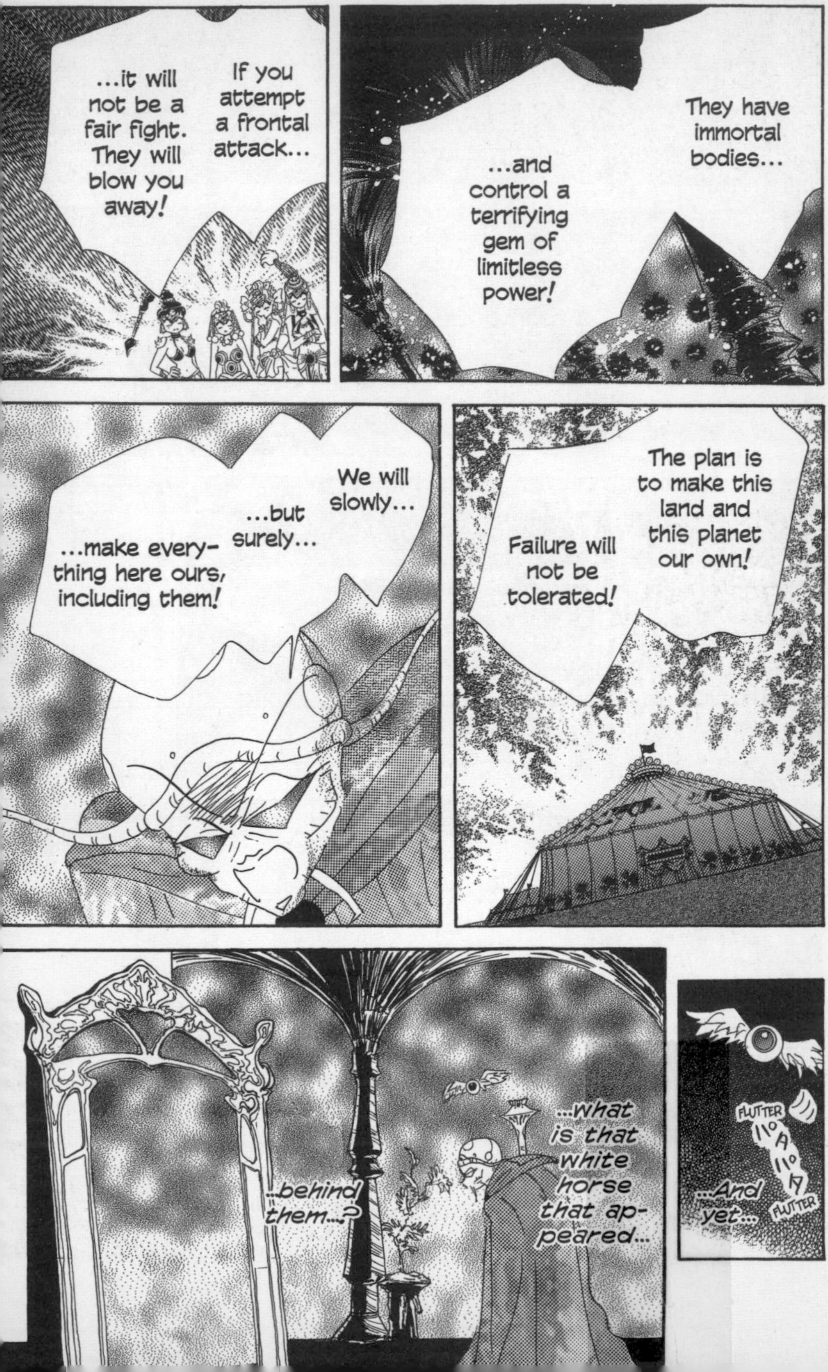
They have immortal bodies...
...and control a terrifying gem of limitless power!
If you attempt a frontal attack...
...it will not be a fair fight. They will blow you away!
The plan is to make this land and this planet our own!
Failure will not be tolerated!
We will slowly...
...but surely...
...make every-thing here ours, including them!
FLUTTER
FLUTTER
...And yet...
...what is that white horse that ap-peared...
...behind them...?

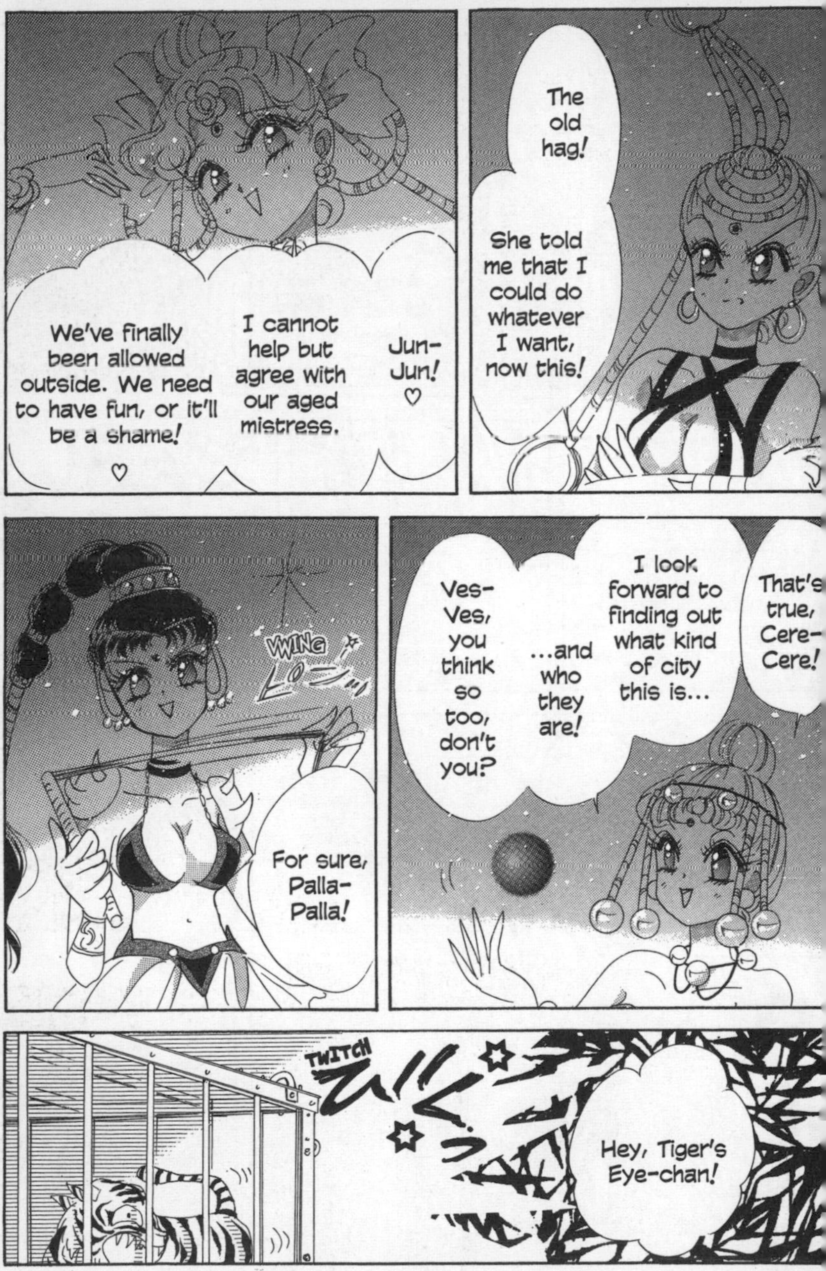
The old hag!
She told me that I could do whatever I want, now this!
Jun-Jun! ♡
I cannot help but agree with our aged mistress.
We've finally been allowed outside. We need to have fun, or it'll be a shame! ♡
That's true, Cere-Cere!
I look forward to finding out what kind of city this is...
...and who they are!
Ves-Ves, you think so too, don't you?
VWING
For sure, Palla-Palla!
Hey, Tiger's Eye-chan!
TWITCH

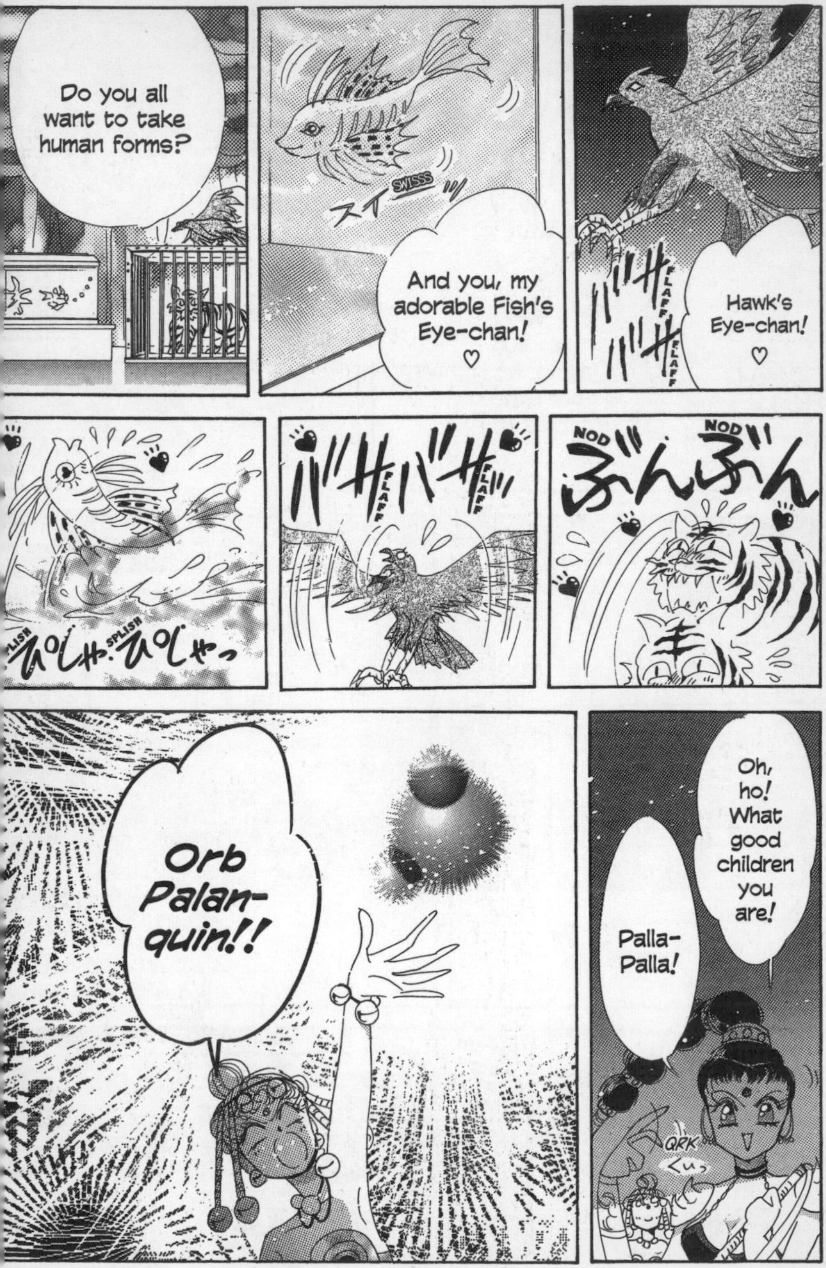

Hawk's Eye-chan! ♡
FLAFF FLAFF
バサバサ
And you, my adorable Fish's Eye-chan! ♡
SWISSS
スイッ
Do you all want to take human forms?
NOD NOD
ぶんぶん
FLAFF FLAFF
バサバサ
SPLISH SPLISH
ぴしゃぴしゃっ
Oh, ho! What good children you are!
Palla-Palla!
QRK
くいっ
Orb Palanquin!!

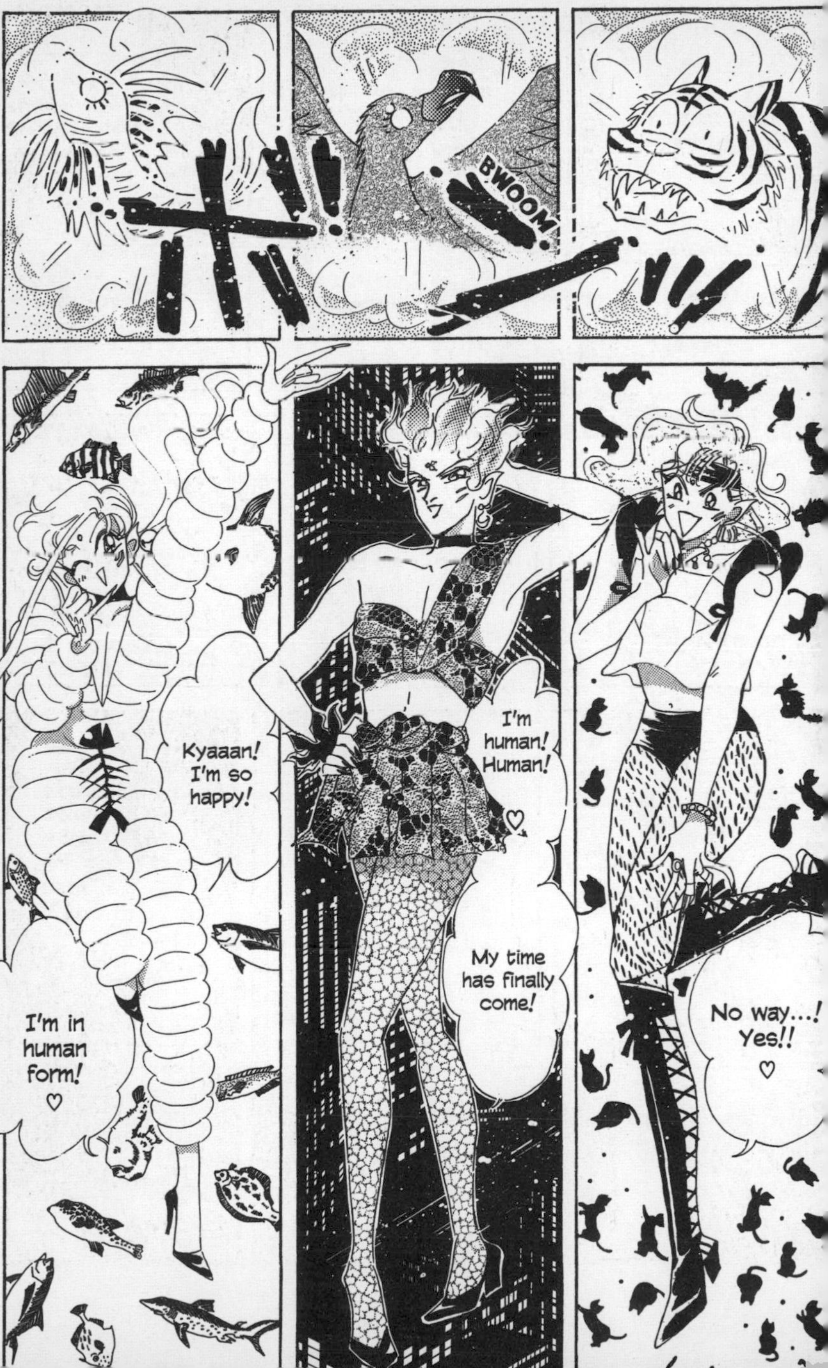
BWOOM
No way...! Yes!! ♡
I'm human! Human! ♡
My time has finally come!
Kyaaan! I'm so happy!
I'm in human form! ♡

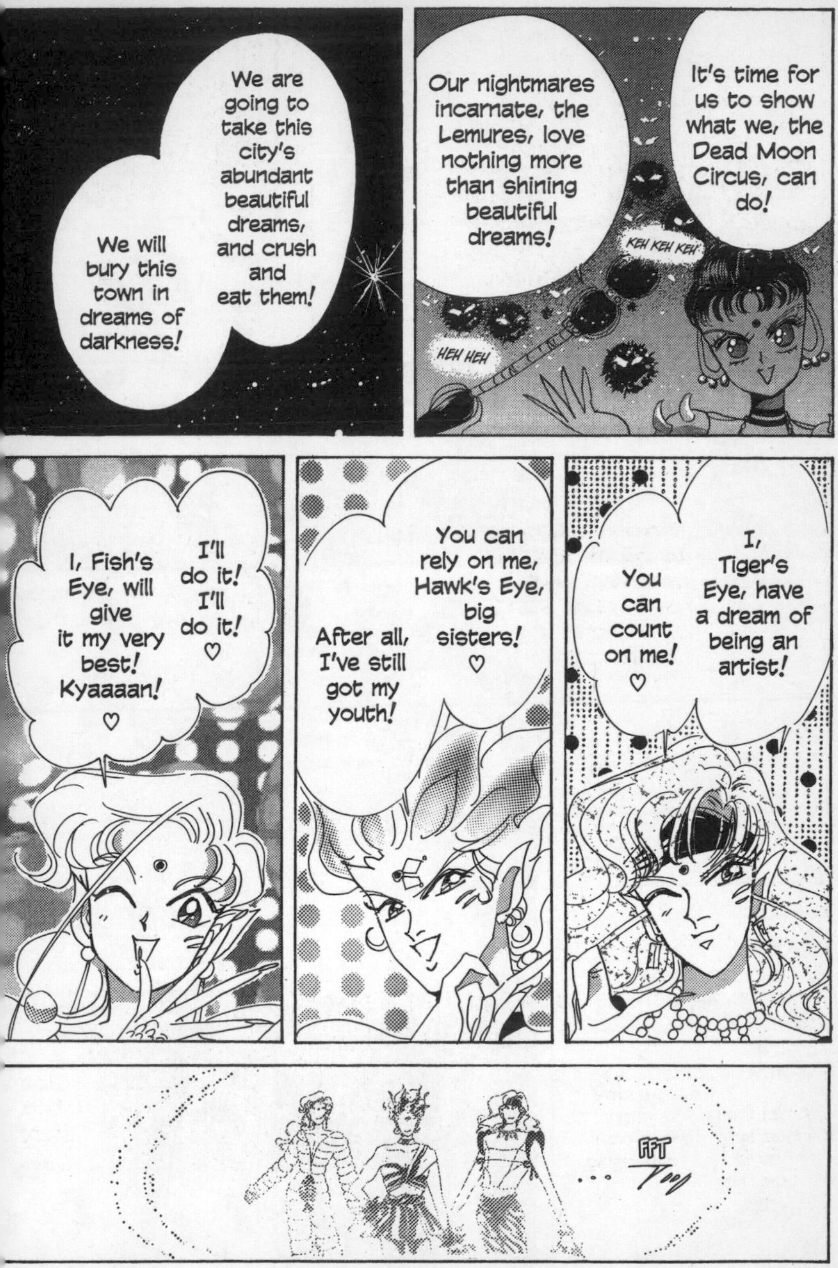
It's time for us to show what we, the Dead Moon Circus, can do!
Our nightmares incarnate, the Lemures, love nothing more than shining beautiful dreams!
KEH KEH KEH
HEH HEH
We are going to take this city's abundant beautiful dreams, and crush and eat them!
We will bury this town in dreams of darkness!
I, Tiger's Eye, have a dream of being an artist!
You can count on me! ♡
You can rely on me, Hawk's Eye, big sisters! ♡
After all, I've still got my youth!
I'll do it! I'll do it! ♡
I, Fish's Eye, will give it my very best! Kyaaaan! ♡
FFT
...

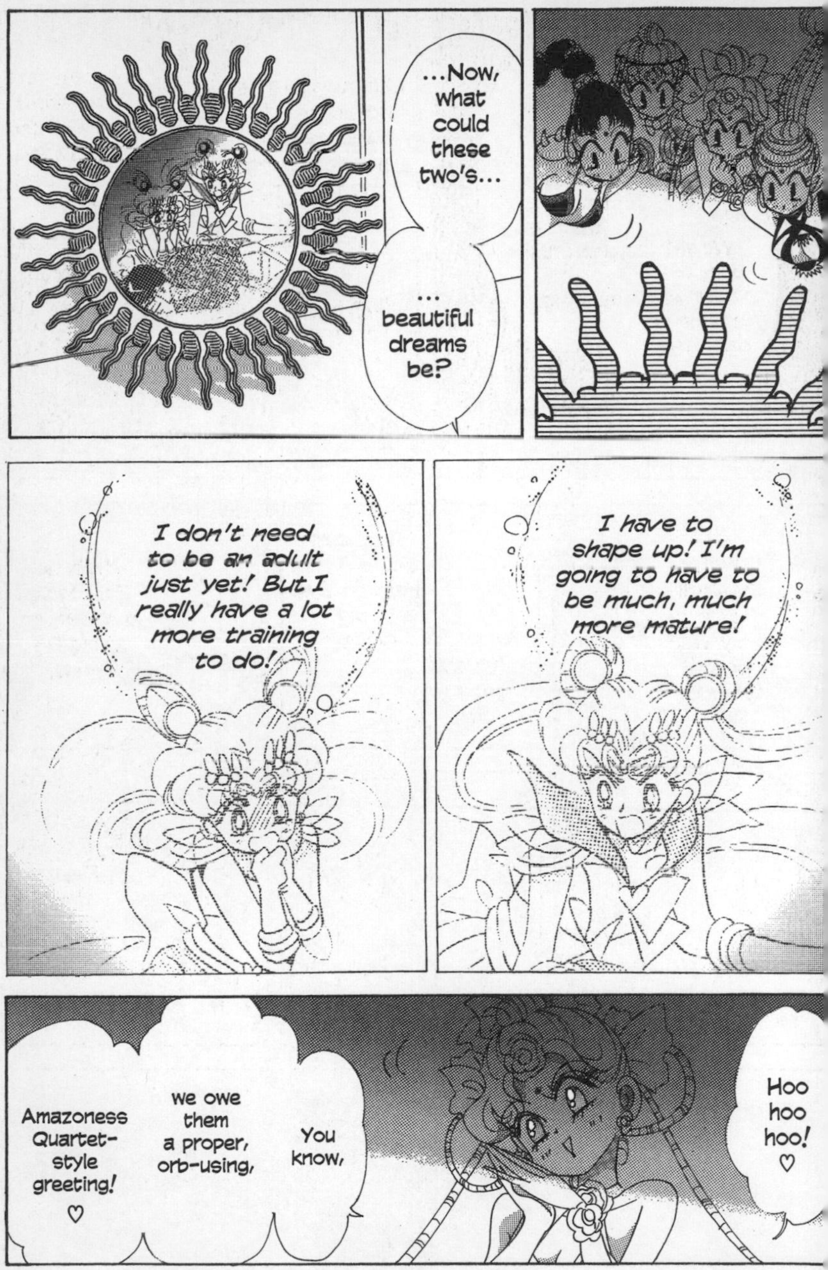
...Now, what could these two's...
...beautiful dreams be?
I have to shape up! I'm going to have to be much, much more mature!
I don't need to be an adult just yet! But I really have a lot more training to do!
Hoo hoo hoo! ♡
You know,
we owe them a proper, orb-using,
Amazoness Quartet-style greeting! ♡

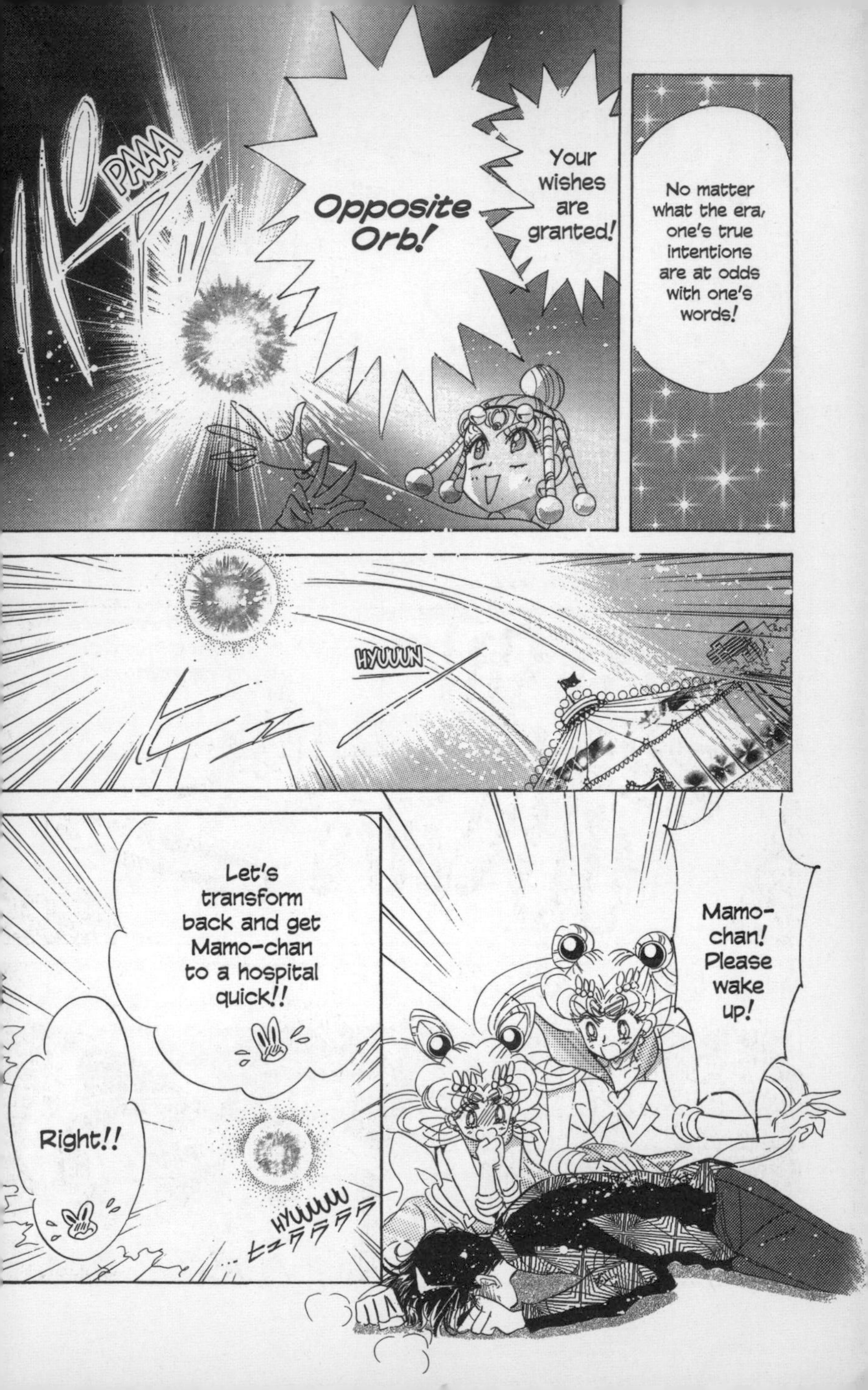
No matter what the era, one's true intentions are at odds with one's words!
Your wishes are granted!
Opposite Orb!
PAAA
HYUUUN
Mamo-chan! Please wake up!
Let's transform back and get Mamo-chan to a hospital quick!!
Right!!
HYUUUU

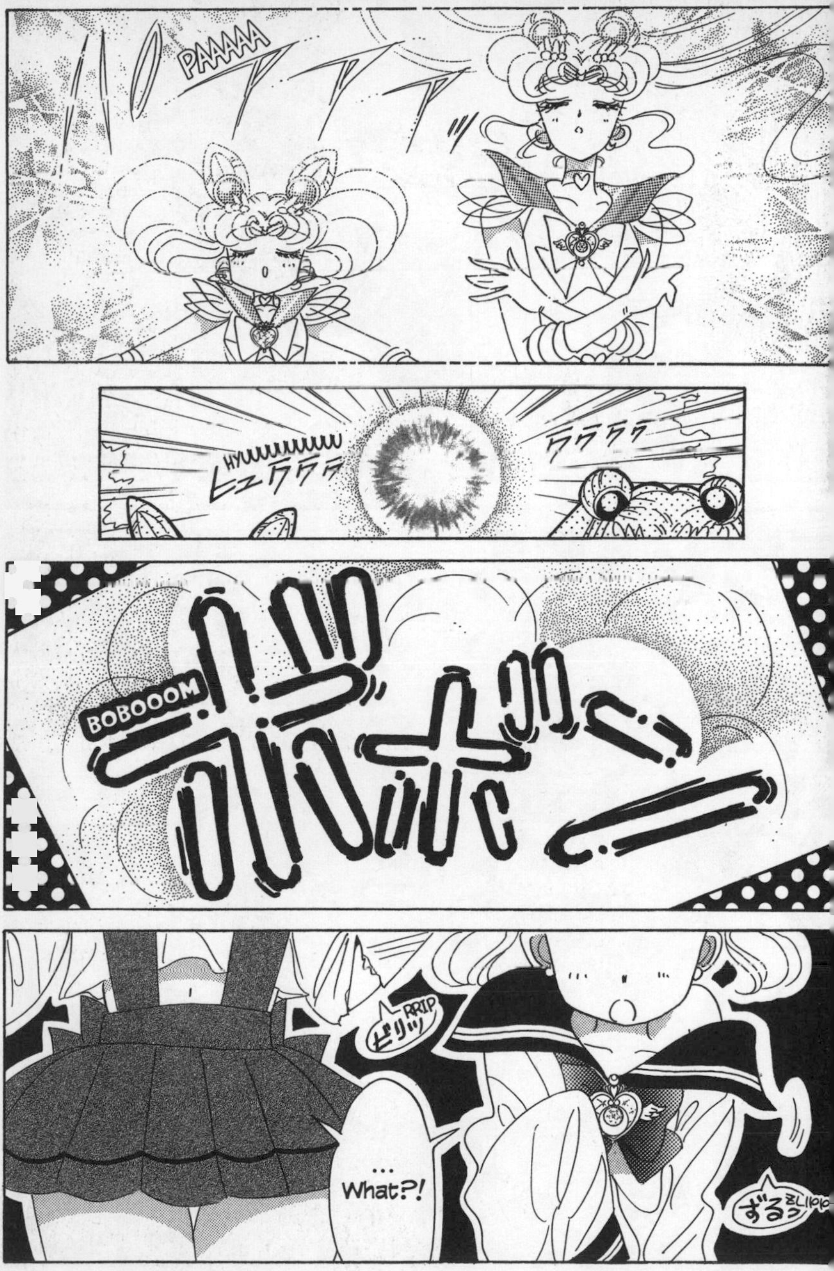
PAAAAA
パアアアッ
ラララララ
HYUUUUUU
ヒュララララ
BOBOOOM
RRIP
ビリッ
ずるっ
... What?!

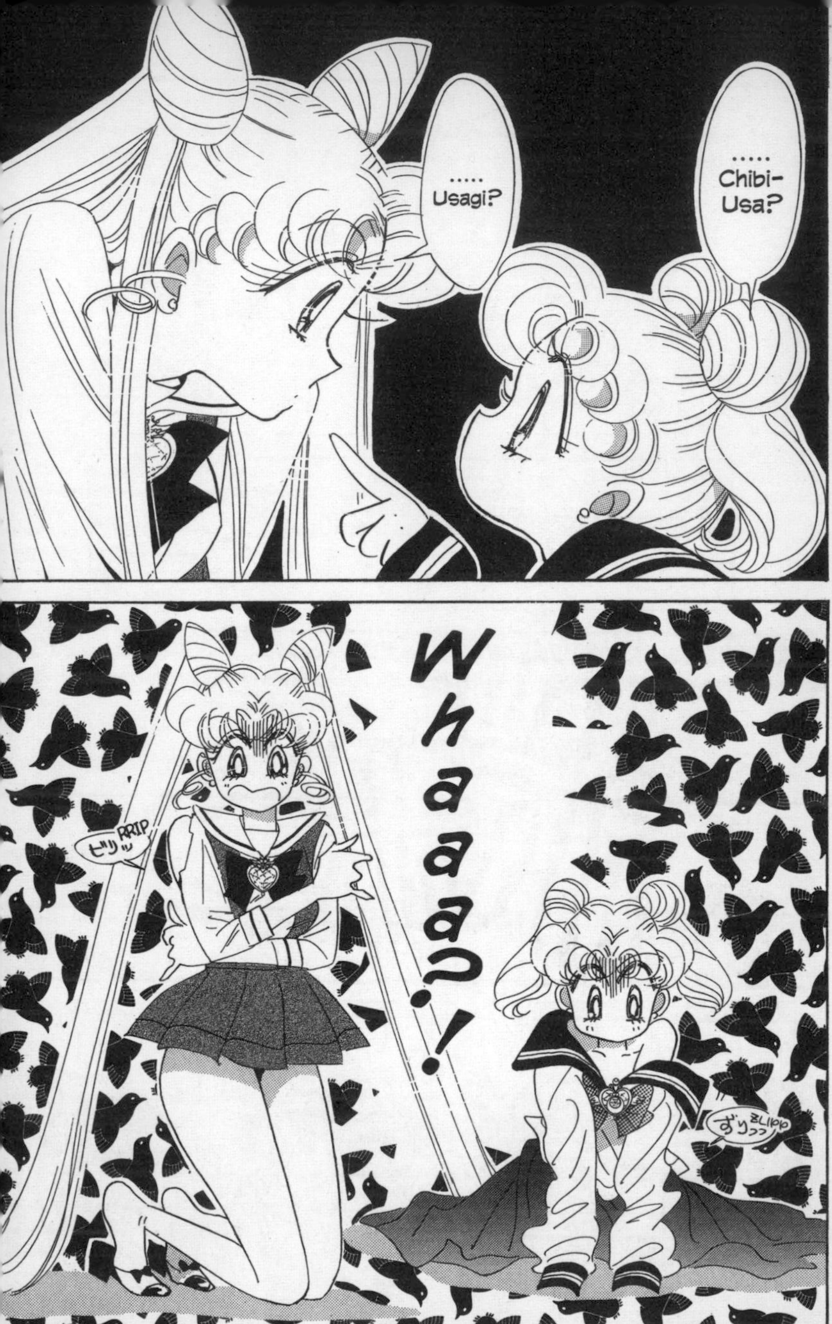

..... Chibi-Usa?
..... Usagi?
Whaaa?!
ビリッ RRIP
ずりっっ SLIPPP

•*to be continued*•

Pretty Guardian Sailor Moon volume 8 is a work of fiction.
Names, characters, places, and incidents are the products
of the author's imagination or are used fictitiously. Any
resemblance to actual events, locales, or persons, living or
dead, is entirely coincidental.

A Kodansha Trade Paperback Original.

Pretty Guardian Sailor Moon volume 8 copyright © 2004 Naoko Takeuchi
English Translation copyright © 2012 Naoko Takeuchi

All rights reserved.

Published in the United States by Kodansha Comics, an imprint
of Kodansha USA Publishing, LLC, New York.

Publication rights for this English edition arranged through
Kodansha Ltd., Tokyo.

First published in Japan in 2004 by Kodansha Ltd., Tokyo, as
Bishoujosenshi Sailor Moon Shinsoban, volume 8.

ISBN 978-1-61262-004-6

Printed in Canada

www.kodanshacomics.com

9 8 7 6 5 4 3 2 1

Translator/Adapter: William Flanagan
Lettering: Jennifer Skarupa